CORPORATE COMMUNICATION

Corporate Communication: Concepts and Practice—a comprehensive and engaging textbook—helps in understanding the underlying concepts and real-life strategies of communication in modern-day corporate set-ups. One of the youngest management disciplines, corporate communication is used by companies to position themselves to the outside world in a highly competitive business environment and to build a "sense of being," on the one hand, and creating a feeling of pride in being associated with the company for various stakeholders, especially the employees and investors.

Some of the functions of corporate communication include identifying and segmenting stakeholders, articulating brand positioning, selecting appropriate channels of internal and external communication, and managing crises, conflicts, and reputations, among others. This revised edition offers a fresh perspective into all basic and critical aspects of corporate communication and incorporates the latest changes in governmental policies and industry trends to aid students adapt to the contemporary business environment and become industry-ready.

This book will be of great interest to students and researchers working in the areas of corporate communication, organizational communication, journalism, mass communication, communication studies, public relations, and human resource management.

Jaishri Jethwaney, currently Senior Advisor for Communication with the Ministry of Health and Family Welfare in its Immunology Technical Support Unit (ITSU), Delhi, India, was Professor and Head of the Department of Advertising and Public Relations at the much acclaimed Indian Institute of Mass Communication where she taught for over two decades.

CORPORATE COMMUNICATION

Concepts and Practice

Third Edition

Jaishri Jethwaney

Routledge
Taylor & Francis Group
LONDON AND NEW YORK

Designed cover image: Getty Images

Third edition published 2024
by Routledge
4 Park Square, Milton Park, Abingdon, Oxon, OX14 4RN

and by Routledge
605 Third Avenue, New York, NY 10158

Routledge is an imprint of the Taylor & Francis Group, an informa business

First edition published by Oxford University Press 2010

British Library Cataloguing-in-Publication Data
A catalogue record for this book is available from the British Library

ISBN: 978-1-032-53723-8 (hbk)
ISBN: 978-1-032-69471-9 (pbk)
ISBN: 978-1-032-69470-2 (ebk)

DOI: 10.4324/9781032694702

Typeset in Sabon
by Apex CoVantage, LLC

To the unsurpassable Jethwaney Kinfolk

CONTENTS

List of tables *viii*
Preface *ix*

1 Understanding corporate communication 1

2 Media dynamics and strategies 22

3 Corporate reputation management 45

4 Employee communication 82

5 Managing government relations 107

6 Writing for media and media relations management 136

7 Corporate communication in brand promotion 161

8 Corporate social responsibility 184

9 Financial communication 204

10 Crises communication 243

11 Corporate communication research 285

12 Laws and ethics in corporate communication 313

Index *359*

TABLES

2.1 Print media press 27
2.2 Magazines 28
2.3 Television 28
2.4 Radio 28
2.5 Cinema 28
2.6 Outdoor (posters, billboards/hoarding) 29
2.7 New media/Internet 29
2.8 Mobile phones and SMS 29
2.9 Employee communication media (house journal, video magazines, et al) 29
2.10 Home pages and company blogs 30
3.1 Impact of good reputation on stakeholders 50
3.2 Benoit's Image Repair Strategies 54
3.3 Simulation of Benoit's Image Repair Theory 55
4.1 Employee communication media 92
5.1 Companies and paid-up capital 111
5.2 Paid-up capital as percentage of GDP 111
5.3 Myths vs. reality 132
7.1 Diamond outlets in 1994 and 1997 181
9.1 Major financial institutions in India 207

PREFACE

Corporate communication has become an established academic stream in most media schools in universities and some MBA schools also. It is widely believed that corporate communication is an offshoot of public relations, as many academic books and learned papers also suggest. One rarely now finds a vertical in corporate Inc. called public relations. It is, however, a dichotomy that corporate communication as a professional movement is yet to reach the magnitude and momentum that public relations did and continues to do so in most countries.

A lot has changed in the last few years that has its ramifications on communication *per se*. Beginning in December 2019 in Wuhan, China up until WHO declared it a pandemic in March 2020, and an official closure given to it in May 2023, there has been nothing like this phenomenon in the last 100 years after the Spanish flu took millions of lives globally. Covid cases are still occurring, but it is no longer a pandemic situation. With the long spell of almost three years, the Covid-19 pandemic has changed the world in more than one way. Pain, suffering, personal loss of family members and friends hung like Damocles' sword on billions of denizens as societies and nations struggled to make sense of the deadly virus when it struck. Even the richest and most advanced countries were ill-prepared to deal with a medical emergency of this kind and magnitude.

Every crisis brings in an opportunity, and this one was no different. What could have taken years, the ingenuity and improvisation skills of our scientists brought to the table the vaccine that was to save millions of lives in a much shorter period than it was speculated. Deaths immediately got minimized, but the pandemic left a labyrinthine trail of ruined families, traumatized children, increase in domestic violence, shaky markets and economies, people losing jobs by the millions, the introduction of "work from home" culture, and many more things. The corporate Inc., first confused, later took up the challenge of rebuilding the lost ground as markets opened and people came out of their homes to shop. Small and medium-sized companies have still not regained from the colossal losses and closure of many enterprises. Governments came forward in most countries to help build economies, but in a situation like the one Covid-19 brought, no effort could be called enough! Covid-19 sent many belonging to the middle class to the poor category, and the poor to extreme poverty in many countries. How the Corporate Inc. communicated with their stakeholders can be an area of empirical research within academia.

Technology, in the meantime, has taken the front seat. The social media platforms have kind of overtaken the classic media like print and electronic in cornering most of the ad budgets in flourishing markets. Social media influencers have become most sought after for pushing brands among their followers. Influencer marketing budget according to industry buzz is anything between USD 5–10 billion in a year. Some social media influencers have more following than well-known celebrities.

AI-led chatbots have every answer under the sun. Just to test how fast and "intelligent" these were, I tried a couple of them to ask the question *What is the state of corporate communication currently?* Within seconds the information with citations came, with a question at the end of the chat: *would you like to know about strategy?*, giving cues on areas. When I wrote Yes on Social media influencers, a complete tutorial appeared! AI bots can be seen in most mainstream news channels, sharing top news and weather news. *India Today* launched SANA for its English and Hindi channels. Odisha Television Network has launched LISA, and lo and behold we had Anjana Om Kashyap, the star presenter of Aaj Taak, introducing her AI version in a program, "Anjana ka AI Avtar, TV pe Pehli baar" in September 2023. While there is no dearth of anchors, the newness of the medium seems to have caught with media also. AI is extensively used in newsrooms for stories.

The WhatsApp forwards have AI bots on everything including religion and culture, spreading the "Gayan," whether one needs or not.

What does all this mean to an average corporate communication professional? In order not to allow oneself to become a zombie, who does not have to use brains, which can be great relief for the lazy, prudence lies in holding on to the basics and strategizing one's own self and not becoming a communication clone dedicated to the AI. Corporate communication managers must understand, assimilate, and analyze the "change" brought on by technology, but at the same time depend on time-tested models and conceptual frameworks on various areas of corporate communication. Technology is only a tool that needs to be befittingly used to fulfill the program objectives, not losing sight of the human side of communication.

Technology has had its tremendous impact on the news media also. Long seen as the "gatekeepers," the news media seems to be losing this coveted role, as the invention of smartphones has led millions of people posting videos of events from ground zero, before any media can reach there.

The corporate communication scholars and practitioners must have a constant watch on the change coming on various fronts and from various forces, both tangible and intangible, and steer their communication accordingly, without losing touch with the ground reality.

Jaishri Jethwaney

1

UNDERSTANDING CORPORATE COMMUNICATION

Chapter objectives

After reading the chapter, you will learn:

What corporate communication is
The evolution of corporate communication and its present-day relevance
Roots of corporate communication in India
The role and scope of corporate communication
Functions of corporate communication
Why the need for corporate communication is felt strongly, especially now.

1.1 Introduction

Corporate communication has come to be recognized as an important part of top management functions. Few organizations use the nomenclature public relations now. However, surprisingly, despite corporate communication, coming of age, the professional bodies continue to be known by the nomenclature of PR, albeit one finds CC professionals floating corporate communication associations. This is an area that needs resolution to avoid confusion among clients and users of services. Due to this vagueness, some feel it's good old PR camouflaged as corporate communication; others feel that PR is but a tiny part of the overall corporate communication, yet others argue that corporate communication is a part of marketing communication. Argenti *et al* have offered the following argument: "Corporate communication can claim historical links to the field of public relations, which has been concerned with the voice and image of big business for nearly a century."[1] Harold Burson, founder chairman, Burson Marsteller, writes, "Corporate communications is one of the many subsets of public relations and under that umbrella you can have relations with advisory services, you can have investor relations, you can have internal communications, marketing support, litigation support, etc."[2]

DOI: 10.4324/9781032694702-1

Cutlip et al share that among the 500 Fortune companies, only one in five use the "public relations" titles. Other commonly used titles are corporate communication, public affairs, public information, or in combination with advertising.[3]

Interestingly, however, the teaching of corporate communication is being pulled out from some journalism schools to management schools.[4] At the same time, courses in public relations have a course or two in corporate communication also.

1.2 Various definitions of corporate communication

Corporate communication is described by some experts as a framework in which all communication specialists, viz., marketing, organizational, and management, integrate the totality of the organizational message, thereby helping to define the corporate image as a means to improving corporate performance.

Corporate communication, according to P Jackson, is the "the integrated approach to all communication produced by an organization, directed at all relevant target groups. Each item of communication must convey and emphasize the corporate identity."[5]

"Corporate communication," defined by Cees and Riel, "is the total communication activity generated by a company to achieve its planned objectives."[6]

> Corporate communication is an instrument of management by means of which all consciously used forms of internal and external communication are harmonized as effectively and efficiently as possible, so as to create a favorable basis for relationship with groups upon which the company is dependent.[7]

According to Fernandez, corporate communication is a long-term strategic initiative usually created within a company to communicate its brand's core message. The success will impinge on the creation of a corporate voice that is "assertive and effective" when addressed to the stakeholders.

As a strategy, corporate communication needs to percolate from senior management to every echelon in the hierarchy. The stakeholders internally would encompass employees and investors, in the external, customers, regulatory bodies, professional bodies, financial markets, special interest groups, shareholders, and potential employees.[8]

Dolphin argues that the corporate communication function "resists a single fixed definition." He feels it is a "dynamic mixture of problem solving skills and insights," which should be viewed as a "process rather than an entity." Corporate communication, therefore, according to Dolphin, has to fulfill three key responsibilities:

> Aiding the management of change
> Helping to define a corporation's role in society
> Assisting the creation of corporate vision and responsibility.[9]

Adopting the earlier information from Finley, Dolphin writes that corporate organizations need to navigate complex public environment which would mean mediating with government, internal stakeholders to manage effects of changing environment and most importantly to operate ethically while also projecting an 'inspiring sense of corporate pride'.[10]

In a nutshell, corporate communications is all about managing perceptions and ensuring that information is disseminated quickly when public interest is involved; a continuous effort is made to maintain a positive image of the organization or person who employs CC; and, last but not the least, there is a smooth and empathetic relationship with varied stakeholders.

1.3 Evolution of corporate communication—the history of public relations

Many scholars feel that corporate communications can't be understood clearly unless its foundation in public relations is analyzed.

Founded in the USA in the first quarter of the last century, the term public relations essentially meant how a company was perceived by consumers and by the public at large. Over the years, its scope has come to include many publics such as employees, shareholders, future employees, bureaucracy, opinion makers, media, wholesalers, dealers, consumers, special interest groups, community, and the public at large.

Efforts at persuading others and influencing public opinion date back to antiquity. The Greeks, though, did not use the term public relations or public opinion but believed in the power of public opinion when they said "*Vox populi vox dei*"—the voice of the people is the voice of God.

Kings often went incognito to feel the pulse of the people about governance and to listen to their grievances.

Ashoka, one of the greatest kings in India, spread Buddhism far and wide through his emissaries. His iron pillars that inscribe the obligations of the government towards its people have stood the test of time.

In the US, the seeds of PR could be traced back to the American Revolution, when the slogan "No taxation without representation" rent the air.

Edward L. Bernays, considered as one of the fathers of PR, contributed richly to reconciling the development of PR. His book *Crystallizing Public Opinion*, which he wrote in 1923, laid down the principles, practice, and ethics of the profession. He felt a PR practitioner was a "special pleader" with two big hurdles to overcome, viz., a) the public's reluctance to acknowledge a dependence on people or groups and b) the establishment of the profession itself.

Amid the Great Economic Depression of 1930s, the governments and organizations felt the necessity for proactive information about the policies and renewed outlook. The governments needed the tool of persuasive publicity for which various kinds of media were needed to reach out to stakeholders.

Back home, fighting the British Yoke, the Father of the Nation, Mahatma Gandhi, exhorted the common man for civil disobedience and non-cooperation against the British government for almost three decades in the last century. His "weapons," however, were non-violence and truth. When the British wanted India to enter the Second World War, the Indian leaders demanded "Purna Swarajay" (Complete self-rule as a bargain) after the war, the process of which began immediately after that and India gained independence on 15 August 1947.[11]

The Bolshevik Revolution of 1917 was indeed a manifestation of people's frustration with the tyrannical Czar and the public's desire to be free. It is, however, a different matter that the USSR turned into a regimented society, until 1989, when people, supported by the right leadership, brought about *glasnost* followed by the disintegration of the country into a number of independent states.

The crash of the financial behemoths in 2008, followed by a widespread global recession, is often compared with the crash of the stock market and the economic depression of the 1930s. The difficult times, as in the past, have necessitated the governments of even capitalist economies to bail out various sectors, like finance, realty, and automobile.

The advent of the twentieth century was marked by the invention of mass communication, beginning with the printing of the newspaper, followed by the invention of the radio, cinema, television, and, later, the Internet, which has disrupted the entire media ecosystem, more specifically the access, reach, and use of media by an average person. The power of the pen came to be recognized when newspapers regularly carried stories on the seamier side of things—the evils of business, the corruption in politics, the double standards in religion, and the exploitation of children, women, and Blacks. The journalists who were writing negative stories came to be known as the "muckrakers." Such articles had a tremendous impact on the public. The organizations and people against whom such dispatches were written felt the need to give their points of view, thus paving the way for the birth of public relations.

Ivy Ledbetter Lee, considered as one of the founders of PR along with Edward Bernays, practiced PR on behalf of some organizations. A financial reporter for the *New York Times*, the *New York Journal*, and the *New York World*, he firmly believed in the need for openness in business to get appreciation and win credibility with the press. When he agreed to handle a crisis for the Pennsylvania Railroad Company, starting his assignment, he put up a "Declaration of Principles" outside his office, which read (excerpts):

> This is not a secret press bureau. All our work is done in the open. We aim to supply news. This is not an Advertising Agency. If you think any of our matter ought to go to your business office, do not use it. Our matter is accurate. Further details of any subject treated will be supported promptly, and any editor will be assisted most carefully in verifying directly any statement of fact. . . In brief, our plan is frankly, and openly, on behalf of business concerns and public institutions, to supply the press and public of the United States prompt and accurate information concerning subjects which it is of value and interest to the public to know about.

Lee's open approach was appreciated by some quarters as it garnered positive publicity for the organizations he worked for, but not all were impressed. Soon critics found holes in the practice of Ivy Lee. He was criticized for not always practicing what he preached. The case in point was about the infamous Colorado Fuel and Iron Company, which later came to be known as the "Ludlow Massacre," which earned Lee the dubious reputation of arranging positive publicity in the press for the Rockefellers, who it was alleged to have hired goons to forcibly put an end to miners' strike that had resulted in 20 deaths, including of 11 children.[12] Lee's actions annoyed the labor supporters who saw him as being anti-union and committed to breaking the strike.[13] Hallahan, however, feels that Lee was not "intentionally deceptive," but at the same time he contradicted his own thesis, which suggests a gap existed between his espoused principles of publicity and actions.[14]

Around the same time, the American Telephone and Telegraph Company (AT&T) felt the need for such a department and even used the term "public relations" for the first time in its annual report.[15]

Lee's contemporary Edward Bernays practiced PR for almost 80 years of his life spanning over 100 years (1892–1995). Argenti *et al* believe that Bernays' several high-profile assignments point to his contributions to corporate communication as practiced today: the Ivory Soap Campaign for Procter & Gamble, the Torches of Freedom March for the American Tobacco Company, and Light's Golden Jubilee for General Electric are definite pointers in this direction.[16]

Let's look at two of his campaigns in a nutshell to draw the connections.

1.3.1 Procter & Gamble campaign for Ivory Soap

The company, to help promote some of its products, including the Ivory Soap, retained Edward Bernays. When he heard that a sculptor by the name Brenda Putnam had asked the company for large number of soaps to use for her work, Bernays came up with an interesting scheme of promoting soap sculpting as a new pastime of American children. Bernays wrote about the campaign thus: "Children, the enemies of soap, would be conditioned to enjoy using Ivory. And nothing would be wasted-soap shavings could be used for washing." The scheme with public participation, comments Larry Tye, was such that it had to be newsworthy.[17]

The campaign helped create a "common ground between the company and its customers: the company's interest in selling soap and the public's interest in having clean kids engaged in wholesome artistic activity."[18]

1.3.2 The Torches of Freedom March and the American Tobacco Company

The *American Tobacco Company* made cigarettes with the name Lucky Strike. Bernays notable effort in this campaign overtly was to make modern women aware of social prejudice of smoking in public, with the aim of increasing sale of cigarettes to women.

He masterminded the strategy along with the CEO of the company and sponsored the event "Torches of Freedom" March in 1929, on an Easter Sunday. A group of women participated in the parade with lit cigarettes, asserting their freedom to smoke openly in public. Bernays is said to have sent 30 women a telegram under the signature of his secretary who was not identified as his own employee:

> In the interest of equality of sexes and to fight another sex taboo I and other young women light another torch of freedom by smoking cigarettes while strolling on the Fifth Avenue, Easter Sunday, we are doing this to combat the silly prejudice that the cigarette is suitable for the home, the restaurant, the taxicab, the theatre lobby but never to never for the sidewalk. Women smokers and other escorts will stroll from Forty-Eighth street to Fifty-Fourth street on Fifth Avenue between eleven thirty and one o' clock.[19]

Larry Tye comments that the entire strategy for the event was scripted by Bernays about where the marchers would join, the route of the parade, including that some women would be escorted by men to reflect many supported their women smoking in public. The media covered the event, and analysts believe that the event was a precursor that brought about change in women's smoking habits.[20]

Kevin Molony argues that Edward Bernays (1892–1995) and Ivy Ledbetter Lee (1877–1934), widely regarded as the two founders of modern PR, are but embarrassing nominations for modern PR people. Bernays, visibly influenced by his famous uncle Sigmund Freud, laid emphasis on mass psychology as a social control technique and by his work for the Creel Committee that was set up by the US government as soon as it entered World War I to disseminate information. Bernays is said to have equated propaganda with PR. In fact, in the first chapter of his second book titled *Propaganda*, the first two sentences sum up his thesis:

> the conscious and intelligent manipulation of the organized habits and opinions of the masses is an important element in a democratic society. Those who manipulate this unseen mechanism of society constitute an invisible government which is the ruling power of our country.[21]

Many scholars feel that the works of Walter Lippmann, a social thinker and commentator, when he wrote his first book *Crystallizing Public Opinion* in 1923, influenced him. Bernays wrote: "The significant revolution of our modern times is not industrial or economic or political but the revolution which is taking place in the art of creating consent among the governed." The two foundational ideas that he took from Lippmann for his PR philosophy were a) a new concept of stereotype and b) a pseudo environment and pseudo facts. By managing stereotypes through news creation, he said that a PR counselor works as a "pleader of public point of view." The PR counselor, he argued, must represent the public to his client and vice versa. They must understand how public opinion is formed and maintained and must understand social psychology and, in particular, stereotypes, which, in his view, were the mental phenomena used by the people in the formation of public opinion. He believed that when a PR counselor creates news, it is strengthened, weakened, or aimed at amending the stereotypes.

A contemporary of Bernays, Ivy Lee also echoed that publicity was essentially a matter of "mass psychology" and people were guided "more by sentiment than mind," a premise used in corporate and brand campaigns even today.

In 1922, when Bernays addressed a young group of students at the Columbia School of Journalism, he exhorted them thus: "You must study human emotions and all the factors that move people that persuade men in any line of human activity. Mob psychology is one of the most important factors that underlay this whole business."[22]

It is not difficult to link the connection of this thesis with today's practice of advertising, PR, and corporate communication.

Dolphin, arguing based on academic literature, posits that public relations and communication have been used interchangeably for long. Similarly, the emphasis placed on certain nomenclatures, he writes, varies according to the country of origin. What used to trade under the name of PR is now variously known as "corporate affairs; corporate communication; public affairs."[23]

1.3.3 Watergate scandal—the precursor of corporate communication

Some scholars believe that the advent of corporate communication as an offshoot of PR came during the Watergate scandal that rocked the USA in the early part of the 1970s. Let's look at the facts:

1.3.3.1 Quick timeline

17 June 1972: five men arrested in a break-in at the Democratic National Committee headquarters at the Watergate Hotel in Washington.

20 June 1972: President Nixon and aide H. R. Haldeman discuss the Watergate; later prosecutors find an 18-minute gap in the tape of that conversation.

15 September 1972: seven men including two former White House indicted in Watergate break-in by Federal Grand Jury.

11–30 January 1973: five men plead guilty to conspiracy, burglary, and wiretapping; two stand trial and are convicted.

30 April 1973: Haldman and Nixon aide John D. Erlichman resign; White House aide John Dean is fired.

The House committee on the Judiciary passed articles of impeachment against President Nixon on 27 July 1974 on the following charges:

1. Obstruction of investigations of Watergate break-in
2. Misuse of powers and violation on the oath of office.
3. Failure to comply with House subpoenas

Richard Nixon, however, chose to resign on 9 August 1974. If he had not, he would have been impeached.[24]

1.3.4 Why is the case important in reference to PR and corporate communication?

The detriment to PR's reputation, according to many analysts, can be attributed to three persons, viz., John Creel, Ivy Ledbetter Lee, and Richard Nixon, all of whom negatively impacted PR's reputation. John Creel, a former journalist who had headed the US propaganda efforts during World War I, used all aspects of media including film, posters, music, painting, and cartoons to ensure public backing of the government's decision to enter the war. After the war, many Americans felt that US involvement was unnecessary. Prior to World War II, Ivy Lee, a journalist turned publicity agent, served as advisor to a German cartel by the German Dye Trust that supported Adolf Hitler's restriction on religion and freedom of press. Because of his friendly relations with Hitler prior to his rise to power in 1933, Lee was often branded as a traitor and called "Poison Lee" by his critics. Similarly, when the Watergate Scandal was unearthed, the cover-up tactics were referred by Richard Nixon as a "PR situation."

Fraser Steital, senior counselor at Burson-Marsteller, believed that the Watergate Scandal gave PR a "black eye." President Richard M. Nixon and his aides used what the people identified as PR tactics to cover up the break-in at the Watergate. To quote Steital, "What Nixon and his henchman wrought was the exact opposite of public relations," unfortunately Nixon reaffirmed the public view when he used the term "a PR situation" in talking about the cover—up tactics.[25]

If one were to analyze the Watergate scandal, it was an issue of unethical practices in the highest echelons of political governance. As the image of the government was involved, the media efforts by the then establishment were referred as PR tactics because Nixon himself called it a "PR situation." Nixon had to resign to avoid facing impeachment. There is no gainsaying that the so-called "PR tactics" would not have saved him from impeachment had he not chosen to resign. The reputation of the PR profession, however, got sullied in the bargain.

It is believed that many PR practitioners got wary of the nomenclature as aspersions were cast on the profession *per se*, and gradually PR metamorphosed into corporate communication, albeit with an expanded mandate to cover many other facets that PR traditionally did not handle, like brand management, corporate social responsibility, care management, etc.

1.4 Roots of corporate communication in India

Public relations, the precursor of corporate communication, has been practiced for long in India. Interestingly, the credit for practicing PR in the formal sense goes to the public sector.

1.4.1 PR foundation in public sector

In retrospect, India opted for a mixed economy model after getting independence from the British yoke in August 1947. The tilt, however, was towards a socialistic pattern, which saw the setting up of a large number of public sector corporations in almost all the facets of the economy, viz., infrastructure, oil, power, steel, heavy machinery, aviation, surface transport, insurance, defense, scientific research, pharmaceuticals, food, hotels, aviation, et al. The first prime minister of India, Jawaharlal Nehru, in fact, was the architect of public sector in India. When Indira Gandhi, his daughter, became the prime minister in the mid-1960s, she only reiterated her faith in the public sector. She surprised everyone when her government, in 1969, did two drastic things: one, the nationalization of banks, and, two, the withdrawal of privy purses from the erstwhile kings, who had joined the Indian union and were receiving some yearly grant that was referred as "privy purses." The grants were a pittance, but the withdrawal sent a strong signal that kings and kingdoms had no place in a democracy.

The public sector, though growing, was often on the media radar, which constantly criticized it for corruption, nepotism, bureaucratization, and losses, among other things. The media treated the entire public sector as a monolith, even though there were some public sector organizations that could truly be treated as "blue chip." On the whole, the public sector was never in loss, but contributed handsomely to the exchequer, but the narrative built by the media was so strong, which, among other things, paved the way for gradually disinvesting of many public sector organizations by successive governments.

Concerned about the growing poor performance of many PSUs and poorer image, Mrs Indira Gandhi, under the aegis of SCOPE (the Standing Conference of Public Sector Enterprises), an association of the PSUs, convened a conference of the CEOs of PSUs in the late 1970s and reviewed the issue. In a path-breaking decision, which kind of laid the foundation for PR, all central PSUs were asked to have a PR department that was to be headed by a professional. Convinced that a motivated force was imperative for the success of an organization, a decision was also taken vide which all PSUs were advised to motivate the workforce and inform them about the company through employee communication media, especially the house journal. Later when she imposed the infamous "Emergency" in 1975, all the PSU boards were asked to introduce "workers' participation" in governance, another path-breaking decision in corporate governance covering the internal stakeholders.

The private sector, on the other hand, always practiced public relations, which often looked after protocol, besides media relations.

1.4.2 Economic liberalization provided impetus to PR practice

Public relations received another spurt in the 1990s when the architect of India's economic liberalization, P V Narsimha Rao was the prime minister, and Dr. Man Mohan Singh, who became the prime minister from 2004–14, was then the finance minister. As the economy allowed FDI (Foreign Direct Investment) in various sectors, many multinational companies entered the Indian shores, bringing along with them the PR culture. The global ad agencies had always been there, but now encouraged by the need for PR, they either strengthened their PR outfits or created them where they did not exist. The agencies, while pitching for accounts, were used to presenting only ad campaigns, but now it was expected that they would provide communication solutions on a 360-degree perspective that included public relations in brand management.

Inaugurating the 15th All India Public Relations Conference on 9 November 1993 in New Delhi, PV Narsimha Rao had this to say of PR:

> You have the magic touch. You can make anyone believe that by using a small amount of hair oil you can get the hair to grow by one foot everyday, by taking some pills which one does not know whether they contain clay or anything else, one can become younger by twenty years within a short time. Now, this is the kind of conviction, a very genuine conviction, which you by your magic touch can bring to bear on the minds of people. What do I need more?[26]

1.4.3 Teaching of PR and corporate communication in schools of journalism

The economic liberalization brought the euphoria about the mass communication job market, resulting in hundreds of private institutes opening shops in metros. Many universities also added PR as an elective subject in journalism courses. The University Grants Commission reviews the syllabus through a committee every few years and sends a model course curriculum to all the universities. Post liberalization, one saw the inclusion of corporate communication and PR as specialized courses in mass communication curricula. The Indian Institute of Mass Communication, a premier institute in the teaching, training, and research in mass communication, also added a full course paper on corporate communication in its PG program in advertising and PR around the turn of the century. Over the years, one has seen that over 300 universities in India have media schools offering full courses at undergraduate and postgraduate levels in advertising, public relations, and corporate communication. Many academics and professionals have added to the knowledge by writing books and empirical papers on corporate communication and encouraging scholars to undertake research projects.

When and how public relations metamorphosed into corporate communication in India, there may be no archival reference, but by and by, it has been seen that companies, both in the public and private sectors, have designated their PR departments as corporate communications departments and PR managers as corporate communication managers.

The professional bodies, as said earlier, however, continue to be referred as public relations societies or associations.

1.5 Various kinds of communication

Marketing communication

Marketing communication consists of those forms of communication that support sales of goods or services. This includes advertising, sales promotion, direct mail communication, etc.

Organizational communication

Organizational communication is used generally to cover public relations, public affairs, investor relations, labor market communication, corporate advertising, environmental communication, corporate communication, etc. Experts believe that organizational communication encompasses a heterogeneous type of activities which have only a few things in common.

Management communication

Management is described as "accomplishing work through other people." Management includes functions like planning, organizing, commanding, coordinating, and controlling. Management communication is used in various staff and line functions in an organization.

1.6 Placement of corporate communication within the organization

There are differing views on where corporate communication is to be placed in the organizational hierarchy. While some feel that an independent department reporting directly to the CEO is the ideal solution, others feel that, since corporate communication is the umbrella term used for various specialists' communications functions in a company, there is no need for a separate department. The corporate communication philosophy implies that various specialists who are in charge of communication of varying kind (reflected in the box) must look at the communication problem of the corporate holistically and ensure that communication from various departments is in harmony and not at variance. To them, corporate communication is a process, a tactic, and not really an independent entity.

For the sake of argument, even if we agree that corporate communication is a process and a tactic, there is no gainsaying that it requires a specific area of understanding, intellect, and skill. Also, as corporate communication communicates on various issues that concern the organization and its stakeholders, an independent department with specialized staff is preferred to render the staff function of aiding and advising the top management and other departments on their issues that require communication intervention. For example, to the marketing department, the corporate communication department can provide support for its brand building communication activities that would encompass events and media endorsements, among other things; for investor relations, it can help in producing appropriate literature and organize events; for HR, it can render help in media interface, especially in times of employee unrest; for a production team, it can help in devising staff motivation programs by using various communication channels. In other words, corporate communication serves as a link both for the internal and external universe of the organization.

Recent research on the corporate communications function reveals that nearly one-half (48 percent) corporate communications officers (CCOs) in the Global Fortune 500 companies report to the chief executive officer. Approximately 42 percent of a CCO's job is strategic, and 58 percent is tactical. Over the next years, they would be focusing more on social responsibility, social media, and reputation. The research done by Weber Shandwick and Spencer Stuart found distinct differences in the perceptions of CCOs from the Most Admired companies versus Contender companies.[27]

1.7 Corporate communication functions

Corporate communication function includes media relations, employee communication, corporate image management, government relations, corporate advertising, corporate PR, brand promotions like events and sponsorships with a view to elicit the desired response from various stakeholders in pursuance of the fulfillment of corporate goals. Some of the strategies and tactics include the following:

- Targeting key trade press to keep the company in focus as far as its brand's equity is concerned
- Working on tactics that bring people face-to-face
- Selecting appropriate media and drafting appropriate messages to reach out to various constituencies
- Creating a strong, positive, and identifiable corporate image
- Building reputation of key executives
- Managing crisis communication
- Assisting top management in change management within and without the organization
- Maintaining investor and shareholder relationships
- Assisting the management in community relations through corporate social responsibility

1.8 Trinity in corporate communication

In pursuance of CC functions, a corporate communication practitioner needs to work on the trinity or troika, viz., audience, message, and medium, to achieve the goals.

1.8.1 Identifying the stakeholders

- The stakeholders or target audience can be defined as those critical groups of people upon whom rests the success of an organization. It is important for the corporation communication practitioner to find where the various stakeholders are located, what their expectations are from the organization, and why the organization is dependent upon them. Every organization deals with a variety of stakeholders that can be broadly divided in to two, viz.,

Internal
External

Internal stakeholders broadly comprise employees, shareholders, and families of employees. The external stakeholders encompass policymakers, opinion leaders, competitors, professional bodies, special interest groups, media, customers (industrial, wholesalers, dealers, consumers), and the public at large.

An organization has certain communication obligations towards its stakeholders that need to be articulated by the corporate communication practitioner. The corporate communication function serves as a link between the management and its different stakeholders. It must ensure responsibility and responsiveness in policy and information to the best interests of the organization and its stakeholders.

Social responsibility, historically ignored by most institutions, is increasingly being viewed as an "investment" in business. This serves as a differential among various organizations. Corporate communication is not image making in the sense of creating a false front or cover-up.

1.8.2 Identifying communication channels

For reaching out to a disparate set of audience, the corporate communication practitioner needs to identify most suitable media vehicles that are accessed by the target audience.

Some of the media for internal and external target audience (TA) include the following:

Media for Internal TA

(Interpersonal communication, brainstorming, house journals, video, idea boxes, intranet, social gatherings, et al). Chapter 6: Employee Communication has been devoted to this aspect.

Media for External TA

(Mass media, conferences, exhibitions, meets, selective media, et al).
The various media vis-à-vis stakeholders will be discussed in greater detail in Chapter 5.

1.8.3 Articulating the messages

An organization communicates constantly even when it may not be formally communicating. People often have a certain perception about the organization that may be based on their experience with its brands, people, or services. Sometimes the perceptions are shaped by external stimuli provided by media or events. Communication during normal times and critical times is the responsibility of the corporate communication department. Before, however, messages are crafted, knowing the minds of the target audience is necessary. Each message that reaches out to a stakeholder group must satisfy its need for information and fulfill the organization's responsibility towards that group.

Research and evaluation need to be in-built in every corporate communication program. It is imperative that the corporate communication department or consultancy must constantly evaluate performance in the following areas, viz., ensuring media mileage, delivery of key messages, market research and surveys, tracking customer/reader inquiries, tracking media opinion, event success, and brand audit.[28]

1.9 Why is the need for corporate communication felt so much, and now?

Organizations today are feeling a tremendous heat due to various reasons. Some analysts feel that an average organization finds itself in a pressure-cooker-like situation. Some of the reasons include the following:

- Big business constantly under attack for various acts of omission and commission
- Challenges of global economy
- Convergence of products and markets
- Growing exposure to information through various media
- Networking of people cutting across barriers of geography, caste, color, and creed
- Issues of corporate governance and corporate social responsibility
- Conflicts and pandemics that have hit an average person like nothing else

1.9.1 Why is big business under attack?

Business generally is under attack from various groups in society for being seen as heartless and bloodsucking. There is a growing perception that the high profits by business often rob the common man of getting goods at reasonable price. There is no gainsaying that if the number of rich people is increasing, so is the number of people living below the poverty line. Thinkers and social critics have often questioned the poor level of consciousness of big businessmen in amassing billions, while their unfortunate brethren go to bed without a square meal, or when millions of children die of malnutrition, and mothers die while giving birth to children due to poor nutrition and scarce medical facilities. At least one-third of the global population lives on one dollar equivalent in a day. Noble laureate Professor Amritya Sen spoke about the need for welfare economics. Many contemporary economists and thinkers are talking about the bottom-up approach and the need for a paradigm shift in this direction. Barrack Obama, in his opening address on 20 January 2009 watched by more than 1.3 billion people around the world, said, "Without a watchful eye, the market can spin out of control. A nation cannot prosper long when it favors only the prosperous."[29]

At macro level, argue Argenti and Forman, corporate communication can be one of the strategies to counteract the persistent scrutiny and negative attention that businesses in general face and at micro level, and corporate communication reflects our interface with both internal and external constituencies.[30]

Famous economist Micheal Shermer's article "Why people don't trust free markets," which drew huge response on his blog, provides interesting insights about people's disdain with big business. To quote Shermer,

> Capitalism may not need apologists and propagandists, but it does need a vigorous scientific and rational defense as evidenced by the fact that so many people still distrust free markets. Market solutions to social problems are generally received with skepticism. Businessmen are distrusted, corporations looked at askance, and there is a well-known resentment against those who have most benefited from markets. (As one New Yorker cartoon featuring two people in conversation reads: "I hated Bill Gates before it became so fashionable.")

1.9.2 Why do people distrust free markets?

Part of the answer, argues Shemer, can be found in history. For a long time, people lived in small groups and communes, from a few to a few hundred people whereby each one knew the other intimately. In most cases they were genetically related. Most of the resources were shared, and wealth was not accumulated. Excessive greed on the part of someone in the group was abhorred, and the guilty punished. Therefore, people naturally respond to a free market system in which conspicuous wealth is paraded as a sign of success with envy and anger. He calls the phenomenon "evolutionary egalitarianism."[31]

Throughout most of the history of civilization, economic inequalities were not necessarily the result of natural differences in drive and talent between members of a society equally free to pursue their right to prosperity; instead, it was "a handful of chiefs, kings, nobles, and priests exploited an unfair and rigged social system to achieve gains best described as ill-gotten."[32]

As more and more people are exposed to the way business functions, especially when scams and fraudulent practices by big business houses, the likes of Enron, WorldCom, Texwell, P. Anderson, and Satyam Computers, surface, business in general is seen as suspect. Public opinion against business builds instantly when people's hard-earned money disappears in the stock market tumble because someone already so rich wished to make more money at the cost of teeming millions by fudging figures and befooling the system! As a fallout, issues relating to corporate governance are debated and discussed at various levels. In fact, soon after Satyam's fraud became public, rival Infosys' spokespersons spoke about the corporate governance imperatives in their company to anyone who was listening.

1.9.3 Challenges of convergence of products and markets

Globalization and the advent of technology has brought about convergence which no one could imagine until a decade or so ago.

The speed at which product and markets are converging is one of the critical trends the marketers must address. Convergence is forcing reinvention of many companies to define themselves and how they would compete in a seamless market scenario.

Following are the outcomes of a changing environment.

- Competition is becoming more multidimensional
- Marketing is becoming much more about market transformation and change
- Branding is going deeper than narrow product association

1.9.4 What will it take to win in a converging world?

- A robust corporate brand management
- A winning customer relationship management
- Customer information management
- Alliance and partnership management
- Management of enabling technology

Harvard Prof. Ranjay Gulati in his book *Deep Purpose: The Heart and Soul of High-Performance Companies*, in the chapter "Are You a Poet, or Just a Plumber?" posits what could be very relevant to the corporate communication narrative. He asks of the top management to define their "Big Story." In other words, to work on a narrative that would reflect the company's real intent. To have a larger impact, the "Big story" he suggests needs to be connected with the narrator's personal story that conveys a sense of urgency. On the crisis front, he recommends re-thinking "in relation to the purpose as moral 'choice points' and take the opportunity to cement the purpose even more in people's minds and establish its continued validity."[33]

1.9.5 Key competitive implications

Competition is becoming more multidimensional. Companies are getting into diverse portfolios. For example, MMTC, which is in the business of exporting iron, ore and other industrial products also produces and sells silverware and gold coins; similarly Coca-Cola and Pepsi which for long were into production and marketing of aerated drinks expanded their portfolio by entering the juices and the bottled water market, Pepsi has also entered the snack category, Sahara India, which began from Financial products, entered into entertainment, real estate, and housing, IFFC fertilizer cooperative got into insurance, ONGC into power projects, and oil companies into retailing, NTPC from its core competency in thermal expanded its portfolio to include hydroelectric power generation, SAIL and NTPC into captive power generation.

There is tremendous convergence in media tools. All the four screens, viz., cinema, television, computer, and mobile, are converging into one. Mobile phones also have Web, music, radio, recorder, and still and video camera options. The pricing is competitive and affordable even for people in the low-income category.

The audience base is converging, cutting across artificial boundaries of territory, castes, color, and creed through social networking sites and blogs.

There is a race for the main service-based customer relationship. Share of product market is superseded in importance by share of customer relationship. Marketing is fast becoming much more about market transformation and change.

Convergence helps break down artificial market borders to better meet customer needs. Branding is increasingly going deeper than narrow product association. It is expected that the brand that goes deeper through the branding of a company's core capabilities, relationships, and way of things would be more successful than the rest.

A world-class capability in customer relationship would go a longer way than being perceived as an expert in a particular product category.

In changing times, communication holds the key in connecting with communities, markets, and minds.

1.9.6 Media exposure: power of public opinion

Media today have become all-pervasive. Communities are connecting through the media like never before. The social networking sites have provided an interactive forum to like-minded people to discuss issues that affect their lives. The 24-7 news channels need stories to keep people's interest alive, and high-society gossip is definitely an important content of media across the board. Media, being in business itself, is perceived to be friendly to business in general as its sustenance rests on the ad revenue, but obliquely it also does "harm" to business when it exposes scams and frauds and write stories on the extravagance of top businessmen and their family members. People, especially the thinking middle class, somewhere feels the riches earned by business houses *per se* are undeserved.

Let's look at the following cases.

When the story of business tycoon Mukesh Ambani presenting a Rs. 242 Crore jet plane to wife, Nita Ambani, appeared in media, followed by younger sibling Anil Ambani presenting a yacht to wife, Tina, costing almost double the cost of the jet, people reacted actively in social circles, not to forget the social networking sites and blogs. Here is a quote from a blogger on Mukesh Ambani's gift during 2007:

> The Reliance Industries chairman will finally have his office in the sky. After he bought the aircraft, Mukesh got it customised at the Associated Air Centre in Dallas, Texas. It has a state-of-the-art business office and cabin management system for games, music, satellite television and wireless communication. But more interestingly, it has a master bedroom, master lavatory with a range of showers, galleys and a sky bar in the forward lounge complete with mood lighting In other words make a grand show of gifting your wife at a rather opportune time, while in actuality gifting yourself an extravagant present. This sullenly brings back memories of that fateful birthday when hubby in his unique wisdom decided to gift me a much prized English crockery set for my birthday! I was aghast. All romantic notions whisked outa the window forever. The poor guy had no clue as to why I was howling . . . blabbering in-between how he does not care for me anymore. Men are at such times, much to our disgust, at a complete loss for words which only makes us howl louder.[34]

Here is a blogger on TIAN, the yacht Anil Ambani presented to his wife, Tina, in 2008.

> Who Loves His Wife The Most, If Only Money Could Tell. . .
>
> Boy, and we thought the economic slowdown had zeroed on to the Reliance brothers too. But we were in the wrong. The business rival brothers are still busy trying

> to outshine one another with expensive presents for their wives. We are sure that you'd remember how Mukesh Ambani, the elder bro, raised many eyebrows when he bought a $52,362,298 worth corporate jet for his wife Nita less than a year ago. Well, now it was time for younger bro Anil to make an impression. And so he did with the super luxury yacht worth $83,784,070 that he got for wife Tina. Unimaginatively named Tian (combining the first two letters from Tina and Anil), this yacht is made in Genoa, Italy and was a long time dream for Tina, which her billionaire hubby finally made a reality. Though much has not been revealed about the super yacht, what we do know is that it is about 34 meters long and cost $47 million to build. Right now, it is anchored near the Gateway of India with plans to test the waters with the couple brining in the New Year. Touché, romance. Let's see what Mukesh has to say to that![35]

Close on the heels of the jet news, media, including television channels, covered the news of Mukesh Ambani building a 27-story mansion in Mumbai for his personal use at a cost of $2 billion, estimated to be the most expensive home in the world.

The property in question, as per media reports, is worth Rs 400 Crores and is located on Altamount Road in South Mumbai. The media provided graphic details of the property. This is what NDTV said about the mansion:

> The house will feature a silver stairway, magnificent crystal chandeliers, six floors just for parking, a panoramic view of the city from 550ft above sea level. A separate gym for each family member, four floors of open-air gardens, a 65-seat theater, complete with a wine and snack bar, a spa, a swimming pool, jacuzi and even a personal helipad. If this wasn't enough, there are also plans to make an ice room, where the Ambanis could beat the heat on a hot summers day. This house named Antilia is expected be ready by next year so that the Ambanis can move in from their current "modest" 22-storey home.

The Waqf board moved the court, alleging that it sold the property so an orphanage could be built. First the high court and later the Supreme Court was moved by the board.[36]

1.10 Corporate governance and corporate social responsibility of business

Corporate governance and corporate social responsibility have become important imperatives for businesses to acquire brand equity. Organizations are very protective about their reputations. However, it is not possible for any kind of communication strategy to camouflage tainted goals and wrong practices for long. Sooner or later, truth surfaces, and that is what the businesses must understand. Many research studies reflect that more and more people like to buy products from companies that are considered ethical and socially responsible. Similarly, a business may also get affected if the public opinion does not support some action of a country. For instance, during the Gulf War, some American brands were boycotted by European consumers.

The issue of corporate governance has been dealt with in detail in the chapter on crises communication, and an exclusive chapter on corporate social responsibility has been included in the book.

1.11 How does a corporate communication practitioner cope with the earlier information and more?

To be successful, a corporate communication practitioner has to be sensitive to understand stakeholders' need for information; he/she should have sharp reflexes to act quickly to a situation, be analytical to make a decision based on the best options in the given situation, and be committed to honest and truthful communication. These traits can be acquired when the incumbent understands the core competence and core values perused by the organization; he/she has a good hang of the market and competition, the unique proposition that the organization has to offer in terms of brand quality, research and development, pricing structure, corporate governance, corporate social responsibility, employee relations, HR policies, and so on and so forth. A corporate communication practitioner has to be proactive in constantly sharing information with various stakeholder groups that reflect the character and ethos of the organization. In times of crises, he/she must respond to the information needs of media as quickly and honestly as humanly possible. This would be possible when the top management understands the role of corporate communication and trusts the parson or agency in charge of corporate communication.

Most of the corporate communication is achieved through media. Therefore it is important that the person in charge of corporate communication understands the media environment threadbare, its sociology, functioning, dynamics, and undercurrents. The following chapter, Media dynamics and strategies, has been devoted to this aspect of corporate communication.

Summary

In this chapter we looked at the roots of corporate, tracking about a century-old relationship with public relations. We looked at various definitions of corporate communication. The chapter discussed the various reasons that have contributed to the poor perception of business among the public. The chapter then discussed the importance of understanding the trinity of communication, viz., message, medium, and audience, before undertaking any program. Functions of corporate communication and its role in a convergent world were touched upon. In the end we discussed why a growing need is felt for corporate communication function among organizations and what it takes to become a successful corporate communication practitioner.

Key terms

Communication channels: various media, like mass media, newspapers, television, radio, internet, cinema, and interpersonal media through which communication is done.

Corporate communication: how a company communicates with its various stakeholders, both in routine and crisis times.

Corporate governance: how a company runs its business both legally and ethically.

Corporate social responsibility: the responsibility of a corporate organization towards society, that goes beyond the obvious.

Corporate image: how a company is perceived by the outside world.

Crisis communication: how a company communicates in times of crisis to reach out to various stakeholders through various means, including the media, with a view to inform how it is handling the crisis.

Investor relationship: relationship of a company with its various investors that would include banks, financial institutions, and individual investors.

Key trade press: financial newspapers, magazines, and trade news channels and financial journalists.

Marketing communication: those forms of communication that support sales of particular goods or services, including advertising, sales promotion, direct mail communication, etc.

Management communication: it encompasses communication used in various staff and line functions in an organization.

Organizational communication: communication that encompasses public relations, public affairs, investor relations, labor market communication, corporate advertising, environmental communication, corporate communication, etc.

Public relations: a deliberate, planned, and sustained effort to create mutual understanding between an organization and its different publics.

Stakeholders: it is defined as those people and groups of people on whom rests the sustenance of an organization.

Concept review questions

Q.1. Trace the roots of corporate communication over the last century, and discuss the differences and similarities between public relations and corporate communication.

Q.2. Define corporate communication, going through various definitions given by scholars over a period of time.

Q.3. Who, in your view, are the various stakeholders for corporate communication? Discuss.

Q.4. Why is the need for corporate communication felt, especially in present times?

Q.5. What role does corporate communication play in the age of convergence? Discuss with suitable examples.

Q.6. Discuss the core functions of corporate communication.

Critical thinking exercise

Follow a story about an organization that has been embroiled in some controversy in various media, including social media, for at least two weeks, and analyze how the organization has responded through various means, to understand the role of corporate communication.

Project work

Meet at least four corporate communication practitioners from the corporate sector and PR/corporate communication consultancies and discuss when and how corporate communication came to be practiced in your country. Discuss whether there has been an expansion of works after the department was designated corporate communication, or if it is the same when it was public relations. Make a list of functions perused by the practitioners, both under PR and corporate communications.

*

Notes

1 Paul A. Argenti and Janis Forman, *The Power of Corporate Communication*, 2002 (New York: McGraw-Hill), pp. 17–18.
2 www.exchange4media.com/PR/Pr_speak.asp?PR_id=69
3 Scott M. Cutlip, Allen H. Xenter and Glen M. Broom, *Effective Public Relations*, eighth edition, 2006 (New Delhi: Pearson Education), pp. 72–73.
4 Ibid.
5 E. Blauw, 1994.
6 Jackson, Paul R., *Corporate Communications* (September 1, 2009). INTERNATIONAL REVIEW OF INDUSTRIAL AND ORGANIZATIONAL PSYCHOLOGY, Gerard P. Hodgkinson & J. Kevin Ford, eds., Available at SSRN: https://ssrn.com/abstract=1508493
7 Cees B. M. Van Riel and Charlkes. J. Fomburn, *Essentials of Corporate Communication-Implementing Practices for Effective Reputation Management*, Routledge, first edition, 2007.
8 Joseph Fernandez, *Corporate Communications: A 21st Century Primer*, 2004 (New Delhi: SAGE Publications, First Edition (2018), Response Books), pp. 224–225.
9 Richard R. Dolphin, *The Fundamentals of Corporate Communication*, 1999 (London: Butterworth-Heinemann), p. 1.
10 J. R. Finley, "The Task and Responsibilities of Business Affairs", *Business Quarterly*, 58, 1994, p. 105 as quoted by R. R. Dolphin.
11 Jaishri N. Jethwaney, Adrash Kumar Verma and N. N. Sarkar, *Public Relations Concepts, Strategies and Tools*, 1994 (New Delhi: Sterling Publishers), pp. 6–7.
12 The incident happened in 1914, but has come alive after almost a century with film footage of the incident and media coverage and the names of those who lost their lives, the memorial in their remembrance and documents relating to the incident on the net. For more details log on to wikipedia.org or simply write "Ludlow Massacre" on the Google search.
13 www.nku.edu/turney/micheal12.htm.
14 Krik Hallahan, *Journal of Public Relations Research*, 14, no. 4, January 2002, pp. 265–315.
15 Ibid.
16 Paul A. Argenti and Janis Forman, *The Power of Corporate Communication*, 2002 (New York: McGraw-Hill), pp. 26–28.
17 Larry Tye, *The Father of Spin: Edward L. Bernays & the Birth of Public Relations*, 1998 (New York: Crown Publishers), p. 157.
18 Paul A. Argenti and Janis Forman, *The Power of Corporate Communication*, 2002 (New York: McGraw-Hill), p. 26.
19 Quoted in Bernays, *Biography of an Idea*, p. 387, reproduced by Paul A. Argenti and Janis Forman, *The Power of Corporate Communication*, 2002 (New York: McGraw-Hill), p. 27.
20 Larry Tye, *The Father of Spin: Edward L. Bernays & the Birth of Public Relations*, 1998 (New York: Crown Publishers), pp. 29–30 as quoted by Paul A. Argenti and Janis Forman, *The Power of Corporate Communication*, 2002 (New York: McGraw-Hill), p. 27.
21 Kevin Moloney, *Rethinking PR*, 2000 (Routledge), pp. 68–72.
22 Quoted by Kevin Moloney, ibid.
23 Ibid., Richard R. Dolphin, *The Fundamentals of Corporate Communication*, 1999 (London: Butterworth-Heinemann), p. 3.
24 Associated Press, 31 May 2005, www.Aponline.
25 Mona Lee and Carla Johnson, *Principles of Advertising- a Global Perspective*, pp. 380–381, https://books.google.co.in
26 Former Prime Minister late Narsimha Rao, while inaugurating the 15th All India Public Relations Conference on 9 November 1993, in New Delhi.

27 11. 32. *Source*: en. Wikipedia.org.
28 Ibid.
29 CNN and other television channels, 20 January 2009.
30 Paul A. Argenti and Janis Forman, *The Power of Corporate Communication*, 2002 (New York: McGraw-Hill), pp. 5–6.
31 www.michaelshermer.com/2008/01/why-people-dont-trust-free-markets/
32 Ibid.
33 Gulati, Ranjay, *Deep Purpose: The Heart and Soul of High Performance Companies*, 2022 (New York: Harper Business), chapter 5, pp. 95–117.
34 *Source*: http://sachiniti.wordpress.com/2007/11/02, posted by Kaveetaa Kaul on 2 November 2007.
35 http://elitechoice.org/2008/12/23/.
36 *Source*: NDTV, 2 May 2008 (With PTI inputs). www.ndtv.com/convergence/ndtv/story.aspx?id=NEWEN20080048618

2

MEDIA DYNAMICS AND STRATEGIES

2.1 Introduction

Media is the conduit through which most of the corporate communication aims are achieved. There are varying media to choose from, each with individual characteristics, importance, and usefulness. Corporate communication professionals need to understand the interdependence of what is termed in the communication parlance as the "Troika" of communication, that is, the need for synergy among three elements—message, medium, and audience; and, more importantly, the dynamics and undercurrents of media functioning in the overall ecosystem.

In this chapter we shall take a look at the various media, their strengths and weaknesses, the dependence of corporate communication on various media, and the reasons of dependence. The alleged "unholy alliance" between corporate communication (including public relations and advertising) and media has been a subject matter of many capricious yet inconclusive debates in media circles and academia. Because corporate organizations book ads in media, it is believed that they have a fair share of voice in what media would write or would be pressurized against writing from the large corporate organizations. The chapter would bring some glimpses of the debate and more.

2.2 The changing media scene in India

India has seen a phenomenal growth in media in terms of expansion, reach, access, and content since its independence in 1947. A free media can sustain itself only in a democracy. As much as the media would like others to believe that it works under no pressure, the fact of the matter is that media in most countries is not as free from pressures as ideally as it should be. There are corporate, financial, and political pressures that most media houses face. According to the 2022 World Press Freedom Index published by Reporters Without Borders on the World Press Freedom Day on 3 May 2022, India was ranked 150 out of 180 countries. Many may not agree, but it does provide a perspective on how the Indian news media is perceived.[1]

DOI: 10.4324/9781032694702-2

The Indian Press has a history for standing up against the power of state in the past. For instance, in 1975, when the then prime minister promulgated emergency and tried to gag the voice of the media by censorship and withdrawing ad support, some relented, while others stood up against the mighty power of the state. Over the years, however, the changing sociology and ownership patterns of the news media, the power of the press recognized by the corporate sector, their relentless efforts at buying media houses, the corporate political nexus has not escaped the attention of the discerning from understanding the compromised status and dwindling independence of media as the unbiased and independent fourth estate that it is supposed to be.

In the following paragraphs, we shall look at the media bandwidth in India and the relative strengths and weaknesses of various media types.

2.2.1 Print media

The world over, particularly in developed Western countries, print readership is on the decline. Philip Meyer has predicted that with the way readership is going down, the newspaper industry in the USA will be extinguished in the 2040s. Closer to home, the Indian print media industry is booming. Statistics reflect that during the year 2020–21, more than 1,525 new publications were added. Interestingly, regional language publications are finding much favor among the readers; therefore, media houses are bringing out editions from the cities where there is sizable population of the people speaking respective regional languages.[2]

The print media is said to be a cost-intensive and low-return business, but it is still attractive to entrepreneurs. The market estimates put the revenue generation of Bennett and Coleman Company Limited that publishes the *Times of India* and other publications at a yearly 25–40 percent.

Interestingly, despite almost over 1.45 lakh registered publications, less than a thousand are members of the India Newspaper Society (INS) and less than 500 of the Audit Bureau of Circulation. According to Khandekar, many newspapers are registered but not published "for purposes other than to make money from the newspapers."[3]

The real change, according to industry observers, in the print industry happened after the lifting of Emergency in 1977. With the change of guard, some regressive laws were repealed, and there was a spurt in circulation and readership, as people wanted to be informed about "what had happened in the proceeding months of the clamp down."[4]

Many magazines like *India Today*, *Sunday*, *Savvy*, *Society* came on the scene, providing interesting in-depth analysis of stories with colorful pictures and graphics. Besides political features, magazines provided the latest lifestyle input to their readers at a cost that was quite affordable. Regretfully, *Sunday*, a very popular magazine was closed.

Color is said to be the next innovation in the newspaper media. The *Times of India* not only pioneered it but also came out with niche supplements on travel, education, fashion, employment with no extra cost to the subscribers. In fact the supplements later became money spinners in those categories for the media house.

As said earlier, one has witnessed a changing ownership pattern in the print media. There has been an increasing big business approach in print media. The government of India opened the news sector for Foreign Direct Investment (FDI) India up to 26 percent in the news and Current Affairs and 74 percent in non-news and current affairs.

In an insightful paper, The Role of Foreign Direct Investment on Press Freedom, Nabamita Dutta and Sanjukta Roy, from the department of Economics, West Virginia University, explored their hypothesis that FDI inflows to an economy would enhance the level of its media freedom, using a panel of 115 countries for a period of 20 years, the sample including high-, middle-, and low-income economies. The results, according to the authors, revealed that greater FDI flows to an economy lead to higher levels of press freedom.[5]

There does not seem to have been any empirical research on this aspect in India since the entry of FDI in the news media sector, but it, indeed, is an interesting area to explore.

2.2.2 The cable changed it all

The country was almost shaken from its slumber when dozens of channels beamed in hotels and people's homes through the cable network post the Gulf War in the 1990s. The doomsayers predicted the death of print medium, which did not really happen because the newspapers changed with the changing times and, for long, went on to get more ad budgets from brand managers. Television in India has seen phenomenal growth and expansion, especially in the last decade or so. Indians have been exposed to the kind of 24-7 entertainment in various languages, including Hindi and other regional language, which was unimaginable until the coming of Zee TV. Zee TV, in fact, can be credited for bringing a revolution of sorts in India.

The other phenomenal change came with the proliferation of news channels. The country has more than 400 news channels in English, Hindi, and other regional languages. The circulation of all put together may not go beyond two digits, but it carries a lot of clout and power. In difficult times, the viewership surges manifold. For instance, during the Covid-19 pandemic, the cumulative viewership of news channels surged from a mere 7% to over 21%. The channels have not been able to maintain it in the post-Covid times.

Despite a low viewership, media planners recommend ad slots in news channels, the reasoning being that news is watched by people who matter in the decision-making process. Because of low reach, the ad tariffs are also attractive to media buyers. In the race to be the number one news channel, one has seen allegations of TRP compromise by a concerned agency in the past. Some channels have been facing cases of criminal conspiracy in courts.

2.2.3 Radio

Radio, which has a potential of reach to almost 90% geographical area and population, unfortunately, has taken a dip in the listenership gradually but is trying to pace up, albeit at a slow speed.

There has been a tremendous network growth of All India Radio (AIR). In 1947, AIR had a network of six stations and 18 transmitters. It reached a 20 percent geographical area and 11 percent population. Now AIR has 223 broadcasting centers covering 91.42 percent geographical areas and 99.13 percent population. However, figures and percentages can be dicey, because, reach is not equivalent to access, access is not equivalent to comprehension, and comprehension does not necessarily ensure credibility. The fact of the matter is that radio listenership has drastically gone down over the years.

According to the Economic Survey 2023, the state-owned All India Radio and the public service broadcaster Prasar Bharati, which has become tech-savvy, reflected in the fact that over 240 radio services of All India Radio are live streamed on NewsOnAir, Prasar Bharati's official app. These streams have many listeners not just in India but globally, in more than 85 countries across the world, it added. The survey, as reported by the media, has appreciated the role of radio, especially the community radio, in connecting people during Covid.[6]

2.2.4 New media

The Internet has changed the world forever with its instant connectivity and reach transcending geographical boundaries. It has changed the way we see and make sense of the world. There has been a growing penetration of Internet in India. As per the latest reckoning, the active Internet user base has been growing at an exponential growth of 20% year on year, reaching to 595 million in 2022. India, according to Nielsen's India Internet Report 2023, had 700 million or more active Internet users aged 2 years and older as of December 2022.

With a fierce competition among various search engines, it is not uncommon to find brand promotion by most of them.

The social networking sites have become the latest rage among netizens. Some of the popular sites include Facebook, Instagram, Twitter, Snapchat that have people from various age groups logging on to share their thoughts and concerns on millions of issues.

Of late, some corporate organizations are also using social networking sites for sponsored debates among chat groups on their brands. This means the people who participate are paid for, an issue that has come under fire from critics.

2.2.5 The cell revolution

Mobile telephony is seen as the fourth screen (cinema, television, and computer being the other three screens), which has hooked an average person like never before. The revolution in the mobile phone segment is seen as democratizing access to communication cutting across the economic divide. As there is cutthroat competition in price from various players and liberal policies of TRAI, it is projected that mobile telephone ownership would grow manifold. From games to Internet connectivity, from commercial messages to social messages, from music download to astrology, you name it, and you have it on the mobile.

India, according to TRAI, recorded a billion mobile phones as of 2022.[7] Smartphone ownership, which is over 50 percent, is going to go manifold, as per industry estimates.

2.3 What are the lessons for the corporate communication professionals?

There is a lot that a corporate communication professional can learn from the environment. The media scene is changing at a very great speed, so it is important to keep pace with the changes, draw lessons, understand the emerging trends in media content, access, reach, and ideology, and prepare media material keeping in view the technological advances, resulting in newer content styles and packaging to suit media needs.

2.4 The future—a decade from now

"The farther away the future, the better it looks" is an age-old adage, but when said for media, it defies all logic. The ever-changing media has brought about so much convenience, so much joy, and so much connectively in an average person's life that the future innovations seem just a blink away. The Net, which was expected to closely bond with varying communities, like-minded people across the world encompassing the poor and disadvantaged, has done so, but it is also a grim fact that, looking at the potential of the Net, especially the social networking sites, the medium has become a tool in the hands of people who navigate a different route, of creating chasms, disseminating misinformation, disinformation, encouraging hatred, misogyny, and vested interests.

If on the one hand the governments and powerful world bodies must listen to the issues raised by people and communities, it is also important that some reigning in of anti-social elements and hate mongers is addressed through the provision of law. The social media operators need also to introspect on what unruly people can achieve through such platforms. Hate speech goes more viral than words of sanity. Filtering of information is the responsibility of the administrators of these platforms.

The world community must be more introspective than it is now, and media houses will also have to employ thinking people and not merely messengers.

Continuing with the trend, people will engage with media more and more—stretching time for all kinds of media in a day. In other words, media will continue to be all-pervasive. The increasing involvement with media and technology, on the one hand, may create excitement, but also a sense of fear about our minds being controlled by technology, a scenario projected by the film *Matrix*. The use of artificial intelligence (AI) and now ChatGPT seem to take away even the routine jobs from our lives. In a media report, which the Punjab and Haryana High Court used ChatGPT in a bail order. Justice Anoop Chitkara uses the AI tool to get a broader picture of bail jurisprudence when an assault is one that involves cruelty, reported the media.[8]

The world may be unipolar or bipolar with varying political structures, but there will always be multiple cultures and diverse engagements with media. Whether we shall have global media structures, segmented structures, or both, the biggest fear of the globe will stem from the political ideologies, marketing strategies, and cultural and religious diversities.

The last decade or so has reflected the near stage-managing of media by subversive forces in many countries. The live coverage of terrorist activities in some cases has brought about intense debate in various circles, including media, on the need for drawing a line. Media, it is hoped, despite its love for reflecting reality, will do some introspection and strike a balance in coverage.

2.4.1 Program content

The content of the programs has drastically changed over a period. The cutthroat competition among the competing brands has made programmers take up issues and use treatment, which leaves much to be desired. It is widely believed that channels will go to any extent to attract eyeballs and raise their TRPs. The news channels, besides news and news-based programs, have included entertainment programs that don't really go with the ethos of an ideal news channel, but who cares? Most of news channels are guilty of programs that raise superstitions among people. All kinds of astrological, numerological, Vastu Shastra, and tarot-card-based programs abound the news channels. Sting operations, a huge dose on non-news input in news channels, frivolous issues, and stereotyping of gender, religion, and politics have become a daily staple in various news channels.

Citizen journalists and stringers are playing an important role in filling the content, making accountability an easy casualty. User-generated content (UGC) is fast occupying space, both on national and local television channels. This may have lent a voice to common people, but the trend has also provided a forum to political adversaries and market competitors to their advantage, which is not really a healthy sign.

2.5 Media characteristics

In the following tables, an effort has been made to provide the relative strengths and weaknesses of each medium, keeping in view its inherent characteristics. When one analyzes, one may find the strength of one medium to be another medium's weakness. To illustrate, newspapers have a better shelf life and can be read at leisure and referred back to when required; hence, it is its strength. This becomes a weakness for television and radio, as once you miss a program or even a part of it, you can't rewind or refer back to it unless the system has an in-built mechanism for recording. To argue further, news coming via the morning newspapers become stale if the television and radio covered the story in their evening bulletin.

All advertising and a lot of corporate communication coverage happens through mass media; hence, media planners and corporate communication professionals need to be very careful in choosing the media, keeping in view the following: the relative strengths

TABLE 2.1 Print media press

Strengths	*Weaknesses*
Message received at home in a relaxed atmosphere	Suffers from literacy barrier
The readers look forward to receiving their newspaper. Has shelf value.	Low shelf life as newspapers become stale in a day
The urge to seek news gives the newspaper a better position to be trusted	Lacks drama and emotion
Reading a newspaper becomes a matter of habit; hence, one can achieve regular attention value	Demonstration of product features not effective
Can cope with detailed coverage	Overtaken by television, radio, and Internet in speed
Written word has more credibility	Lacks empathetic readership
Messages carry urgency	"Bad" news is often considered "good" news
Can be read at leisure	What is of reader's interest is decided by the newspapers
High on national coverage	Average time devoted to newspaper reading is very low; hence, ads and developmental news don't stand much chance of being seen carefully
Local/regional newspapers	
Strong reader loyalty	Small circulation
Local coverage	Potential to be biased
Regional flexibility	Generally poor readership data

Source: Author

TABLE 2.2 Magazines

Generally poor readership data	High production cost
Selective readership	Long copy and cancellation dates
High shelf value	Expensive advertising medium
Create a bond and empathy with the readers	High printing costs
High on style, design, and color	Low on immediate news value

Source: Author

TABLE 2.3 Television

Reaches a wide audience	Expensive for time and production
Sight, sound, and color give dramatic possibilities	Bad quality, transmission problem, and poor anchors may put the viewers off
Larger-than-life image	Too much viewing—bad for the eyes
Achieves viewers' empathy	Tends to make people "home birds" and asocial
High on credibility	High exposure can have adverse effects on impressionable minds
Wide choice of channels without incurring extra cost	High exposure to sex and violence can have adverse impacts on society
A family medium	Transient nature of messages

Source: Author

TABLE 2.4 Radio

Wide coverage	Suffers from apathetic listeners
High OTL among listeners	Audience intently use it as "audio wallpaper"
Inexpensive when compared with TV and press	TV preferred over radio, if there is a choice
Long broadcasting hours	Speed of broadcast (short lead time)
High impact and immediacy	Not a very interactive medium
If used as transistor, a mobile medium	Not very innovative

Source: Author

TABLE 2.5 Cinema

Impact of big screen with sound, movement, and color	TV has eroded the cinema audience base
Attracts young crowd	Slow build-up of audience
Theater viewing is a socializing event	Attendance is low and infrequent
Selective local advertising coverage which can gain immediate impact	Commercials shown either in the beginning or in the interval, when high attendance is not ensured

Source: Author

and weaknesses of various media, their reach, audience segmentation vis-à-vis media access, frequency of readership/viewership, extent of duplication between publications, relative exposure of cinema, radio, television, and the extent of duplication, etc.[9]

Employee communication media (house magazines, video magazines, bulletin boards, et al)

TABLE 2.6 Outdoor (posters, billboards/hoarding)

High coverage and OTS (opportunity to see)	High printing cost of posters unless used on large scale
Large-sized billboards give larger-than-life image	Suffers poor audience research
Sites can be booked very flexibly	On environmentalists' radar as they spoil the landscape
Can create drama with colors and size	Strong winds often damage the boards and lead to accidents
Twenty-four-hour projection	Short-circuiting possible in monsoons
Good reminder medium	Only small messages possible
A community medium	They distract attention of drivers[10]

Source: Author

TABLE 2.7 New media/Internet

Global networking	Low access
Seamless coverage	Information overload
No hierarchical setup for access of information	Banner ad recall not very high
High interactivity	Trolling, stalking, hate mongering
By and large a free-to-access medium	Message spillover to not required territories
Instant connectivity	Not a medium to suit all demographic profiles
A storehouse of knowledge	Requires time commitment
Online marketing profitability	Has taken away business of small players

Source: Author

TABLE 2.8 Mobile phones and SMS

A communication revolution	Nuisance value
Reach not dependent on location	Intrusion in privacy
Reaching the right TA	A possible health hazard
Permission marketing possible	Too many alerts
Emotional connotation	Nuisance from promotional messages
An all-pervasive medium	Increases noise pollution in public places

Source: Author

TABLE 2.9 Employee communication media (house journal, video magazines, et al)

High planning	Controlled media
Pre-test possible	Management interference on content
Reaching the right TA	Enjoys less credibility
The basic aim behind employee media is to create a fellow feeling and a sense of belonging—a family feeling	Requires balance in coverage to avoid annoying a certain section of employees whose views are not included, especially the trade unions
Helps build personal connect	Requires sensitive handling in times of crises
Motivates employees	Receivers often take such media for granted as it generally comes free
Participative	Generally falls short in keeping up with schedules
Feedback possible	Often expensive

Source: Author

TABLE 2.10 Home pages and company blogs

A window to company's ethos, philosophy, vision, and mission	Most of the home pages are not innovative and do not contain much to hold surfers' interest
Help build personal connect with various stakeholders and can be highly participative	The pages are generally not updated for long
Can be updated at a continuous pace without the constraint of space	Often perceived as "management's mouthpiece"
In times of crises, can be a great information disseminator	Low on credibility
Attending to customer complaints and feedback possible	Tracking of blog sphere resorted to by only a few companies

Source: Author

While making the decision on the choice of media, the corporate communication professional will have to consider the following:

1. Most effective media
2. Most efficient media
3. Most credible media

Some organizations have full-fledged corporate communication departments to handle various kinds of media. Sometimes, however, besides an internal department, an external consultancy is retained to give value addition to the internal team, especially in the areas of media tracking, media handling, investor relations, and crises communication, etc.

2.6 Media reach and accessibility in India

An updated knowledge about mass media reach and access is imperative for a corporate communication practitioner. It's important to keep a track of the latest facts, figures, and insights so that while making a media plan, all these issues are taken into consideration. Print medium, which remained the favorite with media planners for long, ceded to television post-satellite revolution in India. Albeit slowly, the Internet seemed to be the medium of times, but it was not much in the media mix until a few years ago; but the latest figures are mind-boggling. Net leads with highest ad revenue, followed by TV and then print. The Indian media is likely to grow by 12–14 percent "to clock **Rs 1.6 lakh crore** revenue in FY24," rating agency Crisil was quoted by the media.[11]

The corporate communication practitioner has to prepare an ideal mix of media for content sharing and engagement with the key audiences.

2.7 The "third party" endorsement –its value in corporate communication and the broad debate

The news that appears in the media is believed to have a third party or neutral perspective of reality and facts. Because the media is neither the sender nor the receiver of news, it is perceived to be independent of the bias, hence making it more credible.

The "third-party" endorsement is believed to be the reinforcement of the news worthiness that the media provides when it publishes or broadcasts stories sourced from a corporate communication and public relations department. There are, however, varying views on the value of third-party endorsements. While some swear by it, others feel that it is overrated to the degree that its effectiveness has become diminished. They believe that people are smart enough to differentiate wheat from chaff, that is, what is objective journalism and what the corporate communication staff pushes.

For long, the tasks rendered by corporate communication professionals were not seen as tangible, while the marketing departments often talked about quantifiable objectives of their job and the data to support their bottom-line approach. However, it is changing now. Free publicity received through the "third-party" endorsement is projected as the measurement of success by the practitioner. It is now commonplace to put up notes to the management on the financial value of such coverage in terms of space measurement and its currency value.

2.8 Ad value of corporate communication

Jim McNamara, talking on the free publicity received in the media known as "measurement by kilogram," opines that a quantifiable method does not indicate the quality of coverage. It also does not take into account whether the intended target audience was exposed to that and, if yes, whether the impact of their attitude towards the company was the intended one.

2.8.1 Defining media measurement

Media measurement is defined as a standardized system for evaluating the effectiveness of communication between two or more organizations and their designated stakeholders through various media channels through pre-determined parameters that would encompass quantity, quality, positioning of news, its tone of coverage, etc.

Analysts often analyze the clippings based on positive, negative, and neutral terms. It is considered positive if it favors the company's point of view; it is negative if it is critical; and it is neutral if it has raised the necessary awareness without taking a positive or negative stand.

McNamara argues that this simple method of analysis runs in to three major challenges to its validity and value:

The simple +ive, -ive, and neutral categorization of media articles runs into the degree of subjectivity. Usually, evaluation is made casually and based on personal judgment. Secondly, the method is crude, as it is possible that a story may have all the elements in it, then how it is to be categorized. Thirdly and most important, categorizing editorial articles as positive, negative, and neutral is a simplistic method of qualitative assessment as it is possible that the so-called positive may not necessarily contain the key message or thrust of a company's viewpoint. Therefore, the article may be categorized as positive but may not be strategically significant.[12]

Let us have a look at what some of the professional bodies have to say on this issue.

2.8.2 The Institute of Public Relations (IPR)

The Institute of Public Relations (IPR) in the USA, in its Guidelines and Standards of Measuring and Evaluating PR effectiveness, says the following:

> Advertising equivalency is often an issue that is raised in connection with media content analysis studies. Basically, advertising equivalency is a means of converting editorial space in to advertising costs, by measuring the amount of editorial content coverage and then calculating what it would have cost to buy that space, if it had been advertising.[13]

The UK Institute of PR Research & Toolkit, supposedly the most comprehensive guide to evaluation and measurement of such coverage, states:

> Despite their widespread use, Advertising Value Equivalency (AVEs) are flawed by the fact that advertising and PR use quite different methodologies, valid comparison therefore is difficult, if not impossible. Opportunities to See (OTS) provides a more useful 'quick hit' quantitative measure (but only of output and not outcome). The public relations industry must get better at providing the worth of PR, and the value of more in-depth use of research, in order to wean both practitioners and clients away from AVEs.[14]

2.8.3 The PR Institute of Australia (PRIA)

The PR Institute of Australia (PRIA) issued a position paper in 1999 stating that it did not believe in AVEs: "The PRIA does not recognize AVEs of editorial media coverage as a reliable or valid evaluation methodology. Editorial and advertising can't be directly compared."[15]

2.8.4 Case study

In a "path-breaking" research, David Michaelson and Don W. Stacks explored the comparative communications effectiveness of advertising and media placement in the UK.

The research was initiated with the following assumptions:

2.8.4.1 Assumptions

Editorial coverage through PR activities has a value that is greater than an equivalent advertisement.

Common assumption is that value of PR placement is upwards of three times greater than an ad in the equivalent space.

2.8.4.2 Reality

To date, this increased value of PR activities resulting in editorial coverage remains an assumption.

2.8.4.3 Test concept

A "created" product was especially placed for this experiment to eliminate bias that may be associated with specific brand preferences. The product was a snack food called "Zip chips" that had no sodium or fats content.

The advertisement and news article were created with parallel messages.

Conducted among 351 adults who read a newspaper at least once a week, 150 respondents were exposed to an advertising message only, 150 respondents were exposed to a news article only, and 51 respondents were not exposed to any test materials and functioned as the central group.

2.8.4.4 Findings

"Zip chips" brand recall was higher than five "competing" national brands.

No statistically significant difference between ad and edit material was observed.

It was found that increased information did not necessarily translate into increased believability.

No statistically significant difference was observed in purchase interest between ad and edit material.

The ad and edit material contributed equally to perceptions of brand attributes on composite and individual questions. Preference for "Zip chips" was identical regardless of source of information. However, there was a high level of uncertainty about the brand because of single ad exposure.[16]

2.8.5 Measurement practices

Globally, many consultancy firms and media monitoring agencies commonly use this method of media content analysis. In the USA, public relations researcher Delahaye and the Reputation Institute have been conducting research on free media coverage and their net positive impact on the reputation of companies in their yearly survey. The survey findings are placed on the public domain, which obviously has wider access and use.

Top ten companies are ranked by free media impressions and Net effect. The Net effect and index is weighted by the amount of positive and negative coverage of a company, which includes print (newspapers and magazines) and television news coverage. Let us see an illustration. During one of the yearly surveys, Walt Disney received 2,085,000,000 impressions, but the net effect was deduced at 212,000,000. It earned the highest score on both counts, so it became the number one scorer. Similarly, Microsoft also retained number two positions on counts, viz., 2,411,000,000 by impressions and 1,78,000,000 by net effect. When one looked at the data of the remaining contenders in the top ten list for rank by impressions, AOL Time Warner, General Motors, Merrill Lynch, Walmart, Citi Group, IBM, General Electric, and Morgan Stanley were named. However, for ranking in Net effect, the positions changed for some, while others disappeared from the list of top ten by Net effect. For instance, General Motors, which had the fourth position by impressions (1,993,000,000), slid to the fifth position in Net effect (1,22,000,000). Walmart, which was at the sixth position by impression

(1,859,000,000), scaled to the fourth position in net effect (119,000,000). Similarly, IBM, which was at the eighth position (1,408,000,000), scaled to the sixth position in net effect (119,000,000), and AOL Warner, which had the third ranking by impressions (2,136,000,000), slid to the tenth position by net effect (87,000,000). The remaining top rankers by impressions, namely Merrill Lynch, Citi Group, General Electric, and Morgan Stanley, did not make it in the top ten by Net effect. Those who did not make in top ten by impressions but by net effect were Intel, General Motors, Home Department, Coca-Cola, and Bank of America.[17]

Now when we look at the methodology, some may find many flaws in it. For instance, one analyst says that outputs do not necessarily become equal outcomes. The ranking of top ten among 100 corporate organizations aims at creating a direct bridge between an organization's excellent media coverage and having the top reputation. The bridge does not exist, because the said survey neither surveyed the media that had written about organizations or the clients who were affected by the goods and services of such organizations. A truly objective poll should ideally include both a quantitative and qualitative survey to map the perceptions of media and consumers. Positive outcomes of any corporate communication program aim at quality media coverage, excellent speaking platforms, increased traffic on the website; while outcomes need to be business goals, such as building a better corporate reputation, increased sales, raising stock price, etc., that any management would look for.[18]

In India, almost all PR, public affairs, and corporate communication firms that work on behalf of various clients undertake media content analysis quantitatively. It is not uncommon to count the number of press clippings and the cumulative column-cum centimeters and positioning after every media interface like press conferences, facility visits, etc. by the corporate communication managers for their management's consumption. The professional bodies, at least overtly, don't seem to have any official viewpoint on AVEs as their counterparts in the western world. One also does not see in India tracking of free press coverage of the corporate sector in general, as in some countries, one example of which has been given earlier.

In the context of the US pattern of research, Steve Farella, president-CEO of one such agency, TargetCast TCM, says,

> It's critical that we take a look at brand impressions from a consumer's point of view not from an agency's point-of-view. We've traditionally taken a look at Nielsen data and CMR data and studied it and, in fact, torn apart advertising campaigns to understand what's going on. But we've been ignoring what's going on in PR, which is becoming a huge part of the business, especially with video news releases.

The key criteria that determine effectiveness of outputs in any communication activity include the following:

- Reaching the relevant target audience or market
- Gaining wide distribution or exposure within those audiences or markets
- Communicating key messages and gaining strong and preferably leading "share of voice" compared with competitors.[19]

2.9 Corporate communication's growing influence in media—the general outcry

The profession of corporate communication/public relations is often criticized for the undue presence of its practitioners in the newsroom corridors, allegedly influencing them for coverage that they may not deserve otherwise, on the one hand, and pressurizing media to hold back information that may do them damage, on the other. This may not really be the rule, but exceptions can't be ruled out. There are many examples to support the criticism. For instance, when the worms controversy in Cadbury chocolates made headlines in many media, a few chose not to report it at all. Similarly, in an accident at a construction site of a major private builder, in which a few workers died in 2007, most of the mainstream media did not reflect the name of the company. Media, in general, has a different rule for the public sector.

The reasons are not far to seek. Some big business houses in India own media outlets; they as well as others who may have no holding in the media business do support media through advertising. Advertising, in a way, subsidizes the cost of media access to the common man. Not too long ago, at least in the Indian context, there was a clear distinction between the marketing and editorial departments in the media, and the twain rarely met. All this, however, has changed with time. The journalists, in their inflated view, always consider themselves to be the drivers of change and watchdogs of society, little realizing that media itself is turning into a market and the content is also driven by market forces. In India, the change, the crossing of the "Lakshman Rekha" between the ad and editorial sanctity became somewhat visible in the 1980s and profoundly in the 1990s, to the extent that media redefined itself and its content. Media were soon seen as brands that were positioning themselves vis-à-vis competing brands, and the bottom line often decided the success or failure of ventures. Those publications that were popular but not successful in monetary terms were closed by the proprietors. The marketing techniques of FMCG goods and some media houses have not been any different.

One of the contemporary and ardent critics of media's growing power and manipulative techniques, Noam Chomsky, along with Edward S. Herman, has propounded the theory of propaganda in media in their widely read and critiqued book: *Manufacturing Consent: The Political Economy of the Mass Media*.

The book created ripples in the world of media, which would ordinarily like people to believe that they are the true watchdogs of society, reflectors of public opinion, a premise questioned by the authors, who argue that the media catered to the interests of the corporate sector, for which they aimed at the articulation of interests of 20% elite class who are relevant to the media; the rest are engaged in inane programs, like soaps and sports, which have become a world unto this class.

To understand who really calls the shots, one must look closely at how society, whether it is the US or any other, functions, argue the authors. The thesis posited by Chomsky and Herman argue that the major decisions over investment and production and distribution and so on are in the hands of a relatively concentrated network of major corporations and conglomerates and investment firms. Mass media aims at mobilizing public support for the special interests that dominate the government and the private sector.[20]

As for manufacturing of consent, the authors talk of two targets of propaganda, one that can be called the political class, the 20% of population that is relatively educated, somewhat articulate and plays a role in the decision-making; and the other, the remaining 80% that follows the orders. The people in the former category, according to authors, broadly, would be those who have managerial functions like teachers, writers, and so on. These are the people who are conscientious about their right to vote and participate in the economic, social, political, and cultural life of their country. The consent of this group is crucial, so, they must be indoctrinated, argue the authors. The remaining 80%, argue the authors, don't think; they follow orders, and they are the ones who pay the costs.

Chomsky *et al* make an institutional analysis of the American national media, both print and television, that follow the propaganda model that sort of sets the agenda that others adhere to. (In the US context, the *New York Times* and the *Washington Post* were referred to as powerful media in the book.). The media, the book argues, does various things like by choice of subjects, by distribution of concerns, by emphasizing and framing issues to fulfill its goals. The media "determine, select, shape, control and restrict," to serve the interests of the dominant elite group in the society. According to the propaganda model, both liberal and conservative media fall within the same framework of assumptions. Which are these agenda-setting media? These are the major commercial corporations that have various business interests besides owning the media that lend them a voice, besides the acquisition of power to set the agenda. The theory posits that there is one set of agenda for the thinking class that also has the maximum purchasing power; the remaining 80% are engaged in issues they feel are most important, like sports and entertainment, that become their physical, psychological, and emotional engagement.[21]

Not all would agree with the authors' thesis. For instance, Walter LaFeber had to say in the *New York Times* in his book review after it had its new edition of the book originally published in 1992:

> The overstatements and the weakness in the 'propaganda model' that the authors try to construct are unfortunate, because many of the book's raw-data comparisons are compelling indictments of the news media's role in covering up errors and deceptions in American foreign policy of the past quarter-century.[22]

Left-oriented thinker Jürgen Habermas, a social theorist, also feels that the media in the USA has systematically worked on the capitalist function. Jeff Nall, positing his argument on Habermas's theory, argues that the liberal model of the public sphere had institutions such as the press bolstering rational-critical debate, but in the hands of private individuals, the press grew so homogenized that it threatened to drown out critical debate, rather than amplify it. As a result, Europe moved to protect the public sphere from the concentration of power into a small number of hands. "Only the United States has allowed the media to subvert its publicist function—the purpose of publicizing a wide-range of ideas and debates—in favor of its capitalistic function—making money," comments Jeff Nall.[23]

If we look at the Indian media scene broadly, what the critics say of media in the West, it makes a lot of sense in our context also. More than 90% of media here are owned by big business. The content of the programs of 24-7 channels, the ad ratio in programs, the dwindling space and time for public interest discourse, the open invitation to corporates to pay for space and time to get positive stories done, are all pointers in that direction. The various entertainment programs that earn TRPs for the media become advertising-revenue-generation machines. Interestingly, the so-called intellectual programs don't generally have many ads, but a cricket match, a football match, or the various retrograde soaps that reinforce age-old stereotypes and build new ones continue to engage the audiences emotionally, thus becoming TRP busters. The media, therefore, is in a win-win situation. It is not uncommon for media to talk about TRPs of some programs in their main news stories to attract those who may not be watching those programs and tell those already hooked on that they were doing fine! In fact, the whole philosophy of TRPs needs to be debated and rationalized if we look at the sample and the geographical area covered for research in a country of 1.3 billion plus people.

Writing about various periods in the media industry in India, Vanita Kohli Khandekar refers to one of the phases that changed the way the media industry would function forever as the "Sameer Jain years" about some three decades ago. Khandekar, quoting Tariq Ansari a senior journalist, argued that the state of the media in general was not any different from what Samir Jain had brought in at the Bennet and Coleman. Using simple marketing techniques, Jain turned his newspapers as brands that needed the caring and nurturing of a product in a fiercely competitive marketplace. His first strategy was to employ people with an FMCG sector background, so that they were familiar with the idiom and nuances of brand management. To quote Khandekar,

> Jain did those things at a time when nobody thought that the "commercial" function in a newspaper had any importance. The notion that there should be a total divorce between a paper's editorial and its marketing was completely shattered by Jain. He made the Times of India the best money making machine that appeased advertisers without qualms.[24]

Sameer Jain closed down all those publications from the stable that were not earning revenue. Some of the popular ones included the *Illustrated Weekly of India*, *Dharmyug*, *Vama*, and *Dinaman*, etc.

Although Khandekar refrains from mentioning the controversial MediaNet strategy of the newspaper, she comments,

> Had they changed completely from being tools of social change to mere reflections of it? Was the purpose only to assemble readers who could then be sold on advertisers? All this talk of treating newspaper like an FMCG seems fine in theory, but there is one critical difference-unlike soap and shampoo, a newspaper is a fodder for the mind.[25]

Unless news media take the readers in their context, they can't relate to it. If the newspapers are becoming glossier, the news programs glamorous but with little intellectual grub, will they not create a generation of socially dead minds? It is a question that only time will answer, argues the author.

A case study on MediaNet has been included at the end of the chapter for understanding its dynamics and undercurrents.

2.10 Do people find corporate news credible?

Former Google CEO Eric Schmidt believed that the Internet had become a "cesspool" of false information, so it was important that filters were applied to sort out the "muck and mire." Brand power, feel many, would be able to bring about some sanity in the matter.

For instance, in 2007, ABC entered a strategic alliance with one of the popular social networking sites, viz., Facebook, which meant that all the users of this networking site had access to ABC reporters electronically. They could view reports and access videos. They could also participate in the live presidential debate in January 2008. This attracted a traffic of over 1.5 million from across the entire world. Later, Facebook did not continue with the alliance on the reasoning that alliance with one media group was not enough.[26]

Edleman, a global PR consultancy, has been conducting a yearly Global Trust Barometer research for the last 22 years (its latest research came in 2022). Interestingly, while some institutions are constantly on the mistrust radar, some which had better credibility have gone down in the esteem. The survey included 28 countries, 36,000+ respondents, averaging 1,150 respondents from each country.

Some highlights:

According to the report, "government and media fuel a cycle of distrust." In May 2020, government was most trusted at 65%, followed by business at 62%, NGOs at 62%, and media at 56%. Come 2022, the figures went down; governments came down to 52%, media at 50%, business to 61%, and NGOs at 56%.

When looking at media and government being divisive, 48% felt government and media were indeed divisive at 28% and 46% respectively; business and NGOs were in a better light at 31% and 29% respectively. Interestingly, 36% perceived the government as a unifying force, 35% media, 45% business, and 50% NGOs.

Fake news concerns have been felt at an all-time high in 2022. Globally, 76% of respondents across 28 countries and many continents feel concerned.

Government in general is not seen as able to solve societal problems; only 44% believe it can, and 42% believe it can execute plans and strategies that would yield results.

People are worried about myriad issues as the world is unfolding before them. Eighty-five percent worry about job loss, 75% climate change, 71% are worried about invasion into their data and personal space by hackers and cyberattacks, 65% worry about losing their freedom as citizens, and 57% about experiencing racism or prejudice.

Respondents in general felt that when government and media feed a cycle of division and disinformation for "votes and clicks," NGOs and business are pressured to take on societal problems beyond their abilities.

In a scathing finding, 67% seemed convinced that society is being lured by journalists and reporters, 66% by government and leaders who they believe do it "purposely" to mislead people by saying things they know are false or gross exaggeration.[27]

The findings are mind-boggling and would make an average person sit up and worry about the increasing trust deficiency in major institutions that are germane to a society. It is a wake-up call to be taken seriously by those who matter. Trust and faith are the ingredients that influence public opinion, as the Romans put it: 'Vox Populi, Vox Dei,' the voice of the people is the voice of God.

Summary

The broad goal behind this chapter was to acquaint the reader with the dynamics of media functioning and the debates surrounding it. The chapter began with an overview of the media scene with the latest data on reach and accessibility and futuristic trends. We then discussed the role and importance of various media in corporate communication, looking at the relative strengths and weaknesses of various kinds of media. This would facilitate a corporate communication practitioner to choose the media carefully and strategically.

Corporate communication values free media coverage, as it is generally believed that editorial endorsement is more valuable than paid communication through advertising. It is commonplace with corporate communication managers and firms to quantify media coverage in advertising equivalency terms to reflect the worth of the effort in money terms. Not all, however, feel that it is the right way of doing it, as advertising and corporate communication carry varying mandates and goals. Views of some professional bodies have been reflected on the issue, in the chapter. Some critics believe that the growing influence of the corporate sector in media corridors has influenced the quality of coverage, which may not always be objective. The debate generated by one of the most ardent contemporary media critics, namely Noam Chomsky, who, in his theory of propaganda, talks of the manipulative power of media, was taken up for discussion. Is corporate media coverage credible? Some viewpoints emerged based on some research studies included in the chapter. The setting up the MediaNet has opened a Pandora's box on media ethics. The case study has been included at the end of the chapter.

Key terms

Electronic media: a term used for broadcasting media, viz., radio and television.
Print media: a term used for newspapers, magazines, journals etc.
New media: refers to the Internet, social networking sites, and the blogosphere.
Media reach: refers to the percentage of people in various SEC categories accessing media.
Media characteristics: refers to the relative strengths and weaknesses of each medium, keeping in view its inherent characteristics.
"Third party" endorsement: the news that appears in the media is believed to have a third party or neutral perspective of reality and facts.
Trade media: used for newspapers, magazines, and news channels exclusively devoted to the financial sector, capital market, investments, and corporate news, etc.
Media measurement: a standardized system for evaluating the effectiveness of communication between two or more organizations and their designated stakeholders through various media channels through pre-determined parameters that would encompass quantity, quality, positioning of news, its tone of coverage, etc.

Concept review questions

Q.1. Define various media and their characteristics.
Q.2. What, in your view, are the futuristic trends in mass media?
Q.3. What are the lessons for a corporate communication practitioner in the ever-changing media scenario?
Q.4. Do you think free media coverage helps in building an organization's image? Discuss with arguments.

Critical thinking exercise

1. Paying for editorial coverage is the latest trend across media. Some say it openly as in the case of the MediaNet; others don't but do practice it. Follow the coverage about a corporate organization on the net for a week, and write your analysis.
2. Follow at least three mainstream/trade newspapers and three channels for a week, and write your analysis of one corporate organization after meeting the concerned corporate communication managers/firms to understand the dynamics.

Case study

What is MediaNet?

MediaNet, an outfit initiated by the Bennett and Coleman company, seeks paid editorial coverage in newspapers from its stable. As per company's sources, the aims behind setting up MediaNet are as follows.

Some highlights

"A futuristic media solution: MediaNet is a true-some integrated value addition process both for the reader as well as for the advertiser. MediaNet also represents future trends in media buying.

Conventional method of media buying has started to give in to a search for media solutions. Advertisers are no longer happy to buy plain conventional units of columns centimeters of advertising space. Buying of media the way one buys pizzas, that is, by the units, may soon become a thing of the past.

"Who would benefit from MediaNet online?

- Corporates who want their "ADDITIONAL" information to be propagated.
- PR agencies that need a single platform to spread a corporate message.
- Small & medium businesses who want to showcase their philosophy and products.
- People seeking updated information specific to certain corporate's and industries.
- Journalists looking at generic industry intelligence."[28]

The website also carries information about its company Optimal Media Solutions Limited (OMSL) that would cater to the clients. Here are highlights of the offerings:

MediaNet services. Business news. From those who make news. Uncensored

Optimal Media Solutions Limited (A Times Group Company) is a leading image building organization. We are looking towards moving beyond the current format of advertising, which is currently used extensively by organizations to improve brand awareness. We at OMS work towards projecting our clients in an informative manner using the (multiple) medium of the Times of India. We provide comprehensive solutions and back this up with an excellent editorial team, which provides solid content. Optimal Media Solutions operates in the metro supplements (for e.g. Delhi Times, Bombay Times etc) of The Times of India.

OMS offers the following properties to clients in the metro supplements:

Front Page Lead Picture: New launches/events.
Page 2/3 (Events Pages): Covering events, parties, and happenings.
Spotlight on Page 2: Features the achievements of an individual based on his profile.
Lifestyle (On Saturdays): Profiling and concepts on brands and individuals (articles/columns). Concentrates on fashion trends, entertainment, beauty products etc.
Travel Page: Published on Wednesdays and Thursdays in the Metro Supplements Customized Concepts: We develop customized articles to cater to specific brand objectives.
What's Hot (On Fridays): Focus on latest happenings/events. Special pages created for channels and details of programs.
Rouge (On Saturdays): Concentrates on women's interest areas.
What's Hot (weekly publication): Features articles on diverse themes like lifestyle, health, travel, etc. in magazine format.

Background:

- OMS functions like an image management agency for clients.
- Understands their unique needs.
- Translates them into editorial concepts.
- We provide solutions primarily on print.

The group attracted criticism from within its own fraternity and others when it launched the Mediated. In fact, the Paper's move triggered an unending debate on the issue of media ethics. Sucheta Dalal puts it succinctly,

> For lay readers, it must be clarified that the sale of news is different and distinct from paid advertisements, advertorials or special supplements, all of which are clearly identified as 'sponsored features,' while paid news is not. Such spurious news has in the past included gushing endorsements of flop movies, fashion and lifestyle products and promotion of hotels and restaurants that enter into a payment arrangement with the organization. The reader has no clue that the adulatory report is nothing but a paid advertisement masquerading as objective reportage or opinion.[29]

India Today, the weekly publication, took up the issue in its editorial titled: "Sacred space: if media sells news columns what's the need for advertisements?" The publication argued that advertisers were interested in media because they proved to be vehicles to reach out to their buyers, because media offered circulation and eyeballs. The journalists, it said, were expected to pursue the path of truth fearlessly, so the marketers got attracted to the strength of those values.[30]

The *Times of India*, responding to various criticisms, wrote an article: "Compete, don't crap: Copycats shouldn't point fingers." It criticized others for copying their style.

The paper said,

> The sluggish fear it. The reactive respond to it. At the Times Group, we pride ourselves upon being at the cutting edge of the third category. The role we envision for MediaNet is that of an auditor, regulating the media's burgeoning interaction with the PR sector.[31]

When Pradyuman Maheshwari continued with his tirade on his blog, years later, the newspaper sent him a long legal notice on threat of libel. He soon closed his blog. His story is quoted by many bloggers all over the globe who have carried on the debate, as one wrote ruefully that as long as people were reading the paper and there was no dearth of advertisers, why would the group care?[32]

Interestingly PR-USA.Net, a network of 12 U.S. state PR sites, search engines, social media, and blogs, provides services to organizations who wish to reach their publicity material on a large scale. The reason why MediaNet has attracted so much criticism is because it has been floated by a media organization, which the critics feel comes under the purview of "conflict of interest."

Let's look at how PR-USA.Net invites organizations and individuals to subscribe to its services. Providing them with various steps of uploading the press releases, it cautions them on the content:

PR-USA.Net

> After your PR is submitted, it will be checked if it contains any forbidden data—adult, violence, racist content, aggressive religious content, etc. If no such problems, it will be published (up to 24 hours).
>
> By publishing your text at this site, you agree that any journalist or media can use it for free. You cannot expect honorarium or other payment from site or from journalists and media that used it.
>
> We distribute press releases to newspapers, magazines, trade journals, TV and Radio. Individual journalists are reached by the Associated Press satellite feed and by email. All press releases are posted to Google News, RSS feeds, search engines and news sites.
>
> We have more customer testimonials than any other press release distribution service! Our customers get noticed by both print and broadcast media. To prove it, we have links to actual newspaper and TV stories done about our customers at our success stories page.
>
> In addition to sending press releases by the AP satellite feed, we target individual journalists by email from our list of 519,000 media contacts. Each press release is sent by itself, not grouped together with other press releases. Our media list is divided into 507 categories so that we can choose journalists that are looking for your news.

Once we have distributed your press release, we will send you a list of journalists that were reached and links to see your press release online. Press releases can be sent within 24 hours or you may choose a later date.[33]

Let us now look at the broader picture. The *Times of India*, because of its bold and upfront attitude of putting the cards on the table, may be criticized, but the fact of the matter is that a whopping majority of media houses do charge for surrogate publicity. The PR/corporate communication firms may not say it openly, but when they are retained by the corporate sector, it is not uncommon to hear them making promise of positive media coverage and "plants" in the media. In fact, their retainership fee takes care of that aspect. It is not uncommon to find interview-based articles with various professionals, especially from the beauty, health, and fitness segment in various media, which, if the grapevine is to be believed, are all fully paid for. The gullible readers and viewers often feel that what appears in the media is included to suit their interest. It has been many years since MediaNet was launched by the Times group, but the discussion among the bloggers and within the media circle goes on unabated. The other view point subscribed by some analysts is that the paper may be criticized for crass commercialism, but the reality is that the Times Group has created a bond with people, especially the youth, which no other paper can claim to have done. Its various campaigns, especially the "Teach India" and "Lead India" have caught the imagination of various age groups like nothing seen before. Its call to switch off lights for an hour at the Earth hour on 28 March saw a drop of 1000 MW in power consumption in one city alone. In fact, the Times group has been able to increase its readership constantly, making its flagship paper, the *Times of India*, one of the top ten newspapers in the country, a feat achieved by only this English newspaper. What more would a company ask for?

Question and practical work on the case study

a) Is paying for editorial coverage fair, in your opinion? If yes, why? If no, why not?
b) Follow the coverage given to one or two corporate organizations or individuals in the paid columns referred to in the MediaNet Services box, and hold a discussion among the peer group on the bias and whether the news seem credible.

Notes

1 www.newslaundry.com/2022/05/03/world-press-freedom-index-2022-indias-rank-falls-from-142-to-150-press-freedom-is-in-crisis, accessed on 27 March 2023.
2 http://rni.nic.in/pdf_file/pin2021_22/Chapter%201.pdf, accessed on 27 March 2023.
3 Vanita Kohli Khandekar, *The Indian Media Business*, second edition, 2006 (New Delhi: Response Books), pp. 20–30.
4 Ibid., p. 31.
5 www.researchgate.net/publication/24112042_The_Role_of_Foreign_Direct_Investment_on_Press_Freedom.
6 https://indianexpress.com/article/business/budget/fm-radio-industry-flourished-388-private-stations-in-2022-june-quarter-economic-survey-8416635/by Amrita Nayak Dutta. New Delhi | 1 February 2023 09:06 IST.

7 www.gadgets360.com/telecom/news/airtel-jio-vi-bsnl-mobile-subscribers-india-1-billion-trai-report-december-2021-2788990.
8 www.barandbench.com/news/litigation/punjab-haryana-high-court-uses-chatgpt-bailorder.
9 Jaishri Jethwaney and Shruti Jain, *Advertising Management*, 2006 (New Delhi: OUP), pp. 291–293.
10 The Supreme Court ordered the removal of roadside hoardings in Delhi in its ruling of November 97. The Municipal Corporation of Delhi issued a notice of 48 hours to advertisers on 24 November to remove unauthorized hoardings or face seizure. Supreme Court's order came in the wake of increasing instances of road accidents, specifically after one of the worst bus accidents in which 28 school children died when the driver, driving rashly plunged the bus into the river Yamuna on 17 November, 1797. Quoting an advertiser, the Times of India in its issue of 23 November wrote, "Accidents take place because drivers drive rashly and not because they get distracted by hoardings", Times of India, New Delhi, 23 November 1997, p. 1. Also see Express Newsline of Indian Express, 24 November 1997.
11 www.cnbctv18.com/business/indian-media-and-entertainment-sector-to-reach-rs-16-lakh-crore-revenue-in-fy24-15572021.htm
12 www.carma.com/resarch
13 www.instituteforpr.org//wp-content/uploads/2002_MeasuringPrograms.pdf, accessed on 28 March 2023.
14 www.ipr.com
15 www.pria.com
16 www.instituteforpr.org/research
17 www.mediapost.com/publications/?fa=Articles.showArticle&art_aid=17559. *note: The Media Reputation Index, a collaboration of Delahaye and The Reputation Institute. Net effect = and index weighted by the amount of positive and negative coverage of a company. Includes print (newspapers and magazines) and television news coverage news coverage*
18 www.measurinupblog.com
19 www.carma.com/resarch
20 Noam Chomsky and Edward S. Herman, *Manufacturing Consent- the Political Economy of the Mass Media* in 1992. Also visit www.chomsky.com.
21 Ibid.
22 www.powells.com/biblio/
23 *www.JeffNall.com* and Jürgen Habermas, *The Structural Transformation of the Public Sphere: An Inquiry into a Category of Bourgeois Society* (Cambridge: The MIT Press, 1991).
24 Vanita Kohli Khandekar, *The Indian Media Business*, second edition, 2006 (New Delhi: Response Books), pp. 33–36.
25 Ibid.
26 www.altemet.org/mediaculture/
27 2022 Edelman Trust Barometer FINAL_Jan25.pdf, sourced on 309.3.23.
28 For details of "MediaNet: In Pursuit of Newer Streams of Content", 27 February 2003, 1002 hrs IST, TNN, log on to www.timesmedianet.com/oms/userfiles/HelpFaq.aspx
29 http://mail.sarai.net/pipermail/reader-list/2003-March/002479.html
30 Jaishri Jethwaney and N. N. Sarkar, *Public Relations Management*, 2009 (New Delhi: Sterling Publishers), p. 14.
31 www.timsofindia.indiatimes.com
32 Anuradha Kher, 15 October 2007, www.ojr.org.
33 www.massmediadistribution.com/home.html; www.Pr-Usa.net.org

3

CORPORATE REPUTATION MANAGEMENT

Introduction

3.1 Defining reputation

Like individuals, organizations too have reputations. A reputation can be defined as the "standing" or an "image" that an individual or an entity has in the perceptions of people who may have a direct or indirect bearing on the effectiveness and existence of that individual or organization. Experts argue that when one talks of 'standing,' it is the goodwill, the equity, the 'fair name,' and 'character' of the concerned that is being talked about. Like individuals, corporate organizations are also protective of their reputations. It is not uncommon to find defamation suits filed by individuals and companies against certain organizations, media, or people when they have felt hurt by what is said or written about them. We have seen a member of parliament being disqualified by the parliament after a local court found the person guilty of hurting the sentiments of a certain community. The party and the person may go to a higher court, but the defamation suit worked against him in the court of law.

Chapter 12: Laws and ethics in corporate communication carries several such case studies, including this one in detail.

Reputation management has acquired newer dimensions in the past couple of decades or so, especially with the proliferation of the Net and social media platforms.

In a time and age that has millions of people connected through the Net, it is not uncommon that celebrities, businessmen, politicians, organizations, and brands are discussed, debated, and criticized through social networking sites. Instantly, communities are formed around issues and individuals who matter. The new-age media has necessitated the need for managing reputations more vigorously than ever before. For instance, when television anchor Barkha Dutt became the target of bloggers post Mumbai terrorist attack in 2008, her company served a notice to a blogger to withdraw the post or face consequences, or when a blogger criticized a newspaper's strategy to charge for business news, he too was served with a notice. He preferred to close his blog. In a media-driven environment, there is no gainsaying that building and maintaining a strong reputation

DOI: 10.4324/9781032694702-3

is key to success in a highly complex and competitive business environment. It holds equally true for media organizations also, as the two cases in point would emphasize.

It is generally believed that positive reputation takes a long time to establish, but one wrong move or a deliberate tirade by an adversary or vested interest, and the reputation can be severely bruised, which may take time to repair, but not always.

Organizations, to be successful, must rely on external research and perception mapping to monitor and improve their reputation constantly. Some practitioners see a great connect between corporate reputation and employees, who can play a definite role in contributing to the positive positioning of their company in the minds of the various stakeholders they deal with. Some others feel that the simplest parameters of judging the corporate reputation of a company is how its stocks are doing and what is the shareholder return on investment.

Many studies suggest that an increasing importance now is being placed on corporate governance by legislators, financial markets, regulators, media, and customers in the boardrooms across the globe.

Former US president Obama snubbed some corporate heads for releasing millions in bonus payments to their employees immediately after the government supported them financially with tax payers' money during the economic meltdown in 2008. Media reported that the AIG distributed $165 million in bonuses even though it received more than $70 billion in federal rescue money. Obama directed the then treasury secretary Timothy Geithner to see if there was any way to retrieve or stop the bonus money. This, the media felt, was "designed as much for public relations as public policy." The controversy escalated when Senator Richard Shelby, ranking Republican on the banking committee, charged Geithner for being ignorant about what was going on at AIG. He was unsparing when he said that AIG executives should take the Japanese approach towards accepting responsibility for the collapse of the insurance giant by resigning or killing themselves.[1]

Anticipating federal restrictions on bonuses, Citigroup and Morgan Stanley were exploring ways to sidestep tough new federal caps on compensation.[2]

Closer to home, beleaguered PWC (Powerwaterhouse Cooper), embroiled in the Satyam Computer fiasco, wished "to be in good books and start on a clean sheet in a key market," as reported in the media. The company announced that post Satyam imbroglio, it would cross-check the audits of all its clients in India. In an exclusive interview to the ET, the then PWC Global CEO Samuel A. Dipiazza said, "We want to convince our stakeholders that the processes at PWC are of the highest quality."[3] Clearly an exercise in damage control after two of its officers were jailed on allegation of collusion with Satayam management in fudging the financial data for years.

3.1.1 Reputation in the Net age

As said earlier, the Net has made our world flat, enabling interaction among global communities, cutting across artificial boundaries, and creating a seamless public opinion on varying issues. This also means that it has given sleepless nights to those who oversee corporate reputation, be they CEOs, corporate communication managers, or professional agencies. Analysts believe that cyber critics often are the activists, disgruntled employees, and customers, who can create a virtual mayhem for organizations through e-mails, chat rooms, blogs, bulletin boards, *et al* that have tremendous reach.

Imagine what a headline like "McDonald's tops index of unethical companies"[4] on the Net can do to the reputation of the company, besides making its management and employees feel terrible. The story appeared on one of the websites that talked about some research conducted by Fraser Consultancy that assessed "42 brands from fashion to food." The story on the Net then went on to say that the report, termed the *Ethical Reputation Index* was based on responses of 13,000 consumers.[5] A case study of McDonald's long legal fight with Greenpeace, an NGO, has been covered in detail in Chapter 8 on corporate social responsibility.

When television was invented, newspapers had to reinvent themselves, because television played havoc with their headlines; now the Net has posed another challenge, creating not only competition for the traditional reporters but also by being a fast medium of disseminating information and by being interactive and seen as empathetic that no other media can claim to be. Millions of people access the Net as soon as anything untoward happens anywhere in the world. Influencers' reach is estimated to be more than the reach of many traditional media in some countries.

What blogger Lee Oden says makes a lot of sense in the age of digital reputation management: "Any company publishing content online or that has customers engaging with content online (producing, interacting, or just reading) is a candidate for an online reputation management effort. That covers just about every company in business?" He recommends that one should not wait until someone decides to launch "a 'yourbrandsucks.com' site. So it is better be proactive than regret later. Listening to "dissenters" and "evangelizing" customers," he recommends, is the first step, before they have a major impact.

The Net has an immense amount of information overload. It is believed that 3.9 billion people, who are nearly half the world population, are posting or uploading videos on the Net constantly, therefore, the importance of monitoring the social media cannot be understated. Media monitoring tools including listening, tracking, and sifting relevant content across a wide range of platforms would be the key to success for corporates. This would also help, especially researchers, to gain insights on social trends and journalists who look for "breaking" news stories. There are many tools to choose from like Google alerts, Sprout Social, Hootsuite, Zoho Social, Meltwater, Reputation, Brandwatch Consumer Intelligence, Semrush, Agorapulse, Sendible, and Brand24, among many more.

Once the company has identified the current and future influencers, addressing their concerns must be the next logical step through community staff.

> Dissenters can be engaged by customer support staff and evangelists are often engaged by marketing staff. Other situations might necessitate legal, PR or product experts. The process of listening, qualifying, and engaging opinionated customers online presents tremendous learning opportunity for companies that want to champion communicating on the social web, suggests Oden.[6]

In an age of instant connectivity, people often turn to the Internet to know about a business or brand as a matter of routine. They also generally look at the reviews, especially of the hospitality industry. Websites like OpenTable, Facebook, and Google are commonplace on their lists. According to a 2021 study, nine out of ten customers look for reviews before they make any purchase.[7]

Companies in e-commerce business, in an age of a hyper social media, have become very sensitive about their reputation which they may have built over decades, but one wrong move can sully their reputation, as Flipkart, Lenskart learned the hard way. In an interesting paper, "Saying 'Sorry': the Role of Apology in Online Crisis Communication" (Mishra, S, 2015), the author has commented that Corporate Inc. in India rarely tender an apology, but social media has brought about a paradigm shift. In the case of Flipkart, one of the largest e-retailers, in 2014, it had announced its Big Billion Day Sale, which ran into trouble because many customers complained of being duped as the prices were hiked up to the maximum retail price, then discounted, which seemed like an eyewash. Both cofounders Sachin and Binny Bansal tendered a long-written apology, saying sorry a couple of times and noting the lessons they had learned.[8]

Another company which has made spectacles a lifestyle personal accessory was also pulled up by netizens for being insensitive in using a natural disaster for brand promotion. In 2015, neighboring country Nepal faced a devastating earthquake which resulted in death and destruction in large measures. Lenskart, at the time of this colossal tragedy, sent a short message service (SMS) the same day that read, "DZ-LNSKART: Shake it off like this Earthquake: Get any Nincent Chase Sunglasses up to R3000 for FLAT R 500 by sending invites to 50 friends@www.lenskart.com/refer-sun."

When the screenshot was shared on Twitter, it brought backlash from people. News media commented on the insensitivity on the part of the company. Realizing the damage to its reputation, the company woke up within two hours, sending apology via SMS and social media: "@Lenskart.com: We regret the wrong choice of words. We deeply apologize for unintentionally hurting any sentiment."[9]

3.1.2 Indian judiciary toughens stand on bloggers

Indian courts are getting tougher on irresponsible blogging. A report by the *Times of India* said that it would no longer be safe to start a blog and invite others to comment, which at times can be "raunchy, caustic and even abusive" under the protection behind the disclaimer that views expressed on the blog are those of the writers. The warning came when the bench comprising Supreme Court Chief Justice KG Balakrishnan and Justice P Saathasivam refused to protect a 19-year-old youth D Ajith from the Southern state of Kerala who had started a community site against Shiv Sena, a Maharashtra-based political party, to get protection against summons received from a Maharashtra court on a criminal case against him. After getting anticipatory bail from the Kerala high court, Ajith had moved the Supreme Court on the plea that the blog comments were restricted to communication within the community.[10]

The Indian Information Technology Act 2000 was amended in early 2009 to keep pace with the international practices. Under the law, Internet users may face libel for what they write themselves, the "intermediaries" who host such content are liable only if they are consciously complicit to the offence or fail to remove the offending material immediately after it is brought to notice by the authorities.[11]

The 2009 amended act introduced Section 66A, which penalized sending "offensive messages." It also introduced Section 69, which gave the government the power of "interception or monitoring or decryption of any information through any computer resource."[12] More about this law in Chapter 12: Laws and ethics in corporate communication.

3.1.3 Reputation management—a big business

In a competitive and complex business environment, managing reputation is not an easy task. Many companies retain specialist reputation management firms to handle corporate communication and reputation management for them. A look at the website of one of the reputation management firms, an arm of a global PR consultancy reflects the way agencies offer niche specialization. Let us look at the offerings:

"Full range of CEO and corporate issues—from creating and maintaining an enduring reputation to recovering reputation after a crisis to managing reputations on-line." Further, it went on to offer the following "products and services":

Risky business reputation online
Safeguarding reputation
Reputation recovery
Building CEO reputation
Reputation Rx
Reputation Xchange
Corporate reputation diagnostic services
Executive thought leadership services[13]

Interestingly, this list, reflected on their website in 2009, has become shorter and more sophisticated in 2023. Let's look at it under its "What do we do?" page on Reputation & Leadership:

- Sustainability, social impact and ESG consulting
- Executive leadership
- Public affairs
- Crisis and risk management
- Geopolitical risk and strategy
- Capital markets communications

Reputation management firms are aware of the views in general of their critics, who believe that such companies manipulate the minds through spin doctoring. The terminology, therefore, over the years, is not as it used to be but has acquired newer terms and nuances, such as advertorials, sponsorship, and paid news often arranged surreptitiously.

George Ludwig, the author of *Power Selling: Seven Strategies for Cracking the Sales Code*, provides some very insightful tips on creating and managing a winning reputation. He writes that it is important for companies to know who they are and what are the areas in which they can bring about improvement. Ludwig recommends that it is worthwhile creating a "world class reputation credo" to be signed by all the employees, that emphasize trustworthiness, which, in turn, is built on a foundation of three personal principles: service-centricity, character, and competence. A person exclusively in charge of reputation management should be employed, which would go a long way in building and maintaining reputation.[14]

"Traits like honesty, integrity, a sense of fair play, and respect for others are vital for long-term success in the 21st century business world," says Ludwig. "Just look at what happened to companies that didn't place these traits on a pedestal. Do you really want your company to end up like Enron or WorldCom? Companies that eschew character for short-term financial gains will lose out in the long run."[15]

3.2 Is reputation management a "spin"?

Media, in general, have a problem believing in the "spin" generated by PR managers on reputation, which, in their view, is often driven by the age-old dictum of *end justifying the means*. They often believe that smart reputation managers spin the facts in a manner that they can create a "world of make-believe" that traps the stakeholders in believing what may be farther from truth. Having said that, the news media over the years, owing to their sociology and ownership patterns, have fallen into the trap, when economics overrides editorial concerns. It is not uncommon for news media, including most mainstream newspapers and news channels, to be working with corporates in building their stories, obviously at a price that may not be divulged.

Sharon Bidder argues that reputation management is an important part of doing business, but reputation management, being a part of PR activities, does little on social responsibility. The aim is often to create credibility through creating an impression of responsibility, through token reforms, code of conduct, and, at times, by aligning the organization with "amenable" human rights and environmental groups. Reputation encompasses many elements that include trust, credibility, responsibility, and accountability. However, when we talk of corporate image, it is what the stakeholders perceive the organization to be.[16]

Companies that have long maintained good reputation are able to hold their fort even when embroiled in a crisis. It is quite likely that the stakeholders would give them the benefit of the doubt. Its failure on that front would be seen as an aberration and not a willful action. The worm-infested Cadbury chocolates case study discussed later in the chapter would bear this out.

Beder suggests the impact of good reputation on various stakeholders in the following table.

One of the strategies adopted by companies allegedly guilty of spoiling the environment is that they fund environmental groups to get their support. It is commonplace to see many large environment groups falling into the trap. From their perspective, they presumably feel that they can influence a company's policy by involving them in their causes. For instance, RTZ (now Rio Tinto), a mining multinational that operates polluting mines in third world countries, donates millions of dollars to various environment groups all over the world, including World Wildlife Fund (WWF).[17]

TABLE 3.1 Impact of good reputation on stakeholders

Stakeholder	*Impact*
Customers	Sales, prices that can be charged, loyalty
Suppliers, clients	Business, loyalty, prices
Investors	Shareholder value higher, more stable
Government	Regulations, license to operate
Neighbors	Support, awards, protests, and complaints
Employees, current and potential	Attract talented staff, morale, loyalty

Source: Author

Greenpeace, one of the largest NGOs in the field of environment, has also, of late, been working with industry and government. Its website claims: "We work with industry and government to find solution." The reason behind the repositioning, as argued by analysts, was when media constantly dubbed Greenpeace as "too radical" and "too negative." Therefore, it reinvented itself as an organization that offered solutions and worked with industries and the government to get desired results in place.

It has fought many a bitter battle, some in the courts of law with a few organizations (for instance with McDonald's, a litigation that went on for years), but when it came to Sydney Olympics 2000, it wrote to some of the official sponsors of Olympics 2000 like Coca-Cola, McDonald's, General Motors, etc., to earn the name of "Green" in the same way Sydney Olympics 2000 did. It said "Greenpeace would like to work with you to explore the areas in which you can make an environmental contribution during Sydney 2000 games."[18]

Greenpeace, for long, has been crusading against the use of PVC (polyvinyl chloride). Nike (which has always been in the eye of the storm for environmental and human rights violations for low wages to workers in third world countries) got a great opportunity to get some accolades from this environmental group. In 1998, Nike announced that it would phase out the use of PVC in its products. Greenpeace's Olympic Report congratulated Nike for "promising to eliminate the use of PVC in its products." The report carried a picture that had Greenpeace presenting a cake in the shape of a green-colored Nike shoe with the text "Greenpeace is calling on other sportswear manufacturers to follow suit and 'just do it!' " (using Nike's signature line). There is no gainsaying that what Greenpeace did for Nike's reputation, no paid promotion by the company could have done! It seemed like a win-win situation for both.

Philip Lesly suggests that the best way to deal with activists is to give them a role. To quote him,

> if a group has legitimate argument and shows it has a sound approach, enlist its leaders. Often, they will make great contribution as employees. They might be retained as consultants, or they may become active in a new working group you set up jointly.[19]

Stauber and Rampton, editors of PR Watch, argue that hiring activists may be a "crude but effective way to derail potentially meddlesome activists."[20] This is not finding a solution to the problem, but avoiding the "nuisance."

It is not uncommon to find firebrand activists of today getting high-profile cozy jobs tomorrow in government committees and global companies.

It is a general belief among critics that most companies don't get to the root of the problem; they just try and manage perceptions, which may be an ad hoc solution and certainly not an ethical one.

Greenpeace, along with many NGOs, came under scanner in India due to a supposed intelligence report on the allegation of disrupting developmental work in the country. As per media reports, the sector in the eye of the storm was Coal. To quote Justin Rowlatt, South Asian correspondent with BBC,

> A secret report from India's Intelligence Bureau, leaked last year, explains why India's government has such a beef with the environmental charity. It said campaigns headed by Greenpeace and other NGOs had drained three percentage points off the nation's

annual growth rate. Greenpeace wouldn't claim to have been anywhere near that influential but its campaign against the coal industry does strike at the heart of the 'Make in India' policy.[21]

3.3 An overview of "rating" research—random glimpses

Companies, especially the ones that are listed on various stock exchanges, are constantly under the glare of policy makers, opinion leaders, media, shareholders, and rating agencies. The rating agencies may or may not be just in the business of research; they, ironically, in general, are financial institutions, corporate communication/public relations firms, research organizations, and media organizations, who, on the one hand, audit the account and manage reputations respectively, but also end up becoming rating agencies. Companies benefit when they get good ratings, which may help them build their reputation. It is not uncommon for companies who get good ratings from known agencies to flaunt the awards in their advertisements and post them on their home pages.

Companies that are poorly rated do suffer from image issues. Both ways, it is a signal for the companies to be constantly on the watch.

Is rating research always unbiased? No debate on the issue can be conclusive, but there is no gainsaying that the prestige of the companies conducting research is also at stake, because they are also in business. Satyam Computers was a recipient of many prestigious awards from some well-known agencies, but what happened to it is now history.

The globally large, three-rating agencies include Moody's, S&P (Standard & Poor with predecessor Poor), and Flitch, all set up in the early twentieth century, in 1900, 1916, and 1924 respectively. In the context of ratings, "Part of the problem", writes the *Guardian*,

> is that ratings agencies are funded by the very companies they rate. If you want to be rated, you must pay an agency between $1,500 and $2,500,000 for the privilege, depending on the size of your company. In theory, this creates a conflict of interest, because it gives the agency an incentive to give the companies the rating they want. It could explain why, for much of the past decade, agencies seemed happy not to question either the risks banks were taking, or the accuracy of their accounts.[22]

In the following paragraphs, we shall have a look at some of these ratings for Indian companies, besides what the people who matter think of reputation management.

3.3.1 CEO survey

In a survey of CEOs conducted by Kor/Ferry headhunters that included a sample of 257 CEOs from all over the world, potential impact of poor reputation was uppermost in the minds of all the CEOs surveyed. Nine out of ten CEOs believed that corporate reputation was somewhat more important today than it was five years ago. When we look at the data in different continents, the sentiment was stronger among European CEOs than their counterparts in the USA.

Two-thirds of CEOs believed that corporate reputation was the responsibility of the CEO, while one in seven placed responsibilities on the board of directors, and just over one in ten said that corporation reputation management was a PR function.

Interestingly, when hiring a CEO, nine out of ten believed that the reputation of a potential successor depended on what his/her previous employer said of him/her.[23]

3.3.2 Ethical companies attract better talent

In another survey by Select Appointments, it was found that three-quarters of people said they would not like to work for companies that were perceived unethical. Yet another survey by web site totaljobs.com found that four out of ten considered a company's corporate social responsibility (CSR) record to be the deciding factor on whether to accept the job.[24]

3.3.3 Reputation and risk survey

The findings of the Ipsos survey, conducted to gauge the reputation and risk—critical to protecting goodwill and equity of corporate brands—show that the risk for global and national corporations is rising because of potential government intervention and tighter regulatory regimes, backed by engaged citizens and social media influencers. Increasingly, in developed countries, Germans and Britons are among the most suspicious of large corporations. The Ipsos MORI Reputation Center illustrated the importance of a new breed of social and political activists (SPAs) that have grown up around the world. These influencers, according to the survey, lead and stir debate and galvanize public opinion by directly and indirectly pressurizing business and government.

The SPAs are consumer-oriented and drive others to reward and punish good and bad corporate behavior. As a result, they are a force to reckon with. Industry and governments can ignore these individuals at their peril, brought out the findings of the research. These were some of the findings of the global market research leader Ipsos' annual survey 2007, in over 20 countries and through 20,000 interviews, measuring the attitude of "engaged consumer citizens" on various things.

At a time when the rest of the world shows an increasing distrust of large corporations, Indians ranked second in their faith in large corporations (62%), first in their faith in campaign groups, and, of all things, second in their faith in the World Bank (63%).[25]

In a global survey conducted in April–May 2022 by Edelman in 14 countries and among 14,000 respondents, Indians have reposed their faith in Indian companies.[26]

3.4 Image Repair Theory

Image repair, re-engineering, image management have become normal buzzwords among communication firms, and they have no dearth of business as there are many who wish to safeguard their "fair name"!

Analysts believe that the concept of image repair in communication traces its roots to sociological and psychological theories. Every time one feels his/her reputation is hurt because "people have come to know" what they believed was a secret known to them alone, the normal human endeavor is to protect it. The strategies vary from person to person, depending on the individual grooming, value system inherited, and the perceived "cost" of not coming clean. Some may listen to the "voice" of their conscience and "confess;" others may deny till proven "guilty." Is it ethical to protect the image when one knows one is on the wrong side? Again, it depends on whether they would wish to get it off their chest, as there seems no escape, or go on protecting the reputation, in which case chances are one may even succeed. Organizations do not behave differently. When an organization's reputation is on the line, image experts use the most suitable strategic route to salvage the damage that aims at preserving the image, despite unfavorable circumstances. Critics often call it the manipulation of minds through words and imagery.

How does an individual or a corporation know that its image is being threatened?

W L Benoit, author of the Image Repair Theory, states there are two criteria to establish that: "(a) The accused is held responsible for an act; and (b) the act is portrayed as offensive. Depending on the criteria, image repair strategies are organized accordingly".[27]

Benoit argues that the response must match the offence. Benoit's taxonomy has five major components: (a) Denial (when an organization outrightly denies that the problem exists or that if it does, it is not hurting anyone). Another variation of denial is shifting blame; (b) Evasion of responsibility (this allows an entity to manipulate public perception so as to relinquish responsibility); (c) Reduce offensiveness (this strategy seeks to offer an alternative perspective to the problem, attempting to make it appear less offensive, which may include stressing only good points, or focusing on more important issues than the events at hand); (d) Corrective action (the organization attempts to repair the damage by taking action to prevent recurrence); and (e) Mortification (the offender apologizes and asks for forgiveness).

Benoit contends that an organization may employ a combination of image repair tactics to solve a problem, but it must be done carefully so that messages do not contradict and senders do not appear to be backpedaling, which only worsens the credibility of the offender.[28]

It is not uncommon for organizations, governments, and especially armed forces to use some of the earlier strategies in creating positive perceptions about themselves and negative ones for the adversary. For instance, the history of Indo-Pak relations is replete

TABLE 3.2 Benoit's Image Repair Strategies

Denial	
Simple Denial	Act did not occur; I did not do act; act is harmless
Shifting Blame	Another did the act
Evade Responsibility	
Provocation	Act responded to prior offence from victim
Defeasibility	Cannot control situation
Accident	Unforeseen consequence
Good Intentions	Meant well in doing act
Reduce Offensiveness	
Bolster	Stress own good points
Minimize	Act is less offensive than it appears
Differentiate	Act is less offensive than similar acts
Transcend	More important issue
Attack Accuser	Reduce credibility of attacker or claim victim deserved it
Compensate	Offer money, goods, or services
Corrective Action	Repair damage; prevent recurrence
Mortification	Apologize; ask for forgiveness

Source: Author

TABLE 3.3 Simulation of Benoit's Image Repair Theory

Denial	
Simple denial	"No fire was started from our side"
Shifting blame	"The enemy started the fire"
Evade responsibility	
Provocation	"We acted in response to the fire from the other side"
Defeasibility	"Couldn't respond immediately to the firing from across LOC because of ceasefire agreed between the countries during the festival season"
Accident	Unforeseen consequence: "While chasing terrorists, some civilians were caught in crossfire"
Good intentions	Meant well in doing act: "We opened fire to chase the enemy to protect life and property"
Reduce offensiveness	
Bolster	Stress own good points: "We always act responsibly unless provoked"
Minimize	Lesser harm than it appears: "Two soldiers martyred against ten of the enemies killed"
Differentiate	Act is less offensive than similar acts: "We received mutilated bodies of three of our soldiers who were held as POWs (prisoners of war), but we follow strict international code of ethics in dealing with enemy soldiers held in our territory"
Transcend	More important issue: "Both sides must honor and respect the ceasefire during the festival season"
Attack accuser	Reduce credibility of attacker: "The bluff of the political leaders from across the border is called, as the "third party" has confirmed interception of talks of terrorist group holed in the hotel with an intelligence officer from across the border"
Compensate	Offer money, goods, or services: "For each civilian killed in crossfire, the family will receive Rs. . . . . lakhs each"
Corrective action	Repair damage; prevent recurrence: "Border fencing recommended to avoid enemy infiltration from across the border"
Mortification	Apologize; ask for forgiveness: "Army sincerely apologizes for two civilians killed in crossfire."

Source: Author

with such examples, especially at the LOC (Line of Control). Let us look at the following simulated illustration based on Benoit's Image Repair Strategies to make sense of the application of the theory.

In an insightful paper, *The Organizational Apology: A Step-by-Step Guide*, *Harvard Business Review* (Schweizer M, Brooks, AW. Galinsky, AD, 2015), the authors recommend that the organizations must take a measured decision on when and why to apologize. The bigger the mishap, the better should be the reason to apologize. Apologizing means acknowledging a mistake. In the medical field, deaths and disabilities do occur, and many a time because of the doctor or hospital's error of judgment or callousness, but doctors are discouraged to tender a public apology as it may embroil the organization in irreparable damage to its reputation, besides making "the hospital vulnerable to a malpractice lawsuit."[29]

In the following paragraphs, we shall take up a few case studies to understand the strategies employed by various organizations in handling reputation and image issues.

3.5 Case studies

3.5.1 Mattel's toxic toys

Mattel CEO Robert Eckert apologized when summoned by a senate committee in September 2007 to explain toxic contents in Mattel toys. Mattel, a $4 billion company that brings smiles to millions of children all over the world, had to retrieve many thousand Barbie accessories and Fisher Prince toddler toys that carried lethal lead. The company also recalled another 20 million potentially dangerous toys.

Mattel's manufacturing troubles in China, according to Wharton Professor Schweitzer, were examples of "failure of competence," which could have easily been prevented. The problem blew out because "the last thing parents want to worry about when they give a child a toy is safety," commented Schweitzer.[30]

The task of communication was tough. It was many-pronged, interfacing with media, lawmakers, opinion makers, special interest groups, irate consumers, and, of course, the media. As far as maintaining data was concerned, it meant updating the recall figures, corroborating it with stocks, complaints diary, as the CEO had to face the media and public with real information for preserving the company's reputation and sales. The CEO tried to stem consumer worries in a video statement on Mattel's website.[31]

Shopping malls had put up notices about recall. Shoppers were given leaflets about the company's decision to recall and where to return the toys purchased by them and provision for store credit against returned toys.

3.5.2 The iPhone price reduction left many customers unhappy

The late Apple CEO Steve Jobs apologized in 2007 for reducing the price of the much-awaited iPhone by about $200 immediately after it was launched for $599. The early hype had created consumer hysteria about the brand. Enthusiastic buyers had queued up for days and many hours to buy the Apple iPhone. The slash of its price by one-third had many buyers seething with anger. Analysts saw the move as compromising on consumer loyalty and risking brand equity. Apple immediately issued $100 store credit to early buyers.[32] The reputation, however, was sullied, as early buyers felt cheated. The $100 credit was half the discount, and that was not in cash, but for buying an Apple product next time.

3.5.3 Challenges of digital media—the Dell story

Dell, who kind of pioneered the use of social networking media for connecting with communities, got itself into a reputation fiasco when its attorney sent a legal notice to a blogger for sharing information that, in the company's view, was proprietary in nature. A blog was posted at consumerist.com with the caption "*22 confessions of a former Dell manager*," which shared about the strategy of discounts and timing of such discounts. The same day, Dell's attorney served a notice, asking the person to immediately withdraw the posting as it contained confidential information that was proprietary to Dell. The text of the posting included the following information:

> Thursday is the first day of new promotion, if you go to the web site at 11.45 p.m. on Wednesday night and again at 1.00 a.m. on Thursday morning, the promotions are different. The catalogue promotion run from the start of the month to the end.

The information, in the meantime, had circulated far and wide among the bloggers who demanded an explanation from the company on its policy. Sensing the heat and to avoid consumer fury, Dell posted an apology on its website immediately: "We goofed. . ."

Company's digital manager said, "We blew it. . . Instead of trying to control information that was made public, we should have simply corrected anything that was inaccurate. We didn't do that and now we are paying for it."[33]

3.5.4 Being large means under focus—the Walmart case study

Set up in 1962, Walmart, a behemoth with 3,700 outlets in the USA and 1,500 in the rest of the world in many countries, is seen as a working class destination for economical goods. It is a highly profitable company earning billions of dollars in revenue each year.

The reputation of Walmart came under scrutiny on various counts that included non-provision of healthcare facilities to its employees, employer discrimination, urban sprawl, and outsourcing and wage suppression. One of the major criticisms against Walmart has been that it may have created some benefits, but the price of those benefits outweighs costs to communities where it is located. It is alleged that because of its lack of healthcare facilities, it has been draining tax bases. Its anti-union policies and hiring policies are also criticized for being anti-labor.[34]

The company has paid millions of dollars to employees who have sued it in the courts of law from time to time.

Nancy D. Davis, in her research paper, mentioned about a study that revealed that there was a shortfall of 2–8% footfalls owing to bad reputation of the company. These shoppers stopped patronizing Walmart after what they read about it in the media. She further pointed out that union-backed groups like "Wake up Walmart" and "Walmart Watch" including elected leaders and NGOs, launched a "sophisticated attack" on the company. The groups' basic aim is to pressurize the company to relent to their demands through media, lobbying, and grassroots movement.[35] The activist groups are seeking support from all the sections of society.

It is believed that the company, until recently, did not have a formal corporate communication or reputation management cell to handle its communication in critical times. Inundated by criticism, Walmart created a "war room" to pre-empt attacks from the activist groups and media and "professionally manage" all discourses about the company through a PR agency, for which it is spending over $10 million a year.

Walmart soon began publicizing its "good works." Its home page reflected on the amount donated by the company on community work and the employment it has generated worldwide. The activists, on their part, had their strategies chiseled against it. Critics such as Robert Greenwald argued through his documentary *Wal-Mart: The High Cost of Low Price* that the company was destroying America with its bullying tactics, low-wage policies, and environmental negligence. One found various kinds of strategies and media mix used by activists to incite negative perceptions about the company.

3.5.5 Worm-infested Cadbury chocolates in India

Just a couple of days before the Hindu festival of Diwali in 2003, Cadbury faced a tremendous loss of reputation, with media talking front page about worms in chocolates, and trade channel CNBC (it was the only trade channel at that point of time in India) literally showing a crawling worm in a chocolate bar.

In retrospect, Cadbury has been not only a leader in the category with 70% market share, it had worked for years and succeeded in getting in to the bastion of traditional *mithaiwallas* to change people's perceptions about preferring chocolates as gifts during festival occasions against the traditional sweetmeats. It's campaign "*khane wallon ko khane ka bahana chahiye*" (any excuse is good enough to eat, for those, who love eating chocolates) has been quite popular with all generations.

The worm controversy erupted in Maharashtra, where the FDA (Food and Drug Administration) collected some samples for laboratory test. The FDA visited some of Cadbury's plants and found a packaging unit in the town of Satara in unhygienic conditions. It promptly seized its license. The company, in the meantime, passed on the buck to retailers, alleging that the storing facilities must be improper, earning the ire of retailers, some of whom withdrew from selling the brand, as reported by the media. The FDA commissioner Uttam Khabargade appeared on a channel, saying, "It was presumed that worms got in to it at the storage level, but what about the packaging? Packaging was not proper or airtight, either way it is a manufacturing defect with unhygienic conditions or improper packaging."[36]

Having goofed up on many fronts, including at the retailers' front, the company put together its act later, after realizing the damage it had suffered. It launched its reputation-salvage strategy, naming it "Project Vishwas" (Operation Faith). In the meantime, it imported better equipment for double packaging. Through the ad campaign Project Vishwas, it informed the consumers about the double packaging that was foolproof against any infestation in future. The new packaging technology increased the cost of production, but the company did not raise the price of chocolates. Project Vishwas also covered its 1,90,000 retailers in important cities and towns. Later, in a very well-orchestrated television ad campaign, it roped in cine actor Amitabh Bachchan to salvage the reputation. In one of the ads in the series, Bachchan was shown visiting the factory to see the process of production. At the end of his conversation with factory managers, while engaged in animated discussion, he picked up a chocolate bar and munched it, saying it was a question of faith of over five decades! The company claimed to have recovered the lost ground in a few months.

The brand, according to many analysts, has been able to create an emotional connect with Indians for a long time, and that perhaps was the reason for the latitude it received from its consumers, who saw it as an exception and not a rule, a lapse and not really a breach of trust.

Interestingly, whenever there is a problem with multinational FMCG products, the Swadeshi forum, which was active in the 1990s and early part of the current century in India, got activated. At the time of the Cadbury fiasco also, they became active, deriding multinationals.

3.5.6 McDonald's' beef-flavored French fries had the Hindus outraged

In 2000, an Indian software engineer by the name Hitesh Shah, working in the US, sent an e-mail to McDonald's asking if its french fries contained beef ingredients, after he read a newspaper article on french fries. He received the reply in the affirmative, saying that, for flavor enhancement, a miniscule beef flavoring was indeed added. In response to Shah's query on why it was not mentioned in the ingredients list, the reply was that McDonald's followed the "Code of Federal Regulations," which is why the ingredients in natural flavors were not broken down to details. Soon an Indian American newspaper carried the story, creating disgust and outrage among the Hindus, especially vegetarians. In May 2001, Hitesh Bharti, a US-based attorney, filed a lawsuit against McDonald's. The company immediately issued a statement that it never claimed that its french fries were vegetarian. Its bluff was soon called when a letter written to a customer asking for a vegetarian menu surfaced, which clearly had reflected french fries as vegetarian.

Public fury escalated as Hindus and vegetarians from various states joined the protests. The enraged people were not satisfied with its apology. The lawsuit went on for close to a year, when McDonald's issued a fresh apology and paid $10 million to vegetarians and various religious groups in a settlement of all lawsuits.

The company also paid to the 12 plaintiffs a sum of $4,000 each in the five lawsuits, posted a new and more detailed apology, and decided to convene an advisory board to advise on vegetarian matters. The company also issued ads in newspapers communicating the following:

> We acknowledge that, upon our switch to vegetable oil in early 1990s for the purpose of reducing cholesterol, mistakes were made in communicating to the public and customers about the ingredients in our French fries and hash brown. Those mistakes included instances in which French fries and hash browns sold at US restaurants were improperly identified as vegetarian. We regret we did not provide these customers with complete information, and we sincerely apologize for any hardship that these miscommunications have caused among Hindus, vegetarians, and others.

All this had its repercussions in India, despite that McDonald's does not use beef or beef products, keeping in view the cultural sensitivities and eating habits of many Indians. Some of its restaurants were vandalized. What went in its favor was that the tests conducted by the Food and Drug Administration research laboratories proved the company's claims of not using beef and the vegetarian nature of its french fries. The company used media vigorously to make its point across various stakeholders. It also used the restaurant space to put notice and issue literature, which also included the paper mat on the serving tray that carried a collage of newspaper clippings on the issue.

3.5.7 Sensitivity in any crisis is a must, whoever you are—the 9/11 experience

When major crises occur involving communities and nations, there is no gainsaying that the actions of organizations, especially the famous ones, are under public scrutiny. Starbucks learned it the hard way. Midwood Ambulance Service was among various rescue groups helping victims in the aftermath of 9/11 in the USA at ground zero, when they needed water for the victims. Located next door, Starbucks, when asked for water, charged them $130 for three cases of bottled water. The rescue team paid from their pockets. Later, when someone realized that they were overcharged, a phone call to Starbucks was treated rudely, not accepting that it could have overcharged. The media got the scent of the story, and very soon everyone knew about it. Thousands of people spoke about the insensitivity of the company on charging for water for injured people, on their blogs. Charging probably was not the issue, as a junior staff may not have had the authority to supply any merchandise *gratis*, but having come to know this, a corrective action could have been taken by the company. Later, when the story got in to the media and grapevine circuit, Starbucks did wake up. The Midwood Ambulance service president shared with Fox News that he received a hand-delivered cheque and a personal call from Starbucks President Orin Smith after reports of the incident became public. "It's totally inconsistent with the kind of behavior one would have expected from our people, so it has been upsetting to learn of this," said Smith in an interview to media.[37]

3.5.8 Managing reputation in a global world—the Hong Kong Disney case

In a global world, brands do transcend boundaries but often have an uphill task of adjusting to varying tastes, cultures, milieus, and sensitivities. Some have done a great job, while others learned through trial and error.

In an insightful paper: "Globalization, Glocalization and Corporate Reputation. What does it mean for the multinational entry?" Robert Wakefield argues that when settling in an alien culture, adopting it could still leave room for a reputation problem. The case study of Disney Corporation throws some interesting lessons for reputation managers.

In September 2005, Disney Corporation opened its new theme park in Hong Kong—a joint venture between Disney and the Hong Kong government. Hong Kong Disneyland incorporated local adaptations "to ensure its Asian guests felt comfortable while still getting an authentic Disney experience."[38]

The company went to the extent of consulting a feng shui master, and, following his advice, it shifted the park many degrees to suit the feng shui requirements and positioned three big boulders to foster harmony with the spirits. The park was given a Chinese ambience with a fantasy garden and musical extravaganza featuring "Golden Mickeys." The park served Mandarin, Cantonese, and English food with a distinctly local flavor.

Accommodating Chinese liking for elaborate weddings, the park also made room for Chinese banquets, where it served shark fin soup, a Chinese delicacy, a must-serve in weddings. Despite all that, Hong Kong Disneyland encountered opposition from various stakeholders and even from across the country. Media highlighted cost overruns and overcrowding in an area that it felt was too small to attract a big crowd. It spoke of noise pollution from the fire display of fireworks, besides labor issues. The most damaging criticism, however, came from the environmental groups. Criticizing the sharp decline in sharks, the environmental groups from all over the world came harshly on how the fishermen were cruel by throwing back the fish into the ocean after chopping off the fin. The park had included the shark fin soup to cater to the local taste; little did they realize that it would boomerang so badly on its own reputation.

Hong Kong Disneyland responded to the controversy, first by giving leaflets describing ecological harm of shark finning, in hopes that it would dissuade shark fin soup orders. It also said in the leaflet that it would buy only from "reliable and responsible suppliers" and would offer non-shark-fin soup options for banquets. All this made no difference to advocacy groups. After months of protests from environmental groups from within and outside Hong Kong, including WWF, Hong Kong Disneyland withdrew shark fin soup from the wedding menu.

This serves a lesson to reputation managers that in a global world, one must look at localization, without losing sight of the wider world.[39]

3.6 Corporate reputation management imperatives

A robust corporate reputation management (CRM) depends on several factors, viz., key performance indicators, competitive edge, product and service range, corporate governance, corporate social responsibility, shareholder confidence, *et al.* A continuous assessment and bringing about change if necessary is required to maintain a positive reputation for a company. In case of a crisis, which can be for any reason, like an organization's internal or external factors, the most important parameter on which it will be judged is how it rebounds and how sensitively and empathetically it deals with victims. How the media reads the performance of a company on these parameters and in critical times becomes an important benchmark of how it is likely to be perceived by various stakeholders.

From the communication perspective, it is important to take care of the corporate reputation both in normal and crisis times. Companies spend a lot of time and effort in positioning themselves in a certain way through words and imagery, for which a winning corporate identity program is necessary. Institutional advertising, also known by varying names as corporate advertising, public relations advertising, issue/advocacy advertising, is used as an important tool.

A continuous exercise in media content analysis, journo tracking, stakeholder evaluation, brand audit, internal communication measurement, opinion polls, crises research, image surveys, etc are used by the companies to keep their finger on the pulse of public opinion.

In the following paragraph, we shall take up corporate identity and institutional advertising. The research part has been dealt with in detail in Chapter 10: Corporate communication research.

3.7 Building corporate identity

3.7.1 Why corporate identity (CI)?

Corporate organizations, like human beings, have identities. All identities are not necessarily inborn; these can be cultivated and acquired with a "desired response" in view. A successful corporate identity is a vital aspect of motivating various stakeholders. A company's name works as its corporate signature. It is given a visual form, either typographically or pictorially. Research indicates that successful companies tend to have superior corporate identity marks, which help in better reputation management.

3.7.2 What is corporate identity?

There are various opinions as to what comprises the corporate identity. The tangible characteristics of corporate identity include color, style, lettering, signature line, stationery, uniform, building, and advertising. The intangible, and equally important to carry an organization through the thick and thin, is the sum of goodwill earned by it over a period through various measures that include the experience the customer has with the company, its products, services, shares/stocks, etc.

Shultz and Hatch, in their book *The Expressive Organization*, feel that the field of corporate identity "has been concerned with the notion of the central or distinctive idea of the organization and how this idea is represented and communicated to a variety of audiences."[40]

Analysts believe that an organization is "an artificial person" in law, so an identity is created. Whatever that organization does or says is articulated through corporate communication, with all its nuances to key stakeholders.[41]

In a paper prepared by the Confederation of Indian Industries (CII) for its two-day summit on "Corporate Image; Going Beyond Brands," in New Delhi in March 2002, corporate image was seen as a strong factor in business performance, communicating the image effectively, a critical aspect of leadership. To have an effective corporate image, the paper said

> communication needs to encompass all characteristics of a business, from name and logo to office technology, to marketing, to vehicles, employees, ethics, product, organizational structure, and advertising. It defines a company's identity by creating a fit between the company and how it is perceived in the marketplace.

According to the CII paper, dealing with a highly skeptical media added a new dimension. The answer did not lie in "burying the collective 'corporate head' in the sand but in communicating, with apparent transparency, and getting it right the first time."[42]

A well-carved-out corporate identity has many benefits, such as the following:

- Motivates people
- Creates a sense of pride and belonging
- Helps build company ethos, culture, and heritage
- Investor relations, public relations, and human resource professionals can bank upon a robust identity to relate to their distinct target audience
- Helps provide a direction to the employees

3.7.3 The value symbols

Symbols lend strong association and recall value to organizations. Various religions have symbols, like Hinduism has Swastika and OM, Christianity has a cross, and Islam has a crescent moon and stars.

Some famous leaders have been associated with symbols, such as Buddha by the palm of a hand, Mother Teresa by a white sari with a blue border, Gandhi by specs, stick, and dhoti, and Nehru by a jacket and a rosebud, etc.

3.7.3.1 Value of symbols

Symbols not only have manifest but emotional value as well. Symbolism, however, has traversed a long journey—from the real to the surreal and impressionistic. In the past, nature was depicted as a real scene; now just a splash of green denotes nature. In the past, faces were close to real; now the proportion may not be there. When creating symbols, simplicity often is a better strategy.

3.7.4 *Aim of communication through devised identity (symbols/pneumonic/mascots)*

The reasons behind creating a strong symbol are the following:

To provoke
To reinforce
To remind
To build a bond
To act

In the sphere of brands, Thums Up, the lovable tiny-tot in Utterly Butterly Amul, Air India's Maharaja, Gattu of Asian Paints, Red triangle of family planning, Tiku-Tiki in the Indian immunization campaign are some strong symbols that define the characteristics of the brand in no uncertain terms.

Analysts put the rationale behind symbols, arguing that while the industry generally can be decoded as the "rational block," the brand often is the "human block." The purpose of corporate identity is to bridge the gap between the two, by "thinking brand and acting corporate." Some of the examples where both have synergized would include the following:

Walmart: Save money. Live Better.
BMW: The Ultimate Driving Machine
Disneyland: The Happiest Place on Earth
DeBeers: A Diamond is Forever
Uber: Move the Way You Want
Nike: *Just do it!*
TATA: We also make steel.
Amway: No pesticides on our farms. You see, we think like a mother; and "We are listening."
ITDC: Incredible India!
SBI Mutual Fund: No boasting. No bragging. No lying. *Soch hamari fayada aapka.*
LIC: We know India better

3.7.5 *Various types of corporate identity*

There are various kinds of companies, some with a single brand, some with a few brands in the same category. There are companies that can truly be called conglomerates, which have many companies with diversified portfolios under them—say from aviation to beer, from manufacturing steel to bottled water. It is important that the corporate identity takes these things into consideration, that is, whether to put all the product and service brands under the umbrella brand or create niche identities for various brands. Let's look at the types first.

Olins classifies corporate identity in three kinds: the monolithic, endorsed identity, and branded identity.

3.7.5.1 Monolithic

In this case, the entire company uses one visual style, encompassing all its brands and services.

3.7.5.2 Endorsed identity

In this classification, the parent company remains prominent; at the same time the subsidiary companies too have recognizable identities and distinct style.

3.7.5.3 Branded identity

In this case, the subsidiaries have carved their own style, and the parent company is not recognizable.[43]

To cite some examples in the Indian context, Maggi noodles, Kit Kat, Nescafe, and Munch, all from the Nestle stable, started under the umbrella brand but now have their distinct identities. On the other hand, when the Tata Group entered the jewelry business under the brand name Tanishq, it did not distinctly reflect the Tata brand, but after a while, it lent its time-tested brand equity when it added "Tata ki guarantee ke saath" (with Tata guarantee). The brand is now distinctly promoted as a Tata brand.[44]

3.7.6 Legal aspects of corporate identity

3.7.6.1 Intellectual property right: its role and relevance in corporate communication

The corporate identity of a company broadly comprises a logo/trademark, pneumonic, words, how they are written, the color scheme, etc. The corporate identity is considered a very valued property of a company which safeguards it carefully. Any infringement calls for legal action. Many battles have been fought on the issue when a successful company found out that its identity had been "stolen" by someone to gain from its success.

In the following paragraphs, we shall look at both the legal aspects of intellectual property rights and communication aspects, especially in the context of corporate communication.

Intellectual property rights (IPR) and their safeguards have gained focus, especially after the Internet united the world in the sphere of boundless knowledge that transcended artificial boundaries. Earlier known as "industrial property rights," the domain has expanded, with new interpretations coming with latest enactments and contests in various statuary bodies and the courts of law.

3.7.6.2 Why do we need to protect intellectual property?

The industrial revolution brought about many similar products that forced their manufacturers to give them a distinct characteristic by way of identity that included a brand name, a distinct monogram, lettering style, etc. Pharmaceutical companies were the earliest applicants for award of patents for their medicines.

Several laws and acts exist that protect new designs, trademarks, and other artistic works that include the Patents Act, 1970, the Designs Act, 1911, which has been replaced with the Designs Act 2000, the Trade and Merchandise Marks Act of 1958, amended in 1999, and the Copyright Act, 1957, amended in 2000, etc.

3.7.6.3 Relevance of IPR in brand management

An advertisement broadly has the following elements, viz., visual, copy, and the mark of identity of the company, besides a mission statement/tagline. Some ads may not have every element referred, but the mark of identity/the brand name, logo, monogram, or trademark invariably has to be there to lend identity to the brand and the company.

3.7.6.4 (I) Defining intellectual property rights

Black's Law Dictionary defines "intellectual property" as (a) category of intangible rights protecting commercially valuable products of the human intellect. Intellectual Property can be defined as a "category of intangible rights protecting commercially valuable products of the human intellect. The category comprises primarily trademark, copyright, and patent rights, but also includes trade-secret rights, publicity rights, moral rights and rights against unfair competition."

In the following paragraphs, we shall briefly describe the four terms to understand their role and relevance in advertising.

(a) Trademark

A trademark is a mark of identity approved by law to be exclusively used by its owner for a period. A trademark can be applied for and owned by a manufacturer, importer, distributor, or even a salesman. Macdonald's, Pizza Hut, Microsoft, Sony, Philips, Wills, Coca-Cola, Pepsi, Microsoft, Infosys, WIPRO are some examples of trademarks.

The definition and implication of a trademark is that it should not be hypothetical, notional, imaginary, conceived, and stored in file. It must be used on goods. Advertising has a very important relevance as the use of a trademark in an advertisement is seen as the "use" in connection with goods/services.

To acquire that status, it needs to be registered. Identity marks, like a symbol, pneumonic, lettering style, or color code may be used with or without registration. If registered, they will be known as "trademarks." Registration of trademarks gives the manufacturer/owner a legal remedy to check unfair practices by unscrupulous traders/competitors.

The trademark law grants a manufacturer or a trader an exclusive right to use the mark of identity for his goods.

The trademark needs to be distinctive and not descriptive. It may not be registered otherwise. Words that are used to describe one or the other qualities of goods like "perfect," "best," "clean," "superb" are not allowed for registration. Despite that, one finds such registration, on the ground that these have acquired distinctiveness with a long use. "Sheen" (that means smoothness, glossiness, and shine on surface) was once registered for a brand of needles.

Devising an appropriate trademark and obtaining registration for the same creates an intellectual property in the trademark. It protects its use by others for similar goods in the same way as it protects any other kind of private property.

(b) Trademark vs. patent

The difference between a trademark and a patent is that the former identifies the origin of the article to which it is affixed, while a patent is a grant from the government. Trademarks have great recall value for the brands and are used by advertisers prominently in the ad campaign along with the tagline/catchphrase.

(c) Once may not be enough: redesigning trademarks

Some companies change their trademarks for various reasons, which include an expansion in their activities, change in the mandate, statutory requirements, or to align with the changing times in terms of design and approach. Britannia Industries went in for a complete overhaul of its identity in the early 1990s. Oil and Natural Gas Corporation (ONGC) has had five logos between 1960–2004. The logic behind its change of logo in 2004, according to the company, was "to reflect the changes while keeping the linkages with traditions and history intact." As if justifying the change, the company, in its publication "ONGC Reports," said in a box item that Exxon, the global energy major, changed names eight times in its 100-year history. The change of logo was announced by large advertisements by the ONGC in the mainstream media.

Canara Bank changed its corporate identity in 2008, for which it ran a full-fledged campaign "We are changing for you." It wished to inform the people about the introduction of superior technology in its transactions, reiterating at the same time its good old service with a smile.

Public sector companies in the 1980s were asked by the government of India to incorporate Hindi also in their identity marks as a statutory requirement. This led to reshaping of logos by various companies.

In the story titled "The Emperor's New Clothes," Brand Equity, ET, argued that a change in the logo had become the "new cure-all for Indian companies." The million-rupee question whether such tactics were effective, however, remained.[45]

Godrej, Shoppers Stop, Ceat, Bank of India, Canara Bank have changed their logos in the last couple of years. Godrej logo was not entirely changed but revamped. Based on research and user perception, the existing logo was given a fresh and contemporary look to express the idea of "brighter living."

McDonald's, Coca-Cola, Apple, BMW logos remain unchanged since their inception. Their logos represent the strong global identity of these brands. Some marketers feel that rehashing the logo can instill new enthusiasm among the consumers, which may not always be true. A change in the logo must be based on genuine reasons and must reflect the new line of thinking, act, or strategy.

(d) Trademark as a brand communication tool

A trademark performs the function of advertising and publicity for a company in bringing about "top-of-the-mind" recall among consumers. Some famous trademarks have become the benchmarks of quality and credibility. Mercedes Benz, Ford, Pepsi, Coca-Cola, Apple, Johnson & Johnson, Marlboro, as global brands, Maruti, TATA, ONGC, Infosys, WIPRO, Airtel, to name a few from the home-grown turf, spell quality and dependability in the minds of the consumers. Despite that Suzuki holds majority shares in Maruti Udyog, its cars now carry the Suzuki trademark, but the company is still known by the old name because of the tremendous faith the users and the market have in the brand.

When Parle came up with a cola alternative to Coca-Cola in the late 1970s, it was named Thums Up. The graphic was of a hand in a thumb-up position. A name that seemed funny for an aerated drink soon gained popularity among the youth who would order the drink making the thumbs-up signal and not asking by name. Its mission statement "Taste the Thunder" synced well with the brand character. The entire advertising of the brand is based on daredevil feats, thus further reinforcing the philosophy behind the trademark. Bought by Coca-Cola, Thums Up continues to be the largest-selling cola drink in the country.

(e) Personal name as trademark

In an interesting case of *DM Entertainment vs. Rajesh Jhaveri*, Daler Mehndi, a pop singer known for his style that came to be referred as "Bhangra Pop," was able to get an action against defendants for registering the domain name "dalermehndi.net," thereby violating inter alia his rights in the name likeness. The court restrained the defendants from using the plaintiff's trademark "Daler Mehndi," thus giving a benchmark judgment by recognizing the celebrity status of an entertainer's personal name as having trademark significance.

Volkswagen issued a display ad in India in leading newspapers in November 2008, cautioning persons and companies who it said was "deceptively using similar marks/logos as their corporate brand/logo in an attempt to confuse the potential consumers into believing that their goods and/or services are produced/offered under some collaborative arrangement."

Global giant Procter & Gamble changed its logo for critical reasons. The company became a victim of wild rumors that it was in league with Satan and was funding the church of Satan. The rumor arose probably from the logo of the company, which had evolved over a century, that showed a man in the moon and stars. To deal with the rumor, the company went to the media and the court to stop the wild charges emanating from certain religious groups. But then, in April 1985, the company gave up the fight and announced that it would remove the logo from its products, thereby avoid unnecessary controversy, despite winning the court case.

3.7.7 Difference between corporate identity and corporate image

Corporate identity, in effect, is how a company *sees itself*, and corporate image is how a company is *perceived* by the world outside.

Physical manifestation (office, uniform, packaging), products, delivery, service, product reliability, advertising, research, and development, after-sales service, competitive edge are important elements in getting a certain image perception from the stakeholders. How well the company handles its after-sales service, how it responds to an irate consumer's complaint, whether its advertising is credible, whether employees feel proud of the company they work for and speak about it to the outside world, and whether its trade partners are happy with it are some of the important considerations in building the image slowly but definitely.

Dolphin posits the argument that corporate identity and image are two different things and should not be mistaken as one. Identity, he says, concerns the presentation of the "corporate persona" of an organization. Image, on the other hand, is "what the organization appears to be—the identity having been established and communicated to various audiences. Unlike image identity does not change from one audience to another. Until such time as it is altered, it remains consistent."[46]

How does one judge that the corporate identity of a company is aligned with its corporate image? Analysts have the following test to know whether both are aligned and what should be done if corporate identity and corporate image are not positively aligned.

3.7.7.1 Situation I

Matching corporate identity and corporate image

The image and reality are accurately aligned. (This means the company has communicated its position and strategies to all key audiences in a positive way. The corporate image thus would help support the corporate strategy.).

3.7.7.2 Situation II

Matching corporate identity and corporate image

In this case, the image is significantly better than reality. (This means that the company has been effective at communicating the desired image, but it has not been able to sustain that position operationally. This is because the company has not understood its identity or that it has been suffering from some complex.).

3.7.7.3 Situation III

Matching corporate identities and corporate image

In this case, the reality is better than or at least different from the image. (This indicates that the company is failing to communicate effectively.).

3.7.7.4 What should be done when one is faced with any of the three situations?

In case of I, there is no need to alter communication.

In case of II, operational problems need to be solved.

In case of III, the communication process needs to become more effective.

Frank Jefkins says emphatically that good image must be earned, it can't be made. A corporate image, he says, is "based on people's knowledge and experience. This may be good, bad, or indifferent. You know all about your business: outsiders know less, and probably much less about it, unless you tell them about yourself."[47]

3.8 Corporate advertising

Known invariably as institutional advertising, public service advertising, advocacy advertising, and social advertising, corporate advertising serves as an important tool of corporate communication in building the image of an organization.

3.8.1 Genesis of corporate/institutional advertising

Roland Marchand, in his research paper *The Inward Thrust of Institutional Advertising: General Electric and General Motors in the 1920s*, finds the traces of institutional advertising in the early part of the last century, when Charles Kettering of General Motors, while addressing a convention in 1927, made an "unusual" proposal. He said, "I think that every 'ad' should be posted in every factory where the product is made." He further said," If that advertising can't make that working force to make a better article after they have read it than they did it before, then you have lost something."

Marchand writes that during the 1920s the nomenclature "institutional" was applied to all forms of advertising that did not primarily aim at immediate sale of products or services. The term also covered various campaigns by utility organizations like meat packers, railroad organizations that tried to enlist the support of the public against certain regulations.[48]

With increasing consumerism and high exposure to media messages, an average person today is more informed than his predecessors, say, a decade ago. The organizations are in public focus all the time. With the constant public scrutiny, an average organization feels like being in a pressure cooker–like atmosphere. Organizations have to do a lot of explanation than ever before. Analysts believe that organizations are being judged not only what they do but also what they stand for. Corporate social responsibility was never such a publicized affair as it is now. Connecting with various constituencies has become a constant endeavor to be "in the good books" with them. Institutional advertising is one of the tools used by corporate communication professionals to provide that X factor and the goodness quotient to their organizations.

Advertising, as we know, is the mass paid communication which "attempts to inform and persuade a large number of people with single communication." Advertising presents a totally controllable message as the advertiser pays for the space or time, subject to the law and the code of ethics governing the discipline. The advertiser also controls the frequency. Advertising is a "mediated" communication, which must be through the mass media like newspapers, magazines, radio, or television, et al. Because of the nature of mass media, advertising reaches many people at the same time with a low cost per opportunity. In corporate communication, on the other hand, the message is invariably sent directly to the media through news releases, press backgrounders, or through invitation to the scribes to press conferences. All these means are not paid for. It is, however, the prerogative of the newspapers and other media whether to accept or reject the corporate information shared with them. They can also publish and broadcast selectively. That's why corporate communication is referred as "goodwill" communication or "third-party" endorsement. The output from corporate communication appears, unlike advertising, with uncontrolled frequency. There is, however, no denying that editorial coverage enjoys more credibility, because of the implied endorsement by the media that carry it. Corporate organizations, however, have often taken the route of paid time and space through corporate advertising to speak positively about itself without any fear of editorial control that happens when they seek unpaid for publicity through third-party endorsement.

In the case of corporate advertising, space and time is purchased in the media using the same parameters of product advertising, but not speaking about any product *per se*. "Corporate advertising," define Argenti and Forman, "is the paid use of media that attempts to benefit the reputation as *a whole* rather than promote its *specific products or services*. Such advertising should brand a company the way that product advertising brands a product."[49]

A corporate ad campaign can be generic in nature to support a product or a sector, such as the World Gold Council encouraging people to buy the yellow metal, or De Beers promoting diamonds, or the National Commission of Eggs Growers (NCEG) encouraging people to take eggs on all days (*Sunday ho ya Monday, roz khao ande*). In all these cases, there are no brands, but products, so when the sector progresses, all manufacturers and brands would.

Leading National Advertisers (LNA), a group charged with reading and tabulating America's top magazines and select newspapers, has a standard definition of corporate advertising:

> To truly be labeled "Corporate" the ad must deal with the company's policies, functions, facilities, objectives, ideas, and standards, build favorable opinions of the company's management, skill, technology, or social contribution, enhance the investment qualities or financial structure of the company or promote it as a good place to work.[50]

Analysts feel that to be truly labeled as such, the institutional advertising must deal with one or all of the following in its communication:

Company policies
Functions
Facilities
Objectives
Ideas and standards
Company's management
Skills
Technology
Social contribution
People's trust [by giving facts and figures]
Financial structure
Clear company's position after a crisis

The Publishers Information Bureau in the United States classifies advertising as corporate when it meets one or more of the following qualifications:

- To educate, inform, or impress the public about companies' policies, functions, facilities, objectives, ideals, and standards
- To build favorable opinion about the company by stressing the competence of the company's management in various fields

- To build up the investment qualities of the company's securities or to improve its financial structure
- To sell the companies as a good place in which to work, often in a way designed to appeal to future employees[51]

Research company Benson and Benson of the United States has identified 14 distinct major topics and more than 200 corporate advertising sub-topics. The company made this analysis in the preparation of its codes for the systematic tracking of corporate advertising:

Subject list:

1. Diversity: Mention various products, services, or concerns incorporated in the text of the ad. List of subsidiaries or data on multinationality are also included
2. Technology: Research, development, or application of quality control
3. Energy: Technology, exploration, conservation, conversion, energy, shortage, or the mention of a specific energy source
4. Ecology: Natural resource, management, recycling, abatement of air or water pollution, or solid waste management
5. Corporate Social responsibility: Grants to sponsor entertainment or education program, employment, or training for minority group, women
6. Consumerism: Communication with a company by the consumer, consumer protection program
7. Major capital investment: Expenditures for projects, facilities, expansion, pollution controls, or energy
8. Financial performance: Reference to earnings or sales, dividend announcement
9. Economic and regulations: Comments on inflation, wage and price controls, legislation, supply and demand, etc.
10. Recruiting and labor relations: Recruitment, working environment, reference to strikes, or employee recognition
11. Acquisitions and mergers: Mergers acquisitions and incorporation announcements and statements for organizational tender offers
12. Name change or protection: Announcement of name change or a new symbol trademark protection
13. Productivity: Increase in human or machine productivity
14. Corporate activity: Information about corporate activities

Over a period, however, corporate adverting has spawned a whole range of labels, such as issue advertising, viewpoint advertising, opinion advertising, advocacy advertising (if you are for the cause), adversary advertising (if you are against the cause), controversy advertising (a neat compromise), public interest advertising, public affairs advertising, public issue advertising, et al.

3.9 Brand image insensitivity

Sometimes, the image of a corporation may be put on block without it doing anything to earn that. The following is a sample:

The Indian Express of 27 July 2008 had the pictures of wailing kith and kin post serial bombing of the city of Ahmadabad on 26 July 2008 on its front page. The incident brought a trail of blood, gore, and mayhem resulting in many innocent people losing their lives and some their limbs. Under the masthead was the banner advertisement: "It is raining free tickets!" with the visual of a smiling model under an umbrella from the state flier Air India. Not that anyone could foresee disasters always and the news that follows, but putting both, the ad and the picture of wailing people, together seemed quite insensitive. What could have been done under the circumstances, since the first page is last to be printed? The newspaper could possibly have gotten in touch with the agency/client to postpone the advertisement. There is this legendary story about the *Times of India*, which did not publish the ad of Colgate toothpaste with the visual of a smiling model on 28 May 1964, after Prime Minister Pundit Jawaharlal Nehru's death on 27 May 1964, without even consulting the company. In the year under reference, even the telephone was a rarity. The publication did not want either itself or the client to appear insensitive when the whole country was mourning the death of its first prime minister, and there were black borders and banner headlines in most of the newspapers. In a time and age of instant connectivity, it would not have been difficult.[52]

Post 9/11, in the USA, *The Times* came out with a special issue on the tragedy, but it was *sans* any advertisements. It is not just the media; even the corporate world would not like to appear insensitive at a time when public opinion is either sensitive or volatile.

Some experts feel that it has become fashionable to launch corporate campaigns even when there may be no need for them. They suggest that a periodic appraisal of such campaigns is necessary to gauge the impact.

Summary

The chapter began with defining reputation and corporate reputation and the need to protect reputation. Corporate reputation management has become a specialization, given the demand from the industry. Many companies commission reputation management consultancies both for normal and critical times. The new age media has created both opportunities and challenges for corporate communication professionals. Therefore, it is important to keep a constant track of how the company is being perceived by various stakeholders.

The theory of image repair was discussed, which suggested various communication strategies and message plans for use in varying conditions. Several case studies were taken up for discussion to understand the strategies adopted by companies to salvage reputation damage.

The chapter then discussed the tools of corporate reputation. The need, role, and scope of creating a corporate identity was discussed in detail. How corporate identity is different from or like corporate image were deliberated upon. Corporate advertising is an important tool for keeping the company in focus about its achievements and what it stands for; therefore, several case studies were taken up for discussion to understand various genres of corporate advertising, viz., institutional, advocacy, public service, et al.

Key terms

Branded identity: when subsidiary companies have carved their own style and the parent company is not recognizable in that identity.

Corporate reputation management: an important management tool to create, enhance, and preserve the reputation of an organization.

Corporate identity: refers to both the tangible and intangible characteristics of corporate identity. The former include color, style, lettering, signature line, stationery, uniform, building, and advertising, and the latter, equally important to carry an organization through the thick and thin, is the sum total of goodwill earned by it.

Endorsed identity: in this case, the parent company remains prominent; at the same time the subsidiary companies too have recognizable identities and distinct style.

Image repair: refers to making use of various tools and strategies to salvage a damaged reputation which may have occurred for various reasons.

Intellectual property right: refers to a category of intangible rights protecting commercially valuable products of the human intellect. The category comprises primarily trademark, copyright, and patent rights, but also includes trade-secret rights, publicity rights, moral rights, and rights against unfair competition.

Institutional advertising: known invariably also as corporate advertising, institutional advertising does not talk about the brands, but the company as a brand aimed at earning goodwill that may come from the company's policies, functions, facilities, objectives, ideas, and standards, management, skill, technology, or social contribution.

Monolithic identity: in this case, the entire company uses one visual style, encompassing all its brands and services.

Concept review questions

Q.1. Define reputation. How is the reputation of an individual different from the reputation of an organization?

Q.2. Why is it challenging and at the same time necessary to constantly maintain a positive reputation in the digital age?

Q.3. Define the Image Repair theory. What are its various segments?

Q.4. What is corporate identity, and what are its various elements?

Q.5. What are the various steps of aligning corporate image with corporate identity?

Q.6. Discuss the similarities and differences between product advertising and corporate advertising.

Critical thinking exercise

Go through at least three case studies from the chapter, and give alternate strategies if you were asked to handle the situations.

Fieldwork

Choose an advocacy campaign from the media, and analyze its aim and the target audience it is aiming to reach. Speak to at least ten members of the supposed target audience to gather insights about the impact or the lack of impact of the campaign on them and why.

Net search

Choose any company that you admire the most. Go to the home page of the company to understand its vision, its philosophy, its various brands and services, and its CSR and how it handles its customer complaints. Having done that, search the Net to find who is saying what about the company. What are the areas that are admired and by whom, or disliked about it and who is saying it. Analyze the input to understand the challenges of maintaining a good reputation in the digital age and how the company has responded to criticism.

Caselets

Analyses of some corporate campaigns

a) "Tata Jaago Re"

Tata group, which is more than a century old in the country, does not generally pick up issues on social or political advocacy through paid advertising but decided to do it around election time with its "Jaago Re" (Wake Up) campaign through its brand Tata Tea.

The "Jaago Re" campaign exhorted the youth to exercise their right to vote. Tata has used a very smart strategy in its "Jaago re" campaign. In the television commercial, there was no mistaking that it was an out-and-out advocacy campaign, with tea as a prop. A young protagonist amidst a group of youth was seen telling a guy "*Boss aap so rahe hein*" (Boss, you are sleeping), then turns towards a girl, repeating it. Irritated, the girl widens her eyes symbolically to say she is not asleep. The protagonist quips, "*Aagar aap election wale din vote nahi de rahe to aap so rahe hein.* (If on an election day you are not voting, you are sleeping.). The paper teacup that he held in his hand had the "Jaago re" website printed, while the protagonist encourages them to visit the site to register as voters.

Another Tata TVC in the series had a politician seeking votes by meeting people personally. The protagonist asks him about his educational qualifications, to which the candidate had no answer. He, in any case, did not think education was required for what he considered was not really a job, to which the protagonist *said* "*Desh KO chalane ka kam.*" (To run the country is indeed an important job.).

As soon as the parliamentary election dates were announced in March 2009, the company upped its campaign by adding the print version also, clearly piggybacking on the television ad. A look at the print campaign (later) would reveal that the ad contains elements of both brand and advocacy advertising. The protagonist's picture reminds of the aim, but various Tata tea brands are also placed in the ad.

Some media reports suggested that the Delhi election held in early 2009 was impacted by such campaigns, as the voting pattern reflected that more youth had exercised their franchise this time.

Analyzing the campaign, the brand equity reflected that while the campaign was on air and print with the parliamentary elections process on in April 2009, more than six lakhs voters registered through its website jagore.com, which was created in association with an NGO by the name Janagraha, based in Bangalore. The article gave an interesting insight about the Net, that is, 30% of all those who visited the jagore site registered for voter identity cards, in contrast to the industry norm that was 0.001%, which was quite an achievement for the campaign. In fact, after the Congress emerged as the largest party, breaking many stereotypes, Rahul Gandhi, the general secretary of the Youth Congress, ascribed the victory to the youth and poor people.

One of the ardent creative brains, R Balakrishnan, known as Balki, and Amer Jaleel, of Lowe Lintas, of which Balki is the chairman, are said to be the brains behind the winning "Jaago Re" campaign, which, interestingly, was conceived after brainstorming over coffee, pointed out the article.[53]

Ironically, about a quarter century ago, Tata Tea was involved in a controversial issue with the Assam government, when it used the paid space but through its attorney. Here goes the story.

During 1998, it was alleged by the state government of Assam that Tata management was supporting subversive elements by financing them and offering its hospitality to certain members of an insurgent group. The government quoted some hospital bills allegedly paid by the company for a relation of a known insurgent who had undergone medical treatment in a hospital in Mumbai. The issue took such a dirty turn that not only the State of Assam but also the central government was involved in the controversy. Noted criminal lawyer Ram Jethmalani issued a large advertisement, which in fact was an open letter to the then Assam Chief Minister Prafulla Kumar Mohanta questioning his allegation against his "client." He challenged the chief minister to reply to him through the same columns, meaning thereby, the advertising space. Not to be left behind, the chief minister took the challenge literally and replied to the allegation through an ad by booking space on the front page, *solus* position (right-hand bottom side of the newspaper, which has the maximum chance of being read but comes at a cost that is normally double the cost for ordinary space). This was a form of corporate advertising, explaining the point of view of the company by buying commercial space.

*b) Lead India (*Times of India*)*

The *Times of India* mounted its "Lead India" campaign in 2008, inviting people to nominate those who they thought had leadership qualities. The media group then organized debates among the selected candidates on a television channel, inviting a panel of judges from a wide spectrum of experts from various fields. The winner was sent to a coveted school abroad to hone his skills in the chosen field. He has since joined a political party, as reported by the paper.[54] The second part of the campaign came through a multi-ad campaign in various media as soon as the parliamentary elections were announced in March 2009. In the ad, people from various strata of society were shown taking oath by placing their hand on their children pledging to vote. Some ads are discussed subsequently.

During the 13th parliamentary elections, Procter & Gamble brand Ariel came out with an interesting advertisement advocating its faith in democracy. The ad had a picture of a hand with a pointing index finger with a black stain (the mark applied by the polling staff to those who go to polling booths to exercise their franchise). The only copy the ad had read, "Perhaps the only stain we respect."

c) Global warming (World Wildlife)

In yet another advocacy issue, the Times group joined WWF, which spearheaded a campaign called "60 Earth Hour."

Roping in popular cine actor Aamir Khan, who is considered a thinking man's actor, the campaign invited people to switch off electricity for an hour on 28 March 2009, branding the hour as WWF Earth Hour from 8.30 pm to 9.30 pm. Choosing the right protagonist is very important for advocacy advertising. In this case, Aamir was chosen, for obvious reasons, over other popular actors like Salman Khan who is often embroiled in controversies; or Shahrukh Khan, who is a brand ambassador to many brands, has great star value, but not seen as intense as Aamir; or, for that matter, Akshay Kumar, who too has great star value and fan following but may not have proved as suitable as Aamir Khan.[55]

*d) Teach India (*Times of India*)*

Through its Teach India campaign, the *Times of India* invited people to join the movement of teaching the underprivileged. It's not just a campaign; it is aimed at being a movement. The campaign received an overwhelming response as soon as it was launched, receiving more than 50,000 volunteers. According to TOI sources, almost 90% of the volunteers had never done any kind of social work before. As Adeline Aubry, program officer, United Nations Volunteers (UNV) Program in India, pointed out, "Teach India has created a new constituency of volunteers." The highest number of students as a percentage of volunteers came forward in Kolkata (29%), but the figure dipped in Delhi (24%), Mumbai (17%), and Chennai (16%). On the upside, employed people showed remarkable enthusiasm. In each of the four cities, the percentage of employed volunteering to teach had far outnumbered other segments like students or retired people. For instance, in Chennai, 53% of the applicants were employed compared to just 3% of retired people, 16% students, and 8% housewives.

TOI's corporate partners, including Cognizant Technology Group, Genpact, Dominos, the Chadha Group, Balaji Infra Projects Ltd, Financial Technologies Group, Lodha Group, Acclaris Business Solutions, Descon (DPSC Ltd), and Xenitis Group, pledged to teaching the underprivileged children on company time as a part of their CSR.

One is reminiscent of a similar campaign years ago by the government, viz., "Each One Teach One." It was a great idea with a desired response from the stakeholders; it won many accolades and awards, but the campaign miserably failed. The reason—the campaign had invited people to ask for a free kit for teaching, and so overwhelming was the response that the agency in charge could not cope with the response. The campaign tumbled under its own weight.

e) Use of corporate advertising to express angst—the Suzuki way

In India, corporate advertising has always been popular. It critical times, some have used it "to be heard" or, as some would say, to settle scores. To cite an example, blue-chip company Maruti Udyog found itself in a quandary when its "other half," Suzuki, feeling wronged, resorted to full page advertisements to put its point across to its various stakeholders. One of its ads in newspapers in November 1997 read: "There is only one company that can capture the global markets. Maruti. There is only one thing that can stop it. Mistrust." The body copy of the ad in two columns, "Disinformation" and "Reality," sought to clarify Suzuki's position but at the same time pointed fingers at "others" for spreading disinformation. The reference was obvious. Analysts felt that a lot of dirty linen was being washed in public. Suzuki's second phase of advertising in early 1998 was, however, on a friendlier note. One of its ads said: "15 years ago, the God of winds brought about the winds of change in India. Let's join together to keep Maruti flying high. Suzuki's promise: All our best to Maruti."

Suzuki that time was the junior partner with less than 50% shareholding. As the brand was phenomenally successful, the government at one point threatened to change the partner firm, if Suzuki was feeling uncomfortable. But not only did it not happen. The government, in a magnanimous doze of liberalization, sold majority shares to the company, and today it is Suzuki and no more Maruti. The name continues because of the immense brand value and strong association people have with the name.

f) Brand promotion through advocacy route—the Benetton way

Some companies, like Benetton, have made use of institutional advertising as a part of their brand strategy. The Benetton's ad philosophy, according to company sources, is based on Luciano Benetton's belief that "communication should not be considered from outside the company but conceived from within its heart."

The brand began its journey with "All the Colors of the World," one of its earlier slogans, which was later altered to "United Colors of Benetton." The concept, feels the company, was so strong that it turned the slogan to its actual logo.

Benetton campaign has undergone three distinct phases:

- The cycle of difference
- The cycle of reality
- The cycle of free speech and the right to express it[56]

During the first cycle, happy groups of multiracial children were shown, followed by couples representing an "all new interpretation of difference." A priest kissing a nun (to reflect religion and sexual conflict) and a white child shown as angel and black as devil (the stereotype of good and evil) were some of the ads, which witnessed tremendous protests.

In the second phase, in a candid commentary on the futility of war, a Benetton ad had a picture of a war cemetery. According to Benetton sources, the ad was published only in one newspaper in Italy, but the whole world came to know about it, as scores of articles in the media appeared in many countries along with the reproduction of the ad.

The other ad that became controversial, at least initially, was the one with a newborn baby attached to the umbilical cord, which Benetton intended as an "anthem to life" but became a cause of much protest. It is a different matter that it later received the due recognition from far and wide.[57]

In early 1992, Benetton ads "changed radically." One ad had the news photo of a real high-drama situation—a man dying of AIDS, which again was criticized, until the parents of the deceased publicly said that their son was being heard more in death than when he was alive.

In the current phase, Benetton campaigns work in alliance with non-profit organizations, large international bodies, adopting various themes such as food, peace, health, et al., making a "different use of advertising."

Oliviero Toscani, the brain behind the provocative yet sensitive campaigns, parted from the company in 2000. Just before that, he happened to come to India, when one found a double- page Benetton ad in the Indian news media, which attracted a lot of attention. The visual comprised a close-up of a healthy palm with some grains of rice placed on it. A small statement accompanied the ad, which read: "One day hunger would be out of fashion"—a very powerful statement, indeed, coming from a fashion company. In an interview with a newspaper, Toscani was asked what the ad conveyed and why only 52 grains of rice were placed on the palm, to which he quipped that he did not know how many gains were on the palm. The hand, he said, could be of a ghetto dweller; it could be of a benevolent person. It could also convey that those who had enough must share with those who did not have. That people really counted the number of grains itself reflected their interest, and they could interpret it according to their perceptions. Toscani said the ad conveyed different things to different people, and so long as they were moved, the purpose of the campaign was served.[58]

j) Cadbury ad

Some scholars feel that the fine line between various genres of ads is fast thinning. A corporate ad could convey a brand in the same manner as a brand ad could easily be interpreted as an institutional ad. For instance, during one of the cricketing seasons in India in 2008, one of Cadbury's ads had a man holding a basket of Cadbury chocolates amidst a community viewing a match on television. As apparent, he wished to distribute the chocolates to people if India won the match. India needed only one run to win, but there was only one last ball to go, but alas! India lost the match, much to the despair of everyone.

A kid picked up a bar from the apparently dejected man, holding the basket, saying they could still celebrate even if it was Kenya. The chocolates vanished in no time. The hapless man kept asking who was Kenya (*Kenya kaun hai*?), to which one of the people replied, "He was just here, he would have just gone here or there" (Abhi yehi tha, yehi kahin gaya hoga), and the person seemed satisfied. The ad has two important points to deliver: one, that no matter who wins, there is always a reason to celebrate. A game is a game, so sportsman spirit is necessary. And, of course, the good old Cadbury's adage "Khane walon ko khane ka bahana chahiye!" Was it a brand ad or an advocacy ad? One could say a brand ad, but with definite underpinnings of institutional advertising.

Another campaign on the brand and corporate borderline is the "Daag ache hain" (Stains are good), a campaign by Surf that has won many awards. In what can be termed as an attempt at advocacy, children have been involved as protagonists to teach a lesson or two to their elders on harmony and environment protection.

k) Ads aimed at behavior change

There are ads that aim at changing the behavior of people. It is important that cultural and gender sensitivity is taken care of in such ads. For instance, the British government's

5.2-million-pound ad campaign, kick-started in early 2009 by the labor ministry encouraging young women to carry condoms, was met with opposition from some groups, reported the *Daily Telegraph*. The campaign implies that men are attracted to women who carry contraceptives: "Men like nothing better than a woman who knows what she wants." Conservative lawmaker Julian Brazier said while condoms did help preventing sexually transmitted diseases,

> it is very sad that the authors of the document do not seem to understand that the problem starts with growing levels of social activity by people with multiple partners. This campaign is contributing to the further growth of the problem rather than to public health.[59]

l) What an idea!

Idea Cellular, an erstwhile mobile brand's campaign "What a great Idea Sir, Ji" stood out in the highly cluttered mobile phone category ad campaigns. Idea's campaign of a rural school through the cell phone with cine star Abhiskek Bachchan as the protagonist had all the ingredients of emotion, drama, and taste of success in a 60-second plot.

A campaign may have a great idea which may not necessarily be implementable, but it sure catches people's imagination. Interestingly, the idea triggered the right response in rural Punjab, where an NGO began a school through community radio, getting great response, as reported by media.

Later, the "idea" was expanded by reflecting the power of SMS and voice phone to gather public opinion before the politician took any decision on various issues of public interest, like opening a mall on agricultural land, sex education in schools, to women empowerment.

Questions on case studies

a) Why, in your view, does a mainstream newspaper like the *Times of India* take up advocacy campaigns?
b) Study the Benetton campaign carefully, and argue on why the fashion brand often took up volatile and uncomfortable issues in building its brand reputation?

Notes

1 The Economic Times, "Outraged Obama Vows to Block AIG Bonuses" (in arrangement with Associated Press, Washington), 18 March 2009.
2 The Economic Times, "Citi, Morgan Stanley Look to Side Sidestep Bonus Caps: Report" (in arrangement with Reuters, NY), 18 March 2009.
3 The Economic Times, 18 March 2009.
4 www.highbeam.com/doc/1P3-1040341721.html
5 Ibid.
6 www.toprankblog.com/2008/11/online-reputation-seo-social-media-pr/
7 www.oberlo.com/blog/online-review-statistics
8 S. Mishra, *Saying 'Sorry': The Role of Apology in Online Crisis Communication in India*. As part of a colloquium titled "Social Media: The New Mantra for Managing Reputation", *Vikalpa: The Journal for Decision Makers*, 40, no. 4, 2015, pp. 455–491.
9 Ibid.
10 The Times of India, 23 February 2009.

11 The Times of India, 26 February 2009.
12 "Amended IT Act to Prevent Cybercrime Comes into Effect", *The Hindu,* 27 October 2015.
13 www.webershandwick.com
14 www.georgeludwig.com.
15 Ibid.
16 S. Bider, "Global Spin, the Corporate Assault on Environmentalism", 2000, Scribe in Melbourne//homepage.mac.com/herinst/sbeder/home.html
17 Ibid.
18 Ibid.
19 P. Lesly, "Coping with Opposition Groups", *Public Relations Review*, 18, no. 4, 1992, p. 330.
20 J. Stauber and S. Rampton, "Deforming Consent-Pr industry's Secret Was on Activists", *Covert Action Quarterly*, no. 55, 1995–96, pp. 18–15, 57 as quoted by S. Beder, ibid.
21 www.bbc.com/news/world-asia-india-32747649. Justin Rowlatt, "South Asian Correspondent with BBC", 16 May 2015, accessed on 19 July 2017.
22 www.theguardian.com/business/2012/feb/15/credit-ratings-agencies-moodys
23 www.management-issues.com
24 Ibid.
25 Sudeshna Sen, The Economic Times, 25 July 2007.
26 www.financialexpress.com/industry/india-on-top-for-trust-in-domestic-companies-followed-by-china-canada-us-and-uk-study/2536103/. The Edelman Trust Barometer Special Report: The Geopolitical Business, which was released here on the sidelines of the World Economic Forum Annual Meeting 2022, reflected how geopolitics has become a litmus test for trust in business.
27 W. L. Benoit, "Image Repair Discourse and Crisis Communication", *Public Relations Review*, 23, 1997, pp. 177–185.
28 Ibid. W. L. Benoit and S. Drew, "Appropriateness and Effectiveness of Image Repair Strategies", *Communication Reports*, 10, 1997, pp. 153–163. As quoted in a research study by Tracie Adams et al in DoD Joint Program in Communication, University of Oklahoma www.ou.edu/deptcomm/dodjcc/groups/98A1/image%20repair.doc
29 The Organizational Apology (hbr.org)
30 http://knowledge.wharton.com
31 www.Mattel.com
32 www.knowledge @Wharton.com
33 www.newscnet.com
34 Ibid.
35 Nancy Diana Davis, in her senior honors thesis on "corporate reputation management, the Wal-Mart Way-exploring effective strategies in the global market place." submitted to Texas A&M University, April 2007.
36 Trade Channel, CNBC and the Times of India, 13 October 2003.
37 www.foxnews.com
38 P. Swann, *Cases in PR Management*, 2008 (Boston: McGraw-Hill) quoted by Robert Wakefield, www.bledcom.com
39 Robert Wakefield, www.bledcom.com.
40 Schulz, Mailken, Hatch, Marry Jo, Larsen, Mogens Holten, editors, *Expressive Organization: Linking Identity, Reputation, and the Corporate Brand* 1st Edition, Oxford University Press, 2000.
41 Richard R. Dolphin, *The Fundamentals of Corporate Communications*, 2001 (New Delhi: Butterworth-Heinemann), p. 43.
42 **"Power of Reputation: CII to Bring Experts Together"**, Posted 5 March 2002, www.financialexpress.com/news/power-of-reputation-cii-to-bring-experts-together/39343/0
43 W. Olins, *Corporate Identity: Making Business Strategy Visible Through Design*, 1989 (London: Thames & Hudson).
44 Jaishri Jethwaney and Shruti Jain, *Advertising Management*, 2006 (New Delhi: OUP), pp. 106–107.
45 The Economic Times, 26 November 2008.
46 Richard R. Dolphin, *The Fundamentals of Corporate Communications*, 2001 (New Delhi: Butterworth-Heinemann), pp. 41–42.
47 Frank Jefkins, *Public Relations for Your Business*, 1995, (New Delhi: Excel Books), p. 12.

48 The Inward Thrust of Institutional Advertising: General Electric and General Motors in the 1920s, Roland Marchand, University of California, Davis/PDF.
49 Paul A. Argenti and Janis Forman, *The Power of Corporate Communication*, 2002 (New York: McGraw-Hill), p. 106.
50 www.lna.com
51 www. Publishers Information Bureau.com
52 The Indian Express of 27th July 2008.
53 Brand Equity, The Economic Times, 29 April 2009.
54 The Times of India, 19 March 2009.
55 The publication reported in its columns in Delhi alone the power load at that hour came down by 1000 MW. Times of India, 30 March 2009.
56 www.benetton.com
57 Ibid.
58 Jaishri Jethwaney, *Advertising*, 1999 (New Delhi: Phoenix Publishing House).
59 The Daily Telegraph, 20 March 2009.

4

EMPLOYEE COMMUNICATION

4.1 Introduction

Among various tasks associated with management, communication is considered the most important, because other management tasks like planning, organization, command, coordination, and control can be achieved only through effective communication. Communication enables management to connect with employees, motivate them, and help them turn organizational goals into their personal goals to achieve the bottom line. While information to employees comes from various directions relating to umpteen official matters, at least one department communicates with employees on issues that go beyond the periphery of "official," that is, the employee communication cell. Some organizations face friction on the issue as to who shall handle that function, viz., marketing, human resource, or corporate communication. We shall discuss this aspect later in the chapter.

One often hears employees being referred to as the "assets" of an organization, and truly so. How seriously an average management practices it may be difficult to answer. An organization comprises people with varying social, cultural, educational, and economic backgrounds who are expected to achieve common organizational goals. This can be seen as a challenge as well as an opportunity. More and more researches point out that internal stakeholders have a great role to play in contributing to the positive reputation of an organization. The CEO often is the torchbearer. His personality, his philosophy, his vision reflects the character of that organization. To cite two examples, N. R. Narayana Murthy, chief mentor of Infosys, is seen as a thought leader, a simple person embedded in middle-class values. Mukesh Ambani, on the other hand, is seen as a shrewd businessman who has expanded his business empire to unlimited heights and lives in uber luxury. Both Narayana Murthy and Mukesh Ambani are successful in their area of activity but are perceived variously.

Lindo recommends four reasons why the internal stakeholders are crucial:

- Internal communication gives employees an interest in corporate objectives. The greater the interest, the more likely employees would be enthusiastic about the long-term objectives of the organization.

DOI: 10.4324/9781032694702-4

- Internal communication enables an organization to gain acceptance for corporate policies and culture.
- Internal communication provides a means by which the organization can win respect for the communication department.
- Internal communication assists in establishing, maintaining, and reinforcing positive relationships with internal customers.[1]

4.2 What is employee communication?

Employee communication is about managing relationships. There is always a tussle, especially among the marketing, HR and corporate communication departments as to who would handle employee communication. As employees are very important stakeholders for an organization, the corporate communication department serves its aim better if it handles employee communication. Corporate communication often uses persuasion to get the desired response, unlike the HR that issues orders through circulars and memos to inform, educate, and communicate. It does not hesitate in quoting rules to make a point that reflects in no uncertain terms as to who really calls the shots. In other words, while other departments interface with employees on "official" matters or hard news, communication that emanates from the corporate communication department is referred to by some practitioners as "soft" news. To illustrate, the HR communication may be about a changed service rule, the finance department about a wage increase or cut in pay, the production and marketing departments may be communicating targets which the receivers are expected to follow. All these issues are often taken up by the corporate communication manager through various channels of employee communication, but in a different tone and tenor. To illustrate, if the production department had communicated certain targets, the corporate communication story could be about a person or a group that fulfilled the target or went above the target in the stipulated time, the reward, the felicitation, besides facts about the targets. This certainly would have a human face and be motivational to one and all than just a circular on the achievement of targets.

Employee communication can be through various media like magazines, blogs, video conferencing, brainstorming, events, idea boxes, intranet, employee radio, and a host of other channels, an area in which the marketing or HR verticals do not possess expertise.

Corporate communication is a top management function, and the CEO needs to interface with the employees both at official and personal levels to create a family feeling and give direction to the organization, as a head of a family would do. Satyam's beleaguered CEO, who was seen as an inspiration by thousands of employees, must have felt let down after the fraud was unearthed and, on top of that, his personal involvement in the scam. In his confessional statement, he had this to say about Satyamites:

> I have promoted and have been associated with Satyam for well over 20 years now. I have seen it grow from few people to 53,000 people, with 185 Fortune 500 companies as customers and operations in 66 countries. Satyam has established an excellent leadership and competency base at all levels. I sincerely apologise to all Satyamites and stakeholders, who have made Satyam a special organisation, for the current situation. I am confident they will stand by the company in this hour of crisis.[2]

The troubles of Satyam employees around that time were far from over. One expected that, with the new management in place, their issues would be addressed. A media report, however, revealed that a quarter of Satyam employees, that is, about 10,000, were seen as "surplus" by its new owner Tech Mahindra, quoting the then CEO Vineet Nayyar who was probably looking for "the least painful way" to deal with the situation. Among the various options, the new Satyam management considered "across-the-board salary cuts, virtual benching of employees and sending some of them on a sabbatical or to work with NGOs", wrote the *Economic Times*.[3]

Companies take great pains to employ the "right kind of people," which include taking references from people who know the candidates. Some companies are even visiting social networking sites to study the profile of a "would-be" employee, to know what they think about, how they respond to issues, and their lifestyles. In the US, writes Sandra Oliver, more than 5,000 organizations have honesty tests, using some form of pencil-and-paper evaluation to enable them to find out the level of an employee's truthfulness or propensity for telling the truth.[4]

Reliance Industries Limited, in one of its corporate sustainability reports, while talking about its various stakeholders, puts them in the following chronological order: shareholders, customers, suppliers, employees, regulatory authorities, communities/NGOs, and trade unions. For employees it says, "We are committed to nurture the talent of our employees and facilitate their personal development. We foster workplaces that are safe, professional and which promote teamwork. We emphasize on cross learning, knowledge sharing, job diversification and developing cross-functional skills."[5]

Marcia Xenitelis talks of the "aha" moment when communicating with employees, especially about change. The "aha" moment, she says, comes when the receiver of the communication has the following expressions:

"Now it makes sense."

"Now I can do something about it."

She recommends conducting focus group interviews among employees to know their communication needs, so that appropriate communication strategies can be devised.[6]

4.3 Genesis of employee communication

Michael C Brandon cited three major phases of employee communication but did not specifically label them, which Lyn Smith now has adapted as follows:

4.3.1 Stage one (pre-1960s)

In this phase the predecessor was industrial relations, goal to improve employee morale; emphasis on individual orientation and camaraderie; attitude—warm and personal; and focus—people.

4.3.2 Stage two (mid-1960s to 1980s)

Here the predecessor was journalism; goal—deliver news; emphasis—facts; orientation—reporting; attitude—cool, skeptical; focus—events.

4.3.3 *Stage three (late 1980s to now)*

During the current phase, the predecessor is marketing; goal—implement strategy; emphasis—organization; orientation—aid to management; attitude—business oriented; focus—strategic objectives.[7]

4.4 Tata's pioneered employee communication and caring

In existence for over a century, the Tata Group has been a pioneer in many things, including caring for its employees. During his tenure, JRD Tata initiated a program of closer "employee association with management" to give workers a stronger race in the affairs of the company. He began welfare schemes in corporate India and the principle of the eight-hour working day, free medical aid, and accidental compensation, which were later adopted by the government of India and made statutory. During his stewardship, JRD Tata, in 1979, instituted a new practice at Tata Steel that a worker was deemed to be "at work" from the moment he left home for work till he returned home for work, which meant the company was financially liable to the worker if any mishap took place on the way to and from work.[8]

The Tatas are also credited for starting the house journal for employee communication way back in the 1940s.

Former Prime Minister late Mrs. Indira Gandhi, a great supporter of the public sector, believed that, to get the best out of the employees and maintain a good image, it was pertinent to have a communication department, headed by a professional. She spearheaded a conference of CEOS of major central public sector organizations in the late 1970s, when two important decisions were taken, among others, viz., a) all central public sector undertakings would have a public relations department that would be headed by a professional and not someone without professional qualifications in communication, and b) all central public sector undertakings would bring out an employee communication journal to keep the staff abreast of the happenings and boost their morale.

4.5 Corporate communication and its interface with other management functions

One of the few generalizations of the profession, believe analysts, is that an organization's reputation in a large measure is dependent upon the conduct of its top management. How they speak about the organization, what they do for its various stakeholders, how they express solidarity and resilience in critical times, and their personal conduct contributes to how the organizations are perceived by their various stakeholders. Media, especially the electronic media, has only brought the issue center stage.

Corporate communication, many believe, is an offshoot of public relations and public affairs, so it is best suited to report as high as possible. Cutlip et al point out that the nomenclatures have changed over a period. For instance, among the Fortune 500 companies, only one in five use the "public relations" titles. Other commonly used titles are corporate communication, public affairs, public information, or in combination with advertising.[9]

Corporate communalization is a staff function that lends aid and advice to the management on issues relating to communication. The success of the department impinges on the support and understanding it receives from various line and staff departments, by timely sharing of information and insights. Let us look at its relationship with various departments.

4.5.1 Marketing

Experts believe that as both the functions aim at reaching out to people, therefore they need to work in harmony and try not tread on each other's toes. As marketing is all about products and consumers, they often feel that corporate communication should be a part of their department in the interest of integrated marketing communication. The major areas of conflict between the two are advertising and publicity, especially product advertising and institutional advertising. In non-profit organizations, the cause of friction is the allocation of funds, raising funds, and reaching out to a variety of publics with educational messages.[10]

4.5.2 Law

In times of crises, especially in case of defamation suits, top management seeks legal aid to get out of the mess. In such times, it generally refuses to speak to the media because the counsel may have advised them to keep quiet. Close cooperation between corporate communication and law is necessary, looking at difficult times, when more and more corporates find themselves entangled on issues relating to safety, environment, health, and resettlement issues, among others. While taking care of the legal aspects, it must be ensured that the human touch is not lost sight of in fighting the cases in courts or through reflection in the media. Stakeholders have a right to redress their grievances through mediation or by filing their case in a court of law, which should not be taken as an affront against the organization, when the case is resolved for or against either of the parties.

4.5.3 Personnel, HRD, industrial relations

As both the corporate communication and personnel departments deal with employees, the risk of friction between the two tends to be high. The employees are governed by certain policies and conduct rules, so if something is written about employees in an emotional tone or tenor in an employee communication channel, the HR often feels that it could be held against the management, especially if the issue was under negotiation with a union.

With time, the roles and expectations of management and employees have also been redefined. The management is increasingly aware that a motivated employee is an asset and can be used as an ambassador of goodwill. If the relationships are stifling within an organization, they inevitably have their echo externally. Who should communicate to the employees? The answer is both the personnel and corporate communication, each having its area defined. While information relating to policies, procedures, welfare activities, and trade union negotiation are HR functions, writing stories on the organization for various mass media, the achievements of some employees, and human-interest stories in media targeted at the internal stakeholders fall in the corporate communication arena. Close cooperation between corporate communication and HR brings about better understanding and respect among employees and serves as a morale booster for them.

A good example of synergy could be found in one of the series of Infosys vacancy ads, wherein an employee's job profile appeared, aiming at enthusing potential employees about the satisfaction they could expect by looking at the happy pictures and job profile of a protagonist in its vacancy ads.

4.6 Outsourcing internal communication

Many companies which may not have an internal corporate communication department often outsource work to an outside PR/CC firm, while others may have an internal corporate communication department but still hire an outside firm to supplement its efforts. In recent times, one has seen some companies, while retaining a specialist PR firm, make them allocate a person to sit in its office as an extra staff support. The person with a certain specialization comes in handy and works as bridge between the retaining organization and the agency s/he comes from.

As we would see later in the chapter, employee communication can become a very creative job encompassing various channels in engaging the audiences. While face-to-face communication, brainstorming sessions, shop floor discussion, and writing for employees in employee-oriented magazines and other media, and idea boxes are better handled by the internal staff, the strategy, the packaging of information, designing of journal, bulletin board, idea boxes, and events can be handled more professionally if outsourced. An ideal team for employee communication would have both internal and external members. When engaging an outside firm, it is important to give it a proper brief and advise it to assign a dedicated staff member to work on internal communication in association with the internal staff.

Cutlip et al propose the following seven conditions for achieving an effective working relationship with internal stakeholders:

1. Confidence and trust between employer and employees
2. Candid information flowing freely up, down, and sideways
3. Satisfying status and participation for each person
4. Continuity of work without strife
5. Healthful surrounding
6. Success for the enterprise
7. Optimism about the future[11]

4.7 Theoretical underpinning of employee communication

Internal communication is about reaching out to the minds of a diverse group of people, with a goal of putting them on a common wavelength about organizational goals despite their varying work profiles, status in the hierarchy, and cultural backgrounds. Giving each employee a sense of usefulness and a feeling of pride in the organization they have voluntarily joined is challenging but not difficult to achieve. Drawing from various sociological and psychological time-tested theories, the people in charge of internal communication can do a fairly good job without sounding too pedantic or official. Scholars, however, feel that this is not an aspect in which much research exists, nor do people deliberately think about it.

Lyn Smith and Pamela Mounter feel that several communication models and schools of thought can be brought to bear on internal communication, but at the same time it may not be easy to sort them out in neat camps.[12]

An understanding of various kinds of organizational culture, however, must precede a deliberation on the theoretical models.

Charles Handy's classic book *Understanding Organizations* (1985) identifies four kinds of organizational cultures, which are discussed subsequently in brief:

4.7.1 Power culture

Small entrepreneurial organizations often have a culture that revolves around the founder. The founder often represents the voice of the organization, at least in the initial stages, so he also controls communications. Even if later a professional communicator was put in place, it is likely that the founder would continue to be the central figure in maintaining internal and external relations.

4.7.2 Role culture

Where bureaucracy heads an organization, it places importance on functions and specialism. Such organizations are often bound by rules and procedures, where everything goes by the rule book. There are laid-out procedures for doing things as well as settling disputes. Large companies and public sector organizations, in general, have well-laid-out policies and procedures for appointments, promotions, retirement, and grievance redressal and conduct rules. Such companies, when referred by critics as bureaucratic, imply that they suffer from "red tape," hierarchies, and delays, etc. Later in the chapter, we shall take up the classic case study of GE, which was turned around by the legendary Jack Welsh, who, among other things, had cut down on bureaucratic tangles within the organization and used communication to bring about change.

4.7.3 Personal culture

Charles Handy posits that within some bureaucracies, one can find traces of yet another culture, which can thrive quite happily within but have little affiliation to the whole. Some cases in point are educational institutions, hospitals, architecture firms, and legal firms, etc. that develop personal culture. In these kinds of institutions, a typical personal culture develops. In such organizations where there is a concentration of professionals, it is not likely that for fulfilling their communication needs they look only inwards. They would rather look outside their organizations to be updated about the latest happenings in their profession.

4.7.4 Task culture

The task culture focuses on the job or project at hand. In such organizations, the project groups based on the task culture are expected to do the job well. According to this theory, for internal communication, this kind of culture would provide fertile ground in terms of material for publication or broadcast.[13]

Let us now have a look at some theories:

4.8 Theories that impact employee communication

As employee communication is all about managing relationships, Treadwell argues that the whole range of applicable theories reflect the cross-disciplinary nature of the profession.[14]

Systems theory: The theory posits the use of the example of living organisms as the analogy. To survive, organisms need to breathe air and take water and nutrients, else they perish. Similarly, employees, just as organisms, also require a positive environment to nourish and sustain them. The health of an organization, believe analysts, depends on its ability to understand, develop, nurture, and maintain these relationships within the system. Everyone has its own thinking about how the organization should respond to his/her needs, so it is important that the organization understands these complexities and respond to them. As the corporate communication practitioners work as conduits between the management and various echelons of employees, they must be sensitive about this aspect. The connectedness means that a shift in one set of relationships can possibly have a major impact on other relationships. For example, the delay in getting to a solution with trade unions would hamper productivity, and thus hit the bottom line. As organisms survive by adapting to the environment, so must the corporate communication department make combinations, permutations with available budget, and time and management constraints to achieve its goals.

Grunig and Hunt talk of the relationship that can be at two extremes—a one-way propagandistic model with no regard for truth to a two-way symmetrical communication founded on mutual understanding and trust.[15]

4.8.1 Persuasion theories

Persuasion theories talk of the importance of how people think and behave, therefore it is imperative that an employee communication manager writes in a manner that would get the "desired response" from the employees. Like the systems theory, persuasion theories also aim at managing relationships.

Centuries ago, Aristotle said of rhetoric a term used for public speaking, a system of logic by which truth could be approached. According to him, there were three persuasive approaches viz., *ethos*, *pathos*, and *logos*. Ethos refers to the character in discourse—an appeal to credibility or authority, pathos appeals to the emotion, and logos is the appeal of a logically developed argument.

Treadwell refers to "the technique of semantic tyranny" that is widely used by government agencies and armed forces, referred to as "bureaucratese." "Without the aid of government spin-doctors" question the authors, "would 'collateral damages' have come to mean civilian causalities, or 'productivity enhancements' mean 'firing people?"[16]

4.8.2 Theories of behavior and attitude change

Albert Bandura's social learning theory posits that people learn from observing others, including characters from their favorite television programs and cinema. Sometimes, it is used as a well-orchestrated strategy to create the necessary hype and aim at better recall. When the movie *Dil Chahta Hai*, a story of young friends, was released, the chief protagonist, Aamir Khan, sported a goatee and continued with it untill the film was released. It almost became a trend. As said elsewhere in the book, he supported separate styles in his later films like *Taare Zameen Par* and *Ghajini*, which also became trendsetters. In fact, as part of the promotional program, the protagonist donned the role of a barber, giving people the style that he sported in Ghajini, just before the release of the film. A college in Bangalore banned students from sporting the Ghajini-style hairdo because it indirectly reflected violence through cuts on the head.[17]

Imagery plays an important role in making a point about the issue on hand and for better recall. Making a caricature of Hitler's persona, especially through his hairstyle and moustache, Charlie Chaplin made fun of the dictator, lampooning him in his highly acclaimed films. That was Hollywood's contribution through communication in critical times.[18]

Martin Fishbein's theory of *reasoned action* proposes that a person's behavior is influenced by a certain social norm attached to it, like women in certain traditional societies do not smoke in public because it is not expected of them to do so, or the public display of close physical proximity by partners. In India, the media has written variously on moral policing against such instances.

Extensively used by advertising fraternities, the theory of cognitive dissonance, propounded by Festinger, explains how people deal with information that is conflicting to them. Dissonance is a common occurrence among human beings who always struggle to reduce it. For example, if there were two options at the same time, the one that is perceived to be more valuable would be preferred. To illustrate, if you have two invites, one for a concert and the other for a lecture talk by a famous author, you will have to choose either of the two, because the timing is the same for both functions. Your mind would struggle and take a decision in favor of one against the other. And you would justify your decision for the comparative value of choosing one against the other. Similarly, if a decision were taken about something, about which conflicting news comes later, in all probability you would avoid reading it to justify your decision. To further illustrate, you bought a car that suited your style and purse. After the purchase, you may come across some adverse comments on some of the components of the car, which you may avoid reading to believe in your earlier decision of purchasing it. Analysts believe that the theory of cognitive dissonance helps the corporate communication practitioner in understanding people's response to messages. Festinger explains that any two perceptions held by an individual would have one of the three possible relationships, viz., *irrelevance*, *consonance*, or *dissonance*. People would go for a persuasive message if it is relevant to them, else it would be ignored as irrelevant. In case, however, the message is seen as relevant, then they would see the message as consonant. If people do not agree or find the information or arguments in the message unacceptable; it would be dissonant.[19]

William McGuire's persuasion *process theory* posits that people go through six steps from first awareness to final behavior response. The process includes the following steps: *presentation*, *attention*, *comprehension*, *yielding*, *retention*, *and action*. When planning messages for the target audience, the strategy must address all the steps to be successful.[20]

4.9 Segmenting internal publics

As in external publics, internal stakeholders are also diverse, so the corporate communication needs to understand the complexities before deciding on the content and channels for transmitting the messages.

Audience is often segmented based on their demographic profiles and psychographics.

An organization that looks like a composite unit from outside is but a bundle of complexities from within. People who work in an organization, when looked at carefully, are divided by gender, age, educational qualifications, hierarchy, location, pay package, and attitudes. At a social level, people tend to be divided by caste, religion, and color. Corporate communication must win over all divisions and diversities, which other departments may or may not be suited to do. A sitting with the HR desk would give data about the entire workforce immediately.

Lyn Smith opines that while working on communication strategies, it would be a good idea to remember the following:

Frontline staff prefers to hear the news straight from line managers.
A mix of media (intranet, publications, audio/visual) would best serve the hard-to-reach groups. Middle managers should be seen as facilitators rather than blockages.
Creative and specialists should be handled sensitively.
She recommends taking in to account diversity (age, gender, race, and culture).[21]

4.10 What to communicate with employees?

Before one decides on the various channels of communication, the pertinent question is what to communicate. In fact, "what" (the content) would determine "where" (channels) to communicate. The corporate communication department should ideally have a small cell within it that would handle internal communication. The choice of people in this cell should preferably fall on "peoples' persons," in other words those with great communication skills and an understanding of the human psyche.

Experts suggest that the senior management should first be encouraged to think about what needs to be communicated. A video or house journal should be seen as a tactic in strategy rather than strategy by itself.[22]

An ideal employee communication should have a mix of stories relating to the organization and employee achievements, viz. how the organization is doing, challenges of time, competitive edge, expectations from employees, futuristic plans, awards won by the organization, etc. For employees, motivational stories on people who made a difference, stories of their courage and grit, their achievements in areas beyond work, like sports, culture, etc., would make readers enthusiastic because such stories concern the people they know personally. Do not forget to include the achievements of their family members, especially children. Devote some space for employees' contribution in writing for the journal or their skills at photography, et al. Everyone wishes to see his/her name in print. It really does not make a difference how well the piece is written; the feel behind it is what matters.

Before we discuss the "where" of communication, let us look at the strengths and weaknesses of employee communication channels.

TABLE 4.1 Employee communication media (house journals, video magazines, interpersonal communication, brainstorming, open days, employees' blogs, et al)

Strengths	*Weaknesses*
High planning	Controlled media
Pre-test of content possible	Management interference on content
Reaching the right TA	Enjoys less credibility
Creating a sense of belonging with the organization	Requires balance in coverage to avoid annoying any section of employees whose views are not included, especially of trade unions.
Helps build personal connect	Requires sensitive handling in times of crises
Motivates employees	Receivers often take such media for granted as often it is provided *gratis*
Participative	Generally, want to in keep the time schedules
Feedback possible	Often expensive

Source: Author

While taking the decision on the choice of media, the corporate communication professional will have to consider the following:

a) Most effective media
b) Most efficient media
c) Most credible media

As said earlier, it is important to know your target audience threadbare so that communication is decided, keeping in view their demographics and psychographics. For instance, in a company like Coal India that has more than five Lakhs employees with over 90% not literate, the choice of media has to be such that it cuts across literacy barrier. On the other hand, in an IT company like Infosys or Wipro that has almost cent percent highly educated employees who are also tech savvy, the choice of media vehicles should ideally be digital.

4.11 Various media for internal communication

Employee communication on the one hand can really be a satisfying part of the corporate communication job, but at the same time it can be critical on the other hand, if a particular group says a trade union would judge any goof up severely if it feels affected by a news item or when its view is not reflected.

There are no two views that corporate communication, of which employee communication is a part, is a top management function. The corporate communication manager, in fact, works as a link between the top management and various sections of employees. In order that communication is not seen as the "mouthpiece" of management, great caution and a balancing act is required. At the same time, the aim of such communication is also to reflect management's perspective and ethos. What would it mean in practice? Let us take a hypothetical case of a company where various unions have given notices for striking work. They may have their reasons for going on strike, and the management has its reason for not relenting to their demands. The management would obviously like to use the channels at its disposal to inform about its action, reaction, and decision. The difficult question here is, do the unions also have the same channels available? In all probability, it's a no. So why should the employees who are represented in unions trust communication that comes from these channels in normal times? This can be a tricky situation for the management, of which corporate communication is also a part. The prudence lies that in crises situations, use the HR and industrial relations channels with the warring employees and not the corporate communication channels. Here is a case study of a company that faced a situation like this. The National Hydroelectric Power Corporation, a public sector enterprise with a workforce of more than 20,000 employees, has several employee unions, many of them owing allegiance to different political parties. Many years ago, while negotiating with union leaders, the HR department called for a photographer from the communication department to take pictures. The management had reached consensus on some issue with the unions. The HR later sent a write-up for inclusion in the employee magazine. As soon as copies of the house journal that carried the story were distributed, it created a ruckus between the management and at least one union that had been on the scene for a long time. The cause of commotion was that the picture that went along with the story did not have the representation of the "oldest" union, but of a union that had just been formed. This union alleged that it was a deliberate act on the part of the management to bring the new union in focus, because the management wished to break the older unions. Now the fact of the matter was that the HR had no role to play in this. The communication department, based on the better resolution of various pictures, selected the picture that appeared in the house journal. The problem needed a quick resolution. The HR consulted with the communication head, who came out with a solution that, under the circumstance, soothed frayed nerves. The department used to bring out two employee magazines, one a quarterly in the magazine format, which had carried the picture, and the other a four-pager that was brought out every month to provide snippets of developments and achievements. So, losing no time, a collage of all the pictures of that day's function, along with the news item, was given prominent position in the publication and brought out at warp speed to salvage the damage. The moral of the story here is that the person in charge of employee communication must be sensitive to both the management and employees' perspectives and, when in doubt, must consult the concerned person in management before making anything public.

Internal communication often requires designing and producing media materials, which broadly include a whole range of employee magazines, films, AVs, instruction materials, safety manuals, corporate identity manuals, bulletin boards, etc. What medium is best for which message and vice versa are eternal questions that constantly haunt professional communicators.

The range of media for internal communications is immense, but not all channels are used by all the organizations. It depends on how much importance the organizations give to the function, the locations of the projects, and the interest the team takes in the activity.

Let us have a look at some of the popular media for internal communication.

4.11.1 Induction literature/information kiosks

When new staff members join a company, it takes time for them to get accustomed to organizational culture. Good companies make all efforts to make new entrants feel comfortable through various means, which may include a welcome letter, an induction training program, literature, or through an interactive medium like intranet, through a QR code, or an electronic information kiosk. All these media are aimed at informing such employees on how the organization works, its hierarchical structure, the decision-making process, its product range, locations, etc.

4.11.2 House journal

A house journal is the most popular corporate communication channel for employee communication. However, not all journals are interesting from the perspective of employees' interest. Bringing out a nicely packaged journal with color- pictures is no guarantee that the journal would be popular. The basic aim of a house journal is to provide a communication forum to employees through which they not only get informed and motivated but at the same time also participate. A journal that has its CEO on various pages is often touted by employees as "His Master's Voice" and would not be respected. On the other hand, a column on a CEO's interfaces with employees on issues that concern them would be appreciated.

The corporate communication head is ideally the editor of the house journal.

House journals come in various shapes and sizes and varying periodicities. The two popular sizes, however, are tabloid and magazine size. With digital media becoming all-pervasive, many companies now bring out e-house journals, which are sent in PDF format via an e-mail or via link or QR code.

A house journal in India needs to be registered with the Registrar of Newspapers if it has some innovative title, because it would need the clearance. In case it is after the name of the company, say, Tata news, or Birla newsletter, it would not need the name clearance. While most of the house journals are *gratis*, some are nominally priced. It would be a good idea to write "For internal circulation" on the cover of the house journal to avoid any problems. If the journal is registered with the regulatory body, then the registration number must appear on the cover or inside of the journal; the statutory information must be published each year, and copies of the journal, as stipulated, must be submitted. Registered journals get some postal discounts.

A house journal can cover topics in several areas like organization's achievements, fulfillment of targets, futuristic plans, human-interest stories, social news, employee contributions, etc. The mailing list may encompass employees, distributors, agents, opinion-makers, and other external publics. Larger companies can have separate journals for internal and external publics. The bottom line for a house journal is that it must satisfy the needs and interests of its readers. Human interest should be the governing principle for stories. Too many uninteresting figures and technical details are unlikely to interest readers.

Large conglomerates often have many house journals coming from their various projects and companies. However, it would be a good idea to also bring out a corporate house journal from the whole group *per se* representing news from various companies, so that the employees have a holistic perspective about the group they work for.

For publishing a house journal, let us consider the following steps:

4.11.2.1 Planning

Develop a concept that serves the company's best interests. The decision about size, format, and periodicity may be taken after a brainstorming session with the team and the management. The popular formats are tabloid and magazine. While getting management's approval, a format presentation should ideally include suggested titles, masthead design, some page dummies, suggested paper, and an indication of the expenditure envisaged.

4.11.2.2 Organizing

Organizing is all about putting together a network. Once the management's approval has been taken, the corporate communication head must set about organizing staff to get going with the job. The greater the frequency, the more likely the need for staff. Depending on the size of the corporate communication department at the corporate office and availability of communication staff at projects, proper networking for news gathering should be made. In the absence of regular staff, it is advisable to develop a band of "freelance writers" from within the organization. It is a great feeling to see one's name in print. The employees will jump at the idea. Discretion, however, should be used in selecting the right kind of people for the job. The immediate step is to work out a strict schedule for collection, writing of stories, production, and printing.

4.11.2.3 Publishing

A professional corporate communication practitioner plans several issues ahead in addition to the one being worked on. As an editor, the corporate communication head must inculcate the habit of reaching out to people and places. It is not possible to write interesting editorials, cover stories, and human-interest write-ups while sitting glued to the corporate seat.

Every good house journal should have a definite "personality," and that is the responsibility of the editor. To bring out the publication on time, one should involve as few management hierarchies as possible for the clearance of the content.

4.11.2.4 Distribution

A journal loses its value if it does not reach the targeted public on time. The quickest and most economical means possible must be selected to reach out to the readers. Some organizations distribute the journal at the place of work, while others mail it to employees' homes. The obvious advantage of the latter is that the staff members are relaxed at home and can read the journal leisurely. Also, the family members can have access to the publication.

To make the publication popular, it is necessary to make it reader-oriented. Organized feedback through a questionnaire survey could be undertaken to examine the extent to which employees are satisfied with the publication. It needs to be remembered that the shorter the questionnaire, the better would be the chances of receiving the response. In fact, a one-page questionnaire should suffice.[23]

4.11.3 Closed-circuit/in-house television

In-house TV is a great medium for linking up a scattered audience in an office and township. Many companies telecast addresses by the CEO to employees and their families during times of crises. The interim management at Satyam uploaded a video on its intranet to address the concerns of employees. The video was later shared with news channels also, to inform people at large about management's initiatives for its thousands of employees.

Some of the leading organizations—to name a few, National Thermal Power Corporation and Steel Authority of ITC—one time had video magazines for employee communication when the medium was popular. The contents generally included management's point of view on various issues, company performance, welfare measures, human-interest stories, and engagement with communities, etc. As long as these continued, the video magazines did not really replace printed house journals but complemented each other.

4.11.4 The new age media

The new age media has brought about a paradigm shift in employee communication. Many companies are now using the digital media to connect with their employees. In the Indian context, several companies, including Infosys, use Internet and intranet to connect to its thousands of employees scattered in various continents and countries.

Satyam Computers, when in exitance, way back in 2008, had launched a web radio station, called Planet Satyam, to connect with its workforce of over 50,000. The station was patterned on YouTube. The station operated from its radio and television studio, located in its Leadership Center in Hyderabad. All the employees could connect live to important internal messages through radio talk shows, panel discussion, and interviews with business leaders.[24]

In recent times, Amazon India and Infosys have started streaming internet radio in their facilities to connect with a disparate set of employees. The radio includes popular music and songs, employee song requests, contests, corporate information, and interviews with employees.[25]

Infosys Intranet connecting its about 70,000 employees across 18 countries is called Sparsh (Touch). It is the company's primary channel of news and official information. It provides a communication platform and networking avenues for Infosys employees. Selected for an award by the rating agency Nielsen Norman as one of the ten best intranet sites for its award "Intranet Design annual 2007: The year's 10 best Intranets." The other recipients included American Electrical Power (US), Comcast (US), Daimler Chrysler AG (Germany), The Dow (US), The National Geographic society (US), The Royal society for the protection of birds (UK), and Volvo group (Sweden).

Among the features that the award recognized were the following:

- User participation and incredible user uptake
- New avenues for publishing and networking
- Content freshness and access to archived content
- Personalized and customized content
- Clean and simple look and navigation
- Attention to design details[26]

4.11.5 Employee blogs

Employee blog is a newer strategy but catching up fast. Sun Microsystems promoted employee blogging, with its former CEO Jonathan Schwartz taking the lead. He left the company in 2010. His blog is said to be visited by thousands of netizens. The blog was created "to improve both communications with the public and collaborations with attitude developers and programmers who author third party applications for sun's systems." When he resigned, he posted the following message on Twitter that read: "Financial crisis/Stalled too many customers/CEO no more."[27]

Robert Scobleizer, an employee of Microsoft, began his blog, called Scobleizer, which contained all sorts of informal and even highly personal information, such as family details and bereavements, information that his salary was "less than $100,000," as well as what came to be closely followed observations on Microsoft's products, which were not always complimentary. Scobleizer's writings, according to analysts, started attracting such high volumes of traffic that any attempts by the software company to stop it were not successful. Analysts feel that the blog did better than harm to the company as Microsoft came to be seen as a cool company against the earlier perception of being monopolistic and a predator. Scoble also left the company.

Southwest Airlines encourages its employees to blog, as it believes it to be another communication tool which can be handled without incurring any additional cost. The employees were skeptical in the beginning, but not anymore. According to the company sources, the site has more than 200 posts and 4,000 public responses in about nine months.[28] "Nuts about Southwest" is accessed by many who share their experiences and their concerns, etc.

According to indiaprblog, some new companies have adopted blogging more rapidly than those that have been on the scene for long. Some of the companies that have adopted blogging include Infosys, TCS, Rediff, Milagrow, HCL, Cleartrip, Gridstone, Frito-Lay, and Naukri.[29]

4.11.6 Ideas boxes

The concept of idea boxes is to create a channel through which the management encourages the submission of innovative ideas in various areas of activities from employees. The ideas are discussed among the management, and those that could be implemented are rewarded. Idea boxes are placed at vantage places for employees to drop their ideas on various subjects that may include improving systems, processes, or even their complaints. When sifted and seen closely, the medium helps in tracking employee perceptions on various issues, areas of concern, and their possible contribution in innovations.

4.11.7 Shop-floor discussions

Shop-floor discussions can be great morale boosters, both for employees and managers.

The discussions can be on many subjects relating to work, targets, or issues that crop up suddenly. Motivating employees is an important task for management, in which corporate communication can play a very significant role, by coining motivational messages that can be displayed. The management often complains about lack of motivation on the part of the employees and forms its own perception about the reasons.

Ferdinand F Fournies lists the following reasons why the employees do not act.

- They do not know why should they do it
- They do not know how to do it
- They do not know what they are supposed to do

- They think your way will not work
- They think their way is better
- They thing something else is more important
- They think there is no positive consequence of their doing it
- They think they are doing it
- They are punished for doing what they are supposed to do
- They are rewarded for not doing it
- They anticipate a negative consequence for doing it
- There is no negative consequence for not doing it
- There are obstacles beyond their control
- Their personal limits prevent them from performing
- Personal problems
- No one can do it![30]

It is important to partner with employees in day-to-day work and brainstorm with them when finding a solution to a problem.

Some companies like the Delhi Jal Board encourages its employees to contribute slogans on safety. The most appropriate ones are later painted on the walls. The employees also get awarded in case their slogans are selected for display. The strategy has helped the company in motivating employees by recognizing their talent and making them conscious about safety norms, which are important from the employees' perspective. The company feels this has helped a great deal, as employees tend to follow the safety norms more sincerely because they believe in what came from them.

4.11.8 Bulletin boards

A bulletin board in an organizational context can be described as a channel for continuous flow of news and messages concerning employees. They come in various sizes and shapes. Some are mundane looking, while others are well designed. The bulletin boards have a fixed periodicity. These are generally placed at the exit gates of the shop floors, but some could even be seen inside the assembly lines.

Apart from circulars and notices, the bulletin boards have become a sought-after medium by production heads for motivating employees to reach the production targets. Giving shift-wise production details on the bulletin boards also encourages competition among different shifts. Rob Frazier, CEO of Colgate-Palmolive, did it with great success. The case study has been added in the chapter. A corner of the board can also be set aside for social news relating to employees and their family members. For instance, if an employee's child topped the examination in the district, his/her picture, along with some news, would not only make the parent feel proud but would please others as it could happen for their children later.

4.11.9 Visits by management

Organizing visits of the top management to various projects achieves two aims from the corporate communication perspectives: one, the employees feel motivated when they are face-to-face with the top management, and, two, these can be turned into a media opportunity to gain some mileage.

It would be a good idea to organize interactive sessions for the project managers with the visiting senior officers. For employees, it can be a gathering followed by participation by employees in cultural activities. This would give an opportunity to the top management to meet the blue-collar workers and mix up with them. Some companies organize open forums, in which employees could share ideas, give suggestions, and vent about their grievances.

4.11.10 Clubs and societies

Talent cuts across artificial hierarchical barriers. To encourage the entire office fraternity, it is important that employees socialize and share common interests through sports clubs, literary societies, etc. This helps build personal rapport and respect among managers and workers for each other as human beings.

At Goodyear Tires, a British company, there is a common canteen for management and staff. It is not uncommon to find them sharing the same table during lunchtime, which obviously leads to socializing.

4.11.11 Open house/events

An open house is a designated day. It could be landmark day, like the foundation day, when employees are invited to come with families, including children, for their day out to visit the plant, participate in various activities, have food, and oodles of fun. The families get a chance to see the place, their spouse/parents work, go around the plant/workplace and get acquainted, and maybe feel proud of their family member and the company.

In a talk show a few years ago with program host Simi Grewal, industrialist Kumara Mangalam Birla shared that on one such open day, as he entered the premises of the plant, he found people in masks going around, leading him to believe that he had come to a wrong place, till he realized that it was an "open day."

Australian airliner Quantas roped in famous actor John Travolta, a trained pilot, to serve as its "brand ambassador at large" on a range of employee and brand-building initiative. The association brought about a lot of media mileage for the company, besides raising employee morale by arranging for John Travolta to meet and speak with Quantas employees in each of the cities on the tour. Travolta spoke about his passion for aviation and special attachment to Quantas. Ogilvy PR handled the campaign in 2002.[31]

4.11.12 Employee involvement in CSR initiatives

Many research studies suggest that one of important factors weighed by people to join a company is its commitment to corporate social responsibility (CSR) and corporate governance record. In an age where an average person has more exposure to the environment in which he/she lives in, many companies are involving them to contribute in issues that go beyond work. This exposes the employees to the contribution of the company in the social sphere; it also sensitizes them to the importance of these areas. Here are a few cases in point where employees have been actively involved.

4.11.12.1 Citibank

Citibank has been celebrating its Global Community Day in November since 2006 with employees, clients, partners, friends, and alumni to give back to communities where they live and work. Taking a couple of examples, the Citibank employees joined thousands of their colleagues worldwide for the company's third annual "Global Community Day" on 8 November 2008 in community development initiatives addressing specific needs including education, housing, environmental protection, child welfare, senior citizen, disaster relief, and healthcare. In India, Citi partners with leading NGOs. In daylong-designed activities, each volunteer team, "an eclectic mix of employees drawn from different Citi businesses across diverse hierarchies and groups, accomplish a clearly defined set of tasks assigned to it.[32] Things changed when the world was hit by the Covid-19 pandemic. Citibank, instead of physical gathering of people, came out brilliantly with its changed strategy, calling it "Global Community Day Reimagined" campaign, vide which Citibank's 63,000 volunteers across 73 countries, contributing a cumulative 1,00,000 service hours participated in the following:

Acts of kindness—from running errands for elderly neighbors and supporting local businesses, to making and donating face masks and writing uplifting letters to those in isolation

Virtual volunteering—activities such as online career counseling, youth mentorship, and résumé-building workshops

Independent service—activities with a community organization of choice[33]

4.11.12.2 HSBC

The bank launched Catalyst, its "employee volunteering" initiative in India in 2007 with the following salient features:

HSBC employees organize a pan India activity in all HSBC branches, encouraging sale of products from NGOs.

Some branches have its employees' educating students on entrepreneurship, work readiness, and financial literacy.

The initiation of the scheme "*Kuchh Dil Se*" encourages employees to voluntarily donate monthly for charitable causes like education and environment protection through a payroll debit. The program has been implemented in partnership with "Give Foundation."

Ninety HSBC staffers ran in the Mumbai marathon in 2008 and raised pledges for SPJ Sadhna School for Developmentally Handicapped, to enable such children to avail of opportunities to study, experience, and enjoy their childhood.

In its HSBC Climate Championship, 2008, employees were encouraged to volunteer in projects to fight climate change and drive environment changes and practices within the organization and participate in a two-week regional filed program in a rainforest in Malaysia.

On the World Environment Day in 2008, about 100 employees across India participated in various environment projects supported by HSBC, contributing 8,000 voluntary hours in the community.[34]

4.11.12.3

Accenture India launched the "Employee Giving Program" across all its workforce at the start of the fiscal year 2006, which enabled employees to lend support to ongoing projects in childcare and education as well as contribute towards relief and reconstruction work during emergencies.

Some companies have initiated "payroll" charities, by which the employees pledge a certain amount that is deducted from their salary. The companies, who often tie up with reputed NGOs, let the employees know the causes for which the donations were utilized.

Summary

In this chapter, we looked at the role and scope of corporate communication in employee communication and the importance of motivated employees in achieving organizational goals.

Theoretical underpinnings in employee communication were deliberated upon after discussing various theories like the systems theory and various persuasion and behavior change theories.

Various channels for employee communication like interpersonal, house journals, idea boxes, events, open houses, and new age media, among others, were discussed with relevant case studies. Strengths and weaknesses of employee media were discussed to facilitate an understanding on choosing the right media.

Case studies of various companies that have involved employees in social philanthropy and CSR initiatives were discussed.

The CEO is the driving force in creating a motivated workforce. Case studies of two legendary CEOs who turned around GE and Colgate-Palmolive have been discussed in detail to analyze how communication was used as a part of strategic planning and marketing objectives in achieving the desired goals.

Key terms

Bulletin boards: described as a channel for continuous flow of news and messages concerning employees, generally placed at the shop floor.

Employee communication: aims at managing a relationship with employees through various forms of communication and media.

Employee blogs: a term used when management encourages its employees to create their blogs and interface with various communities.

Internal communication: refers to communication within an organization.

Internal publics: refers to employees, their families, and other shareholders.

Induction literature: refers to literature especially brought by an organization for distribution among the news entrants, with the aim of acquainting them with the organization.

Information kiosk: refers to the electronic kiosk from which one can retrieve information at the touch of a finger/button.

House journal: refers to a journal aimed at employees or external stakeholders of a company.

Idea boxes: to create a channel through which the management encourages submission of innovative ideas in various areas of activities from employees.

New media: refers to the Internet, social networking sites, and the blogosphere.

Media reach: refers to the percentage of people in various categories accessing media.

Media characteristics: refers to the relative strengths and weaknesses of each medium, keeping in view its inherent characteristics.

Open house: a few designated days in a year when various stakeholders, like employees and their families or neighborhood community or other stakeholders, are invited to the plant for an informal gathering to acquaint them about the company and its processes.

Shop-floor discussions: refers to formal and informal discussions by project management, assisted by the corporate communication department, on motivating employees on various issues.

Concept review questions

Q.1. What do you understand about employee communication? How is it similar or different from communication from other management departments?

Q.2. What are the various strengths and weaknesses of media used for employee communication?

Q.3. What are the various popular communication channels of employee communication? Give salient features of at least four such channels.

Q.4. Analyze in a nutshell various theories concerning employees as discussed in the chapter, and write the insights drawn from them.

Critical thinking exercise

Access house journals of at least three to four companies. Go through them dispassionately to find out what is being communicated from the management's perspective, soft stories on employees and their family members, and employees' contributions, to make a comparative analysis of internal communication among various organizations.

Case studies

Corporate communication, as reflected earlier, is a top management function. If the CEO does not care or understand the value of communication, precious little can be achieved in corporate communication. In such circumstances, corporate communication is employed as a firefighting activity in times of crises. In the following paragraphs, two case studies, viz., GE and Colgate-Palmolive, will be taken up for discussion, wherein both the CEOs not only understood the value of communication but used it strategically in turning around sluggish companies with great success.

The GE turnaround

The turning around of GE by Jack Welch that he headed for two decades between 1980–2001 is legendary and well-documented in his book *Straight from the Gut*, which is referred by millions including management students. Welch is credited for understanding the value of employee communication as a part of strategic planning. How did he go about it?

Cut through bureaucracy

He reduced hierarchical channels from nine to four and six, describing it as "a big company body in a small-company soul" to operate with the agility and nimbleness of a small entrepreneurial firm. Until Welch joined the GE, the company was like any big corporation where written documentation was the order of the day. Welch replaced tons of paper with short "playbooks" that identified important strategies and used these documents as the springboard for strategic discussion with management. Face-to-face talk replaced time-consuming written procedures.

GE today is practically a paperless organization.

Meeting role models regularly

Welch identified 35 top people who reported to him directly and were responsible for explaining and defending their strategic recommendations for their businesses.

He had numerous scheduled and impromptu meetings known as "GE operating system"; these meetings had CEOs, role models, and initiative champions from within GE and outside, sharing the intellectual capital and best practices worldwide. These meetings discussed various issues that included best practices, customer impact, and succession planning, including selection of candidates for leadership training.

Nicknamed by executives as "food fights" or "free-for-all," these meetings would generally begin at 8 a.m. and carry on till 10 p.m.

Making communication activity a core organizational value

This meant repeating ideas to ensure these were heard broadly via the interpersonal route, through shareholder communication, the company's annual report, and in interviews with the press. Welch motivated senior managers, who in turn motivated below-the-line workers. His senior managers, for example, after attending leadership conferences with Welch, would steer such conferences for their junior officers. This surely had a cascading effect.

A constant reminder on expectations

All employees were supposed to carry a wallet-size card that read: "GE leaders. . . always with unyielding integrity to create a clear, simple, reality-based vision. . . and communicate it to all constituencies."

This was an indicator for the top GE leaders to express themselves clearly and succinctly.

Another such card read: "GE leaders. . . always with unyielding integrity have the self-confidence to involve everyone and behave in a boundary-less fashion." This was an indication to democratization—a free flow of ideas from all directions.

"GE leaders. . . always with unyielding integrity are open to ideas from anywhere. . . and committed to work out," said the GE employee value card. "Work out" meant a forum for brainstorming and decision-making for employees and their bosses. The work-outs, according to employees, resembled a grueling oral examination with questions and recommendations hurled at managers by their subordinates.

A workout included a three-day session where 40–100 employees would brainstorm on how to improve their business. The unit boss would set the agenda and then depart, leaving a facilitator. At the end of the workshop, he/she would join the group when recommendations would be made based on discussions. If a problem needed further probing, a small group would go in to it, till the next workout was convened.

In about a decade, 2,00,000 employees underwent the workout sessions. This resulted in openness, transparency, and respect for people across various echelons and a show of free flow of communication where everyone mattered. The areas of discussions included improving productivity, quality, and customer and supplier relationship.

Corporate communication lessons

Jack Welch established a strong partnership between communication and strategic planning, making communication activity a core contributor in transforming the company and sustaining its vitality.

Colgate-Palmolive

Robert Frazier did at Colgate-Palmolive, when he joined in 1996, what his contemporary Jack Welch had been doing since 1980 at GE—the use of communication to turn around a sluggish company into a dynamic volcano with a highly motivated workforce.

Defining the problem

When Frazier joined the company, he became aware that the key people were not happy because the company was not meeting its key performance indicators (KPIs). There was hardly any communication within the company, and whatever was emanating did not seem accurate. Frazier, an engineer by profession, did not have any formal training in communication, but that was no constraint for him, because he had identified the problem and knew communication was the imperative.

Using marketing strategy

Calling it "Internal Marketing Campaign," based on the marketing strategy: "Here we are; Here is where we want to be," he made a simple proposition for people to understand the problem and the goal. He believed that a turnaround could happen only when employees recognized their role as the key to success; they were to see themselves as the solution bearers. To involve them, he went about teaching them about business, finance, gain sharing, industrial pressure, and competition. He would say, "It never occurred to me that I was involved in any kind of employee communication activity. My goal was to turn Colgate-Palmolive Morristown factory in to a global business."[35]

The daily "check-ins"

To put his vision into practice, he started what was called the daily morning "check-in" routine. In a room that was asymmetrical without any windows, with some furniture lying disorderly here and there, twenty employees would come and stand, making a kind of circle, to discuss what happened yesterday and what was planned for the current day. Frazier would walk in, which was not with a view to alert the employees or he expected to receive pleasantries; he would join the talk as others would. The group would then leave and get on the day's business, becoming aware that their contribution mattered. The stand-up forums, against formal meetings, feel the analysts, were his first credo.

Shop-floor communication

White boards full of information revealed details of breakdowns, goals, sick leaves, birthdays, vacation schedules, and numbers of units coming from various assembly lines. A large race car billboard depicted productivity of each assembly line relative to the others. Each employee could see where his/her race car was. Banners were hung from the walls, extolling virtues of open communication. Alongside were inspirational messages encouraging people to push forward their next goal. The energy and enthusiasm were visible in the plant for anyone to see. In Frazier's words, "the people who work for us are not stupid. Very soon they could see a direct connection between what they were doing and success for the business."[36]

CEO interfacing with employees directly

He led the communication portfolio by interfacing directly with employees at an interpersonal level and through the company newsletter. In fact, his front-page article became a source of knowledge about the company and a great source of inspiration for employees. He shared with them where they were and where they were going in terms of asset utilization, the quality of products, material losses, financial results, and teamwork. In terms of the turnaround, it brought about following changes: asset utilization went up by 48%; production volume by 67%; the number of cases produced per person increased dramatically by 64%. The cost per case decreased by 42%, and cases rejected decreased by 82%. Interestingly, these results became possible mostly with the same people who worked before Frazier's arrival.

Argenti and Forman feel that the lesson learned from this case study is the criticality of specific market orientation for an effective employee communication program.[37]

A CEO can truly bring about change through communication if he believes in the power of communication and by involving employees in the big picture.

Questions on case studies

a) What, in your view, are the similarities or differences in the strategies employed by respective CEOs of GE and Colgate-Palmolive in achieving the desired goal?
b) Go through the following two books carefully, and write an analytical review on the books, especially on how the commitment of the top management in internal communication was leveraged in making a motivated workforce at GE and Southwest Airlines:

1. *Straight from the Gut*: Jack Welch
2. *Nuts! Southwest Airline's Crazy Recipe for Business and Personal Success*: Kevin and Jackie Freiberg

Notes

1 D. Lindo, "Have You Checked Out Your Public Relations Recently?", *Supervision*, November 1995, in Richard R. Dolphin, *The Fundamentals of Corporate Communications*, 1999 (London: Butterworth-Heinemann), p. 24.
2 R Ramalinga Raju's confessional letter to the board and regulatory bodies. Full text appears in chapter 9.
3 The Economic Times, 23 May 2009.
4 Sandra Oliver, *Corporate Communication*, 1997 (London: Kogan Page), pp. 40–41.
5 "My Reliance, My Life: Corporate Sustainability Report, 2005–06", https://www.ril.com/Sustainability/CorporateSustainability.aspx.
6 www.employeecommunicationtips.com
7 Adapted from 'from the three Bs to the high Cs, communication World, April/May, 1997, in Lyn Smith with Pamela Mounter, *Effective Internal Communication* (New Delhi: Kogan Page), pp. 8–9.
8 www.tatasteel/100.com/index-jrd.asp
9 Scott M. Cutlip, Allen H. Xenter and Glen M. Broom, *Effective Public Relations*, eighth edition, 2006 (New Delhi: Pearson Education), pp. 72–73.
10 Jaishri Jethwaney and N. N. Sarkar, *Public Relations Management*, 2009 (New Delhi: Sterling Publishers).
11 Scot M. Cutlip, Allen H. Center and Glen M. Broom, *Effective Public Relations*, seventh edition, 1994 (Englewood Cliffs, NJ: Prentice-Hall), p. 261.
12 Lyn Smith with Pamela Mounter, *Effective Internal Communication*, 2008 (New Delhi: Kogan Page), pp. 29–30.
13 Charles Handy, *Understanding Organizations*, 1985 (London: Penguin).
14 Donald Treadwell and Jill B. Treadwell, *Public Relations Writing*, second edition, 2005 (New Delhi: Response Books), pp. 6–7.
15 J. E. Grunig and J. T. Hunt, *Managing Public Relations*, 1984 (New York: Holt, Rinehart & Winston).
16 Donald Treadwell and Jill B. Treadwell, *Public Relations Writing*, second edition, 2005 (New Delhi: Response Books), pp. 10–12.
17 Campus Fatwa on Ghajini Style (indiatimes.com).
18 The Great Dictator: The film that dared to laugh at Hitler—BBC Culture.
19 L. Festinger, "A Theory of Cognitive Dissonance", in Donald Treadwell and Jill B. Treadwell (Eds.), *Public Relations Writing*, second edition, 2005 (New Delhi: Response Books), pp. 14–15.
20 W. J. MacGuire, "Theoretical Foundations of Campaigns", in R. E. Rice and C. K. Atkin (Eds.), *Public Communication Campaigns*, 1989 (Thousand Oaks, CA: Sage), pp. 43–66.
21 Lyn Smith with Pamela Mounter, *Effective Internal Communication*, 2008 (New Delhi: Kogan Page), p. 28.
22 Ibid., pp. 73–74.
23 Jaishri Jethwaney and N. N. Sarkar, *Public Relations Management*, 2009 (New Delhi: Sterling Publishers).
24 infotechindiatimes.com
25 Corporate Audio Streaming Connects with Staff—Radio World.
26 www.infosys.com and indiaprwire.com
27 Jonathan I. Schwartz—Wikipedia.
28 www.indiaprblog.com/2008/05/
29 Ibid.
30 www.leadership.com
31 www.ogilvypr.com/case-studies
32 www.businessindia.com
33 Reimagining Ways to Give Back for Global Community Day (citigroup.com).
34 www.hsbc.co.in
35 Interview with Rob Frazier by authors in 1999 in Paul A. Argenti and Janis Forman, *The Power of Corporate Communication*, 2002 (New York: McGraw Hill), p. 145.
36 Ibid., p. 146.
37 Ibid., pp. 144–149.

5

MANAGING GOVERNMENT RELATIONS

Chapter objectives

After reading this chapter you will learn the following:

What is meant by government relations and why corporate organizations need it
How the relationship with government is strategized and pursued and who does it
Various tools of government relations like lobbying, public affairs, and issue management
Government relations—imperatives
Case studies in government relations

5.1 Introduction

Business in any society functions and operates under various legal frameworks and regulations. Business has a great role to play in a society, but its sustenance and growth depends on its relationship with various stakeholders, including the policymakers and opinion leaders. For smooth sailing and expansion, business organizations constantly strive to influence legislation to suit their interests, including their bottom-line. Relationship with the government works at various levels, viz., formally through the government relations cell or a public affairs/PR consultancy; through the chief executive officer; and through industry associations. Most organizations, in the Indian context, especially those in the private sector, simultaneously work at these three levels. For successful government relations, organizations use various strategies and tools to impress upon the government. Lobbying, invariably referred to as public affairs, forms the crux of effective government relations management.

Is government relations management a part of corporate communication? In a broader sense, yes, but in many companies, the government relations' officers work independently

DOI: 10.4324/9781032694702-5

of the corporate communication department. Critics argue that this could be so because the companies may want to keep the dealings with the government a secret.[1]

In this chapter we shall, first, look at the corporate sector evolution and growth in India in a nutshell and the various sectors in the economy and their need to interface with the government. This would be followed by some glimpses of various national business associations that have been formed to look after the interests of the sector, their missions, and mandates. The chapter would then discuss in detail the evolution and process of lobbying, issue management, followed by steps in government relations. A few case studies have been included at the end of the chapter to facilitate easy understanding of the process of government relations.

5.2 Business and government—a symbiotic relationship

Business is an essential part of any society. Various forms of governments apply varying kinds of controls over business. Even countries that are capitalist in nature also exert influence on business, both in normal and critical times. Every country has a set of rules, regulations, and regulatory bodies for regulating business. In many countries, companies can be formed only through government laid-down procedures. Companies, especially in the business of tobacco, liquor, pharmaceuticals, and banking/finance face more regulations than their counterparts in other sectors.

No society can function without a robust economic system. The 2008 recession saw the US government bailing out some sectors with taxpayers' money, which led a newspaper to comment that the US government's action was reminiscent of the erstwhile USSR. Closer to home, in the Satyam fraud case, the central government swung into action immediately by replacing the board of directors with its nominees as a first step. Just in a matter of three months, the company was sold through a process of bidding.

To understand the role of government relations, we shall look at the corporate sector in India, various industry bodies who, on behalf of the industry, not only do intense lobbying to influence policymaking but also seek the support of the government when the going gets tough.

5.2.1 Some glimpses of the growth of the Indian corporate sector

When India achieved freedom from the British in 1947, the country received a truncated economy, aggravated by a divided country. About 500 small states joined together to make the union of states, called India. The resources in various states obviously were not similar. India opted for a mixed economy but modelled it with a slant on welfare economics, creating the public sector, whose prime objective, unlike the private sector, was not necessarily profit making. The phase between 1947 and 1991 generally gives an impression that there was complete government control of business. The period is also invariably referred as the "License Raj," meaning thereby that, for anything, one needed government's license, thus scuttling the growth of private entrepreneurship. The 1990s is referred to as the "era of economic liberalization," which meant the closure of the license system.

Surjit Majumdar, in his insightful paper, comments that despite the so-called government control, the private sector grew by leaps and bounds between 1947 and 1991, because both autonomy and the state's role had their limitations.[2]

Analysts believe that if politicians and bureaucrats use the ploy of controls to obtain different kinds of favors for themselves or their political outfits, out of the same process, businessmen also play the regime of controls to their own advantage.

India witnessed an initiation of planning through five-year plans to boost various sectors, especially infrastructure and industry. The growth in its infant stage itself received a rude shock in the 1960s, when both China and Pakistan engaged the country in two wars. The decade also witnessed severe drought conditions in the country. India received food grain support from the developed world to fulfill the needs of its growing population. When Lal Bahadur Shastri took over as the prime minister after the death of the first prime minister and the architect of public sector, Pundit Jawaharlal Nehru, his mission statement was "Jai Jawan, Jai Kisan," eulogizing the importance of the defence forces and agriculture. His untimely death brought Nehru's daughter Indira Gandhi as the prime minister, who brought about some landmark changes that shaped the Indian economy for more than two decades. Some of the immediate actions included giving the agriculture the much-needed push, what came to be known as the "Green Revolution," nationalizing of banks, withdrawal of privy purses (a grant given to kings who had merged their kingdoms) of the erstwhile kings, which many thought was symbolic to bring home the point that there was no place for kings and kingdoms in a democracy. Public sector also received a great impetus in the two decades following the ascent of Indira Gandhi.

Some stringent controls in the shape of monopolies and restricted trade practices (MRTP) and Foreign Exchange Regulation Act (FERA) were promulgated. The period also saw the setting up of cooperatives in the areas of fertilizers, dairy, and sugar to boost the rural sector. The 1970s witnessed the setting up of oil, gas, and power companies in the public sector, inviting major investments. The coming of Rajiv Gandhi in 1984 ushered in an era of IT and telecommunication, which, in a way, was responsible for the telecom and IT revolution in India in the 1990s. It not only made the country an undisputed leader in the larger global perspective but also connected teeming millions within the country through wireless cell phones at an affordable cost, cutting across the economic divide.

5.2.2 Growth of public sector in India

Public sector in India touches an average Indian as nothing else does, because public sector companies produce literally everything under the sun, to put it proverbially, from missiles to matchboxes. Globally, the role of the public sector enhanced after the industrial revolution, first in Great Britain, followed by Europe. Even the USA, that has the lowest share of the public sector in the GDP, has some public sector organizations occupying monopolistic positions, like the National Aeronautics and Space Administration (NASA), US Postal services, nuclear power research projects, and defense industries. India, in contrast, has an impressive share of public sector share in the GDP. The economies of Brazil and Argentina are stated to be modeled on the Indian pattern.

In retrospect, the share of the public sector was at 70% of all investments during the first five-year plan in 1951, which came down to 30% in the tenth five-year plan. The investments, however, have continued to grow, from Rs. 29 crores in 1951 to 21,58,877 crores in 2020.

The following box gives a glimpse of the central public sector state as of 2020–21.[3]

- **Total Paid-up Capital** in all CPSEs as of 31.3.2020 stood at Rs 3,10,737 crore.
- **Total Financial Investment** in all CPSEs was Rs 21,58,877 crore.
- **Capital Employed** in all CPSEs was Rs 31,16,455 crore.
- **Gross Revenue from Operations** of 256 operating CPSEs during the financial year 2019–20 was Rs 24,61,712 crore.
- **Profit** of 171 profit-making CPSEs stood at Rs 1,38,112 crore in financial year 2019–20.
- **Loss** of 84 loss-making CPSEs was Rs 44,817 crore in financial year 2019–20.
- **Reserves and Surplus** of all CPSEs stood at Rs 9,57,579 crore as of 31 March 2020.
- **Net Worth** of all CPSEs was Rs 12,35,706 crore as of 31 March 2020.
- **Dividend** declared/paid by 105 CPSEs in financial year 2019–20 stood at Rs 72,136 crore.
- **Contribution of all CPSEs to Central Exchequer** by way of excise duty, custom duty, GST, corporate tax, interest on Central Government loans, dividend, and other duties and taxes stood at Rs 3,76,425 crore in financial year 2019–20.
- **Foreign Exchange Earnings** of CPSEs through export of goods and services stood at Rs 1,21,756 crore in financial year 2019–20.

Sixtieth annual public enterprises survey 2019-20

The 1956 Industrial Policy resolution paved the road map for the public sector in India with the following broad objectives:

- To help the rapid economic growth and industrialization of the country and to create the necessary infrastructure for economic development
- To promote redistribution of income and wealth
- To create employment opportunities
- To promote balanced regional development
- To assist the development of small-scale and ancillary industries
- To promote import substitution and save and earn foreign exchange for the country

The industrial policy of 1991, in contrast, spoke of the need to review the investments in the public sector; to refer the chronically sick public sector enterprises to the Board for Industrial and Financial Reconstruction (BIFR) and other similar bodies created for the purpose. It also talked of the need to create a social security mechanism for protecting the interests of those affected. To raise resources, it talked of government shareholding to be offered in mutual funds, financial institutions and among the general public, and workers. It also spoke of the need to make public sector boards more professional and to be given greater autonomy.

If one were to look at the quantum, the public sector enterprises have been miniscule in number when compared with the private sector, but in terms of investments, the public sector has clearly overshadowed the private sector.

Here are two tables that reflect the registration of companies over a period of four decades and their paid-up capital and paid-up capital of companies as percentage of GDP.

TABLE 5.1 Companies and paid-up capital

Year	*No. of companies at work*		*Paid-up capital (puc) (in crores)*	
	Govt. companies	*Non-govt. companies*	*Govt. companies*	*Non-govt. companies*
1956–67	74	29283	72.6	1005
1960–61	142	26007	477.2	1271.5
1970–71	314	30008	2064.4	2439.2
1980–81	851	64706	11442.2	4914.1
1990–91	1167	223285	40424.4	18636.2

Source: *Handbook of Industrial Statistics*, 1992

TABLE 5.2 Paid-up capital as percentage of GDP

Year	*PUC as % of GDP at market prices*			*PUC as % of aggregate PUC*		
	Govt. companies	*Non-govt. companies*	*All companies*	*Govt. companies*	*Non-govt. companies*	*All companies*
1956–67	0.59	8.23	8.82	6.74	93.26	100.00
1960–61	2.95	7.85	10.79	27.29	72.71	100.00
1970–71	4.78	5.65	10.43	45.84	54.16	100.00
1980–81	8.41	8.61	12.03	69.96	30.04	100.00
1990–91	9.23	3.49	12.72	72.56	27.44	100.00

Source: *Handbook of Industrial Statistics*, 1992

5.2.3 The boom in the service sector post liberalization

The decade of the 1990s saw a rapid privatization of the corporate sector. The issue of privatizing the public sector for the first time could be traced to the manifesto of the Bhartiya Janta Party during the 1989 elections. The party questioned the logic behind setting up of hotels and the bread industry in the public sector. The elections gave a boost to BJP's fortunes as it won many more seats compared to its poor performance in the 1984 elections. The congress, which created and nurtured the public sector, which had been in the saddle throughout the period from 1947 until 1991 (with brief spells of two non-congress governments), became the architect of liberalization, inviting criticism from the *Swadeshi* lobbies. Some public sector companies were axed during the liberalization phase. The media in general wholeheartedly supported the privatization of the public sector. According to Chalapati Rao and Guha, the liberalization and Foreign Direct Investment (FDI) policy of the government of India enabled many foreign controlled companies that were established or converted into subsidiaries, even including the fully owned ones.[4] First-generation entrepreneurs like Narayana Murthy, Ramalinga Raju, Sunil Bharti set up Infosys, Satyam, and Bharti respectively, getting into big league in IT and telecommunication in the private sector. Later, older, and established companies like Tata, Birla, and Reliance also entered the service sector. Analysts believe that the expansion of the service sector was not really the result of any conscious decision of the government, but a product of the tendencies emanating from the Indian economy and its interactions with the global economy.[5]

The realty sector became an important area of private sector expansion. The capital market witnessed many frauds, paving way for regulation of the sector. The chapter on financial communication may be referred to, to understand the evolution of the capital market in India.

With various sectors in place, viz., public, private, and cooperative, there has always been a need to connect with the respective stakeholders. Of the three, both the public sector and the cooperative sector have been relatively reticent in connecting with its audience. As said in Chapter 1, Mrs. Indira Gandhi took steps to invite the CEOs of the public sector organization to impress upon them the need for communication with various stakeholders, including the need for image makeover of the public sector, which resulted in central public sector enterprises setting up public relations departments.

The cooperative sector has been communicating at the grassroots level, primarily through various traditional and folk media, to connect with its audience. Interestingly, however, the corporate offices of most of the companies in the cooperative sector are in the capital cities in plush offices, with some exceptions. A general lack of accountability has witnessed the cooperative banking sector falling prey to capital market scams more than once.

The private sector has been the most vocal of the three sectors in projecting its concerns and voicing its point of view from time to time. The private sector associations like the FICCI, CII, and ASSOCHAM have become powerful lobbies reflecting the concerns of the private sector. To influence policymaking and legislation, they have been bringing out many research papers, organizing conference and colloquiums, and involving the political class to bring home their points. In the following paragraphs, we shall look at, in a nutshell, their missions and mandates on government relations, followed by public sector association SCOPE and cooperative union, viz., NUCI's role and scope.

5.3 Industry associations and their role in government relations

5.3.1 FICCI

Set up in 1927, on the "advice of Mahatma Gandhi," FICCI claims that its history is very closely interwoven with the freedom movement. FICCI's website reflects that it is inspired by "economic nationalism as a political tool" to fight against discriminatory economic policies. It has Mahatma Gandhi's quote with his picture profile (reproduced in the box).

FICCI has a membership of over 1,500 corporate organizations spanning large, medium, and small enterprises and over 500 chambers of commerce and business associations. Claiming a clout with the government, the following quote from its home page reflects its say in the economic policies of the country:

> FICCI has played a proactive role in evolving the economic policies of the nation both in the pre-Independence and post-Independence period. The Government has been consulting FICCI while evolving and implementing all major economic policies of the country. The Government of India Act of 1936, Bombay Plan, Five-Year Plans, etc. are some of the major economic policy instruments that were discussed threadbare in the FICCI forum. That partnership between the Government and FICCI continues. Thirty-four specialized committees of FICCI on diverse segments of the economy

grapple with sectoral issues on a day-to-day basis to provide solutions to business and to suggest pragmatic policies to the Government.[6]

> *I cannot forget the services rendered by the commercial class, but I want you to make Congress your own and we would willingly surrender the reins to you. The work can be better done by you. But if you decide to assume the reins, you can do so only on one condition. You should regard yourselves as trustees and servants of the poor. Your commerce must be regulated for the benefit of the toiling millions.*
>
> Mahatma Gandhi
> Speaking at FICCI's 4th Annual Session on 7th April 1931

5.3.2 Confederation of Indian Industries (CII)

CII works "to create and sustain an environment conducive to the growth of industry in India, partnering industry and government alike through advisory and consultative processes." Founded over 114 years ago, the business association has a direct membership of over 7,500 organizations from the private as well as public sectors, including SMEs and MNCs, and an indirect membership of over 83,000 companies from around 380 national and regional sectoral associations.

About its government interface, CII writes on its home page: "CII catalyses change by working closely with government on policy issues, enhancing efficiency, competitiveness and expanding business opportunities for industry through a range of specialized services and global linkages."

5.3.2.1 CII campaigns

In the last few years, CII claims to have stepped up its engagement on a wide range of issues that it identifies as being of national concern and priority. The CII in the last couple of years has launched two campaigns, viz., *Brand India* and *Integrity India*.

Through the Brand India Campaign, the CII strives to build brand salience for India by positioning it as a "Globally Competitive and sound Investment destination and as a Reliable Partner to do business with."[7]

The Integrity India Campaign takes on the challenge of "working to improve probity in public life by putting the issue of Integrity center stage."[8]

5.3.3 ASSOCHAM

The ASSOCHAM website claims to represent the interests of more than 3,00,000 direct and indirect members. Its mission

> as a representative organ of Corporate India, ASSOCHAM articulates the genuine, legitimate needs and interests of its members. Its mission is to impact the policy and legislative environment to foster balanced economic, industrial and social development.

> We believe education, IT, BT, Health, Corporate Social responsibility, and environment to be the critical success factors.[9]

ASSOCHAM has 60 expert committees covering various economic activities in India, especially in the field of information technology, biotechnology, telecom, banking and finance, company law, corporate finance, economic and international affairs, tourism, civil aviation, corporate governance, infrastructure, energy and power, education, legal reforms, real estate and rural development, etc.

ASSOCHAM exhorts the policy makers, business houses/entrepreneurs and students (the future of India) "to grasp the golden opportunity of leading the country in the resurgent India."

All the three major industry associations have their roots in the pre-independence India.

5.3.4 Standing Conference of Public Enterprises (SCOPE)

Standing Conference of Public Enterprises (SCOPE) is an apex professional organization representing the central government public enterprises. It has also some state enterprises, banks, and other institutions as its members. SCOPE is an offshoot of "New Horizon," a society that was established in New Delhi, India on September 29, 1970 for promoting better understanding among the public about the individual and collective contribution of the public sector in building the industrial base of the country. Within a short span of three years, the founding fathers, according to SCOPE sources, visualized a greater role for this society and converted it into an apex body for all central public sector enterprises. SCOPE thus came into being on April 10, 1973. The government of India formally recognized it on 8 November 1976 by a decision of the Union Cabinet.

SCOPE sustains itself through a membership fee that comes from various PSUs. It also has a few state-of-art SCOPE complexes that are rented out to some PSUs for their corporate offices.

Its mission is "to facilitate the endeavors of its members in improving their overall performance and to promote their legitimate aspirations by strengthening their effective and sustained engagement with stakeholders."[10]

Among various areas that include corporate governance, etc, the role and scope of work reflected on its home page also includes "Interfacing with the government, regulatory bodies and policy makers for creating favorable policies and a regulatory framework to safeguard the interests of public enterprises and improve their competitiveness."

Although there is a general criticism of SCOPE among many CEOS that it is not proactive in putting forward the issues relating to member PSUs and that it did not create public opinion to oppose disinvestments of PSUs through the liberalization phase, there is no denying that being created by the funds of the public sector that are owned by the government, SCOPE can hardly criticize the decisions of the government, unlike the private sector associations, if need be. Nonetheless it does use its good offices to persuade the government on various issues. A list of issues which SCOPE discussed with the GOI over the last decade or so includes the following:

5.3.4.1 Priority issues discussed with the government

1. The future of presidential appointees on the boards of the companies being privatized
2. Adequate incentives and special provisions to encourage professionals with a proven record, who can take up the challenging assignment of effecting turnaround of sick and non-profitable enterprises.
3. Review of the move to roll back the retirement age of presidential appointees from 60 to 58 years
4. Removal of restriction on employment of board level executives after retirement/ resignation
5. Labor reforms
6. A road map for disinvestments/privatization
7. Review of strategic sales of profit-making enterprises
8. Offering shares of the companies to be privatized to the profit-making blue-chip PSEs and the public
9. Methodology of valuation of the assets and market goodwill of the companies being privatized.[11]

Some of its other activities in the recent past include the following:

5.3.4.2 Interactions and submissions to parliamentary committee

SCOPE had submitted to the parliamentary committee on PSUs various documents submitted by SCOPE to the government from time to time on "Financial Restructuring and Disinvestment."

SCOPE had also recently submitted a memorandum to COPU on disinvestments and privatization of the Indian public sector.

5.3.4.3 Presentation before the disinvestment commission

SCOPE made a presentation before the Disinvestment Commission. The commission, in its reports, included most of the suggestions given by SCOPE.

Department of Public Enterprises

The following two bodies are crucial to public sector functioning and their monitoring.

5.3.4.4 The Department of Public Enterprises (DPE)

The Department of Public Enterprises is the nodal department for all Central Public Sector Enterprises (CPSEs) and formulates policy pertaining to the role of CPSEs in the economy. The DPE also acts as the interface between the various parliamentary and government organizations and the CPSEs.[12]

5.3.4.5 Committee on Public Undertakings (COPU)

In the Indian Parliament, the Committee on Public Undertakings (COPU) has members from various political parties. If the public sector companies are anxious about anything, it is this committee that keeps them on their tenterhooks. The COPU keeps a close watch on their functioning and can be very unsparing in its criticism. The COPU, from time to time, visits some of the PSUs, especially those that are problem-ridden. COPU submits its reports to the parliament. The COPU, at the same time, can be a great source of support, if handled properly. A case study of handling a COPU visit has been added at the end of the chapter.

5.3.5 National Union of Cooperatives in India (NUCI)

The Indian Cooperative Movement is said to be the largest in the world. More than a century old, the movement has grown both in size and volume of business, encompassing activities that include agriculture, horticulture, credit and banking, housing, agro-industries, rural electrification, dairy, consumers, tribal, agri-business, weavers, HRD, and information technology. There are about 5.5 lakhs cooperatives in the country with a membership of about 20% population, that is, 23 crores. The cooperative movement touches the entire nook and cranny of the country, which is claimed by the NUCI to be 100%.

Located in the capital city of Delhi, the NUCI, from time to time, organizes seminars, which are attended by representatives of cooperatives from various parts of the country. It also organizes training programs, especially for employees looking after PR and communication for various cooperatives to enhance their skills.

While there are some success stories in the cooperatives, especially the Anand, many cooperatives have been in the public glare for various problems, including political interference, nepotism, unprofessional attitude, and lack of accountability. The cooperatives have not really been a priority area for the government for long.

The NUCI has formed a group of PR practitioners representing the cooperative organizations to address their image issues.

Most large private sector organizations have government relations officers to liaise with the government at three levels, viz., local government, state government, and central government. One does not find such a post in any public sector organization. Some, however, do have liaison offices, especially those public sector organizations that are not located in the capital city of Delhi. The liaison offices in such cases look after the hospitality of visiting officers, handle protocol, and fix meetings with ministries, etc.

The readers are advised to consult Chapter 9 on financial communication along with this one to understand the functioning of the Ministry of Corporate Affairs and other regulatory bodies.

Those handling government relations often use lobbying/public affairs as a strategic tool to influence policymaking and legislation. In the following paragraphs, we shall look at the evolution and process of lobbying and various cased studies to understand its functioning.

5.4 Public affairs/lobbying

The professions of public affairs and lobbying are often referred interchangeably. However, some scholars feel that a public affair is more than just lobbying, which only aims at influencing legislation by various means. Public affairs, on the other hand, is broader based and includes varying target audiences. Some argue that the nomenclature public affairs have been taken from lobbying, a profession not viewed favorably. Lobbying generally does not draw positive comments from the media. This, feel practitioners, is largely due to lack of knowledge about the function and misperceptions surrounding it. Similarly, public affairs as a profession is also not well-known due to limited exposure of the common man.

Stuart Thomson and Steve John argue that public affairs goes further than lobbying. Public affairs does not only include influencing decision-makers but also policy makers/bureaucracy, influential bodies, regulatory authorities, commercial bodies, and an organizations' various other stakeholders. All these put together only help achieve the desired policy outcome. Media is also an important influencer in the entire gamut of activities. When media covers a story, politicians and other influencers take note of it. Public opinion formation through media often applies pressure on the decision-makers.[13]

When a public affairs strategy is used, many believe, it can protect an organization from the perceived threat of a new policy initiative or regulation. It can also help the organization against any adverse comment made by government, officials, politicians, and others in the industry that matter in public perception. As soon as Satyam Computer's fraudulent practices were exposed in India, it became a free-for-all situation, when industry stalwarts from sister IT firms commented adversely but at the same time did not spare any effort to tell the world that they followed the best practices. Similarly, politicians, representatives of regulatory bodies, and anyone who mattered commented, little realizing that the fate of over 50,000 employees who were not party to the fraud hung in thin air.

For instance, as soon as the UPA, led by the Congress, won the elections in May 2009, most of the news channels in their discussion programs had representatives from the industry who were asked to reflect their expectations from the government, given that this time the Congress was returned with a better score. It was clear that now that the major party in the UPA had more seats than last time, it may not pursue a "common minimum program" that was acceptable to its other partners. When translated, it would mean more economic reforms, as the Left parties did not form part of the UPA. Similarly, when the BJP government was elected in 2014, there was an atmosphere of mistrust in the UPA government. The media wrote extensively 'Policy paralysis.'

Public affairs help organizations to be on the vigil in the face of ever-changing social, political, and economic environment, so that they can clarify their stand, change strategies, and ensure protection of reputation of individuals and organizations. Public affairs practitioners often use the art of issue management to achieve the desired goal. We shall discuss issue management later in the chapter.

Public affairs/lobbying is said to be dynamic, so the tools and strategies are constantly updated to suit the political processes.

It is believed that lobbying/public affairs is more widely accepted and practiced in the USA as a business practice. The reason is not far to seek. It has to do with the funding of political campaigns, where, in most parts, it is through the political action committees, individual donations, and corporate donations. Public affairs firms work overtime to ensure funding of candidates right from the stage of primaries. In fact, the worth of a candidate is gauged from the amount of money he/she has been able to accumulate all through.

When we look at India, most of the funding of election campaigns is from the big business houses, but always clandestinely. Immense amount of lobbying takes place, but interestingly, there are no independent lobbying firms, as lobbying is not accepted as a profession in India. The political parties do the lobbying themselves. The government of India announced the introduction of electoral bonds "to cleanse the system of political funding in India." The bonds come as promissory note, coming through a bank account, but without the payee's name. The purchaser can buy only after fulfilling the KYC norms. The electoral bonds have a life of 15 days,

> during which it can be used for making donation only to the political parties registered under section 29A of the Representation of the Peoples Act, 1951 (43 of 1951) and which secured not less than one per cent of the votes polled in the last general election to the House of the People or a Legislative Assembly.[14]

There is wide criticism of electoral bonds as it is alleged that most of these are going to a dominant political party. Some NGOs have gone to the supreme court on the usefulness of these bonds in cleansing the system.

The Supreme Court is in the process of deciding whether the current scheme facilitates anonymous corporate funding to political parties and whether it was wrongly certified as a Finance Act. The Court's decision will affect transparency in election funding, believe the analysts.[15]

Many years ago, one of the industry associations held a conference for reaching consensus among its members on political funding to regularize the system and make the issue transparent.

4.00 Lobbying and Public affairs

For this chapter, we shall use lobbying and public affairs as synonymous, without getting into the literal meaning of both the terms.

5.4.1 Defining lobbying

Defining lobbying, the official website of the British Parliament explains: "Lobbying is the practice of individuals and organizations trying to influence the opinions of MPs and Lords. Methods of lobbying vary and can range from sending letters, making presentations, providing briefing material to Members and organized rallies."[16]

There is a difference between lobbying and petitioning. Lobbying is an attempt to influence the opinions of MPs and lords on specific subjects. On the other hand, petitioning involves making a request to the House of Commons to act on a specific issue, which is presented to the House by an MP, often on behalf of their constituents.

Milner defines lobbying as

> any action designed to influence the action of institutions or government. That means it covers all parts of central and local government and other public bodies. Its scope includes legislation, regulatory and policy decisions and negotiations on public sector contracts or grants.[17]

Sauza and Dale feel that

> lobbying is an important part of the democratic process. Always has been. Always will be. There is nothing wrong with paying consultants for practical advice. Businessmen,

charities, and trade associations are not experts on the political system so they pay people who are.[18]

Ian Greer associates got into controversy in the "Cash for Questions" scandal in 1994 that rocked the conservative government. Money was said to have been exchanged for MPs asking questions in the parliament as a part of the lobbying campaign. Two members of the British parliament, viz., Graham Riddick and David Tredinnick, both conservatives, were found to have taken money for asking questions. Similarly, Neil Hamilton is said to have accepted gifts in exchange for political and parliamentary activity from Mohammed Al Fayed, the owner of Harrods. It is widely believed that instances such as these eventually led to the historic downfall of the conservative government in the 1997 general elections in the UK.[19]

The Indian Parliament faced the same sequence in 2005 when a sting operation by a news channel exposed 11 members of parliament, ten from the lower house and one from the upper house, taking money for asking questions. Called *Operation Duryodhana*, the sting operation was steered by Cobrapost and Hindi Channel Aaj Tak and lasted for eight months.

In all, more than 61 questions were submitted by 11 MPs, of which 25 were tabled in the parliament. While most of the questions had some element of public interest, it did reflect enormous lobbying efforts by some organizations.

All the 11 members of parliament who belonged to various political parties that included the Congress (I), BJP, RJD, and BSP were expelled from the Parliament.[20]

5.4.2 Lobbying in the West

The history of lobbying can be traced back to many centuries. The nomenclature is believed to have come into practice when people with business and social interests met parliamentarians in Britain, in the lobby of the parliament building, to be handy with information and arguments for those members of parliament who were arguing on the concerned bills. These people came to be known as lobbyists.

Lobbying, however, has become a full-fledged discipline in the last few decades or so.

There are said to be about 35,000 public affairs firms in the USA, and industry participants through lobbying may be over 1,00,000. In the US, many former elected representatives and diplomats work for various lobbying firms.[21]

5.4.3 History of lobbying in India

Harold Gould's book *How South Asians Forged an India Lobby in Washington* is an interesting study of some Indians and organizations who created a lobby in the USA, in pre-independent India, to fight for civil rights of about 5,000 South Asians and aiming at using US government's pressure on the British parliament to emancipate India from its yoke.

Gould talks of the one-man army, Sardar Jagjit Singh, popularly called JJ, who, according to the author, was the "maestro of the final phase of the Indian lobby's trek through American history." He was both shrewd and a visionary, who aligned politics with economics, when, in a statement before the US Congress in 1945, he said, "The 400 million East Indians represent a great untapped trade reservoir." He further said, "There exists a great demand for American goods." Gould feels that the India lobby reached its peak activity during World War II, by which time the Indians had learned the dynamics of systems that worked, how media functioned on stories, and political networking.

A confidential note by the US special envoy to the pre-independent India by the name William Philips, addressed to the US President Franklin D. Roosevelt, worked immensely in India's favor. The note, it is believed, was intentionally leaked to a columnist of the *Washington Post*, which created the right noise in circles that mattered. The note was critical of British policy towards Indian freedom. The note said that the policy relating to war efforts in Asia were in jeopardy because of the arrogance and intransigence of the British government. The note suggested that the British must declare their intent to grant independence to India after the War. The publication of the news came as a windfall to the India lobby.[22]

India has come a long way in adapting the sophisticated art of lobbying both within and outside the country, in managing issues that affect it.

Richard Holbrooke, a well-known Pakistan sympathizer, became the new US envoy to South Asia in February 2009, but India, mercifully, was not a part of his portfolio. Many ascribe this to the great lobbying efforts by the India lobby. This also came as a sharp departure from President Obama's previously stated approach of engaging with India, Pakistan, and Afghanistan in the regional dialogue.

India has been resisting for many decades the internationalization of the Kashmir issue. If it were included, the whole process would have been a nonstarter. When in the past there was speculation about former President Bill Clinton being made the envoy to Kashmir, India made its stance very clear. In no way was India ready to equate the Kashmir issue to what Pakistan was doing in Afghanistan. India's former security advisor Brijesh Mishra once categorically stated, "No matter what government is in place in India, India is not going to relinquish control of Jammu and Kashmir. This is written in stone and cannot be changed." Daniel Markey, a South Asian analyst, ascribes this to India's lobbying efforts. To quote him,

> They have a fairly effective lobbying machine. They have taken a lot of notes on the Israel model, and they have gotten better. . . some of the lobbying effort is obviously done through the companies, but a lot of it is direct government to government, people talking to each other. The Indian government and those around the Indian government made it clear through a variety of channels because of the Clinton rumor and they came out to quickly shoot that down.[23]

As soon as Barak Obama took over as the president of the USA, and unveiled his government's policy towards the Indian subcontinent and New Delhi, the government of India spared no effort to ensure that relations with the new regime and the new Congress remained on the same footing as under the Republicans for the last eight years. According to official lobbying records, as reported by media, India had already spent $2.23 million since 2005 on lobbying in the US. The expenditure mainly focused on getting the Indo-US civilian nuclear deal through the Congress. The lobbying firm, Barbour, Griffith, and Rogers (BGR), included former US ambassador to India Robert Blackwell and former house foreign affairs committee staffer Robert Walker. The former, however, left BGR in 2008. The new lobbying firm for India in the US since August 2008 is Patton

Boggs. It is believed that the democratic leaning of the firm was behind retaining it to give India "advice" and push its interests in Washington, where the Democrats hold sway.[24]

Incidentally, the US senate unanimously adopted a resolution, which received bipartisan support, condemning Mumbai attack on 26 November 2008, praising India's restraint. The house of representatives later adopted a similar resolution.

With the new administration in the saddle, it is expected that expenditure on lobbying may increase, and India would like to focus on issues that are against the Indian interests, especially the IT sector, outsourcing.

On the corporate side, if there was one lobby that was constantly engaged to safeguard the interests of tobacco growers and companies making cigarettes, it has been the tobacco lobby, until the advocates fighting their battle for decades were successful in getting the act passed, banning not only advertising on mass media but also making public smoking an offence and reflecting boldly on cigarette packs that smoking caused cancer.

5.4.4 The process of lobbying

The process of lobbying is long, cumbersome, and complex, involving robust strategy and interpersonal networking, besides media handling skills.

The first step is to identify people and institutions that are likely to be helpful in the pursuit of the chosen issue. Having identified them, it is important for the lobbying firm to carry out research about the stand and position taken by these people and institutions in the past on similar issues. Soliciting the support of the identified individuals, who are important opinion makers/elected representatives of the legislature, who would be particularly sympathetic to the cause and influence their peer group on the organization's behalf, is imperative for the success of any lobbying effort.

5.4.5 Making of public policy

A lot of policy agenda is initiated by the party in power, keeping in view the requirements of various sectors and, at times, also to fulfill its poll promises.

Government, comprising politicians and civil servants, is generally responsible for thinking through and drafting the bills. Many a times, the policy needs inter-ministerial input, which is time-consuming and needs great networking capabilities to influence bureaucrats and politicians, especially from the finance ministry, when finances are involved. However, all policies do not have to do with politics alone. Procurement, investments, mergers, pricing, government funding, law and order, international relations, environment protection, etc. are also areas of policy considerations.

The civil servants report to politicians, some of whom work as ministers in various ministries. Each ministry has a minister with a possibility of some junior ministers. A civil servant, called the Secretary to the Government, heads the ministry. He/she has several junior civil servants for assistance.

In the legislature, besides the treasury benches comprising the party in power, there are other political parties. It is important for the lobbyists to keep a track of various important persons in opposition parties who matter. When a bill is discussed in the legislature, support of various sections is ideal, which may not always happen as members often follow the party line. However, on some bills, the members cut across party lines, especially those that have to do with national sovereignty, social issues, etc., but not always.

For instance, when the left parties abandoned the UPA coalition government in 2008 over the issue of the Nuclear Proliferation Treaty (NPT) with the USA, the government had to face a vote of no confidence. Immense amount of lobbying could be seen when an unlikely partner, the Samajwadi Party, lent support to the beleaguered UPA government and steered it through amidst allegations that cash was exchanged for buying support of some legislators. The sting operation also had some footage reflecting "horse-trading." In fact, lobbying is a constant activity in coalition politics, for which, the help of professional lobbyists may not necessarily be sought.

Many governments in democratic countries, including India, put bills in the public domain for feedback and suggestions of civil society before these are discussed in the parliament to become acts. Many a times, bills are presented by private individuals/NGOs for which they need to do a lot of lobbying within the legislature for the passing of the bills. For instance, some bills spearheaded by private intervention that included bills on domestic violence against women, indecent portrayal of women in media, child rights, withdrawal of advertisement on cigarettes and liquor from media space, to name a few, have been passed due to immense pressure and lobbying and advocacy efforts by the non-governmental organizations.

5.4.6 Media and lobbying/public affairs

Media has always been an important tool in public affairs. It is important for the public affairs company to understand the media matrix, the ownership/sociology, its functioning, political ideology, if any, and the undercurrents. A good hang of various kinds of media, national and regional, mainstream and language, besides information about important journalists, political correspondents, foreign desk correspondents, strategic analysts, editors, in fact all who matter in terms of their opinion and clout, will be an important step in taking up an issue for lobbying.

Analysts feel that the public, politicians, and media are intrinsically linked, so cannot be dealt with in isolation of each other. Media, with its tremendous clout, is often able to exert pressure on the political class. Similarly, the public can be involved in giving a larger-than-life imagery to issues. Road shows, rallies, candle marches, signature campaigns are said to be very successful in enlisting the support of the political class.

Media in India successfully lobbied to scuttle a regulation that would have curtailed its freedom of expression. Post 26/11 (Mumbai siege by terrorists in 2008), the Information and Broadcasting Ministry of India prepared a draft order restricting media covering live terrorist attacks, which could not even be discussed amidst immense pressure from the various media houses who called it "Media Gag Order." A representative body of media met the prime minister, who promised them that nothing would be implemented until it had the broader consensus of the media. Tremendous lobbying by the media resulted in its being put on a back burner. Some media representatives, however, did feel that certain restrictions in the interest of national security were needed, but self-restraint by media would be a better strategy. In retrospect, the infamous Emergency promulgated in 1975 in India put censorship on media, but some brave heart media houses like the *Indian Express* and *The Statesman* refused to bow down. When some of their stories were censored, these newspapers would leave the space blank rather than edit or redo such stories.

The blank space on various pages day after day said it all, which had a tremendous impact on people's psyche.

Media abounds in stories about how companies use their lobbyists and liaison officers who move in the corridors of power to get things done for their companies. In an interesting article, "MNCs fine tune the great Indian 'jugadd' mantra," Nandini Sen Gupta and Vivek Sinha wrote that "managing the environment" was still considered a huge competitive advantage in India. The authors commented that it was important for the government to know the antecedents of those who lobbied on behalf of various companies. Even cross-checking with embassies, they commented, was not a bad idea. The story quoted Ramesh Adige, board member, Ranbaxy Labs, who said,

> In general, the governments, both central and state, should know exactly whom they are talking to. They should seek a board authentication from the person that he is representing the MNC, otherwise anyone can walk in with a visiting card, making any claim. In addition, the embassy should be activated so that they are in the loop and are aware of the negotiations as they play out to avoid any mishaps.

Indian bureaucracy, commented the scribes, performed abysmally low when it came to transparency and uprightness, if the ratings of various international surveys were to be believed.[25]

Business organizations keep a constant watch on politics and influence legislation when their interests are at stake. One of the largest and respected companies in India, namely the Tatas, faced a typical problem in the 1970s for which they did immense lobbying to avert the nationalization of its Tata Iron and Steel Company Limited (TISCO). This was more than four decades ago, when not many talked about advocacy and lobbying. The company came out with flying colours in managing an issue to its advantage. The case study has been included at the end of the chapter.

5.5 Issue management

Issue management is an important part of government relations. An issue can be a long pending one, seeking a resolution or something that may erupt instantly. Organizations take a call on whether to go alone or go through a trade organization/industry association to handle the issue with the desired objective of a favorable outcome. Let us understand what is an issue and what are various steps in managing an issue.

5.5.1 What is an issue?

An issue can be defined as an ongoing public policy dispute affecting performance of an organization, a long-term social or political problem that defies solution. Reservation for Gujjars, Yamuna pollution, road rage, domestic violence against women, female feticide, public health, environment pollution, the NPT between India and USA, or the alleged decision of nationalization of TISCO in the 1970s would all qualify as issues that require management.

A review of literature, however, reveals that there is no clear consensus on defining what really is an "issue." Various perceptions exist on the definition of an issue. Some feel advocacy advertising, corporate planning, crisis management, public affairs, public policy is nothing but issue management. Issue management requires management of perception to reach a desired goal. It often needs the use of integrated communication tools that may include one or all of these.

There is a growing consensus that a "client context" is necessary for issue management. Each issue that needs to be managed shall have many factors touching it and several areas that encompass it viz., social, political, and economic contexts.

An issue generally involves a complex set of target audiences that need to be identified. Often positions are taken about "abettors" and "victims" in a crisis that demands careful and sensitive handling. Media generally takes a certain stance on an issue that has the potential of coloring judgment of various stakeholders.

5.5.2 The issue management process

5.5.2.1 Step one

Problem definition/identification of the problem

Issue management process begins with the environment scanning. A dispassionate SWOT analysis of the situation is a must. Many kinds of perceptions could be floating around the issue that needs to be studied. The research team in charge needs to "collect" all the perceptions, sift, analyze, and reach a conclusion as to which perceptions are based on reality and which ones are based on hearsay, the grapevine, or a deliberate effort of the adversary to use misinformation to color perceptions. This would help in working out the communication strategy and content of the message.

5.5.2.2 Step two

Analysis

After understanding what the problem is, it is important to know the source of the "existing" perceptions. These could be the result of a media reportage, grapevine, hearsay, a piece of legislation, utterance by an important personality, who commands credibility among the people, people's own experience with the product, person, or organization. While analyzing, it is important to find out the missing link or the deliberate effort, which may have been involved to mislead the people or a deliberate communication gap that may have been created.

With these two steps, one would have a fair idea about the "current mindset" of the people.

5.5.2.3 Step three

Identify your stakeholders

In issue management, people and institutions whose support is required need to be identified to precision. The existing perceptions of such people and institutions on the issue on hand and the reason why they should support the cause and their previous stand that is reflected in the public domain need to be established through research. Who their possible influencers are need also to be found out. What their expectations from you are is another area that needs to be addressed and probed.

5.5.2.4 Step four

Developing strategy

Determine what you want to change—a decision about the "current mindset" vis-à-vis the "desired mindset." The uni-focus goal in every case of perception management must be to ensure that perceptions surrounding an issue or an organization must match the reality.

5.5.2.5 Step five

Action programming

Seek creative solutions to the proposed change management program. Advertising, public relations, lobbying, and the other below-the-line activities, depending on the strategy and requirements, need to be decided upon. Choose the best media vehicles that would reach the largest number of people in your designated target audience group in a short time at the lowest cost, to achieve the desired reach.

5.5.2.6 Step six

Evaluation

Carry out a constant evaluation while the campaign is on. Bring about change in strategy or messages, if needed, to avoid possible damage.

According to many theorists, people are likely to suppress dissonant messages while preferentially selecting information favoring their position to reinforce their current viewpoint. If changes in public opinion occur, the crucial element of determining public opinion is the residual amount of persuasive force, however small, which can override the reinforcing information, since this is the effect which will cause opinion alterations.

A few cases in point would further clarify this.

5.5.3 When an organization became a victim of the grapevine

ICICI bank found itself in the center of rumor-mongering when the global financial services sector, embroiled by the Lehman bankruptcy in late 2008, triggered global recession. ICICI bank's stock plummeted in no time.

The bank acted fast to manage perceptions through a 360-degree communication plan. One saw the CEO and other senior officers on almost every possible news channel to give their stand on the issue. The company issued advertisements, perked up its marketing strategy and customer calls, among other things. The festive season in India starts with Dussehra, Diwali, and Eid in October/November every year. The bank's customers received an interesting text message that read: "Your deposits with ICICI Bank are safe. Your bank is well capitalized, with good liquidity. Please do not listen to baseless rumors.

Happy festive season." The bank spent millions of rupees in ad campaign that it called "Customer Education Series" on generic banking issues.

5.5.4 Influence of perceptions on policy decision

At times, perceptions influence policy decisions. More than two decades ago, Binaca, a popular toothpaste, became the "victim" of a legislation which ordered the banning of toothpastes with fluoride content. The scientific research findings around that time had reflected that if very young children consumed toothpaste with fluoride content in a certain quantity while brushing, it could prove fatal for them. Ironically, the USP of the brand was "Binaca with fluoride" (*Fluoride yukt Binaka*). The company had no choice but to stop the production of the brand.

The experience of Anand, the second largest dairy movement in the world, is another case in point. Intensive media education and media advocacy, amidst opposition due to ignorance and resistance from vested interests, were made use of to bring about an acceptance of a great idea whose time had come—the innovative dairy movement that had millions of people participating in it.

5.5.5 Perceptions in politics

It is believed that election campaigns are games of smart perception management. The "spin" is used to suit the prospects of the party against the adversary.

There is this interesting case about perception management during the Delhi assembly elections in 1998, when the generally ubiquitous onion became dearer, making it beyond the reach of the common man.

The price of onions had shot up when the election fever was at its peak. Onion has a very typical connotation in the Indian social milieu. It is seen as a poor man's staple that goes with his bread [*pyaz* aur *roti*]. The Congress was able to spin this in its favor. Its entire campaign revolved around the onion, which suddenly went missing from the poor man's palate. The analogy was used to bring home the point that the ruling party was unable to control the prices of the essential commodities, though the fact was that the price of essential items like rice, pulses, etc had not gone up. Despite the party in power talking about it, the mood was such that no one was listening. The humble onion proved to be the nemesis for the incumbent party, because of the use of smart imagery by the competing party in reinforcing the perceptions of the electorate. The BJP lost the election and has not been able to get back to power in Delhi since then.

In 1914 the BJP used "policy paralyses" as a metaphor for the incumbent UPA government in its election campaigning to create a perception that the government's functioning was paralyzed on major issues. The Congress suffered its worst defeat at the hustings.

5.5.6 When perception was managed unethically

On 10 October 1990, a 15-year-old Kuwaiti girl—Nayriah-al-sabah—testified before the US Congress about the atrocities that Saddam Hussein's regime was committing against Kuwaiti citizens. She specifically mentioned that Iraqis were taking Kuwaiti babies from incubators in area hospitals. Her testimony caught the imagination of the people as her face and tearful disposition was vividly caught by the camera. It, in fact, became the language of government's call to arms. Her testimony came to be referred to as the "Incubator Atrocities." Many senators voted for war and cited the story. It came to notice later that a group called the "Citizens for a Free Kuwait," which was represented primarily by wealthy members of the Kuwaiti ruling class, paid PR firm Hill & Knowlton $10.5 million. The aim of the PR strategy was to "offset unfavorable publicity about Kuwait's form of government as well as its human rights record." It was also revealed that the girl who testified was the daughter of the Kuwait's ambassador to the USA. There was even a doubt if the girl was in Kuwait at the time of the alleged atrocities she described. Amnesty International had a difficult time corroborating her allegations. The Kroll Report that came out in 1992 concluded that there had been no mass scale atrocities on babies. It is, however, a fact that seven babies died because medical equipment was moved from a hospital.

The PR agency later admitted having coached the girl about the incubator imagery. The agency defended its action in the interest of drawing public attention. Analyzing the case study wherein perceptions were managed intentionally, Thomas J. Mickey questions the use of signs and visual imagery, which may or may not represent reality.[26]

Perceptions are said to be sensitive to events and happenings and can be formed instantaneously. At the same time they are never permanent, if managed well, especially in the case of wrong perceptions.

5.6 Government relations—imperatives

Dealing with the government is challenging, if not difficult. The bureaucracy generally is criticized for red tape and a rule-bound attitude towards issues. The bureaucrats are trained to strictly go by the rule book. The bureaucracy, by and large, commands a lot of clout in the power echelons, as they formulate all policies and procedures. Therefore, it is important for those who handle government relations to understand the functioning of government and the use of protocol in interfacing with them. The following steps would help:

5.6.1 Set objectives

Government relations are dynamic and not always easy to handle. Work out long-term goals and short-term objectives, keeping in view the overall vision and mission of your organization.

5.6.2 Identify issues

It is important to identify issues from an organization's perspective that need to be handled. There may be issues that emerge from time to time, due to change of environment. These also need to be articulated and strategies worked out to be handled at policy level.

The party that forms the government, its agenda, its relationship with business must be studied and kept in view. Go through the election manifesto of the party in power and major opposition parties in the parliament to understand what would be pushed by the government and where would the support or opposition come from.

5.6.3 Identify the concerned nodal ministry and officers

Every business, whether in the public or private sector, is handled by a nodal ministry, like steel, water, defence, power, industry, HR, labor, etc. Depending on the business of the company, that ministry would be most crucial for maintaining relations. A ministry is headed by a senior bureaucrat, known as Secretary to Government of India, who is assisted by various joint secretaries that have deputy secretaries and undersecretaries. Within the ministry, there are several desks, the lowest rung officer being the section officer, who happens to be the most important link in a ministry. Officers handling government relations need to maintain cordial relations with the concerned desk officer and the concerned bureaucrats that handle the relevant sector. All these officers can be put on the mailing list for posting company literature and regularly sent invites for various functions.

Every ministry is headed by at least one minister. There can, however, be more than one ministers in larger ministries called the union minister and state minister. Interaction with ministers and their secretarial staff, some of who could be from bureaucracy, is often maintained by the CEOs.

The earlier information holds good for maintaining relations both at the state and central levels.

5.6.4 Identify allied ministries and regulatory bodies

Besides the nodal ministry, Ministry of Corporate Affairs, Ministry of Finance, Ministry of labor and Employment, and regulatory bodies like the Registrar of companies, the SEBI, the NSE, if the company is a listed one, are the key government bodies a company needs to liaise with.

5.6.5 Make a list of crucial elected representatives

Know about the members who return to state assemblies and parliament representing various political constituencies from various states. Identify those constituency areas where your organization's projects are located. Also identify the major contenders who lost the elections. Make a mailing list and keep them abreast of your organization's activities through literature and personal contact. Send them invites when any milestone is achieved. They can work as an influential pressure group within the parliament and state legislatures, and those who lost this time could win next time. In a time when parliamentary proceeding are live on television in India, it has been seen that the various parliament members make an effort to speak about issues concerning their political constituencies and often on developmental projects. The government relation's officers can lobby with the ministers and members of parliament to take up issues that concern their organization during parliamentary discussions.

5.6.6 Work on contact program

Establishing contact with policymakers is central to government relations. Once you have identified the key personnel as discussed earlier, you need to work on approaching them proactively in normal times by keeping them informed about the company through personal contacts, meetings, presentations, and literature. In times of crisis, one must work on a crisis communication plan to elicit their support. When Pepsi found nuts and bolts in its cans, it was the FDA that did a lot of talking on its behalf, thus restoring the confidence of the people. In India, when both Pepsi and Coca-Cola were embroiled in the pesticide controversy based on an NGO's finding, the parliamentary committee went into the issue.

5.6.7 Handle COPU visits carefully

Those working in the public sector organization may have to handle the COPU visits to their projects, as a team member. This is slightly tricky and sensitive, because the committee generally demands such visits when there is negative feedback on a particular project. The COPU chairman can be a member of parliament from an opposition party, and that is what requires sensitivity in handling. A case study of NHPC has been included at the end of the chapter on one such COPU visit.

5.6.8 Government relations to safeguard interests within the sector

The general perception is that government relations management is needed by an organization or a trade association with the policy makers. However, there are instances when groups within these sectors and trade associations have tried to elicit government support for their vested interests. While some sectors, especially the media, abhor any kind of government interference, it is not uncommon to find journalists' unions seeking government intervention on pay fixation from their management, or the film industry seeking government support to fight elements within their fraternity, like multiplexes as the fight between Bollywood producers-distributors and multiplexes in May–June 2009 reflected. The United Producers and Distributors' Forum (UPDF), to avoid problems in the future, proposed a government cell. As soon as the new government took charge, the UPDF president began his lobbying, garnering media mileage prior to his coming to Delhi to meet the finance minister and the information and broadcasting minister. Mukesh Bhatt, the then president of UPDF, appeared in the media space, talking about his mission and proposed meeting with the prime minister, besides the concerned ministers. The story reflected that he had met the prime minister before the election, who told him that with an impending election, he could not take a decision. With the same party in power, albeit with a better mandate, the then president of UPDF took the opportunity to remind the prime minister of his promise. To quote Muksh Bhatt, "After his (Dr. Manmohan Singh) party won, I sent him a letter reminding him of the promise. . . The idea behind the independent government cell is that it can safeguard our interests."[27]

5.6.9 Critical factors in managing government relations

Ogilvy Government Relations, a part of Ogilvy Public Relations Worldwide, believes that there are two critical factors in managing successful government relations, viz., knowledge and experience. The agency claims that "through high-level service on congressional staffs, in agencies and the Executive branch, Ogilvy Government Relations team members are deeply knowledgeable about the way government actually works, day in and day out."

The following quote is important to understand how a consultancy handles government relations on behalf of its clients:

> Ogilvy Government Relations approaches government relations from a simple premise: actions by federal institutions have the power to either hurt or help clients. These actions may take the form of high-profile legislation that earns front-page coverage in major newspapers. Or they may be arcane regulatory or policy implementations at the agency level. At either extreme, it is vital to have representatives in the Nation's Capital who can help clients both reduce the risk to their organizations and manage legislation and regulation in an opportune manner. In order to accomplish these objectives, Ogilvy Government Relations concentrates on four key disciplines.[28]

The framework is based on four key activities:

1. Resource Overview: as a starting point, the agency undertakes a SWOT analysis of the client's issue through in-depth interviews with its key leaders and staff members, thereby making an outline of tasks to be performed.
2. Project Development Report: it recommends a strategy based on resource review, followed by a schedule of putting the projects into action.
3. Goals and Benchmarks: these are clearly defined to evaluate the impact of efforts and adjust, if required.
4. Continuous Communication: there is a continuous dialogue of government relation's team with the client to build "a strong working relationship with each other—and with Capitol Hill and federal agencies."[29]

Summary

In this chapter we discussed the meaning, role, and scope of government relations. We looked at an overview of the evolution of the corporate sector in India and their need for interfacing with the government to look after their interests. There are several trade associations like the FICCI, CII, ASHOCHAM, SCOPE, and Association of India Cooperatives that constantly lobby with the governments at various levels to influence legislation. While some associations are strong and proactive, others are reticent when it comes to pushing the agenda of their sector. The chapter looked at the various tools like lobbying and issue management used in government relations. Case studies of Tata and NHPC, each from a private and public sector, were taken up for discussion at the end of the chapter.

Key terms

Government relations: maintaining a continuous dialogue with policy makers and opinion makers with a view to influence policy/legislation in favor of the company or sector.

Issue management: an issue is defined as something that has policy repercussion. Issue management can be defined as managing a controversial issue to the advantage of the client/organization.

Lobbying: the practice of individuals and organizations trying to influence the opinions of MPs.

Public affairs: influencing decision makers, policy makers/bureaucracy, influential bodies, regulatory authorities, commercial bodies, and an organization's various other stakeholders.

Perception management: managing the first conscious activity in the mind about *an object* or *an issue—an impression*, before it becomes an opinion and conviction.

Concept review questions

Q.1. Define government relations and various steps for an effective government relations management program.
Q.2. Define lobbying. How is it different or like public affairs?
Q.3. When and how did lobbying come to be recognized as an important tool of influencing legislation? Write your answer with some cases in point.
Q.4. Define issue management and various steps to map and influence the perception of the concerned target audience group.

Critical thinking exercise

1. Follow up stories in financial media, say from 15 February, a fortnight before the budget is placed by the finance minister in the parliament, to see various lobbies working through industry associations and media on issues that are being pushed to influence the budget. Sometimes lobbying continues between the times the bill goes from Lok Sabha to Rajya Sabha. Go through the budget carefully to see what all has been accommodated to understand the impact of lobbying and who was pushing it with what benefit.
2. Follow up the efforts of the India lobbyists with the new US administration in keeping India's interests in focus in varying fields, especially on outsourcing and our stand on Kashmir, terrorism, and neighboring Pakistan.

Case study: averting the nationalization of TISCO

Tata Iron and Steel Company Limited, the largest steel company in the private sector, had a turnover of Rs. 23,000 million, employed 75,000 employees, and had over five lakhs shareholders at the time of the problem in the late 1970s.

The problem

After the infamous Emergency promulgated by Mrs. Indira Gandhi in 1975, she announced elections in 1977. Much to the chagrin of the ruling Congress party, it lost the elections, and a coalition government comprising several small parties, India's first experiment in coalition politics, was in the saddle under the banner of Janata Party. As soon as it came to power, its intention of anti-multinational and large private sector companies became visible. The Coca-Cola and IBM were the two major global giants that left the Indian shores, lock, stock, and barrel. The government contemplated taking over or nationalizing TISCO. The company management and its various stakeholders, including its 75,000 employees and 500,000 shareholders at the time, had reason to be anxious. The company found out that its customers and the general public were sympathetic towards the company and did not support its nationalization. The government apparently had no reason except to achieve political mileage. TISCO had long been a very respected company for its vision, its technical competence, and welfare activities. It commanded great brand equity.

The company undertook an integrated communication approach that included lobbying, advocacy, and public relations to reach out to various stakeholders with its points of view. The stakeholders the communication program targeted included shareholders, employees, trade, opinion makers, government, politicians, bureaucrats, and the general public. The subsequent table reflects the issues that were taken up for perception management.

Broad strategy

The basic objective behind the 360-degree communication campaign was to stop the government from taking over TISCO by influencing the thinking of different target groups through various media and well-thought-out strategies. The "selling proposition" of the program, as the company called it, was the following:

> TISCO is not only a superbly managed steel company, it is also a unique example of a company which has recognized that its social commitments extended beyond its employees, to the community and its rural population around it. Jamshedpur city, created by TISCO, is the living embodiment of our nation's dream of a better life for our people. India needs many more Jamshedpur today.

In the print media, a six-ad campaign was released reflecting facts about TISCO governance that laid emphasis on employee welfare, community development, rural development, shareholder trusteeship, and, above all, its superior steel technology.

TABLE 5.3 Myths vs. reality

	Government attitude	*TISCO's stand*
1.	Pre-conceived notion: Big business means exploitation	Large business does not exploit
2.	Prejudice: Big business hinders national progress in a socialistic economy	Big business helps national, industrial, and economic progress
3.	Suspicion: The company fills its coffers	The company contributes immensely to labor welfare and community development
4.	Belief: Taking over or controlling TISCO's operations is necessary	Controlling or taking over of TISCO's operations is against national interest

Source: Author

A 10–15-minute talk show in television had a prominent political commentator interviewing public personalities on topical issues concerned with nation building, which had the necessary rub-off on TISCO as a company that contributed to the nation building.

The company termed advocacy and lobbying as the "non-public media" that "formed the main thrust of TISCO's program." Company's liaison office in the national capital, Delhi, was activated to do the necessary networking. A pre-defined list of members of parliament and members of legislature of concerned states of Bihar and West Bengal were sent literature including advertisement pull out to keep them briefed about company's stand. Chairman of TISCO, JRD Tata, one of the highly respected business leaders in India, sent a memorandum to the concerned ministry, following up with personal letters to the members of parliament, highlighting TISCO's contribution in the national, industrial, and social fields.

The company created several awareness programs for the employees, which covered various operational activities through audio-visual means.

For the shareholders, the company brought out a specially designed annual report with pictures and a company mission for the task. It organized an exhibition and an audio-visual presentation during its annual general meeting to keep the members informed of the developments.

All the shareholders were given a handout which reflected the government's attitude and the company's stand, outlining the role they as a group can play in helping the company in its problem.

Third-party endorsement through editorial support was constantly maintained. Letters to editors from friends and the general public were organized to be sent, journalists were taken for facility visits to the TISCO factory in Jameshdpur. Regular meetings with senior correspondents and various editors were arranged in three metros, viz., Delhi, Mumbai, and Calcutta, to keep them posted and enlist their support. The media persons were also mailed company literature during the campaign period.

JRD Tata, during his visits abroad, spoke to media about India, its industrial progress, and the government's role in the development which indirectly reflected Tata's role also in the nation building.

Industry support was enlisted through workshops and seminars on the steel sector and private sector's contribution to that. Films and audio-visuals were shown at various clubs like rotary and Lions Clubs to reach out to people whose opinion mattered.

Before the government could make its stand clear, though the tirade stopped thanks to the superb communication strategy of the Tatas, the government fell, and the congress-led government bounced back, and with that, the thought of nationalizing big business also died down.[30]

Case study of COPU visit to Salal HE project in J&K

The National Hydroelectric Power Corporation, a central public sector enterprise that was set in the mid-1970s, had a few projects that were embroiled in various geological and technical problems, besides some of them facing the ire of insurgency within some states where the projects were located. The Salal Hydroelectric project, located in the state of Jammu & Kashmir, also had myriad challenges, besides that it was governed by the Indus Water Treaty with Pakistan, as the river Chenab, on which it was constructed, ran through both the countries. The treaty meant that a team of Pakistani engineers would visit periodically to ensure that there was no change in the design of the project. The COPU decided to visit the project in the mid-1980s. The general perception, reinforced by varying media reports, was that the project had a long way before it could be completed. Rarely did media talk of the immense geological problems the project was facing, or the innovations introduced by the organization in surmounting the technical snags. The project is located about 70 kilometers from the neared rail and airhead in the district Reasi. The present author comprised the team to manage the visit of one such COPU at the site. The team, under the chairmanship of the CEO, brainstormed on the issue, the possible queries that could come from the COPU members, and how to make NHPC's viewpoint clear, despite all the criticism, most of which was based on ignorance, misperceptions, and, in some cases, due to vested interests of local business and political interests.

As a hydro project is generally spread over a large territory, with different project components like tunnels, penstocks, dam, reservoir, powerhouses at various places, one cannot not get a holistic view at one place, so the first step in communication was to make a tabletop working model of the project in fiber glass to give a complete picture of the project, indicating problem areas. Flip charts were made to introduce various work components. A special presentation through OHP (overhead projector) was made, titled *Misperceptions VS. Reality,* appearing side by side that reflected the areas of misperceptions and NHPC's take on them. A short video of work progress was especially prepared for sharing with the team. The presentation room also had a pinboard carrying still pictures of various work components. Not to hide the criticism, some media clippings were also pinned on another board to generate discussion.

The visit was kept a secret, so that the local media did not crowd the place even before the NHPC team made the formal presentation. The local media, of course, got to know and met some members later.

The team, when it landed at Jammu, was taken to the company guesthouse in Jammu where a minute-to-minute program was drawn about what would be done, including hospitality and presentation. The team listened very carefully to the presentation by the CEO assisted by the project chief and asked many questions, made notes, etc. After about four hours, the team was taken to the project site by cars. The road to the project is quite difficult and uncomfortable. On the first day, the team was taken to one of the sites and to some crucial ones the next day, when one of the members asked if on the way back they could go via the Vaishno shrine, which was arranged instantly. It was during the 30-kilometer-long track both ways that the NHPC and COPU teams broke the official barrier and discussed myriad issues ranging from hydropower to spiritualism, from tacking on foot to using mules. Walking for miles together and sharing meals created a sense of camaraderie with the COPU team, which also had an octogenarian member of parliament, who walked all the way, giving tips on how important it was to take small steps and not fall prey to taking a rest in between that would make further walking painful. The team, though, did not share much about their impressions about the project while being there, but back home, NHPC found its efforts bearing fruit when COPU submitted its report. The basic premise from NHPC's perspective was not to be on the defensive, or hide facts, including sharing information on some calculated risks taken. NHPC top brass shared with the visiting COPU team everything, including the difficulties of working in a terrain that was not easy, the geological surprises that were encountered at every step, which were not envisaged when the project started, and, of course, the innovations that were making the difference. The issue of cost and time overruns was dealt with, keeping in view the information earlier. The COPU, it is believed, gave a very balanced report to the government on the project.

Case study discussion questions

Q.1. Critically analyze the Tata nationalization case study. Do you think the present-day media options, especially the Internet and social media platforms, could have given the company a better edge to fight its case more strongly? If yes, how, and which media would have been more useful? If no, why not?

Q.2. How, in your view, was the COPU visit handled? If you were in charge, what else could you have done? Discuss.

Notes

1 The author's request to a few government relations and corporate communication officers of private and multinational companies to share their government relations' model or strategies failed on the plea that it was dynamic and could not be put in as many words.
2 Surojit Mazumdar, "The Corporate Sector and Indian Industrialization-a Historical Perspective", in *Indian Industrial Development and Globalization*, 2009 (New Delhi: Academic Foundation), pp. 193–233.
3 Press Information Bureau, pib.gov.in.
4 Chalapati Rao and Atulan Guha, "Ownership Pattern of the Indian Corporate Sector-implications for Corporate Governance", ISID Working Paper 2006/09.
5 Surojit Majumdar, "The Corporate Sector and Indian Industrialization-a Historical Perspective", in *Indian Industrial Development and Globalization*, 2009 (New Delhi: Academic Foundation), p. 228.
6 *Source*: www.ficci.com
7 ***Source***: www.cii.in
8 Ibid.
9 *Source*: www.assocham.org
10 *Source*: www.scopeonline.in
11 Ibid.
12 http://pib.nic.in/release/release.asp
13 Stuart Thomson and Steve John, *Public Affairs in Practice: A Practical Guide to Lobbying*, India edition, 2008 (New Delhi: Kogan Page), pp. 1–5.
14 Electoral Bonds_Press RELEASE_2-1-2018.pdf (dea.gov.in)
15 Electoral Bonds—Supreme Court Observer (scobserver.in)
16 www.parliament.uk/about/contacting/lobbying.cfm.
17 C. Miller, *Politico's Guide to Lobbying*, 2000 (London: Politico's Publishing), p. 4.
18 C. Sauza and I. Dale, *Directory of Political Lobbyists, 1999–2000*, 1999 (London: Politico's Publishing), p. 1.
19 Stuart Thomson and Steve John, *Public Affairs in Practice: A Practical Guide to Lobbying*, India edition, 2008 (New Delhi: Kogan Page), p. 5.
20 For details of the Sting operation, including the names of the MPs and questions asked, log on to www.cobrapost.com.
21 S. Harrison, *Public Relations-an Introduction*, 2000 as cited in K. Milner, *The Growth of Consultancy Lobbying Firms in UK*, 2006. Leeds Business School, UK, as quoted by Thomson, Stuart and John Steve in Public Affairs in Practice: A Practical Guide to Lobbying, Kogan Page, 2007.
22 Harold Gould, *How South Asians Forged an India Lobby in Washington*. Gould A Harold, Sikhs, Swamis, Students and Spies: The India Lobby in the United States, 1900–1946 First Edition, Sage Publications, 2018.
23 https://www.peoplesreview.com.np/
24 The Economic Times, 29 January 2009.
25 The Economic Times, 21 July 2005.
26 The PR Review [Fall 1997].
27 The Times of India, 9 June 2009.
28 www.ogilvygr.com/what.cfm
29 Ibid.
30 Adapted from the case study that was published in volume II of PR Case studies, brought out by the India Foundation for Education and Research, 1992.

6

WRITING FOR MEDIA AND MEDIA RELATIONS MANAGEMENT

6.1 Understanding media in the context of corporate communication

Today media is all-pervasive. It has become a vital source of information for people. It is a key industry and source of employment and profit. Media has provided a platform for major social, political, and economic debates. It is a source of entertainment for billions of people.

The perception about the impact of media generally oscillates between two extremes—that "it has a great impact" to "it does not impact lives." The bias of the content often determines how the audience would perceive media. Many research studies contend that media does influence and is also influenced by society. Media both mirrors and reflects society. Media is not outside of society; it too is a social institution, linked with other social institutions, sharing common history and culture. People working in media come from the same social milieu and inherit the value system the same way others do.

McQuil ascribes five important attributes of mass media that lends it significance.

1. ***A power source***: Media is the primary means of transmission and source of information in society.
2. ***Media is in an area of public affairs***: Government organizations and the corporate sector, because of various regulations, are often in the media glare.
3. ***A definition of social reality***: Media is a forum where the changing culture and the values of society and groups are "constructed, stored and visibly expressed."
4. ***A primary key to fame and celebrity status***: First they were people from the entertainment industry, later the sports persons, now even corporate honchos, who have acquired celebrity status in the media.
5. ***A benchmark for what is unusual***: It is not uncommon for media to define morality and ethical norms on various issues, especially environment protection, labor, corporate governance, etc.[1]

DOI: 10.4324/9781032694702-6

6.1.1 *How does corporate communication fit in the scheme of things for media?*

The raw material for media is information that comes from various sources and what the reporters gather on their own. In other words, media depends both on primary and secondary data. Reporters sometimes may use one source in filing their story or multiple sources for making investigative stories. Corporate communication is a platform for accessing both kinds of sources of information for the media. Let us look at more closely the various sources of information for media.

6.2 Primary sources for media

6.2.1 *Personal contacts*

The worth of a journalist is gauged from his networking capabilities and grooming of sources through personal contacts. It is important to keep a diary of contacts, both telephone and e-mail contacts, in soft and hard copies. Contacts are crucial to the very sustenance of a journalist. Good journalists even keep a note of the area in which various persons will be useful while maintaining their contact list.

6.2.2 *Tip-offs*

Tip-offs are an important source of "breaking news" for the media. It is not uncommon to get tip-offs and cues from anonymous callers in the newsroom. Such calls come from various sources, like someone who could be a disgruntled employee or a whistleblower, while some could do it for excitement. When socialite Sheetal Mafatlal was caught at the Indian customs in June 2009 for walking away without declaring jewelry worth lakhs of rupees, the custom officers revealed to the media that it was on a tip-off from the Mafatlal family itself.

The subversive elements often have been informing the media houses in the nick of time about imminent terrorist attacks to create anxiety among people. It happened in the case of both Gujarat and Delhi bomb blasts (2008).

6.2.3 *Crime and emergency calls*

Most media houses make mandatory calls to the local police room to know about accidents, crime, thefts, etc. a few times a day. The journalists on the beat often visit the police PR cell for briefing and the place where the event happened.

6.2.4 *Politicians*

Journalists on the political beat are regular at meeting up with politicians. It is also not uncommon for politicians to invite journalists when they wish to share something or for informal get-togethers on festive occasions. A journalist has an uncanny sense about what will make news, so they find news ideas even during informal meetings.

6.2.5 NGO sector

NGOs are generally the advocates, who keep doing a lot of research to prove their point when advocating for or against an issue. They can be a great source of information for journalists.

6.2.6 Academia and experts

On an issue that needs expert comment or an academic perspective, journalists keep in touch with various experts and academics to make interesting news stories. Electronic media often invite such people in their programs.

6.2.7 Press conference, press meets, and facility visits/press junkets

The journalists get invited to various press conferences, one-on-one press interfaces, and are also taken by corporate sector to their plants and by politicians to trail the campaigns. These are occasions when a bright journalist can go beyond the official press note to make an interesting story.

6.3 Secondary sources for the media

The expression secondary source implies that the information already exists somewhere, say books, journals, the Net, newspapers, news releases, et al, which need to be accessed for use. Let us look at some of the secondary sources journalists rely on.

6.3.1 Press release

A press release is a written official document that comes from an organization to the media with a request for publication. The journalist and the copy desk, when including the facts and figures, ascribe it to the source. We shall discuss about press releases and its various kinds later in the chapter.

6.3.2 Wire services

Media houses often subscribe to various wire agencies for news. Gathering information for a newspaper is a Herculean task. Therefore, media uses various ways of getting stories. Wire agencies, at one time, supply stories to many media at a pre-determined yearly fee. The stories, when they appear in newspapers, carry the byline of the source. In India, many wire agencies exist that include both national and international. The prominent Indian wire agencies include the PTI (Press Trust of India), UNI (the United News of India) both in English and Bhasha, and Univarta in Hindi. There are many other smaller ones who supply feature service and news clippings to electronic media. Indian media also sources releases from some overseas agencies like Reuters, AP, AFP, and ANI.

6.3.3 Parallel media

With the proliferation of various media, especially the on-line media, it is not uncommon to access information from company sites, citizen journalists'/bloggers' sites, and corporate blogs. It is commonplace for print media to look at the various news bulletins of the electronic media on a day to expand on some interesting stories for their next day publication. Similarly, electronic media reporters often see interesting stories in the print media to cover them in detail in their various bulletins during the same day.

6.3.4 Letters to the editor

It is common for media to receive letters and e-mails from their readers and viewers, either commenting on certain coverage or giving their viewpoint. Many a times, some well-known people also do that. Publication of such mail or taking them up in the news bulletins also fills space and time, besides reflecting the public opinion.

6.3.5 Pre-scheduled public events

These occasions can generate many interesting stories. For instance, most papers carry a "Today's engagement" column that has the listing of important public functions in the city.

6.3.6 Newspaper advertisements

Ads, especially those that reflect mandatory information, public notices regarding bankruptcy, tender notices, *et al* can be sources for further investigations writing.

6.3.7 Corporate literature, annual reports, and global and country reports

Organizations often share corporate literature including annual reports and global and country reports to journalists on the beat. It is not uncommon to find critical stories appearing in the media based on facts and figures from these publications and their interpretation.

On the part of the corporate communication professional, he/she also needs to know the various genres of information that could go to the media at various points of time, like:

- Spot news
- Backgrounders
- Information for a feature
- Rejoinder
- Denial
- Facts and figures
- Pictures, graphs, and charts

6.4 Writing for the media

A corporate communication professional must do a lot of writing. Such writing is not generally ascribed to him/her, but facilitate narrative in the media about the company. The media writing would broadly cover the following:

1. News releases
2. Press handouts

3. Press notes
4. Rejoinders
5. Features

6.4.1 Factors for writing effective press releases

A news release must meet the basic news criteria. Some of which include the following:

6.4.1.1 Timeliness

Timeliness implies that the event is new. Timeliness may also depend on what is happening in the world around you and within your organization.

6.4.1.2 Relevance or consequence

Events and organizations have relevance if the media can see a potential impact on their readers and viewers.

6.4.1.3 Proximity

It implies that the news is local or has a local connection, if using local media. If the news were of national and international importance, the mainstream media would often take it.

6.4.1.4 Prominence—the VIP impact

Generally, people attract attention, and important people attract more attention. A visit by a minister, an international expert, or a celebrity would have news value for the media.

6.4.1.5 Rarity/Unusualness

People enjoy a break from the routine, and so do media. Small unusual events lighten a page or a program and help the media fill empty space. For instance, the *Times of India* has a "Bizarre" column that includes unusual stories from all over the world.

6.4.1.6 Human interest

Readers are interested in other people, even if they are not related. The daily work, triumphs, tragedies, and relationships of people being people have an inherent reader or viewer interest. Media and PR can both contribute in this regard.

6.4.2 Why are releases often rejected?

The expression "Unadulterated Garbage" is commonplace in media circles for most press releases. The media does not take many press releases seriously. The reasons are many, some of which would include the following:

- Badly written
- Organizational bias

- No reader interests
- No link with the area
- Old story
- Too long

In the following paragraphs, we shall discuss the various kinds of writing for the media. First the press release.

6.4.3 Various kinds of press releases

There are many kinds of press releases, some of which are discussed subsequently:

6.4.3.1 Announcement release

A new product, the opening of a new plant, an innovative drug, the latest annual report, and a new policy are occasions for an *announcement release*. For instance, the new "three-in-one anti-retroviral drug" for HIV patients would qualify for an announcement press release. The appointment of TRAI (Telecom Regulatory Authority of India) secretary, or the new board of directors appointed by the government in Satyam Computers, or manufacturing the world's cheapest car by Tata, the Nano, would qualify as an announcement release.

6.4.3.2 "Created press release"

An announcement often is not attractive enough to catch media attention. Hence some "dressing up" is done to get good coverage, or get coverage when there is "news lull." Inviting a celebrity or an expert to the premises often attracts media attention. For instance, the chief minister giving the first polio drop on "Polio Ravivar" or protagonist Amitabh Bachchan doing the honors can be a good material for a "created press release" as well as photo opportunity. Universities and colleges often invite their famous alumni to felicitate them on the annual alumni day, an exercise in image build-up. For instance, the Hindu College felicitated a number of its famous alumni on the Golden Jubilee Function of Old Student's Association in April 2009. The picture that accompanied the story had Imtiaz Ali, the director of Hindi blockbuster *Jab We Met*, Arjun Rampal, the *Rock on!* star, and *Slum dog Millionaire* co-director Lovleen Tandon, who have been in the news for their contribution to the Indian cinema. The story also reflected the names of some other famous alumni who may have not been able to make it to the event.[2]

6.4.3.3 Spot press release

While the earlier two can be planned, as the name suggests, "spot" release is written spontaneously, more often when a crisis happens, like the closing of a plant, adverse effect of a drug resulting in deaths/ailment, accident in a factory, an airplane crash, etc. All these occasions would call for informing the public through the media. In case of major accidents or other kinds of emergencies, calling for a press conference may be a better option. If that were so, a written press handout should also be distributed to the reporters.

6.4.3.4 Response news release

The media has many sources of information, and often news about an organization reaches them from sources other than corporate communication. A consumer activist group, an environmental lobby, or a competitor may make an adverse comment on your organization. On such occasions, the corporate communication manager will have to be ready to come up with a response release.

6.4.3.5 Feature news release

Developmental stories and features on topical issues can be worked at leisurely and supplied to the media. Media often takes up these stories for weekend reading or as fillers on weekdays.

6.4.3.6 "Bad" news release

In a reactive situation, especially a crisis, much like the spot release, the organizations volunteer in supplying news not so conducive to their image, but in the interest of sharing information and winning credibility of being the first to share information. A crisis always attracts media attention, so instead of media asking for the happening, it works better if the organization volunteers with the news. In the early 1990s, when the public sector company National Thermal Power Corporation (NTPC) had an accident during the trial runs of one of its plants located in Kahalgaon in Bihar, killing some, including Russian engineers, the company immediately sent video coverage, visuals, and a news release to media even before the news spread. It invited a lot of positive comments from the media for their proactive approach. The *Economic Times*, in fact, wrote an editorial on it.

6.4.4 Press handouts

A press handout is generally distributed to press persons at a press conference. The handout contains salient points of the issue for which the press conference has been invited. It is the job of the PR person to keep the issue in focus. A press handout also helps the scribe in quoting the source of news, if he missed any point during the conference.

6.4.5 Press notes

PR and media persons are interdependent on each other for news. In a press conference or during a press brief, the chief executive throws insights about various issues, which the reporters may be noting down. Smart corporate communication practitioners also note down such things and prepare a press note, which may be given exclusively to someone on demand. This would ensure accuracy on what the spokesperson said. In fact, as far as VIPs are concerned, press notes generally are given to scribes at the end of such meetings, to avoid being quoted out of context. Often, we hear spokespersons complain for being misquoted in the media.

6.4.6 *Rejoinders*

Rejoinders and denials are not similar. News from a competitor may attract a rejoinder. A factually wrong news item may invite a denial from the aggrieved party. It is very important to look at the news item microscopically and be sure before responding with a rejoinder on which would be a better strategy, taking it up with the media or keeping silent. Similarly, in case of a denial, be sure before you deny to the media that what the spokesperson said was untrue. Many a times, the scribes record interviews, either seeking prior permission, or without a formal permission. There is no point losing face when the media can prove your claim otherwise. To cite the example of Mr. Varun Gandhi, a BJP candidate for the 15th parliamentary elections in 2009, he was jailed for a "hate speech" he indulged in against a community. As soon as the opposition and the community representatives against whom he allegedly spoke against raised their voice, he complained of the footage being doctored by his opponents. The tape was called for by the Election Commission, who, after examining it, seemed convinced that the footage was original and not really doctored. There is a lesson for spokespersons and their media relations officers here. They need to realize that times have changed and recording both sound and visuals, cumbersome before, is very easy now. So the prudence lies in being careful, because denial would be more damaging than keeping quiet when one knows the truth about one's own doing.

6.5 Style considerations

Individual media have their distinctive styles and conventions of writing and broadcast. If one has to send a general release, then following a generic style is a safe bet. Some media houses have stylebooks, but not all have. Those who have to write or supervise media writing, it would help if a regular reading of some important newspapers and watching news channels is undertaken to absorb the style of individual newspapers and channels.

6.6 Structure of a news release

Most writers speak of the foolproof "five Ws and one H" formula to cover an event. These covers *who*, *what*, *when*, *where*, *why*, and *how*.

Which "Ws" are to be given preference in the first and second lead is a matter of judgment. Perception about this varies between the organization that issues the release and the media that receives it. To illustrate, it is not uncommon for organizations to start the release with what its CEO has to say. The media generally prefers to pick up the crux of the story, if it has readers' interest in it. The quote, if found suitable for the story, is then taken. It also depends who is saying it, the CEO of an unknown company or a stalwart like Ratan Tata or Narayana Murthy.

6.6.1 *The lead*

The news lead must meet the basic media requirement of getting the story across in the first sentence or two.

Some experts talk of the "20-second rule." If you have 20 seconds to tell a friend about your story, what would you say? Write that down, and you have the first draft of a summary lead.[3]

6.6.2 *The body*

What is the story about? A summary lead should contain that. What is in it for the reader? Provide a reason for further reading, followed by more details about the happening, building on the first lead.

The last paragraph often should contain general information or background about the source of the news, person who is the focus of the story, etc. For example, if a news release is about the launch of a new movie by a production house, the last paragraph should ideally contain the background about how long the production house has been in business, how many movies it has made, including some very successful ones. The names of the partners, or which company owns that production house, can also be indicated.

6.6.3 *Inverted pyramid*

There may be many ways of writing a press release, but one must bear in mind that the media is always short on time; hence, it is important that you write a release that is newsworthy and written in "media style," that is, the way a reporter would write his/her story. Over a period, press releases written in "inverted-pyramid" style have gained acceptance in the media circles.

6.6.3.1 What is an inverted pyramid style?

An inverted pyramid style of writing posits that the most important information in the press release need to be covered in the first one or two paragraphs to cover the essential "Five Ws and one H." As you proceed writing a press release, you must ensure that you write from the most important facts to the less important facts, as symbolized by the inverted pyramid. The wider base at the top signals the inclusion of most important facts. As the width of the pyramid keeps shrinking, the facts also must be lesser in significance.

If the press release is written in this professional style, it helps the news desk or the reporter picking up the story as soon as it reaches him, without wasting time in trying to find news from a long press release. It is generally said that the reporters and the news desk use their scissors mercilessly when they do not find relevance in the story in the first or second paragraphs of the news release.

The media may or may not take your headline, but the news release must always carry a headline so that the crux of the news is reflected instantly.

Many research studies suggest that most press releases never see the light of the day. They are binned without a second look. Some of the reasons for rejection, as said earlier, also include the following:

- The release has blatant publicity stuff for which paid space could have been the answer
- It does not have news value from media's perspective
- It is an old story
- It is badly written

In a nutshell, keep in mind the following when writing a news release:

EXHIBIT 6.1 CHECKLIST ON NEWS RELEASE WRITING

1. Write tight and get to the point
2. Avoid vagueness
3. Do not be redundant
4. Write for your readers
5. Proofread, read aloud, and let it sit
6. Do not plagiarize
7. Story should answer the five Ws and H, but not necessarily in one paragraph

The next exhibit has all the elements that should find place in a news release.

EXHIBIT 6.2 MODEL NEWS RELEASE FORMAT

Organization's name (use company letterhead preferably)
Address
Date
Contact:
Name
Phone (office/after-office hours/home)
Fax
E-mail
News release: For immediate release/or for publication/broadcast on or after. . . (indicate time and date)
Leave space for sub-editor to write headline
Headline (optional, but it's better to write)

Lead paragraph: (this must attract reporter's/news desk's attention immediately. It must encompass the story and make the sub-editor decide why he should include the story in readers' interest. Always double-space the story. Leave a couple of inches margin on the left for editing marks. Use the inverted pyramid format for the story.

When the press release ends, write "ends," or put a star mark to indicate closure. At the beginning of the page, write a key word and page number/total pages.

6.7 Ground rules for news release for broadcast media

From the point of view of news, the content of news release for print and broadcast media would be the same; however, in practice, the content of the release would be driven by the audio/video availability. Rarely would a television channel take a dry story, unless it is too critical and the visuals are not available. Many channels run such stories with "file shots"/stock shots. Broadcast writing is writing for sound/visuals. The writing for broadcast should be able to capture speech and speech patterns so that copy sounds natural when spoken on air. One also must be able to write to time. Any normal story would be taken for between 30–60 seconds. As the listeners and viewers of broadcast media can't see the attribution marks ("") so one has to be careful. Use one of the two alternatives:

Use direct attribution: for example, the CEO. . ., Mr. . . says that. . .
Use actualities—that is, a tape of the CEO making the statement

Write out numbers from one to nine and numerals for numbers from 10 to 999. Write words for numerical figures that are long, complex, or may not be obvious to the speaker, such as thousands, millions, second, third, fourth, etc. Write years as numerals, such as 2009.

6.8 Feature writing

Feature writing is an important part of corporate communication writing. Features can be written for both mass media and media for internal communication like house journals aimed at employees.

6.8.1 What is a feature?

From the corporate communication perspective, a feature story is one that does not have topical relevance, or urgency, but has appeal for readers. One scholar has defined features as those stories, which focus on a special angle of the news, for example, human interest stories, profiles, issues, or general topics. Features can be written on a variety of subjects like people, case studies, research findings, history of a brand/organization, special/commemorative occasions, etc.

The greatest difference between news writing and feature writing, according to analysts, is the style of approaching the subject. While most news releases are bound by the Five Ws and one H or the inverted pyramid style, a feature can be creative and innovative in approach to hold people's interest. A feature writer can use narrative lead, chronological lead, descriptive lead, anecdotal lead, or a teaser lead to attract readers' curiosity and interest.[4]

An important difference between a news item and a feature is that in the former, the climax is at the top, while in the latter, the climax can be gradually built until the end to retain readers' interest.

6.9 Managing media events

There are two kinds of events, one the "created" and the other "spontaneous" or "reactive." The former is planned to get the desired media mileage as a deliberate effort on the part of the organization, and the latter is organized to meet an urgency or in the aftermath of a crisis to give an organization's point of view.

Let us look at some of the media events.

6.9.1 Press conference

Press conference is an occasion when an organization invites a cross section of media reporters through a formal invite at a designated time and place. A press conference is held for various reasons, viz., to declare profit and loss account of the company at the end of a financial year, to release some important report of public interest, demonstrate a new product or express solidarity among the top management after some fiasco, to clarify a misperception floating in the media to answer media queries. A press conference is generally used as an occasion for release of news simultaneously to all media, provided the subject is newsworthy. Most organizations organize at least one press conference yearly as a proactive corporate communication strategy to declare their profit and loss position. At other times, a press conference is organized after a crisis has happened and the organization wishes to share its point of view to its stakeholders through the media. The corporate communication manager, in fact, is the MC (the master of ceremonies), being solely in charge of organizing the press conferences from the word go to the follow-up with media.

6.9.1.1 When should one organize a press conference?

The answer is, not very often. A press conference should ideally be organized when the press release cannot be substituted for it. In other words, only if a discussion is warranted between the organization's spokesperson and the media should one call for a press conference. The key to success of a press conference depends on the teamwork.

Consider the following preparations for holding a press conference:

Pre-event
Event
Post-event

6.9.1.2 Pre-event preparations

- The purpose of calling the press conference and what desired response the management is seeking should be discussed threadbare. This will clear the haze and help in formulating the strategy.
- A decision about the spokesperson, that is, who would address the conference, may be taken, keeping in view the purpose of the said conference. Remember, the corporate communication manager should never address the press conference. The spokesperson should ideally be the head of the organization or a department. (Some exceptions, however, are seen in practice in India, as far as the armed forces and the Ministry of External affairs are concerned. The person designated as press officer or public relations officer does the routine press briefing.).
- Prepare a press kit that should ideally have a press note, pictures/graphs, literature about the organization, a writing pad, and a pen/pencil.
- Make the list of invitees from the media carefully. The list should comprise those who cover your organization.
- Decide on the venue. Make sure that it is suitable for the media.
- Decide for transport of media persons from a convenient place to the venue and for the return journey.
- Decide on the timing. It should neither be too early nor too late in the day. The conference should end at such a time that the media persons are able to get back to their place of work to file the story on time.

- Arrange for hospitality. Depending on the timing, it can be a lunch or high tea. The venue should ideally be next to the press conference.

6.9.1.3 Event

The room where a press conference is being held must be comfortable, with good acoustics and enough seating capacity to accommodate the invitees. It should not be too large to look empty and not too small to be inadequate for all those who arrive.

The head table can have three to four chairs. The spokesperson may have his deputies sitting on either side. It is not unusual to let the subject expert speak, should a question from media so demand.

If the seats don't have a fixed microphone system, then a wireless microphone should be handy to be passed on to the journalist who is asking the question. Someone from the corporate communication department must be on his/her feet to pass on the microphone to various journalists.

As a corporate communication manager, you must be in command of the entire situation. After the spokesperson and media have taken their seats, formally introduce yourself and the spokesperson and others occupying the chairs on either side of the spokesperson. After his initial address, which can be verbal, or a PowerPoint presentation, invite the media persons to ask questions. It is always better to set a time frame for the conference to continue. Depending on the occasion, a time span of 45 minutes to one hour should suffice.

Normally, once the press conference begins, the corporate communication manager could also take a seat and watch the proceedings and get up to announce that there was time for the last two to three questions. Sometime, however, you may have to interject or ask a "friendly" journalist to ask a question (this generally is briefed beforehand), when the spokesperson has been pushed into a corner by a reporter's question.

It helps if the corporate communication person has a good rapport with the media persons. This cannot be achieved in a day but requires concerted efforts over a period. Press conferences should not be the only occasions to meet media persons. There is no gainsaying that it serves the organization's cause better if it has a friendly media.

6.9.1.4 Post event

Ensure that journalists who had availed of your transport facility are dropped back. It is possible that there may be some more who may have not used your facility while reaching but would like to be dropped back; do plan when such requests come at the last minute.

Follow up stories the next morning, both in terms of coverage and qualitatively. It is possible that some papers, which were represented, did not cover the story. The reasons could be various, viz., the journalist did not file the story, he filed it but the story was not included as a deliberate choice of the desk, or it was removed at the last moment because of space constraint. Should the corporate communication manager take this up with the concerned media? There are two schools of thought, one that feels that it is the prerogative of the journalist or the media house to include the story or not—the corporate communication manager should not ask them about it; the other, especially the one represented by corporate communication and PR firms, who are more aggressive, feel that there is nothing wrong asking those journalists, because they have a client to answer back to.

6.9.2 Press briefings

A press briefing is different from a press conference in that it is informal and does not require elaborate arrangements. Press briefings can be both proactive and reactive. By proactive, it is meant that certain clarification or points are required to be given after a crisis. In this case, certain media persons are invited for the press briefing. In a critical situation, it is also prudent to supply a written statement to avoid misquotation. In case of a reactive press briefing, a reporter could seek an audience with the chief spokesperson for getting certain clarifications or to have spokesperson's byte before filing the story. Similarly, if a spokesperson has been misquoted, he calls for a press briefing.

6.9.3 Press tour

A press tour varyingly known as facility visit or a press junket, especially in the West, is much like the press conference, except that it needs elaborate arrangements. It requires a press party to be taken either within the city or elsewhere, including overseas. The occasions that warrant such visits include a landmark achievement/commissioning of a plant or an accident at site. Both kinds of occasions require careful handling.

While inviting reporters to join the facility visit, it is advisable to write to their editors or chiefs of bureau of various newspapers and programs in charge of radio and television channel. In normal circumstances, sufficient notice must be given, because the concerned reporter may have to be spared for several days from the place of work, if the press party is going out of station. Here is a checklist in Exhibit 6.3 for the press tour.

EXHIBIT 6.3 CHECKLIST FOR FACILITY VISIT FOR MEDIA PERSONS

Occasion
Invitation
Arrangements (transit/boarding/lodging/hospitality)
Preparation at site
Press backgrounder
Briefing press party at site
Site visit
Embargo for news (In case of accidents, arrangements for facilitating reporters to send dispatch from site to respective offices (Internet/direct-dial telephone/fax/etc.).
Follow-up

6.10 Media relations management

Media relations management is said to be the proverbial "Achilles' heel" for many a corporate communication practitioner. Effective media relations management is challenging, if not impossible, to handle. The success of a corporate communication manager, for whatever reasons, is often gauged by the management on his getting positive publicity for the organization. A bad media report on a day means he must answer to the management on something that was not his doing anyway.

Before one embarks on media relations, it is very important to understand media, its sociology, its expectations, and its limitations.

Media provides a very important bridge between organizations and its various stakeholders. Hence, there is no *avoiding* or *evading* the media. It is important to understand media requirements and respond to their information needs and at the same time mentor them to suit your organization's communication needs. It is important to bear in mind that media is nobody's friend, but at the same time it is not unfriendly. Media has a job to perform. News, as someone has said, is oxygen for the media. Being of help to media in providing facts as they are and sending as fast as one can not only helps media perform its job but also makes the practitioner a credible source for it.

There is a general feeling that a reporter can "place" the news in the newspaper. If you were to ask a media practitioner, he would categorically tell you that a reporter hardly has this kind of clout. A reporter can only file his/her story in a credible and convincing manner; the "placing" of the story is the prerogative of the sub-editor or sectional editor of that edition. It boils down that when a corporate communication manager is giving a story to the media, it should have the facts, figures, arguments, logic, credibility, and, most importantly, the capacity to influence readers to the extent that the sub-editor decides to include it.

The other important issue for consideration is the timing of information delivery to the media. In the print media, each page in a newspaper and each news item in a newspaper page have a deadline. To illustrate, each news item in a paper needs to pass through the hands of the chief sub-editor and the composing assistant. The computer has cut short the need for the composing assistants now. In most newspapers, the reporter's story reaches the sub-editor electronically. The setting of the page would, however, require someone to decide what would appear where in a page, and that is where the role of the sub-editor comes. The corporate communication person, hence, must know the right time for his organization's news to reach the media house and sub-editor's desk. This would mean that he must feed the reporter well in advance so that he makes the story and send it to sub-editor's desk well on time. It should be neither too late or too early, to avoid it is being "killed."

"As with all relationships," write Argenti and Forman,

> media relations is a two-way street, requiring positive efforts on your company's part to ensure success. The media typically does not get excited about the good things the companies do. . . If negative media interest develops, solid relationships and open lines of communication with various messengers of the media will be of great use to your company.[5]

6.10.1 How to cultivate effective media relations

Effective media relations are the key to successful corporate communication. However, it is a long process to build a relationship with the media fraternity that is based on mutual understanding and trust. The following issues are crucial to effective media relations.

6.10.1.1 Develop your organization as a beat

The foremost quality of a corporate communication manager is to think and work like a journalist. The first step is to develop the organization he/she is working as his/her beat as a journalist would do. Gather information, understand the dynamics, and visit sites to see the production process, learn technical jargon, and understand innovations, so that when writing for the media, it would be possible to convert the technical and difficult information in a generalist fashion. Most of the journalists are not experts in the field they report on, but they are able to convert the technical jargon in common man's language. For instance, during the economic recession, it was not uncommon to find newspapers explaining in their various stories the meanings of various terms like "inflation," "deflation," "recession," with illustrations on what it would mean to people's lives.

Having done that, study the sector in which you are placed, the competition, the size, the market, the futuristic projections, the expert view, etc. All this comes with time, but only if one is interested. It is important for the corporate communication manager to not only be knowledgeable but also perceived as someone who knows the subject and can be of help to the media. Providing information to a journalist and at times telling him where to source information from and who to contact for that story would gain him/her great respect.

6.10.1.2 Create a media cell within the corporate communication department

As a first step, it is important to create a media cell with persons who are most suitable for the job. If someone from the media has joined the corporate communication department, then he/she will be suitable as such a person would have the firsthand experience of media functioning and dynamics. He/she also would have many friends in the media, so facilitation is easier. If you do not have someone from media joining the department, then pick up persons who have good writing skills, are voracious readers, hardworking, with sharp reflexes, and extroverts, but at the same time cautious and mature. In case you have an external firm also helping in the media relations, an ideal combination would be a team from both sides.

6.10.1.3 Maintain media archives

It is important to keep a track of what appears in the media and archive them for future reference. This serves as a gold mine for the department as one can flip back and see how different media covered the organizations at various points of time and how the scribes handled the issue. The DMRC (Delhi Metro Rail Corporation) maintains the archives impeccably by cataloguing news clippings and binding them chronologically.

6.10.1.4 Good media relations depend on your synergy within the organization

Corporate communication is not just about communication per se but understanding the need and value of communication for various processes, achievement, and the uniqueness of products and services of an organization. For instance, in a marketing-oriented organization, it is marketing that needs to drive communication. Understanding the dynamics and the nuances and imbibing the spirit in media stories will help attain organizational goals. Working in isolation of key functions will deny corporate communication its due role and recognition.

6.10.1.5 It is the quality and not quantum that matters

It is not uncommon to hear from corporate communication managers after every event about how many clippings they were able to generate. Many convert the space into advertising equivalency to impress upon the management the value of the coverage in money terms. Remember that it is the quality and not quantity that matters.

A common joke about certain companies in media corridors is the quantity of press releases they churn out, which may not even deserve a second look. One scribe put it bluntly when he said: crying wolf does not help them. When the wolf really comes, there is no one to help them, meaning when there is genuine story, it too has chance of getting killed. In an age of fierce media relations by PR and corporate communication firms, it is not uncommon to see this happening, because they get paid on a pre-commitment of certain coverage.

6.10.1.6 Understand journalists' needs

The raw material for a journalist is information, for which he literally would "beg, borrow or steal," as goes the maxim, to write his story. Understand his genuine need, so you can provide him with relevant and timely information. But in case you cannot, make it very clear to him; he would appreciate an honest refusal. A journalist is a professional whose entire existence depends on good stories, so he would get to the bottom of the story anyway. It is said that once a journalist, always a journalist. Therefore, you must not share anything off-the-cuff and then expect him not to include it in his story.

6.10.1.7 The unchangeable truth about media

A corporate communication manager must understand some ground realities about media. They will run their newspapers and channels as any other business.

The consumer (viewer/reader) will be the epitome of focus (to give him/her what he/she expects or decide on their behalf what is good for them—an area that is critical but cannot be denied). When in crisis, there would be media encroachment that needs to be appreciated from media's perspective.

6.10.1.8 Handling negative press

It is impossible not to get negative press sometime, either for something the organization was guilty of or on a perception of wrongdoing. Both situations need careful handling. In a crisis, some damage is inevitable, but it is important to keep the human concern topmost. The organizations must be very careful about the use of words and imagery in such times. The issue has been dealt with in greater detail in Chapter 10: Crises communication.

The biggest impediment in media relations, according to Sandra Oliver, happens to be the perceived perception about corporate communication and public relations being manipulative in projecting the organization in a certain way to achieve positive coverage.[6]

6.10.2 Interdependence of media and corporate communication

Corporate communication and media are inseparable, because most of the corporate communication is achieved through media. There is no denying that the most important information resource for the media is the individual, both the authorized one who speaks on behalf of the organization, and also the one who provides a "tip-off," he/she could even be an adversary. Therefore, it is important for a corporate communication practitioner to be an important source of information for a journalist, who covers his/her organization. Without the reporter, the corporate communication person is without a medium through which he/she could get mileage for the organization, similarly, without the official information source, the reporter is without an important authorized source. Some journalists may like to gather information from various sources, which include staff, moles, obtain leaks, rumors, or bits of information, but there can be no substitute for an authentic and reliable news source. There is no denying the fact that no matter what non-newsmen think, all reporters the world over value trustworthy news sources above mere informants, rumormongers, and malcontents.

There are some press release dissemination services that the corporate commensuration professionals and agencies can make use of for wider reach. A mention has been made in Chapter 2 of one such agency floated by several PR firms, bloggers, and search engines put together called the PR-US Net, which promises dissemination at a price. In the Indian context, the Times Group has launched MediaNet that allows paid publicity to corporate news that it calls "uncensored." This, of course, has met with severe criticism from within the media itself. For details, refer to Chapter 2: Media dynamics and strategies.

6.10.3 What do media expect from corporate communication?

Having said that, media and corporate communication are interdependent; each has certain expectations from the other. Let us have a look at what media expects from corporate communication:

- Media expects up-to-date information
- Media expects nothing to be hidden from them
- It expects the corporate communication manager to provide information faster, accurately, and truthfully
- Concoctions and half-truths are abhorred by the media

Remember, corporate communication is only one source of news for the media, there is no stopping a journalist to use more than one source for the story. If a scribe does not find a corporate communication manager useful, he/she will be bypassed next time.

6.10.4 What does corporate communication expect from media?

- Corporate communication professionals expect media to trust them.
- They expect media to understand and appreciate their professional role as well as constraints.
- They expect media to give the organization's perspective in the story and not be judgmental.
- They expect media to check back on facts, especially when the story being written has a negative slant.

6.10.5 Strategic media handling

It is very important to make use of a strategy for arranging media coverage. There are certain do's and don'ts in media handling, some of which have been articulated subsequently:

1. Do not choose a day for a press release or press conference when there is something big happening in the city/country, for instance an Olympics inaugural, a polling day, announcement of election results, an international summit or some untoward emergency, which has kept the media busy. Chances are, you will not have many reporters coming for the conference or attending to your press release.
2. Include visual and graphics in your news release. Try to put assorted visuals along with a general press release so that most of them get "exclusive" pictures. Reporters generally drop pictures that come along with news releases in the belief that the same may have gone to 20 others. Inform the reporter about the exclusivity of the visual. If there are statistical diagrams and charts, send a soft copy or a Link to drive for high resolution pictures/video/graphics.
3. Update your media list periodically. Journalists also change desks and jobs.
4. Organize media facility visits to your plant occasionally so that they can get the realist part of the story and, in the process, build transparency between the organization and the media.
5. Brief the spokesperson about the journalist, his writing style, and his political leanings, if relevant, beforehand. A mock interview is not a bad idea for the novice in media interface.
6. For an exclusive interview with a reporter, send background information to the reporter in advance. This often sets the tone for discussion, and the interviewee also starts confidently.
7. The corporate communication officer should invariably be present in all briefings and media interaction with the organization's spokesperson.
8. Be an avid media consumer and observe writing styles, program formats, and issues undertaken by the electronic media. In critical times, compare various newspapers/media on their perspective on the issue.
9. Build a good working relationship based on trust with the media staff, in particular the reporter assigned to cover your organization.
10. Submit only "fresh" news.
11. Use the "5 Ws and one H" in news reporting, that is, who, what, when, where, why, and how, as discussed previously in the chapter.

12. Use material that will be of interest to the public.
13. Be accurate—check and recheck figures, facts, spellings, dates, locations, and names.
14. Avoid technical terminology/jargon.
15. All copy should be typewritten or computer-generated. Leave at least two inches margin on the left of the page for copy-editing.
16. Learn to observe deadlines. This is critical not only for daily newspapers and 24-7 news channels but also for weekly or biweekly publications.
17. Present your case well. Do not insist media on including certain facts; it may not be appreciated.
18. It is not a good idea to criticize the media, but in case of some serious error, do take it up with the concerned media house.
19. If "news" is only to achieve an organizational end, then it is a good idea to issue it as a paid advertisement.
20. Visuals. Large newspapers send a photojournalist along with the reporter to cover a story that needs visuals. However, keep assorted pictures ready for distribution. Provide digital images of photographs if requested by a newspaper. JPEG format is most often used in 300 dots per inch (dpi). This resolution level is required for print reproduction. If a photo shoot is taking place within your facility, photo releases, signed by photo subjects, need to be released.

Write the names of the people in a photograph from left to right. Do not write on the back of the bromide. Type the names and paste the paper on the back of the bromide. The best option is to send digital images.

Be careful about spellings and designations of people appearing in the picture. Double-check if in doubt. Exhibit 6.4 is a ready reckoner for handling media in a crisis.

EXHIBIT 6.4 CHECKLIST FOR HANDLING MEDIA IN A CRISIS

1. Make quick analyses of the situation. Know the truth first to be able to handle the issue intelligently, quickly, and in the interest of the organization. If the problem persists for long, it is useful to get a perception study from an outside expert/organization to gather honest insights about the problem.
2. Announce an emergency telephone number and website so that the affected/interested people and media can be in touch.
3. It serves the cause of the organization better if a single contact person answers to the media.
4. Hold a press conference if necessary. At the same time, it is recommended to avoid holding the press conference if a press release can serve the purpose.
5. In case of deaths, express empathy and concern, even if the organization was not directly involved in the calamity.
6. Always make positive statements about the organization and programs.
7. The organization has to honestly give a feeling that any problem is of utmost importance to it.

8. Have an action plan ready. The public and the media would always want to know what are you doing to avoid similar eventualities in future.
9. Reach the media before it reaches you.
10. Be committed to open and honest communication.
11. Every situation has more than one perspective. Knowing the exact truth and circumstances under which the eventuality happened takes time. Hence don't immediately admit or pass on blame to others. It will not only be seen hasty but also insensitive.
12. Tell the facts as they develop. Rely on investigative sources for details.
13. Never say "no comment."
14. Issue a prepared statement to the media as soon as possible, and follow-up.

6.11 Preparing the spokesperson for media interface

Not many spokesperson are enthusiastic, giving media interviews. Ask an average CEO; it is the last thing on his/her wish list. As much as they would like to keep media at arm's length, it is not possible, because that is one of the prices of being at the top. If we look at the flip side of the argument, it is through media that one can reach out to a large section of people and establish a great reputation for the company. The shareholders can feel reassured when they look at the sincerity and honesty of the top brass when quoted in media. Difficult as it may be, it is not impossible to cultivate a healthy relationship with media, based on mutual trust and confidence.

It is one of the foremost tasks of the corporate communication manager to aid and advise the top brass on media handling and prepare the spokesperson on media interface.

Let us look at the areas.

6.11.1 Face-to-face interview

There are occasions when the spokesperson may face a reasonably large media group when addressing a press conference, while at other times he could be having a formal or informal chat with a reporter on a one-on-one basis. Both kinds of media interface need a good amount of preparation. There may come a situation when a spokesperson is facing a large bevy of journalists; it is here when the corporate communication manager needs to curate it strategically. On the part of the spokesperson, there is always a first time, and if someone says he was not nervous facing the news media persons the first time, he is lying. It needs a good amount of homework to be confident and on the mark.

The first step is preparing well on the subject/issue for which the press conference is being organized. Remember, a good outcome comes only through teamwork. It would be a good idea to get all the concerned experts and think of all the possible questions that could possibly be asked by journalists. There is nothing wrong to have the subject experts sitting on either side of the spokesperson in the press conference, who he can rely on when needed.

6.11.2 When facing many journalists

In case of a press conference organized after a crisis, the tone and tenor of media will be different. There will be a volley of questions, some straight, some not so. There is possibility of allegations, charges, etc. Maintaining calm, poise, and balance is very necessary. Journalists often ask provocative questions to provoke the spokesperson in giving them a good sound bite. The spokesperson needs to be advised that questions rarely appear; it is the answer that may bring damage if one is not careful. If there are television cameras rolling, it is even more important to keep a watch on both verbal and non-verbal communication, including facial expression and gestures, because they would communicate more loudly than words. Former Home Minister Shivraj Patil was accused of being indifferent during the Delhi blasts in October 2008, because the media felt he was busy changing his dress for so many times, going from one venue to the other. It was unfortunate to trivialize the issue to that extent, till he called some select media reporters in his office the next day to give them a bit of his mind. His body language reflected his anger and annoyance. He said defiantly that what was wrong if he changed his dress during the day. Did the media find him drinking or playing cards on that day to create so much uproar? Interestingly, rebuked by the home minister, the story was buried by all and sundry. This could be an exception, because a very senior public figure was involved; the CEOs can never get the chance to reply angrily.

6.11.3 One-on-one interviews

In case of a one-on-one interview with journalists, it is important to brief the CEO about the journalist, his writings, and political leaning, if any. The CEO must be told to try and avoid giving any off-the-cuff/out-of-context remarks, as often these become the headlines. If he does not wish to be quoted on a certain issue, the journalist must be informed in advance. In most cases, the journalist would respect that, but he may not if the real "meat' in the story came from that information.

Journalists, in general, do not appreciate if you were to tell them how to use the quote or see the manuscript before they file the story.

In case of a television interview, it would be worthwhile to brief the CEO about the program format, the kind of audience that is going to watch the program, and a good rehearsal on both verbal and non-verbal language. The television house has the editing facilities, and it is not uncommon to find the answer coming in pieces, changing the whole context. Experts suggest that if one restricts the time of each sentence to a maximum of ten seconds referred to as the "Ten-Second Formula" by some, it would be very difficult to edit it. Television producers and scribes in India often appreciate Mr. Lalu Prashad Yadav for his short and succinct bites that defy all chances of being edited.

6.11.4 Telephonic interviews

In this day and age of media proliferation and 24-7 news channels, it is not uncommon for spokespersons to receive calls for a sound bite on some issue that may concern that organization's product or policy. The CEO must be advised on how to respond to such requests. Senior journalists do not appreciate if they are asked to be routed through the corporate communication manager or the PR firm. However, if the CEO wishes to give a prepared answer, he can always tell the scribe to allow him sometime, as he is busy in something, unless the call has come for an ongoing crisis in which his organization is embroiled. It will be insensitive not to respond to the call or take time, unless some facts are requested, which may take some time to gather. Checking the antecedent of the caller is not a bad idea. If the call is routed through secretarial staff, then it is easy to tell the scribe to leave the number, as the CEO is busy or on other line. Probably, the telephonic interview would be taped, if sourced from a media house, so the spokesperson must be careful in giving his viewpoint.

6.11.5 Interviews by e-mail

It is not uncommon for journalists, especially from periodicals, to send a list of questions to an organizational head for inclusion in a feature-based story. In this case, the receiver gets enough time to prepare and send answers to the requesting scribe. It would be a good idea to check back the e-mail ID. Any good journalist would invariably use his/her official e-mail ID to establish credibility, and not use the personal one.

In the age of new media, it is possible to address the media through video conferencing, connecting with many places, countries, and continents. Many companies are even trying the route of social networking sites, interfacing with communities to keep a finger on the public opinion pulse.

Journalists can at times be demanding and intimidating, little realizing that an average person does not enjoy being under the media lens. Helen Sissons puts it very aptly when she writes,

> Journalists forget sometimes that for many people being interviewed by the media can be a daunting experience. It may be the first time they meet journalists, we owe it to people who talk to us to be fair and accurate and to respect their confidence.[7]

Having said it, there is no wishing away media. So the best course is to understand the importance of media in giving your organization the necessary mileage, appreciate journalists' need for information, and prepare well.

Summary

In this chapter, we looked at what can truly be said to be the heart and soul of corporate communication practice, viz., writing for media and media relations. We looked at the interdependence of media and corporate communication and the need for mutual respect for each other's domain.

A corporate communication practitioner must do a lot of writing for the media, which is not ascribed to him/her. Various kinds of media writing like press releases, rejoinders, and features were discussed with tips on style and content.

The chapter then moved on to the handling media events. How to organize press conferences and facility visits were discussed in detail, with some hands-on tips on effective handling of events.

One of the important tasks of a corporate communication practitioner is to aid and advise the top management on media interface. Hands-on skills were discussed on "grooming" the spokesperson in handling media effectively.

Key terms

Announcement release: a new product, the opening of a new plant, an innovative drug, the latest annual report, and a new policy are occasions for an *announcement release*.
"Bad" news release: refers to an organization issuing a press release after a crisis voluntarily and proactively in the interest of sharing an adverse happening with the public at large.
Denial: a factually wrong news item may invite a denial from the aggrieved party through a press release.
Electronic media: a term used for broadcasting media, viz., radio and television.
Feature news release: refers to writing a developmental story on a topical issue.
Inverted pyramid style: it is defined as writing the most important information in the first one or two paragraphs to cover the essential "five Ws and one H" (who, what, when, why, where, and how).
New media: refers to the Internet, social networking sites, and the blogosphere.
Media reach: refers to the percentage of people in various SEC categories accessing media.
Media characteristics: refers to the relative strengths and weaknesses of each medium, keeping in view its inherent characteristics.
Media relations: a term used for maintaining a working relationship with representatives of the media fraternity who cover the organization.
Press briefings: a press briefing is different from a press conference in that it is informal and does not require elaborate arrangements.
Press conference: press conference is an occasion when an organization invites a cross section of media reporters through a formal invite at a designated time and place.
Press handouts: generally distributed to press persons at a press conference.
Press notes: generally written by the corporate communication manager while the spokesperson is interfacing with media. It is handed over to the scribes so that the spokesperson is not quoted out of context.
Print media: a term used for newspapers, magazines, journals, etc.
Press tour: it refers to an event when a press party is taken either within the city or elsewhere, including overseas, to cover an important occasion.
Response news release: issue of a press release in response to an adverse comment in the media from a competitor and NGO or an individual whom the company feels is not based on truth.
Rejoinders: news from a competitor may attract a rejoinder.
Spot press release: refers to a release written spontaneously when some emergency has occurred.
"Third-party" endorsement: the news that appears in the media is believed to have a third party or neutral perspective of reality and facts.
Trade media: used for newspapers, magazines, and news channels exclusively devoted to the financial sector, capital market, investments, and corporate news, etc.

Concept review questions

Q.1. Why, in your view, is media important in the practice of corporate communication? Discuss with examples.
Q.2. What are the various forms of press releases? Discuss all with an example each.
Q.3. How is a press release different or like a press note? Elucidate.
Q.4. Describe various kinds of media events in corporate communication.
Q.5. What are the various steps in organizing a press conference?
Q.6. How would you prepare the CEO for an interface with the media?

Critical thinking exercise

1. Watch an interview-based program on any mainstream news or trade channel carefully. If need be, record it to view it later more closely to analyze the verbal and non-verbal language used by both the interviewer and the interviewee.
2. There are several interview-based programs on various news and trade channels. Who, in your view, is the best interviewer, and why?

Notes

1 I. D. McQuil, *Mass Communication Theory*, 1994 (London: Sage) as quoted by Sandra Oliver in *Public Relations Strategy*, second edition, 2008, CIPR (New Delhi: Kogan Page), pp. 94–95.
2 The Asian Age, 12 April 2009.
3 Donald Treadwell and Jill B. Treadwell, *Public Relations Writing*, second edition, 2005 (New Delhi: Response Books), p. 238.
4 Ibid., pp. 270–271.
5 Paul A. Argenti and Janis Forman, *The Power of Corporate Communications*, 2002 (New York: McGraw-Hill), p. 225.
6 By Sandra Oliver in *Public Relations Strategy*, second edition, 2008, CIPR (New Delhi: Kogan page), pp. 96–97.
7 Helen Sissons, *Practical Journalism*, 2006 (New Delhi: Sage Publication Ltd.), p. 179.

7

CORPORATE COMMUNICATION IN BRAND PROMOTION

7.1 Introduction

Corporate communication, as we discussed in the first chapter, is the sum of communication activity generated by an organization to interface with its various stakeholder groups. Corporate communication integrates with marketing communication to support brand communication through various routes such as consumer public relations, media endorsements, sponsorships, and events. In the following paragraphs, we shall look at these corporate communication tools in brand promotion activities.

7.2 Consumer public relations

Consumer public relations, according to experts, is a part of the function of the corporate communication professionals who work in tandem with marketing and advertising departments to create a carefully tailored promotion program.[1]

Marketing planning encompasses various tasks like conception, pricing, promotion, and distribution of a product. Consumer PR is an important tool of promotion in the mix that aims at connecting the brand with consumers in a subtle manner.

A consumer PR campaign, when taken along with advertising, can be more effective than advertising, operating alone. Marketing, according to Harrison, can be befittingly assisted by brand public relations in three circumstances:

- Building and maintaining awareness
- Repositioning
- Overcoming negative perceptions[2]

Analysts believe that consumer communication has evolved from its narrow specialist function to becoming an indispensable component of overall marketing strategies.

Philip J. Kitchen and Don J. Shultz have argued about the emerging "turbulent" relationship between marketing and PR with the emergence of a newer discipline called

DOI: 10.4324/9781032694702-7

consumer PR. In a roundtable organized by *Advertising Age* journal for a special section on PR, a few marketing and strategy experts were invited to debate and deliberate on the role of PR in marketing. Some interesting viewpoints emerged.

One of the participants in the roundtable, David Selby, then chief marketing officer and senior VP of Potbelly Sandwich Works, felt that both PR and marketing were inseparable and needed to be integrated. PR, in his view, needed to look at long-term objectives on programs undertaken by them. For instance, the events in support of a brand did create the necessary buzz and hype, which may also result in media talking about it, but PR, he argued, must put a discipline and process in place that can think two or three steps ahead of the immediate need to understand how a brand will be maintained over a period.[3]

Jim Speros, who worked as the chief marketing officer, US, at Ernst & Young, almost echoed the same sentiment when he said that PR inputs do result in media coverage, but what was the return on investment? It was not about how many clips one got, he argued, but about whether the marketing mix in totality resulted in a surge in sales. Speros was emphatic when he said that whether it was advertising or PR, the state of the art was just not there. He reckoned the issue of press releases to "flash bulb marketing" without any follow-up. Great brands, he argued, were built over a period with sustained activity.

Andrew Kritzer felt that it was easy for marketers to have control of content in advertisements, but in PR one did not necessarily have any idea what spin was going to be put by various media on the information one was providing.[4]

There are PR diehards who feel that corporate PR has been an integral part of brand building for long enough to question its efficacy now. Critics of advertising argue that the big bang approach of advertising should be replaced by the slow build-up used by public relations to have a long-term impact on building strong brands. Public relations is seen by them as an important part of integrated marketing communication (IMC), which encompasses coordination and integration of marketing communication tools, avenues, and sources within a company into a seamless program that maximizes the impact on consumers and other end users at an effective minimal cost. The ideal marketing mix includes product, pricing, promotion, distribution, advertising, consumer promotion, personal selling, direct marketing, and public relations.[5]

With a plethora of products under various corporate brands, it is only prudent to create a sense of identity among the consumers about the umbrella brand. In the Indian context, Tatas probably is one of the strongest corporate brands that has transcended geographical barriers and is considered one of most respected brands not only within the country but also globally. The sheer brand name Tata is seen as a promise of quality, from soaps to jewelry, from trucks to hospitality, from steel to departmental stores. Tatas have never been aggressive in their communication, but whenever required, the brands have used advertising, albeit with "Tata ki guarantee ke saath" (with the guarantee of Tatas) or "A product from Tatas" accompaniment.

Post imbroglio over the Hindenburg report, the Adani Group in May 2023, at its completion of 35 years, came out with a PR campaign across media, "*Hum mushkilo ki nahi sunte, karke dikhate hai*" (Undeterred by challenges, we deliver on our commitments). Curated by Ogilvy, media reported, "The company celebrates the resilience, determination and indefatigable."[6] The campaign, in its 100-second TVC, brings home the point that when people did not believe that Adani's could do certain things, they did it (like power generation, packaged food, airports, etc.).[7] The campaign, in a way, must be a morale booster for its employees, besides sharing with other stakeholders, especially people in general and detractors of the group on its achievements.

In the survey conducted by the *Advertising Age* journal, it was found that senior marketers were divided on the role of consumer public relations in the overall marketing mix. Eighty three percent (83%) felt that PR was effective in creating awareness, 67% felt it provided credibility, 61% felt it educated customers. On the other hand, only 28% felt that PR input helped in prompting trial for a brand/service. Similarly, only 22% each felt that PR was able to persuade skeptics or drive sales. On asking how the PR firms contributed towards the marketing programs, 67% cited media contacts, 48% cited creative ideas, 45% said PR was like "arms and legs support" and strategic thinking, and only 29% cited PR's role in gathering competitors' and industry insights.

On a question about the role/s in which PR could be effective, 76% marketing experts saw PR value in supporting marketing, 72% saw it in product launches, while 65% saw PR's effective role in supporting the corporate brand. Surprisingly, fewer at 55% were impressed with PR's role in crisis management and 57% about corporate reputation management.

The survey was distributed to select *Advertising Age* subscribers. Of the more than 130 respondents, 41% described themselves as VP (marketing), 21% as chief marketing officers, 17% as presidents or CEOs. The largest respondents at 39% came from the consumer goods category, 22% from the industrial sector, 9% from healthcare, and 8% from technology.[8]

When the recession phase in 2008–09 affected sales across both FMCG and white goods, resulting in a slash of advertising budgets, some companies tried to keep their pots boiling by interfacing with their consumers through means other than advertising. The use of online marketing and use of social media in promoting brands is fast becoming a major part of consumer connect globally. When the Covid-19 pandemic spread its tentacles across the world from 2020–22, markets went behind many decades. In an atmosphere of lockouts, despondency, loss of jobs, companies both in white goods segment and FMCG, in general, kept away from advertising, bringing the entire media to a distress situation as their sustenance largely depends on revenue from advertising. Many in journalism and advertising lost their jobs.

7.2.1 Active consumer

Today's consumer has the tech command in her hand. The net, social media platforms, the multifunctional mobile, the media player, the digital television with a remote to order what she wishes to access make her a master of her choice. The customer care mechanisms put in place through professional BPOs make her life easier than before. The customer marketers are fast learning that they need to largely abandon "tried-and-no-longer-true" mass marketing techniques to identify the niche landscapes and determine how to connect with each customer individually with niche messages. Technology has made it possible to focus on key constituencies.

According to Gooderham, the consumption behavior of today's young generation is driven by two considerations; they are less trusting of business, and, second, they want business to help them make "guilt-free" purchases so that they can buy without bothering about the impact on their health and that of the planet. He argues that with this new consumer psyche and values, marketers can deliver it through innovative consumer connect that influences stakeholder opinion and behavior, while at the same time protecting the reputation of the organization.[9]

7.2.2 Changing styles of buying and selling

The real marketplace now has active competition from the virtual marketplace. For instance, when it all began, the eBay, an online mart, became immensely popular because of the various niches it provided to the customer and the unprecedented control over the purchasing process that it offers. About 200 million eBay buyers and sellers ran their own marketplace, finding the products that suit their needs, setting up ranking and feedback systems that have established trust in the market, controlling both products that are offered and the prices they are willing to pay. In fact, e-Bay can be credited for selling cars via the Internet for the first time. But as soon as the dealers felt that their role was being circumvented, they too joined the bandwagon of eBay to offer the cars nationwide in the US, creating their own niche and revenue system. Later, Amazon, Flipkart, Blinkit have completely changed the way an average consumer engages with the market. The coming of Unified Payment Interface (UPI) via the phone has only facilitated the transactions. The business of offline players and small shopkeepers has been affected immensely, but thanks to the digital economy progressing fast, roadside vendors and hawkers have got on to the UPI bandwagon.

Companies are engaging with their customers, especially Gen Z, in varying ways. PepsiCo company relied a great deal on bloggers to set Super Bowl advertising slots. Even just five days before the event in February 2009, the company was waiting for a response from the bloggers to decide which ads will best align with consumer interests. The company, in a press conference, unveiled the 3D versus Alien ads at the end of January 2009.

7.3 Caselets

7.3.1 Gillette sensor

In 1998, Gillette had to suspend its campaign of razor Sensor, because the company could not cope up with an unprecedented demand in the US. When it came to the UK launch, the company began with a low-key consumer brand PR, including a bit of women's press advertising. Countrywide advertising had the input based on research on what men and women considered a good pair of legs. Within three months, the sensor accounted for 40% of the razor market, demonstrating the impact of brand PR.[10]

7.3.2 Subway

Subway is the largest sandwich franchise and leader in the crowded quick-serve restaurant category globally. Subway repositioned itself using the PR route. It made Jared Fogle, the celebrity weight loss hero, its brand ambassador. The PR agency positioned Subway as a leader in addressing the growing obesity facing many Americans. It created a multi-layered integrated campaign to kick off Subway's partnership with the American

Heart Association as the national sponsor of American heart walks. Its media options included in-store promotion, spokesperson appearance, and targeted media relations. Jared visited schools, talking about his battle with weight loss. Promotional opportunities also included events such as the *American Idol* sponsorship and major league baseball balloting. The company also introduced several interesting products alongside. The campaign managed to receive a lot of coverage in top broadcast and print media that included the *Wall Street Journal*, the *Boston Globe*, *USA Today*, *Newsweek*, and *New York Times*. Stories were also carried in *CNN Headlines*, *Larry King Live*, the Jimmy Kimmel show, *MSNBC Live*, CNBC's *Squawk Box* and *Fox & Friends*.[11]

The toxic contents in mettle toys had parents worried, the reduction of iPhone prices within a week of its much-awaited launch had early buyers fuming, the worm-infested Cadbury chocolates had the multinational worried about its image, and Dell threatening to sue a blogger are some of the case studies in consumer public relations that have been included in details in the chapter on managing corporate reputations, which may be read along with this chapter.

A multi-pronged approach is required to get the mind share of the consumer in a highly competitive and media-cluttered environment. Let us look at some of the changing paradigms.

7.4 Innovative strategies in reaching out to customers

Marketers in India are also finding innovative methods to catch up with potential customers, which may not involve any formal media use. "Your next coffee break at work may be sponsored by a beverage company," said an interview-based article, as companies are trying hard to get at the captive and focused audience to sell their brands. The companies are focusing more on the BPO firms where the employees are said to have high consumption patterns. On this phenomenon, analysts believe that for promotional activities that require captive audience, or for products which need an explanation, office premises are preferred more than the shopping malls as they may have higher foot falls, but the attention span of the visitors is far lesser.

In an interview, late Anand Halve of Chlorophyll communication reasoned that some products have characteristics, which allow them to market themselves to a group in a defined environment; for example, the Gym becomes a perfect fit for promotion.[12]

The much-hyped Hollywood film *Snakes on a Plane* is believed to be as much the creation of fanatic consumers as it was Hollywood's technology. The hype generated by the bloggers forced the producers to retain the title *Snakes on a Plane* instead of the contemplated title *Pacific Air Flight 12*. The movie is believed to have been altered, which involved many days of extra shooting to fulfill growing fan expectations.

By entering some personal data, consumers could send a friend a customized voice message from Samuel L. Jackson, the film star, referring to the friend's name, job, car, and buddies.[13]

The promotion of any new movie now needs new technology-enabled public relations that include trailers, curtain raisers, audio clip, graphics, customized net sites, collaterals, main protagonists appearing on television reality shows, talk shows, news channels, and travel to various cities to connect with the audience. When *Delhi-6* was released in February 2009 in India, it preceded with all kinds of promotion stimulating the appetite of the people to watch the film. The hero of the film, as reported by the media, went to various cities, claiming to be the highest in a day, accomplished by any actor in the world that was to earn him a place in the *Guinness Book of Records*! This itself became news, earning more publicity footage for the film.

The disruptions in conventional marketing, feel many analysts, mean that across the board, organizations must change their mindset about technology and consumer PR. Having said that, the traditional expectations from PR—the third-party endorsement through media, building events, and activities to extend their news values to additional audiences—remain crucial. However, who the third party is, what comprises news, and where to organize the event in the tech age are issues that need to be understood and addressed to get the desired results. Similarly, the endorsement need not necessarily come from celebrities, but maybe someone who the audiences connect with emotionally.

Case study

Since the augmentation of the Net access, a lot of promotional activities can be seen on the Net. Film producers seem to have made the most of it. The first film to go whole hog on promotion was *Slum Dog Millionaire*. Many have joined the bandwagon.

Creating the necessary buzz—the *Slum Dog Millionaire* story

A click on a search engine produced 28,100,000 results for *Slumdog Millionaire* in 0.17 seconds on the eve of the Oscar Awards function on 22 February 2009. Millions of reviews, trailers, comments, good wishes, and criticism adorned the net.

Did the team create the hype intentionally that was responsible for the generation of tremendous interest in a film that exposed the underbelly of a metropolitan of a developing nation, only the strategists could tell? It was a clean sweep for the film at the Golden Globe Awards in the USA, followed by awards in multiple categories at BAFTA. It also won the National Board Review (NBR) award, which generally is said to be a precursor to winning the Oscar.

Much before the film was slated for release in India, the announcement of these awards created the necessary curiosity, including what superstar Amitabh Bachchan had to say about the film on his blog. In an interview with the director, Danny Boyle, and actor Anil Kapoor on mainstream Indian television channels, Kapoor refused to comment on Bachchan's criticism, while Danny said the issue was clarified with Big B, who had posted the following on his blog, "If SM projects India as (a) third world, dirty, underbelly developing nation and causes pain and disgust among nationalist and patriots, let it be known that a murky underbelly exists and thrives even in the most developed nations."[14]

Some criticized the film director and producer for exploiting the gullible children who worked in the film. Boyle said ahead of awards, "We also put in place an educational plan for the children which we are sticking to and we will be there for them long after the fuss has died."[15]

Based on the novel Q&A, by Indian writer Vikas Swarup, the success of the film brought about interesting tie-ups with NGOs in the field of child rights and use of consumer PR and appropriate media vehicles. Internet mart eBay India and Plan India, an NGO working in the field of child rights, invited people to be the "owner of a collector's copy of the famous Slumdog Millionaire novel authored by Vikas Swarup." It offered the copy "autographed by the film's stars crossed-over lovers, Dev Patel and Frieda Pinto." The charity auction was live on the portal eBay India starting from February 16–28, 2009 bidding starts at Rs. 270/-."[16]

Those who wished to watch the film on television, TATA SKY with its DTH charged just Rs. 25/- for a day, which in a way increased the target audience for the film. In fact, the moment one switched on the television, the *Slum Dog* promo with the "Jai Ho" number was telecast, both in English and Hindi. It received tremendous response from the subscribers.

The film is said to have benefited a great deal from W.O.M.M (Word of Mouth Marketing) that encompassed buzz, blog, trailers, viral, grassroots, cause influencers, social media, ambassador programs, consumer-generated media, and mainstream media, including a star cast director appearing on news channels and more. Consumer PR strategies need to be blended well with other promotional activities to achieve synergy. The example of *Slum Dog Millionaire* can be highly valued by product marketers.

What was responsible for generating such a huge curiosity in the film: the international recognition ahead of its release in India, the Oscar nominations (ahead of the awards), the debate it generated on exposing the underbelly of Mumbai, important characters played by slum children, or a smart marketing strategy? Whether it was one or all can be an interesting issue to address in brand management.

Salaam Bombay! probably was the first film with an Indian theme that used aggressive marketing and PR strategies in their race to the Oscars in 1988, where they succeeded also, as we read in the case study earlier. Fourteen years later, in 2002, Ashutosh Gowariker's film *Lagaan*, which seemed to have good chances of making it to the Oscars, went overboard in its promotional strategies and tactics.

Sony Pictures took charge of promoting the film. The lead protagonist Aamir Khan gave multiple interviews to international media, the film was screened at many theaters, and a local PR agency was commissioned to handle various aspects of public relations. The agency spent another USD 2 million on promotion. There was a lot of buzz and curiosity for the film, but it lost the battle in the end. In retrospect, the first film from India that was nominated for the Oscars way back in 1957, the iconic film *Mother India*, entered the fray without any publicity and lobbying, but still was nominated, though it did not win.

The fourth film that made it to the Oscars in 2023 is none other than *RRR*.[17]

Despite that *RRR* was a roaring success in the country and overseas, the film was not the official entry of the country to the Oscars. *The Kashmir Files* was the official entry at the Oscars. The film *RRR* has grossed over USD 170 million worldwide and has also remained in Netflix's top ten for 14 weeks, as analysts put it, making it exactly the kind of international phenomenon that leads to awards.[18]

Many in Hollywood started evincing interest due to the scale, grandeur, and storyline of *RRR*, and, of course, the music, especially the song "Nattu, Nattu." When Rajamouli and his team were in LA, Jennifer Beals, the Flashdance star, one of the many fans of the film came to meet him. She later hosted her own screening of *RRR*, she told the *Times*. "It's over three hours long, but you're wishing it was three more hours. I want to see it over and over again, and now I feel sort of evangelical about it." Media reported that Beals was not alone in championing the cause. The Russo Brothers, news DC Studios cohead James, and *The Black Phone*'s Scott Derrickson, who called it "an awesomely outrageous roller coaster of a movie," illustrated the sentiment in a tweet with a GIF of Jr. NTR slow-motion knee-sliding out of the reach of a leaping tiger, surrounded by a wall of flames. Many fans of the film scouted for the film with the hashtag "RRR for Oscars."[19] All the efforts that were not aggressive in a literal sense, but subtle and organic in truth, bore the desired fruit. SS Rajamouli's *RRR* created history by being the first Indian film to win an Oscar. The "Naatu Naatu" soundtrack by Keeravani Was was awarded the Best Original Song Award at the 95th Academy Awards.[20]

7.5 Third-party advantage—through media endorsements

PR helps in creating awareness through third-party endorsement in media, reinforcing credibility to the paid form of communication. Involving journalists in the buzz around a product often pays off richly in brand building.

Media endorsement techniques, however, have stretched out to include many things that include media houses offering editorial package along with ad bookings, social networking sites paying to chat groups on discussing/endorsing the brands, product placements in films and television programs, celebrities talking about brands and issues as a part of the narrative, etc. Let us look at a few cases.

7.5.1 Reebok on a fast track

Reebok roped in film actress Bipasha Basu and cricketer MS Dhoni in a campaign that was launched in mid-2009, even before the ad could register; various lifestyle channels and mainstream newspapers were splashed with ad endorsements. In fact, Zoom, an erstwhile film-based channel, ran a few-minutes story with a curtain raiser, raising viewers' curiosity when the program anchor naughtily questioned who Bipasha was chasing, leaving behind her then-boyfriend John Abraham. The commercial shot outside India had the onlookers watching Bipasha and Dhoni running at breakneck speed, sometimes over the cars, till one knew it was a Reebok ad.

7.5.2 Honda's launch of Jazz

Similarly, when Honda launched its car Jazz in June 2009 in India with a very interesting commercial, in which every passing car along Jazz evaporated in thin air, it had its endorsement the next day in mainstream media. *Business Standard*, an economic paper, ran a picture on page one and a story appearing on an inside page. The picture of Jazz had two gentlemen posing along with it, viz., Fumihiko Ike, Honda Asia Oceania Operations, and Masahiro Takedagawa, president and CEO of Honda Siel Cars India limited, at the launch of the Jazz.

This was followed by its weekend motoring that carried the lead story "Jazz Attack!" with six pictures of the car and a Q&A about its various aspects, including pricing.[21]

7.5.3 TUMS—the twin advantage

In the USA in the early 1980s, the antacid market was quite cluttered in the country. For a new antacid to be launched, a genuine product differentiation was important. Smith-Kline briefed its R&D department to evolve a product with dual benefit. Soon it came out with a calcium-based antacid called TUMS with the desire of offering consumers a dual benefit—acidity relief and at the same time calcium for the bones.

This way the consumers could be told about taking only one pill for two problems and therefore allay their fears over multiple self-medication issues that were emerging.

However, calcium deficiency was not a big issue at that point in time in the US. Acidity, on the other hand, was a known and established ailment for which people self-medicated frequently, making antacids a high-selling category.

The company realized that the dual benefit would be lost on the consumers unless an education program around the gravity of calcium deficiency was implemented.

A broad-based consumer PR activity around osteoporosis and its debilitating effects preceded the conventional launch. Media carried third-party endorsements, including interviews with doctors, to bring about credibility to the whole issue.[22]

7.5.4 Product placement

Sometimes product placement is subtle and at other times blatant. Critics argue that product endorsements can take care of the cost of the film in many cases, so the producer is not worried about the fate of the film at the box office.

The history of the product placement can be traced back to the 1950s in the film *The African Queen*. The all-time innovative product placement anywhere in the world happened in the movie *I, Robot* in 2004, with the high-end car brand Audi's endorsement. Audi RSQ played the central role in the futuristic film, which was very different placement when compared to the BMW Z8 in the film "*The World Is Not Enough*." Audi, in fact, was designed and shaped for the film, keeping in view the storyline, the props, the ambience, and the expectation. The carmaker is said to have worked with the movie director Alex Proyas and the set designers. This resulted in innovations of sorts that included RSQ sports coupe, spherical wheels, mid-engine design, butterfly action doors, a color-changing luminescent paint job, and a low sleek profile.

One has witnessed product placements in Indian movies that encompass coffee houses, pizza brands, gutka brands, bikes, cars, and what have you.[23]

7.6 Area of discord

In the past, journalists would often take a story on a brand that was innovative, keeping in view readers' interest. Critics believe that crass commercialization and cutthroat competition has changed it all. Now editorial space can be bought to lend credence to flop brands and fledgling companies. There is a growing discontent about it within a section of media practitioners also. In all this, it is unfortunately the PR that is at the receiving end. This is an area that media needs to address and may be included it in its code of professional ethics.

7.7 Sponsorships

Sponsorship refers to the monetary support by an organization to an activity of another organization for an event with a definite commercial objective in mind, but at the same time to create goodwill with the organization that has requested for sponsorship.

Webster's Dictionary defines sponsorship thus: "a person or agency that undertakes certain responsibilities in connection with some other person or some group or activity as in being prominent endorser, advisor, underwriter, surety etc."[24]

7.7.1 Connecting with the youth

In is not uncommon to see college students looking for various sponsors during their college fete. Many companies, especially in the FMCG sector who target youth for their brands, come forward to sponsor various events in high schools and colleges. The sponsorship may include one or all of the following: sponsoring a concert, thereby all the expenditures, including fees to be given to the band, are taken care of; a banner on the wall that reflects the sponsorship, and if media covers the event and provides some glimpses, the banner ensures good visibility for the sponsoring organization. Some sponsorship may mean sponsoring the alumni dinner, awards for winners of competition, or paying for advertisement in the media about the event. In these kinds of sponsorships, the organizations don't pledge much amount, but when it comes to sponsoring national and international sporting events, the stakes are quite high on both sides. Any sponsor who decides to sponsor such an event looks for measurable commercial return in exchange of investment.

Sponsorships, feel experts, are an excellent way of positioning one's business or a brand for developing relationship marketing strategy. The effectiveness of a sponsorship is difficult, if not impossible, to measure against expenditure on other promotional activities, including advertising.

7.7.2 Improving public perceptions

Companies that are trying to improve their public perceptions generally like to earn goodwill through sponsorships. Multinational companies, especially in the FMCG sector, have earned the ire of some communities and certain lobbies in the past. For instance, Coca-Cola, which is seen by some a symbol of economic imperialism, has had to face a lot of resistance from certain groups in India on the issue of scarcity of groundwater, which they alleged was because of Coca-Cola factories in certain states, especially in the south. The India Resources Center, an NGO, claimed that it ensured that Coca-Cola was banned from the "Make Poverty History March" in July 2005, wherein close to 300,000 people participated in Edinburgh in Scotland.[25]

The Coca-Cola Company has undertaken various rain-harvesting projects in some Indian states to gain favorable public opinion. The case study may be referred to in the chapter on corporate social responsibility.

During the Beijing Olympics, some traditional sponsors like the McDonald's developed cold feet when a section of public opinion reflected that China should not have been given the Olympic mantle due to human rights violations in Tibet. The company perhaps did not wish the adverse public opinion rubbed on it. The only Olympic-themed UK activity was a press competition to win a trip to Beijing. In the US, however, it promoted its Southern-style chicken with athletes on the packaging. In Australia, it ran the "flavor of the Games" promotion.[26]

McDonald's renewed its sponsorship contract for five years with football's world-governing body, FIFA World Cup and FIFA Confederations Cup, which includes the selection of marketing assets and perimeter board, as reported by ANI.[27]

"Ferrari to close down London" was the headline of newspapers a few years ago. The reason was to allow oil giant Shell to film a new commercial to promote its long-term sponsorship of Ferrari F1 team. The ad is believed to have cost the company two million pounds. The commercial had the Ferrari cars racing through a selection of the world's most famous cities including London, New York, and Sydney with the aim to showcase Shell's V-Power high-performance fuel.[28]

Corporate organizations bet big time money on winning athletes on sponsorships. Michael Phelps, the US golden boy, was no exception after his phenomenal eight-gold medal tally in Beijing Olympics 2008. A few months later, a tabloid by the name *Screws of the World* published a picture of Phelps with his baseball cap worn back to front, using a lighter to send smoke along his glass bong at a party, where he was reported dead drunk. The news sent shock waves among his several sponsoring companies. Marketing pundits got busy predicting the fallout if the story proved right. Big corporate organizations are believed to be sensitive about any issue involving drugs, particularly if their product is bought or directed at children. Phelps that time around was said to be worth millions in sponsorships. Some of the brands he endorsed included Hilton Hotels, Omega watches, Kellogg's cereals, and Speedo swimwear. In fact, Speedo swimwear paid him USD 1 million as bonus for bagging eight gold medals in swimming. Phelps was also chosen as the face of Mazda, earning him a handsome fee.[29] Many of his fans did not believe in the negative story on him, if the response on social networking sites was any indication.

When beleaguered company Morgan Stanley laid off 5,000 employees at the end of 2008, the government, as a bailout package, paid it a few billion dollars from taxpayers' account. It earned the wrath of some elected representatives and others for its insensitivity in trying times, when it held a three-day conference in a five-star hotel in Palm Beach in Florida, splurging in a lot of expenditure. It tried to defend its position, saying it was a strategy to promote the company, but there were not many takers for that. Congress elect Cummings criticized the company for sponsoring such a lavish event "when people in the Main St. were struggling to make ends meet."[30]

The Oscars ceremony is one of the most looked-out-for events in the cinematic world, thanks to seamless media and entries from the developing world making it broad-based. While there was a lot of hype and buzz around the Indian entry *Slum Dog Millionaire* and documentary *Smile Pinki* in 2009, media reported low-key responses from the sponsors. Was it recession, or were they the kind of films that were not glamorous per se, or was it the changing of guard in the US, with Obama snubbing Wall Street honchos for taking away billions in bonus while the taxpayers paid the bail-out amounts? It was difficult to say, but ABC reported about a 21% fall in the ad revenue from sponsors.

Cosmetic giant L'Oréal dropped its sponsorship, giving a hole of over $20 million to ABC that telecasts the ceremony live. General Motors, another big sponsor, announced months in advance that it was not sponsoring the show. American Express, another big spender, bought only one slot.

The reason ascribed by some film critics was that the Oscars functioned better when there were mass-market films that dominated the nominees' list, which was not the case this time. T. Alfred, on the *Dallas Morning News*, reasoned that the response from the sponsors was not encouraging because the films in the reckoning were "smaller, more boutique films." He further said, "There is no *Titanic*. There is no *Lord of the Rings*."

Whatever the critics' points of view or the sponsors' woes, the Indian entry *Slum Dog Millionaire* bagged seven Oscars, and the documentary *Smile Pinki* won the eighth one. India brought back home eight Oscars, first time in its history, which was enough reason for people to rejoice and media to increase their TRPs!

7.8 Online sponsorships

Online sponsorships are fast catching up with companies for two reasons: one, Internet access is growing manifold, especially among the youth; two, the medium proves quite cost-effective when one looks at the constant exposure and seamlessness of the medium.

7.8.1 What is online sponsorship?

Online sponsorship is not very different from "real" sponsorship. Ryan and Whiteman define online sponsorship as "the linking of a brand with related content or context for the purpose of creating brand awareness and strengthening brand appeal in a form that is clearly distinguishable from a banner, button or other standardized ad unit."[31]

For the advertisers, comments Chaffey, the online sponsorship has the benefit that their name is associated with an online brand that a site visitor may already be familiar with. On the other hand, some companies go in for co-branding, as HSBC cards once had with Yahoo!'s money trusting service.[32]

In online sponsorship, the company that sponsors and the organization that has received the sponsorship put the necessary information on their websites in an interesting manner. So every time a user wishes to know about that event through a search engine, many pages open, including that of both the companies. In online sponsorship, chances are that there will be a mix of appreciations and criticism, as netizens, especially bloggers are very active on registering their views, that would be seen by many, who may agree or not agree, but get exposed to varying perspectives on the said sponsorship. But that's part of the game!

There is so much clutter on the websites that there is always a question mark on the effectiveness of this medium. Many innovations are happening to make it clutter-free. For example, Volvo conducted a very interesting study to understand both the branding value of advertising sponsorship on the Net as well as the difference between the value of "exclusive" sponsorship (when an ad is displayed exclusively on a website) in contrast to "shared" sponsorship (when several ads appear on the same page of different brands). The International Advertising Bureau reported that in a sample of 1,514 visitors, exclusive online sponsorship produced considerable lift as compared to negligible lift from shared sponsorship.[33]

7.8.2 Brand promotion events

Corporate communication has long been organizing media events that encompass press conferences, press meets, and press junkets/facility visits. Of late, its services are much in demand for brand promotional events. Every event, if carefully planned and executed, has the potential of enhancing the brand image and recall for the company. For this chapter we shall concentrate on brand promotion events only. Chapter 6, on "Media writing and media handling," discusses the planning and execution of various media events.

When events are used for brand promotion, it is important to ensure that the said event enhances the brand salience and that events are not added just for short-term hype.

Corporate organizations make two-pronged use of events in brand promotion, viz., sponsoring certain events to get the necessary mileage through sponsorship, and events that are specially created for a brand launch or brand promotion. The bottom line for any promotional event, however, is to draw customers, especially the potential ones.

Organizing an event is a web of complex activities that requires precision management. Events may not always result in monetary rewards, but effectively organized events help in directly communicating with the target audience and are believed to be a good return on investment in the long run. An event not only helps interface with potential customers but provides instant feedback and insights about the market trends.

7.8.3 Defining event management

Event management is defined as the application of management practice of project management to the creation and development of festivals and events. Event management can be said to be a way of outsourcing occasions that are either social or business or a combination of both. The range of events can be from small birthday parties, marriage ceremonies, to large-scale political rallies, international sporting events, concerts, or academy awards nights, etc.

The selection of venue, the invites, the sets, the décor, the music, the entertainment, the stage, the anchors, the celebrities, the seating arrangements, the protocol, security, parking, media coverage, the follow-up form parts of event management. Event management involves meticulous planning, financial resource management, and rigorous discipline. Large event management companies often subcontract work, keeping in view the niche specialization of these firms.

Many enterprising NRIs in the US have made events surrounding singers, dancers, film actors, and religious personalities from India a big business venture. The tickets for such events range from USD 25 to 100 per person. A look at some of the tabloids brought out by the Indian community in New York (generally distributed *gratis* from Indian restaurants and religious places), for instance, reflected dozens of events from East to West coast from August to September, when the weather is generally pleasant.

A successful event manager must be creative, innovative, with an analytical mind, sharp reflexes, problem-solving capabilities, but, above all, a sharp sense of judgment with extraordinary man-management skills.

Billions of dollars are spent globally on events of varying kinds and magnitude. The Indian event industry, which was Rs. 5000 crores in 2016,[34] grew to over Rs. 10,000 crores in 2019–20 and is poised to grow further at 25–30% in 2023, as per market trends.[35]

7.8.4 Concept to commissioning

An event begins with an idea, a concept that is converted into something tangible. Event organizers are now taking up projects from concept to commissioning, which means they are taking charge of the entire gamut of work involved in organizing events, right from giving the client the objectives of the proposed event, theme selection, planning, inventory, selection of venue, getting clearances from authorities, setting up of venue/décor, guest list, invitations, hospitality arrangements, security, publicity, etc. A lead time of six to 12 months may be required for an event of international or national magnitude. A sporting event of international nature like Olympics or Commonwealth games may need a lead time of two to three years for infrastructure development, if required, besides other arrangements to make the event international in stature and experience.

When ASIAD 82 was organized in India, large scale infrastructure activities were undertaken that included the creation of the Asiad Village to lodge athletes and organizers, construction of new stadiums and refurbishing of old ones, construction of roads leading to various sports venues, beautification of monuments, planting of trees, besides a host of other things. In fact, India started its color television experiment during the ASIAD 82.

Later the Commonwealth Games in 2010 (CWG 2010) were held in Delhi, India from 3 October to 14 October, attracting over 6,000 athletes from 71 Commonwealth countries participating in 21 sports and 272 events. The multisport event was humongous in every respect when compared with the ASIAD 82. According to various estimates, the event cost the Indian taxpayers over USD 10 billion.

The Commonwealth Games attracted a lot of international media interest due to varying reasons, including charges of nepotism, corruption, and delay in the completion of the works, hygiene and security of athletes, drawing strong response from social media against some media stories. The government of India, in a very interesting move, allowed only public broadcaster Prasar Bharti to cover the event. Hundreds of private channels were left gasping at the loss of opportunity. The inaugural event was so beautifully choreographed and curated that the critics did not have much to complain about.

CWG 2010 resulted in large-scale infrastructure development, including world-class multistory buildings for providing accommodation to the visiting teams and organizers. Dozens of flyovers were constructed, and the metro covered hundreds of kilometers connecting various sporting sites.

When any developmental work takes place, it is not without inviting the ire of some groups. The organizers faced criticism from some environmental groups for creating housing projects on the dried Yamuna riverbed. The lesson drawn is that it is important to be prepared for any crisis when organizing a large event. As is the common knowledge, an investigation committee was set up immediately after the games were over to go into the charges against the organizers.

7.8.5 Use of technology in events in the digital age

Innovation in technology has affected the way events are now conducted. It is not uncommon to see hand-held devices of varying kinds, computers that connect to several central servers, dozens of cameras from various directions shooting the event, especially sports, instant editing facilities, deployment of drones for shooting, live telecast, and teleconferencing facilities. For sporting events, the GMS (Games Management System) seems a solve-all device that addresses accreditation, games result management, information dissemination, and facilities management.[36]

The accreditation device looks after registration for all kinds of individuals, like athletes, event organizers, officials, media, support, and security staff, including volunteers.

The games result management has many sub modules of the result management that caters to the conduct of the games based on international federation rules. The module has the capability of automating various stages like draws schedules, result capture, ranking, and medals, etc. It also supports end of the event and post-game reports for all the events conducted during the sports meet.

An information dissemination device distributes information across to various media like web pages, computer information system, source board interface, television interface, SMS interface, WAP interface, and interface with e-mail system.

7.8.6 Facility management

Facility management includes management of accommodation, transportation (information regarding vehicles deployed), human resources (information regarding the skills of persons available), VIP protocol, inventory control of equipment deployed at the games site, and arrival and departure of athletes.[37]

7.9 Caselets in event management

In the following paragraphs, we shall look at some of the case studies of events that were sponsored by organizations and some events organized around various brands for brand launch or brand promotion.

7.9.1 Coca-Cola sponsorship of events

Coca-Cola remains as one of the largest global sponsors of multiple events, especially sporting events. The company sponsors events both at local as well as global levels, calling sporting events as "a natural fit." By matching the brand with world events, the brand is expected to benefit from the exposure and association with world standard events. On the other hand, when it supports local events, the brand is exposed exclusively to a local market, thus making the brand seem local. All the local offices of the company are mandated to participate and support local communities—be it sports, fashion, or music, keeping in view the following broad objectives:

To create unforgettable teen moments linked to Coca-Cola
To ensure 'Coca-Cola' is viewed as making everyday life more interesting and fun
To communicate the dynamics and leading attributes of the brand
To be seen as a national sponsor at local level and a global sponsor at international level.[38]

The company ensures that the attributes of the product suitable to sports sponsorship are highlighted by positioning Coca-Cola as an icon and leading brand that "mentally and physically boosts consumers, associations with major sporting events."[39]

Coca-Cola has long been associated with global sporting events since 1928. Some of these include the Olympic games, the FIFA World Cup, and Special Olympics. The company has aided about 200 National Olympic Committees, assisting thousands of athletes in their training.[40]

7.9.2 Innovative event management through youth

Red Bull energy drink enjoys a good market share in the segment in UK, Europe, and USA. It has entered the Indian market also.

Brainchild of Dietrich Mateschitz, an Austrian who had quite liked a Thai energy drink that had immediately cured his jet leg, he approached the manufacturers of Krating Daeng, Thai for Red Bull, for the possibility of a similar drink for a wider market. The brand was launched in 1992 in the European market, followed by its entry in the US in 1997. The company did not undertake the traditional route of mass advertising, but made inroads into the youth bastion through events. Under the strategy, students and disk jockeys (DJs) were hired to host parties where the drink was sold. The craze for the drink soon caught on as youngsters mixed it with vodka, paving way for a "drug-free way to enjoy partying late in to the night without loss of energy."

Red Bull also innovated some exciting events called Red Bull Air Race and Red Bull Street Style 2008, held in many countries to find the world's best soccer players. Riding on the success of these events, the company sponsored mainstream events like Formula 1, by keeping up with its edgy and youthful positioning.[41]

Analysts believe that the brand did not spend a lot of money in the traditional promotional activities, but innovated strategies and tactics to create the necessary buzz and acceptance for the brand, positioning it differently from soda drinks. In a guerilla style, they target men in the 18–35 age category at college parties and bars that offered free samples. From 1980s to current times, the brand has made a history of sorts by almost shunning mass media campaigns.[42]

7.9.3 Brand promotion through media

Volkswagen very interestingly integrated its strategy with PBS (Public Service Broadcasting), when it launched its three new models in 2003 in the USA. It chose exclusive sponsorship of PBS' s *The Blues*, a landmark seven-part television series chronicling the evolution of American art form and its influence on artists across the musical spectrum. One of the most successful promotional components of the Blues project was the year-long "On the Road" tour, which brought *The Blues* to nearly 50 film and musical festivals across the country. It provided Volkswagen the opportunity to interface with tens of thousands of potential buyers.

7.9.4 Raid de Himalayas

The number of sponsors for motor sporting is increasing in India constantly. Some of them include, MRF, JK Tyers, Kingfisher, Tatas, Maruti Suzuki, and Castrol, who have been associated with the automobile industry, except Kingfisher which is in aviation. Maruti Suzuki, for the last decade, has been organizing the sporting event that includes its own vehicles also in the adventure sport category.

The Raid de Himalaya rally has been organized since 1999 by the Himalayan Motorsport Association formed in the same year. The motor sporting begun with an aim of conducting motor sporting events in the Himalayan regions of Himachal Pradesh, Jammu, and Uttarakhand, and has been a great hit with motor rally enthusiasts in India. Maruti Suzuki has supported the Raid de Himalaya from its inception in 1999 and nurtured it to the mega motorsport fixture that it enjoys today. Raid de Himalaya "is rated amongst the top ten toughest rallies in the world and given its high international standards it sees participation from abroad as well," as reflected on the company website.[43]

According to the company sources, it had requests from motoring enthusiasts from across the country for a car rally with lower level of competition, stress, and difficulty, but one which would allow the participants to enjoy the journey in a stock car, without the expensive modifications that rally cars are compulsorily subject to. More importantly, it said

> the idea is to enjoy the vast cultural heritage of a land that is exotic, beautiful and awe inspiring to say the least; without having to sacrifice the family car in the attempt! At the same time, it is necessary to introduce an element of competitiveness that would make this rally much more than a tour.[44]

7.9.5 Brand launch through road shows

Road shows are seen as an important way of brand activation by analysts as the customer gets a personal experience of the brand. The "Drive it like you hate it" campaign by Volvo in the US, through consumer engagement, ad support, and experiential events, managed to connect the American consumer, making the brand a huge success.[45]

TVS Scooty launched its new brand Streak through road shows in four towns of Gujarat in January 2009. Driven primarily by young women, the event involved them in the road shows for five days in each of the following towns: Ahmedabad, Vadodara, Surat, and Rajkot. The road show had 20 young girls driving Streak, followed by horse-driven chariot with cheer girls. The cavalcade also had a float with a promotional design and material. The idea behind the show was to create necessary buzz and communicate with young women en route, at some pre-determined venues, through games and contests.[46]

A lot of creativity is required in organizing promotional events. Since liquor cannot be advertised in mainstream media in India, the companies often organize events for some inane contests or for distributing awards, more often inviting celebrities to gather necessary buzz. It is not uncommon for them to publicize the events through mass media. Such events are organized to introduce their new brands of spirits. One finds a total lack of strategy and finesse in such events. In one such event, one of the former Ms. World was invited. Much to the embarrassment of the event managers, she came in an Indian ensemble that did not go well with the theme and the ambience. To top it all, she was reluctant to play host by serving the invitees, who had paid to have a glimpse of her and be served by the celebrity!

TAG Heuer sponsored a polo match at which former Ms Universe cine star Sushmita Sen and the famous Hindi film star Shah Rukh Khan arrived and were paraded on elephants and horses. How it lent support to the brand or helped it sell more watches is not easy to comment. Incidentally, Polo sports seems to be attracting a lot of corporate sponsorship. It's not uncommon to see organizations sponsoring the event on a daily and weekly basis.

Columnist Shobha De expressed her disgust when many companies did not hesitate to reflect their logos prominently to gather mileage in events post 26/11 in the city of Mumbai that was trying to recover after the heinous terrorist strike on 26 November 2008.

Narrating one such instance, she wrote in her column that she received an e-card that had a "blob of blood at the top, that left a trail which ended with the name of the PR agency, hired to handle the event and the celeb list." A mile-long scroll was kept alongside the Marine drive, on which citizens had to put their signature to reflect their collective angst. The scroll, she said, turned out to be a brand promotion device for "unimaginative and cold-blooded marketers." After every few meters, there was a logo of a sponsoring company![47]

What a lack of sensitivity and imagination! In retrospect, when 9/11 happened in the USA, many right-thinking companies pulled out their ads from news channels in order not be seen as insensitive in trying times when the news was somber. In fact, *Time* magazine came out with a special issue on 9/11 that was *sans* any advertisements.

Brand promotion through sports players and sports venue

While one watches live one's favorite sports, it also seems like a brand promotion show with sports persons wearing jerseys with brand logos; their bats and wickets also carry the brand promotion material. The sports of cricket and football attract the maximum brand promotion from the corporate world, especially from companies manufacturing sports goods and accessories. The sponsoring organizations wish to paint everything with their brand logos, from sportswear to sports articles, not to forget the ground. A continuous exposure of brands for days across dozens of channels, the Net, and reproduction of sports persons pictures in print media ensures top-of-the-mind exposure and recall to the brand.

In a nutshell, event sponsorship and the use of events for brand launch and brand promotion need a lot of thinking, planning, and strategy formulation to achieve the desired marketing goals. Events planned without any sense can boomerang and bring negative publicity to the brand.

Summary

In this chapter we have discussed various tools and strategies used through corporate communication to achieve organizational goals. These broadly include employee communication, issue management, perception management, public affairs/lobbying, promotion, and brand-related events. Media-related events and the subjects of employee communication and corporate reputation have been dealt with in respective chapters as indicated earlier. The chapter discussed the role of consumer PR in corporate communication, the need for connecting with the consumer, and the changing paradigms in ensuring consumer connect in the digital age. Later, two more tools, viz., sponsorship and brand promotion events, were discussed in detail with case studies.

Key terms

Corporate reputation management: an important management tool to create, enhance, and preserve the reputation of an organization.
Consumer public relations: creating a carefully tailored promotion program aimed at consumers.
Employee communication: refers to communicating with internal stakeholders, viz., the employees, through various media with a view to create among them a sense of belonging for the company.
Event management: the application of management practice of project management to the creation and development of festivals and events.
Online sponsorship: the linking of a brand with related content or context for creating brand awareness and strengthening brand appeal that is clearly distinguishable from a banner, button, or other standardized ad unit on the Net.
Sponsorship: refers to the monetary support by an organization to an activity of another organization for an event with a definite commercial objective in mind, but at the same time to create goodwill with the organization

Concept review questions

Q.1. What are the various tools of corporate communication that are used for brand promotion?
Q.2. What is consumer public relations, and how does it help in maintaining relations with the customers?
Q.3. Define the role and scope of promotions in achieving goodwill for an organization. Discuss with relevant case studies.
Q.4. Discuss the difference between sponsoring events and creating events for brand launch or brand promotion, with suitable illustrations.
Q.5. Track various brand promotional events of an FMCG product or a lifestyle product through print, electronic, and Web media, and write your analysis.

Critical thinking exercise

If a brand is undergoing a crisis (for example pesticide controversy among colas), do you think the company should suspend its brand promotion till the controversy settles down? Validate your answer with reasoning.

Case study in consumer PR: diamonds—a woman's best friends

The diamond market has seen a tremendous growth in the last half century or so. The industry pegged the global diamond market at USD 89.18 billion in 2019 and expects it to expand at a compound annual growth rate (CAGR) of 3.0% from 2020 to 2030. Analysts put the growth factor mainly to the rising demand for diamonds from emerging economies, especially India and China, both incidentally the most populous countries in the world.[48]

In India the craze for diamond seemed to be industry induced in the late eighties and nineties, as an interesting case study later will reflect how an aspirational middle class woke up to the craze of owning the diamonds. Gold was traditionally considered women's "Streedhan" and an asset. It is a known fact that Indians all along have been crazy for gold. According to the World Gold Council, Indian households own over 25,000 tons of gold as of 2019, which was equivalent to 40% of the country's GDP.[49]

Gold has seen an unprecedented rise in price over the years. But something else was also making its presence felt, first in the mind space, then in real terms—the diamonds. When the winds of liberalization swept the country, along with many international brands in fashion and lifestyle products, one witnessed a generic campaign on diamonds: "A Diamond Is Forever" (Heera hai sada ke liye) from De Beers.

Three baseline surveys to map the attitudes of consumers towards diamonds were undertaken in 1993, 1994, and 1995.

Highlights:

1. *The diamond acquisition study*—1992 and 1995: both the studies measured the market quantitatively and provided insights for developing strategy and program development. The study looked at gathering data on what was acquired, at what cost, who made the purchase decision, and consumer attitude towards gold, diamonds, and other precious stones.
2. *The Trade structure study*—1994: it was a census of jewelers in 53 large cities of India to find out their turnover, stocking pattern for gold and diamonds, and the sources from which they procured it.
3. *The brand tracking study*—1996: the first annual study was taken up in 1996, followed by another study in 1997, to understand consumer attitudes towards diamond jewelry and recall and comprehension of advertising campaigns.

Based on the studies, the following insights emerged for defining the diamond market:

1. The wedding segment as measured that would address the newlywed
2. The non-bridal segment, singles, and post marital acquisition
3. The elite segment, which buys high-value pieces from time to time[50]

The Diamond Promotion Service (DPS), besides advertising efforts, undertook trade education and contact programs through hundreds of interactive programs educating the retailers on how to gauge diamond quality and undertake promotional activities.

One found gold shops introducing diamond jewelry, with promotional schemes like "kitties." Women were encouraged to pay just Rs. 1000 per month for 12 months and collect diamond jewelry worth Rs. 14,000. The kitty would open every month in the presence of various subscribers. The one who won the kitty would get away with diamond jewelry worth Rs. 12,000/- without having to pay any more subscription. Only the last few ones who were not successful would get jewelry for what they paid for + Rs. 2000/- more. This was a kind of win-win situation for everyone. Mehra Sons probably was the first jeweler to introduce this with its diamond brand Enchante. This scheme is now being perused from international brands like Orra to a small jeweler tucked in a busy market in a city or a small town. Diamonds have become an important part of jewelry of an urban woman, because they come at an affordable price tag and, in many cases, buy-back guarantee.

TABLE 7.1 Diamond outlets in 1994 and 1997

City	*1994 diamond outlets*	*1997 diamond outlets*	*1997 vs. 1994 % growth*
Mumbai	398	701	76%
Delhi	362	930	157%
Kolkata	198	246	24%
Chennai	202	264	31%
Bangalore	157	322	105%
Jaipur	59	220	273%
Ahmedabad	64	87	36%
Hyderabad	67	138	106%
Coimbatore	88	160	82%
Pune	61	78	28%

Source: Author

In order to encourage young girls, the "My first diamond" scheme was also introduced at a price of a couple of thousand rupees. One finds a spurt in ad campaigns around Valentine's Day every year.

The initial study threw interesting data on diamond outlets as reflected in the following table.

The total number of jewelers went up from 1656 to 3146 during the period, a 90% increase. Over the years, almost all shops retailing in gold in cities and even towns have diamond jewelry.

The brand promotion was supported by media endorsements through the consumer PR route. The Diamond Information Center was able to place, in 1996, 125 print placements, 150 minutes of free airtime, adding up to ad value of Rs. 3.47 crores. The total investment, as worked out by the DIC, was only one-fifth of it.[51]

Besides generic campaign, many retail outlets also advertise branded diamonds. Tanishq, a Tata company, has been in the forefront. Interestingly, the value of presenting and owning a diamond has been used in service brands also. In the past, a pension fund ad had a retired man presenting a diamond to his wife, to which she quipped, "*Heera, iss umar mein?*" (Diamond at this age?) Only to get a reply from her loving husband that the diamond did know her age (*Heere ko tumhari umar ka kya patta!*). The craze for diamond as an expression of love cuts across all age groups.

Question on the case study

Do you think marketers and promoters play with the aspirations of gullible consumers in buying things they may not need? Discuss in the context of the previous case study.

Practical exercise

Speak to ten young working women and ask them what a diamond means to them and when they acquired their first diamond and whether the ads for diamonds have any impact on the purchasing behavior.

Notes

1 Richard R. Dolphin, *The Fundamentals of Corporate Communications*, 1999 (London: Butterworth-Heinemann), pp. 86–87.
2 S. Harrison, *Public Relations- an Introduction*, 1995 (London: Routledge).
3 Philip J. Kitchen and Don J. Shultz, *Raising the Corporate Umbrella: Corporate Communication in the 21st Century*, 2001 (New York: Palgrave).
4 Advertising Age, 24 January 2005.
5 Jaishri Jethwaney and N. N. Sarkar, *Public Relations Management*, 2009 (New Delhi: Sterling Publishers), pp. 190–191.
6 "Adani Group Rolls Out #Humkarkedikhatehain Campaign to Celebrate 35 Years of Service in India", *The Financial Express*.
7 "The Adani Group Spends 35 Years Believing That Nothing Is Impossible", *Campaign India*.
8 Paul Holmes in Advertising Age, 24 January 2005.
9 www.tlg.ltd.com.
10 A. Mitchell, "A Subtle Approach to PR", *Marketing*, 28 April 1994, p. 53.
11 Cerrell Associates, www.worldcomgroup.com/casestudies.
12 Ibid.
13 Ibid.
14 www.theguardian.com/film/2009/jan/14/amitabh-bachchan-rubbishes-slumdog-millionaire, accessed on 23 August 2017.
15 Times of India, Indiatimes.com, 9 February 2009.
16 www.indiaprwire.com.
17 www.indiatoday.in/magazine/society-the-arts/films/story/20020318-lagaan-as-race-for-oscars-draws-to-a-close-aamir-khan-proves-his-marketing-acumen-795737-2002-03-24.
18 www.indiewire.com/awards/industry/rrr-india-oscar-snub-1234764557/
19 www.latimes.com/entertainment-arts/movies/story/2022-10-26/james-gunn-dc-studios-troma-timeline.
20 www.thehindu.com/entertainment/movies/oscars-2023-rrr-creates-history-naatu-naatu-wins-best-originalsong/article66612385.ece#:~:text=SS%20Rajamouli%27s%20RRR%20has%20created,in%20Los%20Angeles%2C%20United%20States.
21 Business Standard, 13 June 2009.
22 Jaishri N. Jethwaney, Adrash Kumar Verma and N. N. Sarkar, *Public Relations Concepts, Strategies and Tools*, 1994 (New Delhi: Sterling Publishers), p. 192.
23 http://money.howstuffworks.com/product-placement5.htm, accessed on 23 August 2017.
24 www.merriam-webster.com/dictionary/sponsor, accessed on 24 August 2017.
25 www.indiaresourcecenter.org.
26 www.brandrepublic.com.
27 www.aninews.com, 9 July 2006.
28 www.autotalk.com/ferrari
29 www.chat.mapple.com, 9 January 2009.
30 www.fertilethoughts.com.
31 Ryan and Whiteman, 2000, quoted by Dr. Dave Chaffey at www.markeeting-insights.co.uk.
32 Ibid.
33 Ibid.
34 www.ey.com/in/en/newsroom/news-releases/events-and-activation-industry-grown-at-15-to-inr-4258-crore-in-2014-15-ey-report, accessed on 23 August 2017.
35 "Event Industry Is Poised to Grow at a Rate of 25–30% in 2023: Deepak Choudhary", outlook india.com.
36 www.cmcltd.com/service_offerings/event_management.htm
37 Ibid.
38 www.coca-cola.com.
39 Ibid.
40 Ibid.
41 blog.freshegg.com.
42 Kaleigh Moore, "Red Bull's Approach to Marketing: Then and Now", BANKNOTES | BANKNOTES, hashtagpaid.com, 28 June 2022.

43 www.marutisuzukimotorsport.com/rallies/raid-de-himalayas.aspx, accessed on 23 August 2017.
44 www.raid-de-himalaya.com/2006/choice.htm.
45 https://econsultancy.com/blog/66013-brand-activation-and-its-role-in-driving-consumer-engagement-and-awareness/, accessed on 24 August 2017.
46 www.eventsfaqs.com.
47 Indiatimes.com.
48 "Diamond Market Size, Share & Growth Industry Report", 2030, grandviewresearch.com
49 "Indian Households Have Stocked Up to 25,000 Tonnes of Gold: World Gold Council", *Business Today*.
50 Pran K. Chaudhury, *Successful Branding*, 2001 (Hyderabad: Universities Press), p. 70.
51 Ibid., pp. 77–78.

8

CORPORATE SOCIAL RESPONSIBILITY

Chapter objectives

After reading this chapter, you will learn:

What corporate social responsibility (CSR) is
CSR definitions
Genesis of CSR
Theoretical underpinning of CSR
Various phases of CSR in India
Global practices in CSR
CSR and Companies Act 2013—implications

8.1 What is corporate social responsibility (CSR)?

Corporate social responsibility (CSR) is a much-talked-about phenomenon in boardroom discussions since the passing of the Companies Act 2013 in India, which has made it mandatory for all kinds of companies to implement CSR if they come in the purview of the set indicators. Corporate social responsibility means different things to different organizations and people. In the absence of a universally accepted definition for CSR, there are lots of myths surrounding the term. Some organizations claim that caring for employees, giving them bonus, equal pay for equal work, keeping reservation of jobs for people from socially and economically weak backgrounds, and subsidizing food on premises is fulfilling CSR. Others feel that caring for employees is mandated and in the interest of the organization to retain talent; what it does beyond that, for communities, who may or may not be its customers, is what comprises CSR. In fact, profit was considered a "dirty" word in public sector boardroom discussions, especially in the 50s to 70s. For long, the Indian public sector *per se* carried a perception that it was created

DOI: 10.4324/9781032694702-8

with a social responsibility mandate, so earning profit was not necessary for them, until it received a big jolt post liberalization when the government went on a selling spree of "sick" units.

Critics argue that many companies undertake CSR activities to transfer funds to avoid taxes, while others argue that a robust CSR policy and practice is nothing but a good business sense. It builds an organization's image, which ultimately gets converted to a better bottom line for it. In other words, CSR is about how companies manage the business processes to produce an overall positive impact on society.

8.2 Defining corporate social responsibility

Philip Kotlar and Nancy Lee define corporate social responsibility as a "commitment to improve community wellbeing through discretionary business practices and contributions of corporate resources."

The World Bank has defined CSR as operating a business in a manner that meets or exceeds ethical, legal, commercial, and public expectations that society has of business. Companies see CSR as more than a collection of discrete expectations that society has of business. Leadership companies see CSR as more than a collection of discrete practices or occasional gestures, or initiatives motivated by marketing, public relations, or other business benefits. Rather, it is viewed as a comprehensive set of policies, practices, and programs that are integrated throughout business operations and decision-making processes that are supported and rewarded by top management.[1]

Mallen Baker refers to CSR as "a way companies manage the business process to produce an overall positive impact on society."

Archie Caroll describes CSR as a multi-layered concept that can be differentiated into four interrelated aspects, viz., economic responsibility, legal responsibility, ethical responsibility philanthropic responsibility. At the bottom of the pyramid is economic responsibility, followed by legal and ethical responsibility. At the top of the pyramid is philanthropic responsibility.

The World Business Council for Sustainable Development, in its publication *Making Good Business Sense*, by Lord Holme and Richard Watts, used the following definition. "Corporate Social Responsibility is the continuing commitment by business to behave ethically and contribute to economic development while improving the quality of life of the workforce and their families as well as of the local community and society at large."[2]

Public sector corporation Bharat Petroleum Corporation Limited (BPCL) defines CSR thus:

> At BPCL we believe that it is equally important to return to society. Which is why, we believe some of our finest achievements aren't those found in our balance sheets but those, in small towns and villages spread across India. Our involvement in sharing this wider responsibility dates way back to 1984, when in pursuance with our philosophy "to give back to the society/community our best", we aimed to help the people enrich their lives, be it our employees or their families also extending the scope of definition of families to those that we saw beyond our glass cabins in these rustic surroundings, and thus started our romance. Today, we term them as our extended family i.e., our villagers from rural areas.[3]

8.3 Genesis of corporate social responsibility

The concept of CSR is not new, except probably the term. Its roots can be traced to all religious scriptures that exhort people to share their fortunes with the less privileged ones. Businessmen over the years have indulged in philanthropic works of various kinds. It is said to have happened as an act of corporate social responsibility when in the 1790s England witnessed the first large-scale consumer boycott over the issue of slave-harvested sugar which finally forced the importer to have free-labor sourcing.

Ida Tarbell's 1904 work *The History of the Standard Oil Company* (Rockefellers) helped lead to the decision of the Supreme Court of the United States to break up the company on antitrust grounds. Similarly, Upton Sinclair's 1906 book *The Jungle* led to the passage of the Pure Food and Drugs Act and the Meat Inspection Act by the United States Congress. These can be seen as early attempts to mandate socially responsible corporate behavior.

Corporate social responsibility (CSR) in India, feel analysts, can probably be traced back to when the Tata Iron and Steel Company (TISCO) was set up in 1907. The Jamshedpur plant today is seen as a gigantic social outreach program that covers 600 villages in and around its manufacturing and raw materials operations through initiatives in the areas of income generation, healthcare, and education.[4]

The term CSR came to common use in the 1970s, and by the 1990s the concept was fully recognized. As per research, in 1977, less than half of the Fortune 500 companies mentioned the term CSR in their annual reports, but around 1990, 90% of companies in the Fortune 500 list reflected CSR and their goals in their annual reports.[5]

8.4 Theoretical underpinning of CSR

Bryane Michael refers to three schools of practice in CSR, viz., the neo-liberal school, the state-led school, and the "third-way" school. Let us look at how these schools look at CSR.

8.4.1 The neo-liberal school

The assumption in this line of thinking is that the adoption of CSR policies by business is rational and profitable in the long run. These policies, the author argues, result in product demand factors of production such as labor and capital. CSR here is seen as a larger branding strategy. Engaging CSR programs, marketing them, and auditing them results in creating respect and equity for such organizations. Therefore, it attracts demand from those market segments that wish to do business with socially sensitized companies. The chapter has reflected findings of research studies that clearly indicated that people preferred to buy products from the company that they perceived was socially responsible and ethical.[6]

8.4.2 State-centered school

Advocates of this school believe that national and international policy makers should actively promote CSR obligations. It is argued that when there is intervention from the policy makers, people benefit. International bodies like the World Bank, the UN, and the

EU have been playing an active role in promoting CSR. Companies, especially those that are large and international, sign in many international protocols so that these are seen as benchmarks by employees and clients.

8.4.3 The "third-way" school

Many analysts see the third sector, meaning the civil society organizations (CSOs) and the non-governmental organizations (NGOs), as the real motor driving the CSR. Given the overall presence of NGOs and CSOs in their CSR programs, companies reflect the changing times and expectations. The Delhi government's Bhagidari (partnership) scheme with the resident welfare associations (RWAs) bore fruit in better governance. When the Congress (I), led by Chief Minister late Mrs. Shiela Dikshit, brought home victory the third time in a row in the 2009 Delhi elections, the analysts commented that it was because of her bonding with the masses through various partnership schemes with CSOs and NGOs. The AAP government has also put in place many schemes in a participative mode.

Before the municipal elections in December 2022, the party promised to give the RWAs the status of "Mini Councils," empowering them financially and to decide the civic body's policies, reported media.[7]

Over the years it has been seen that many donor organizations, including the UN, have transferred funds to NGO partners and not state players in development projects, in the belief that there would be less bureaucracy and efficient functioning of schemes at the grassroots level.

8.5 Various phases of CSR in India

As per the "Altered Images: the 2001 State of Corporate Responsibility in India Poll," a survey conducted by Tata Research Institute, the evolution of corporate social responsibility has witnessed the following pattern:

8.5.1 The ethical model (1930–1950)

This model promoted the concept of "trusteeship" revived and reinterpreted by Gandhi. Under the notion, businesses were motivated to manage their business entity as a trust held in the interest of the community. The efforts of the Tata group in the beginning can be said to be inspired by this model.

8.5.2 The statist model (1950–1970)

Under the aegis of the first prime minister, Pundit Jawaharlal Nehru, the model came in to being in the post-independence era when the government went in for a mixed and socialist kind of economy. The important feature of this model was that the state ownership and legal requirements decided the corporate responsibility.

8.5.3 The liberal mode (1970–1990)

This model was propounded by Milton Friedman. According to this model, CSR is confined to its economic bottom line, which implied that it was sufficient for business to obey the law and generate wealth, which, through taxation and private charitable choices, can be directed to social ends.

8.5.4 The stakeholders' model (1990s–present)

The model came in to being during the 1990s because of realization that, with growing economic profits, businesses also have certain societal roles to fulfill. The model expects the companies to perform according to "triple bottom line" approach. The businesses are also focusing on accountability and transparency through several mechanisms.

Corporate social responsibility (CSR) is an integral part of corporate governance. CSR is now widely regarded as the *mantra* whereby organizations, as a matter of principle and practice, consider the interests of society by taking responsibility for the impact of their activities on customers, employees, shareholders, communities, and the environment in all aspects of their operations. This obligation is seen to extend beyond the statutory obligation to comply with legislation and sees organizations voluntarily taking further steps to improve the quality of life for employees and their families as well as for the local community and society at large.

Experts feel that CSR is a business imperative. Whether pursued as a voluntary corporate initiative or for legal compliance reasons, CSR will achieve its intended objectives, only if businesses truly believe that CSR is beneficial to them.

8.6 CSR and myths

There are lots of myths surrounding the CSR. Some feel that because companies put in the resources, it is up to them to decide the *modus operandi* of CSR, which may not be true. The stakeholders need to be involved from the beginning to make it successful. Some feel that CSR is interchangeable with corporate sponsorship, donation, or philanthropic activities.

8.6.1 CSR—a business imperative

There are several reasons for companies to include CSR as an important part of governance.

Globalization has brought in seamless markets, global resource outlets, especially for production of goods in poor nations where the labor is cheap. For instance, advocacy groups in the USA, at one time, were able to convince many youths to boycott Coca-Cola at college campuses as it was draining away the groundwater in various places, thus creating scarcity of water for the poor in India. Nike was lambasted for allowing children in poor countries in its production outlets.

Over the years, there have come into existence international legal instruments and guidelines such as SA 8000, a social performance standard based on international labor organization's conventions. International organizations such as the UN and Organization for Economic Cooperation and Development have developed compacts, declarations, guidelines, principles, and other instruments that set the tone for social norms for organizations. All these are advisory in nature but carry a lot of weight.

One of the UN SDGs (Sustainable Development Goals) is poverty alleviation. Many state governments are asking businesses to be aware of their impact on society.

Salman Khursheed, immediately after taking over as the minister for corporate affairs and with a dual charge for ministry of minority affairs in UPA II government that came in to being in 2008, called upon the industry leaders to give adequate representation to candidates from the reserved categories. His ministry had called for data from the industry. The media quoted the minister on this, thus, "We are talking about affirmative action here, engaging [the industry] through dialogue."[8]

Global Compact, a voluntary initiative by the UN, is concerned with the social legitimacy of businesses. The Global Compact is a framework for businesses that are committed to aligning their business operations and strategies with ten universally accepted principles that companies are expected to follow in the areas of human rights, labor standards, environment protection, and anti-corruption.

The scandals involving corporate behemoths like the Enron, WorldCom, et al have reduced public trust in companies and shaken confidence in the regulatory bodies to book the guilty. Many companies are now going overboard in making their policies and processes open for public scrutiny. As soon as the Satyam Computers fraud surfaced, it sent shock waves in the IT sector; many, like the Infosys and Wipro top brass, started talking about parameters of corporate governance in their companies, to distance themselves from Satyam, which they wished people to believe was an exception and not a rule. It must, however, be said to the credit of the government of India and the regulatory bodies that within three months of Satyam Fraud, the guilty were booked, and a new bidder was given charge to manage the company.

The US President Barack Obama's lashing out at the Wall Street bankers on 29 January 2009 reflected the changing times and expectations of responsible behavior from the Corporate Inc. in trying times of economic recession. He branded all Wall Street bankers as "shameful" for giving themselves $8.14 billion in bonuses as the economy was deteriorating and the government was spending billions of dollars to bail out some of the prominent financial institutions. Then Vice President Joseph Biden was more unsparing when he said that such people needed to be jailed. "There will be time for them to make profits and there will be time for them to get bonuses," Obama said. "Now is not that time. And that is the message that I intend to send directly to them." The news of bonuses, however, came before the official announcement that the US economy had shrunk by 3.8% in the October–December quarter, its worst show since 1982.[9]

Fleishman-Hillard Inc., a public relations firm in the USA, conducted a survey on corporate social responsibility of business vis-à-vis people's expectations, including the role of media and technology in informing people about what companies were doing. The survey, conducted in 2007, threw some very interesting insights.

> There has been a steady drumbeat of media coverage on environmental issues over the past year and, clearly, those are important issues. But our findings again this year indicate that for most Americans, social responsibility begins with a basic concept—companies should treat their employees well.
>
> *(Dave Senay, president and chief executive officer of Fleishman-Hillard Inc.)*[10]

The survey reflected that treatment of employees was considered an important part of CSR in the USA. For the second year in a row, respondents said that when it came to how they defined "corporate social responsibility," a company's treatment of its employees and its involvement in the community counted more than its environmental stewardship. In addition, nearly 40% of Americans indicated that treatment of employees was more important to them than a company going beyond the law to protect the environment (15%).[11]

Americans of all political persuasions, reflected the research findings—95% of Democrats, 82% of Independents, and 65% of Republicans—said that it was either very or extremely important for Congress to ensure that companies were addressing social issues. In addition to looking for more government oversight, 77% of surveyed American consumers believed that there was a need for global standards for corporate social responsibility (an increase of 12% over last year's results). Furthermore, two-thirds of respondents indicated that they would make purchasing decisions in favor of a company that met such global standards.[12]

8.7 Global practices in CSR—some cases in point

Corporate social responsibility is a concept with a growing acceptance within Canada. CSR, however, frequently overlaps with similar approaches such as corporate sustainability, corporate sustainable development, corporate responsibility, and corporate citizenship. While CSR does not have a universal definition in Canada, "many see it as the private sector's way of integrating the economic, social, and environmental imperatives of their activities. As such, CSR closely resembles the business pursuit of sustainable development and the triple bottom line."[13] In addition to integration into corporate structures and processes, CSR frequently aims at creating innovative and proactive solutions to societal and environmental challenges.

More than 225 investment companies with assets over US $3 trillion, including Morgan Stanley, Goldman Sachs, and AIG have signed the Carbon Disclosure Project, under which the companies are requested to share carbon emission data by posting it publicly for all investors. In 2005, the project launched the Climate Leadership Index for companies with leading climate strategies.[14]

India has been doing its bit on this front. It received accolades from the three top NGOs, namely, Germanwatch, Newclimate Institute, and the Climate Action Network (CAN), who in their report published in the Climate Change Performance Index (CCPI) in 2023 ranked India in eighth position among 63 countries.[15]

One of the early supporters to the Kyoto Protocol, in USA, 279 cities signed the Kyoto Protocol. The state of California has passed a legislation to reduce emission from all industries by 25% by 2020.

The State of California sued six of the world's largest automakers including General Motors (GM), Ford, Chrysler, Honda, Toyota, and Nissan on the grounds that greenhouse gases from their vehicles have caused damage to the environment worth billions of dollars. The lawsuit, according to media reports, is the first of its kind to focus on manufacturers' liability for damages caused by their vehicles.[16] The Kyoto Protocol only bound the developing countries. Later, the Paris Agreement in 2016, which, in a way, superseded the Kyoto Protocol, fixed on both developed and developing countries to reduce carbon emissions. The Paris agreement has 194 nations as signatories, which are required to work towards the goal of "preventing the global average temperature from rising more than 2°C above preindustrial levels and pursuing efforts to keep temperature rise below 1.5°C."[17]

Around the same time, Richard Branson of the Virgin Group donated a projected US $ 3 billion over ten years from his five airlines and train company to the development of low carbon energy resources such as wind turbines, cleaner burning aviation fuel, and "cellulosic ethanol." The Virgin Group has also launched Virgin Fuels company that will invest up to US $ 400 million in biofuels.[18]

According to the Foundation for CSR research, a positive correlation between CSR and financial performance is pointed out. Thirty-one new studies conducted between 1996 and 2005 have reflected "a positive correlation between CSR and financial performance. Additionally, a study of superstar companies (P&G, etc.) showed that companies that consistently considered a wide range of stakeholder opinions outperformed the S&P 500 financial index by more than twice the average." A CSR Europe poll found that 70% of European consumers said that a company's commitment to social responsibility was an important factor when they bought a product or service, and one in five would be willing to pay more for products that were socially and environmentally responsible. This was in line with a 1999 study that showed 86% of European consumers would be more likely purchase a product from a socially responsible company.[19]

India Inc. waking up to the CSR call—provisions in the Companies Act 2013

The Ministry of Corporate Affairs notified Section 135 and Schedule VII of the Companies Act 2013 as well as the provisions of the Companies (Corporate Social Responsibility Policy) Rules, 2014 which came into effect from 1 April 2014. The Ministry's Website has a PDF file on FAQs on CSR. It is a copy of the letter sent to all stakeholders.[20] Some salient points from the notification include the following: The CSR rules are applicable to every company registered under the Companies Act 2013, and any other previous laws in India apply to companies in the following situations, when the net worth of a company is Rs. 500 crores or more; or a turnover of Rs. 1000 Crore or more; or a net profit of Rs. 5.00 crore or more, in any financial year. The expenditure on CSR will not be deemed as a business expenditure. There is no specific tax exemption on CSR spending. Activities that benefit the employees will not be considered as CSR activities. Contribution of CSR funds can be transferred to a trust/society only if created for the CSR work and not to any existing one that a company may have. The CSR policy and activities will be displayed by the company on its website. Reporting of CSR is mandatory in the board's report to the shareholders. Foreign companies shall contain an annexure under Section 138 of the Act that will reflect the CSR work undertaken. If a company spends some excess amount on CSR, it can't be adjusted in the coming years; however, an amount spent less in a year can be carried forward to the next year. Companies are fully competent to engage third parties for monitoring the efficacy of their CSR activities; the government has no role in monitoring it. Under the provision of the act, boards of companies are entitled to decide on whether to use the CSR amount in supplementing a government scheme. While the companies are expected to encourage employees to get involved in CSR work, their contributions will be pro bono and not monetized as CSR expenditure.

Let us look at Clause 135 in detail.

1. Every company having a net worth of rupees five hundred crore or more, or turnover of rupees one thousand crore or more or a net profit of rupees five crore or more during any financial year shall constitute a Corporate Social Responsibility Committee of

the Board consisting of three or more directors, out of which at least one director shall be an independent director.

2. The Board's report under sub-section (3) of section 134 shall disclose the composition of the Corporate Social Responsibility Committee.
3. The Corporate Social Responsibility Committee shall:

    a) Formulate and recommend to the Board, a Corporate Social Responsibility Policy which shall indicate the activities to be undertaken by the company as specified in Schedule VII;
    b) Recommend the amount of expenditure to be incurred on the activities referred to in clause (1); and
    c) Monitor the Corporate Social Responsibility Policy of the company from time to time.

4. The Board of every company referred to in sub-section (1) shall:

    a) After taking into account the recommendations made by the Corporate Social Responsibility Committee, approve the Corporate Social Responsibility Policy for the company and disclose contents of such Policy in its report and also place it on the company's website, if any, in such manner as may be prescribed; and
    b) Ensure that the activities as are included in Corporate Social Responsibility Policy of the company are undertaken by the company

5. The Board of every company referred to in sub-section (1), shall ensure that the company spends, in every financial year, at **least two per cent of the average net profits** of the company made during the three immediately preceding financial years, in pursuance of its Corporate Social Responsibility Policy: Provided that the company shall give preference to the local area and areas around it where it operates, for spending the amount earmarked for Corporate Social Responsibility activities: Provided further that if the company fails to spend such amount, the Board shall, in its report made under clause (o) of sub-section (3) of section 134, specify the reasons for not spending the amount.

Explanation.—for the purposes of this section "average net profit" shall be calculated in accordance with the provisions of section 198.

Schedule VII of the Act delineates the various activities that the companies can undertake under CSR.

Schedule VII

Activities which may be included by companies in their corporate social responsibility:

1. Eradicating extreme hunger and poverty
2. Promotion of education
3. Promoting gender equality and empowering women
4. Reducing child mortality and improving maternal health
5. Combating human immunodeficiency virus, acquired immune deficiency syndrome, malaria, and other diseases

6. Ensuring environmental sustainability
7. Employment enhancing vocational skills
8. Social business projects
9. Contribution to the prime minister's National Relief Fund or any other fund set up by the central government or the state governments for socio-economic development and relief and funds for the welfare of the Scheduled Castes, the Scheduled Tribes, other backward classes, minorities, and women
10. Such other matters as may be prescribed

In the government's FAQs, it has been indicated that while there will be no government monitoring of CSR activities, the provisions of the act allow enough safeguards on the implementation of the CSR Act.

The government of India began the mandatory CSR activities with the public sector in 2010, making the Department of Public Sector Enterprises (DPE) responsible for working out the guidelines, etc.

In March 2010, Department of Public Enterprises (DPE) issued a set of guidelines on corporate social responsibility in order to formalize the way CSR is done in the Public Sector Undertakings (PSUs). This move led to the formation of the National Corporate Social Responsibility Hub (NCSR Hub), which would perform the following functions:

- Nationwide compilation, documentation, and creation of database
- Advocacy and research
- Preparation of panels of implementing organizations/monitoring and valuation agencies
- Promotional activities, including production of short films, printing of brochures, pamphlets, etc.
- Conferences, seminars, workshops—both national and international
- Act as a think tank
- Any other matter as entrusted to it from time to time by the Department of Public Enterprises (DPE)

National CSR hub

The NCSR Hub was formally launched on 21 March 2011, to focus on the mammoth task of developing a strategic framework for CSR in India. It was expected that the National CSR hub will "use critical inputs for generation of new approaches that are relevant to business in current social change and development concerns" with the following functions:

- "Nation-wide compilation, documentation, and creation of database
- Advocacy and Research
- Preparation of Panels of Implementing organizations/monitoring and valuation Agencies
- Promotional activities, including production of short films, printing of brochures, pamphlets etc.
- Conferences, Seminars, Workshops—both national and international

- Act as a Think Tank
- Any other matter as entrusted to it from time to time by the Department of Public Enterprises (DPE)."[21]

Later UNICEF organized a consultation with a cross section of large NGOs, UN bodies, and PSEs in three metros, viz., Delhi, Mumbai, and Kolkata. The deliberations resulted in deciding the following tasks for the National CSR Hub:

Guidelines

Loss-making CPEs not mandated to earmark any specific budget;

The implementation of CSR will be a part of the MOU signed between the respective CPSE and the government of India.

The performance of CSR activities would be monitored by the concerned ministry periodically.

CSR budget, expenditure, and performance would be reflected in the annual reports of the CPSEs.

The CSR projects would be independently evaluated by an independent, outside agency.

The passing of Companies Act 2013 created quite a flutter in the corporate circles as nothing would be allowed to be kept under the carpet. *Forbes India* conducted a survey to find out what would be the scenario post—Companies Act 2013. The subsequent table reflects the CSR spend by some top companies and the gap.[22]

The earlier research found some interesting and innovative programs undertaken both by public and private sector companies. For instance, Ashok Leyland operated a FunBus in Chennai and New Delhi, with a hydraulic lift for differently abled children. Children from primary schools run by municipal corporations and orphanages were picked up on a day's picnic. The company also ran an AIDS awareness program that covered 3.5 lakh drivers. The Axis Bank ran Balwadis for children from slum clusters. The bank also had skill development programs PREMA and Yuva Parivartan in motor driving, welding, mobile repairs, and tailoring for young men and women. Hindalco's CSR spanned 692 villages and 12 urban slums and reached out 26 lakh people. The activities included construction of check dams, ponds, bore wells, to provide safe drinking water. Infosys Science Foundation gave away the annual Infosys Prize of honor to outstanding achievements in science and engineering. The company supported causes in healthcare, culture, and rural development. Nanhi Kali, a program run by the KC Mahindra Education Trust, supports education of over 75,000 underprivileged girls.

Tata Consultancy Services' (TCS) Computer Based Functional Literacy (CBFL) programs for adults has benefited 1.2 lakh people. The program, available in nine Indian languages, is spread in a number of states.

Healthcare is one of the main concerns in CSR for Tata Steel. The Tata Steel Rural Development Society aimed to improve the agricultural productivity and raise farmers' standard of living.

Public sector oil company Bharat Petroleum's rain harvesting project, appropriately titled BOOND (drop), in association with the Oil Industries Development Board, selected drought-stricken villages to bring them water. Indian Oil Corporation, another

SR NO.	COMPANY	REVENUE	AVG PAT	ACTUAL SPEND	2% OF PAT
1	INDIAN OIL CORPORATION	442,459	7,783	83	156
2	RELIANCE INDUSTRIES	368,571	21,138	288	423
3	BHARAT PETROLEUM CORPORATION	223,315	1,438	8	29
4	HINDUSTAN PETRO-LEUM CORPORATION	195,891	1,118	27	22
5	TATA MOTORS	170,678	8,437	15	169
6	OIL & NATURAL GAS CORPORATION	151,121	23,660	121	473
7	STATE BANK OF INDIA	147,197	13,056	71	261
8	TATA STEEL	135,976	3,895	146	78
9	PNB GILTS	104,628	29	NA	1
10	HINDALCO INDUSTRIES	82,549	3,597	28	72
11	COAL INDIA	78,410	11,759	119	235
12	BHARTI AIRTEL	71,506	6,511	33	130
13	MMTC	67,023	129	3	3
14	NTPC	66,366	9,334	49	187
15	LARSEN & TOUBRO	64,960	4,818	70	96
16	ESSAR OIL	63,428	-201	NA	N/A
17	MAHINDRA & MAHINDRA	63,030	2,948	22	59
18	MANGALORE REFINERY & PETROCHEMICALS	57,214	1,066	NA	21
19	TATA CONSULTANCY SERVICES	48,894	8,935	51	179
20	BHARAT HEAVY ELECTRICALS	50,654	5,823	37	116
21	STEEL AUTHORITY OF INDIA	51,428	5,153	61	103
22	GAIL (INDIA)	44,861	3,891	54	78
23	STERLITE INDUSTRIES (INDIA)	43,116	6,831	7	137
24	CHENNAI PETROLEUM CORPORATION	45,397	392	3	8
25	ADANI ENTERPRISES	39,416	1,940	14	39
26	ICICI BANK	37,995	6,366	24	127
27	PUNJAB NATIONAL BANK	37,447	4,460	NA	89
28	WIPRO	37,308	5,152	NA	103
29	MARUTI SUZUKI INDIA	40,050	2,162	12	43
30	JSW STEEL	36,964	1,569	32	31
31	INFOSYS	33,734	7,128	26	143
32	STATE TRADING CORPORATION OF INDIA	30,905	60	NA	1
33	CANARA BANK	30,816	3,313	NA	66
34	BANK OF BARODA	30,488	4,262	NA	85
35	RUCHI SOYA INDUSTRIES	30,332	167	0	3

Source: Forbesindia.com

oil behemoth in the public sector, ran the Indian Oil Foundation (IOF), which worked towards the preservation and promotion of India's rich heritage. It also offered 150 sports scholarships to promising youngsters. ONGC's CSR program offers community-based healthcare services in rural areas through 30 Mobile Medicare Units (MMUs). In the Northeast, ONGC-Eastern Swamp Deer Conservation Project works to protect the rare species of Easter Swamp Deer at the Kaziranga National Park in Assam.[23]

Natural gas behemoth ONGC, as per a PIB press release of June 2023, is funding the construction of National Disaster Mitigation Centre and Yatri Niwas in Sidhra, Jammu, to cater to the needs of thousands of pilgrims who visit the Amarnath shrine each year. The public sector broadly will be "providing accommodation for 30,000 tourists in a year, thus staggering the movement of tourists and pilgrims." The press release further shared that ONGS Disaster Management Centre will play

> a pivotal role in providing essential amenities such as lodging, sanitation, and safe drinking water. It will serve as a central hub for distributing vital information and delivering relief measures during emergencies. Additionally, it will contribute to traffic management and ensure a seamless tourist/pilgrimage experience, with a special focus on facilitating boarding and lodging facilities for needy tourists/pilgrims.[24]

What is CSR implementation scenario post Companies Act 2013 in India?

It is mandated in the act to undertake independent third-party research on the efficiency and efficacy of CSR activities. However, there is not much literature available in the public domain on this aspect. In the following paragraph, a few glimpses of the 2019–20 KMPG research are provided to give a sense of the CSR landscape in India.

1. More companies complying to section 135 of 2013 Act.
2. More than 30% companies had more than three meetings of the CSR committee.
3. There has been a 323% increase in companies disclosing their outreach programs in their annual reports.
4. Seventy-six percent of companies spent 2% or more on CSR during 2019–20, the period of study.
5. Forty-one percent of companies have aligned their CSR to UN SDGs.
6. INR 30577 was spent cumulatively by 100 companies on CSR during 2014–19.
7. Seventy-five percent of CSR projects were accomplished with partners, a reflection of SDG 17.
8. A 150% increase in the number of companies who have decided to spend 2% on CSR
9. A 220% increase in expenditure under schedule vii (3) relating to "reducing inequality" at companies with women as chairpersons of CSR committees
10. Eighteen percent of companies have CSR foundations.[25]

Earlier in 2008, ASSOCHAM and KPMG conducted a survey on the state of CSR in India. In the white paper that came out after the survey, it was pointed out that only 27 companies responded to the call for sharing CSR date, out of which data was compiled for 24. The ASSOCHAM site, that time, claimed to have three lakh members. The white paper did not mention how many members were approached to participate in the survey.

The ASSOCHAM and KMPG study throws some interesting facts about CSR initiatives of some Indian companies and multinational companies operating in India.[26]

Some highlights:

8.7.1 Thematic areas

The companies took up a diverse thematic area that encompassed health, education, livelihood, poverty alleviation, environment, water, housing, energy, and microfinance. Some companies also included women empowerment, child development, and development and infrastructure support. While some companies chose to narrow their focus, others took a broader view. Out of 24 companies which sent their data, 16 followed on three to five thematic areas.

Among 58% of the sample, there is a separate CSR department that takes care of the activities.

8.7.2 Public-private partnerships

The importance of building a strong public-private partnership as well as working closely with NGOs as implementers was preferred by as many as 67%. More and more companies were communities from the catchment area of a company who had a direct effect of business on them. Out of 24 corporate organizations surveyed, five worked towards the benefit of employees, neighboring community, and the general public.

8.7.3 Transparency and accountability

Sustainability reporting (SR) at the time of the survey was gaining recognition as a value-added tool for displaying a corporate's commitment towards transparency and accountability towards its stakeholders.

Public disclosure and reporting were the other metrics used to compare the CSR initiative of companies. Twenty-five percent reported as per GRI rules, 21% were signatory to the Global Compact, 21% brought out a separate CSR report, and only 8% mentioned about their CSR initiatives in their annual reports.

ASSOCHAM's white paper referred to the term corporate citizenship that was then gaining ground. Quoting Boston college center for corporate citizenship, the term is defined as "a business strategy that shapes the values underpinning a campaign mission and the choices made each day by its executives, managers and employees as they engage with society." The key principles of corporate citizenship include the following:

- Minimize harm
- Maximize benefit
- Be accountable and responsive to key stakeholders
- Support strong financial results

Corporate citizenship, like CSR, focuses on the membership of the corporation in the political, social, and cultural community, with a focus on enhancing social capital.

Even though there was growing evidence of the usefulness of CSR from charity to a long-term strategy, many still believed CSR was linked to philanthropy.[27]

Amendments in Companies Act 2013 relating to CSR

The Ministry of Corporate Affairs notified the amendments, which came into effect from 22 January 2021.

Highlights

- Where the CSR spending does not exceed Rs. 50 lakhs, there would be no need for a CSR committee. In such cases, the board of directors will discharge the function.
- If there is any unspent amount from an ongoing project, the same shall be transferred within a period of thirty days from the end of the financial year to a special account to be opened by the company in any scheduled bank for that financial year, which will be designated as "unspent CSR Account" and that amount must be spent on CSR within three financial years. If not, then that amount will be transferred to #Fund specified in schedule VII within a period of 30 days from the date of the completion of the third financial year. Further, if the company does not have any ongoing project, it must, within a period of six months of the expiry of the previous financial year, transfer the unspent amount to a #Fund specified in Schedule VII.
- Funds disbursed and utilized towards CSR activities henceforth shall be certified by CFO or financial head.
- The company shall mandatorily disclose the composition of the CSR committee and CSR policy and projects approved by the board on its website for public access.
- Every company having an average CSR obligation of Rs. 10 crores or more in the three immediately preceding years shall undertake impact assessment through an independent agency of their CSR projects having an outlay of rupees one crore or more, and which has been completed not less than one year before undertaking the impact study. The amount on research can be booked as CSR expenditure, but it should not be more than 5% of the total CSR expenditure for that financial year or fifty lakh rupees, whichever is less.[28]

8.8 Who gives how much in India?

According to a story in *IndiaCSR*, the CSR budget of some of the Indian companies for 2021–22 is reflected subsequently. The list includes companies with varying business interests, from banks to technology firms, from oil and gas companies to conglomerates; the CSR spend ran into hundreds of million rupees. Here is a glimpse of the top ten CSR spends. Top of the list is occupied by Reliance Industries Limited, with a CSR budget of 737 crores; close on the heels is HDFC bank, with a CSR budget of 733.86 crores; the third position is taken by Tata Consultancy Services Limited, with a CSR budget of 716 crores; public sector behemoth Oil and Natural Gas Corporation Limited spent 436.02 crores on CSR; Infosys Limited, with a CSR budget of 396.7 crores, at the fifth position, was another major player in the technology industry; ITC Limited, at a CSR budget of 354.27 crores, was another leading conglomerate with a diverse range of business interests; Indian Oil Corporation and NTPC, two other public sector organizations, spent Rs. 323.14 and Rs 281.08 crores respectively on CSR during the year under review;

occupying the ninth and tenth positions among top CSR spenders, Tata Steel Limited spent Rs. 266. 57 crores, and ICICI Bank Limited spent Rs. 261.73 crores.[29]

For individuals with riches, an act of corporate social responsibility may mean an act of philanthropy. Analysts argue that philanthropists are different from philanthrocapitalists in their almost businesslike approach to charity.

In their book *Philanthrocapitalsim: How the Rich can Save the World*, authors Mathew Bishop and Michael Green note that new billionaires use big business strategies and expect results and accountability.

When asked by media in 2006 on what social responsibility he felt towards the country of his birth, Steel magnate Lakshmi Mittal replied, "I am still very young, I still have a few years' work to do before I can consider it."

In June 2006, Warren Buffett, one of the richest men at the time, pledged to donate the bulk of his $44 million to a charitable foundation run by Bill Gates.

It is estimated that Warren Buffet has pledged $46 billion for healthcare and anti-poverty programs.[30]

Bill Gates has stepped down from Microsoft to concentrate on the Bill & Melinda Gates Foundation.[31]

Gates, whose net worth is estimated at $104 billion, announced in July 2023 that he was giving $20 billion to the Bill & Melinda Gates Foundation (BMGF), which he runs with his former wife, Melinda French Gates.[32]

Corporate philanthropy is not new in India. The Tatas and Birlas have been contributing for long in various sectors, including endowments in educational institutions, by giving scholarships to meritorious and needy students, in performing arts, and religious and social activities. The media, however, hardly wrote about it. Publicity about such acts, feel many, is important as more and more people can be roped in to make the world a wee bit more comfortable for those who remain on the fringes of the society.[33]

8.9 Designing a CSR project—the imperatives

The following checklist will be useful for initiating a CSR program.

CSR initiative steps:

1. The first step ideally is taken by the board of directors to decide on a CSR initiative. It must be a well-thought-out decision, based on a sound economic model so that there is no going back. This can begin with the preparation of a "social responsibility inventory" of what the company may be doing until then.
2. Select a person to oversee the CSR, who would prepare a proposal on various areas the company can think of in CSR. This needs to be based on a clear picture of the country's socio-economic matrix, the Planning Commission's Five-Year Plan outlay and, if possible, a good look at the UN Sustainability Goals, of which India is a signatory. A CSR program that is not embedded in social reality may not be of much relevance. Enter the area that makes a difference in the lives of people. Select the area of operation around your projects or at places that need to be reached on priority.
3. Conduct a social audit to know exactly what is required and not necessarily what you wish to do. For example, the board may have taken a decision to open schools in, say, 50 villages. One way is to go ahead and open the schools, the other is do a

baseline survey, conduct a social audit to find out the demographic profile of area, look at the gap. It is possible that there may be plenty of schools already, but they need to build infrastructure or they have dearth of funds for paying teachers' salary. So prudence would lie in partnering with existing systems to strengthen them, rather than opening new schools.

4. Review the audit and reach a decision on what can be best suited. Create a sustainability model, so that after a period the stakeholder community can run the initiative on its own, and you can move to other areas.
5. Involve the concerned ministry and local government and grassroots level Gram Sabha in designing the project.
6. Involve all the levels of employees in your CSR initiative. It would not only be fulfilling for them but they would feel a sense of pride in a company that goes beyond the obvious.
7. A CSR plan needs to translate into concrete actions by identifying the team that would be responsible and accountable for making it happen as envisaged with well-laid-out goals, financial resources, deadline, and priorities sorted out.
8. It is important that the CSR initiative should reflect the company's ethos and not dilute its brand name value.
9. A partnership model with NGOs can be considered, instead of going it alone.
10. A continuous appraisal is required to sustain the CSR initiative. A suitable audit methodology may be made a part of the program.
11. Transparency and honesty of purpose would take any CSR initiative soaring high. Put your CSR work details on the public domain; say it on your website. This would not only create a good image for the company but would also make people in charge accountable.

Novel idea of setting up social stock exchange

Mooted in the union budget of 2019–20, the idea behind setting up a social stock exchange in India was to "enable entities involved in social activities such as charitable trusts and non-profit organizations (NPO) to access the capital market for funds."

The Securities and Exchange Board of India (Sebi) gave in principle its approval to the National Stock Exchange (NSE) for setting up the exchange in December 2022. A statement from the NSE read,

> For eligible NPOs, the first step for onboarding starts with the registration on the Social Stock Exchange segment. Post registration, NPOs can initiate the fund mobilization process by issuance of instruments such as Zero Coupon Zero Principal (ZCZP) via a public issue or private placement.[34]

The concept is new, and its success can be gauged after one sees the activity in the stock market in a few years and with the mobilization of money.

Summary

In this chapter we defined corporate social responsibility (CSR) and its role and scope. The genesis of CSR was traced to more than 200 years ago, when people refused to buy sugar that was processed by slaves, forcing the importer to change the inhuman practice. In India, the Tatas are credited for taking CSR initiative, though initially it may not have been called by that name. We looked at the theoretical aspects of CSR and various stages of CSR in India. Best practices and the growing awareness about CSR as a business policy were discussed. The CSR survey, including the ASSOCHAM and KMPG white paper, was also discussed in detail to appreciate the development of CSR in India. Several CSR case studies of companies of various sizes and hues were taken up for discussion.

Key terms

Corporate social responsibility: operating a business in a manner that meets or exceeds the ethical, legal, commercial, and public expectations that society has of business.

Corporate governance: a term used for the legal and ethical norms followed by a corporate organization.

e-Choupal: spearheaded by ITC, the e-Choupal leverages information technology to virtually cluster all the value chain participants in the rural hinterland of India by delivering the same benefits as vertical integration does in mature agricultural economies like the USA.

Social audit: refers to conducting surveys among the communities to make needs assessment.

Critical thinking exercise

Chose a sector, say automobile, IT, FMCG, etc., and analyze the CSR initiatives of at least three to four organizations from that sector to look at the thematic areas taken up by them and how they go about practicing CSR. Draw your conclusions about various activities and whether these synergize with their corporate goals. Speak with, say, ten to 15 people to know whether they are aware of the CSR initiative by these companies and if it is important for them to buy products from a company that is socially responsible. You can access their CSR initiatives from their websites and annual reports. Some companies also bring out sustainability reports that are often available in the public domain.

This exercise can be taken up in groups, so that meaningful discussion is held after the insights are available.

Field work

Get in touch with an organization that runs a CSR program nearby. Take a brief from the CSR officer on the program, and know whether the CSR initiative is run by the company itself or with a partnership with some civil society organization, the objective behind the CSR, and budget pledged.

Visit one of the areas, talking to the beneficiaries, and find out whether they are aware about who is responsible for the project and whether their participation in the projects is sought and if any feedback has been taken from them. Speak with the local block development officer and Gram Sabha head to know whether they have been involved in the CSR initiative. Make an analytical note on how lives are being touched or not through the CSR efforts.

Questions

Q.1 Define corporate social responsibility. How it is similar or different from corporate citizenship, corporate sponsorship, and corporate philanthropy?
Q.2 What are the myths surrounding the practice of CSR? Discuss.
Q.3 What have been the various stages of CSR in India?
Q.4 Which Indian company, in your view, is doing excellent work in CSR, and why do you think so? Put forth your arguments based on facts.
Q.5 Go through the UN Sustainable Development Goals (SDGs), which can be accessed on the UN website, and discuss the areas that need to be taken up by companies on priority in their CSR programs.

Notes

1 "Business for Social Responsibility", www.bsr.org.
2 mallen@mallenbaker.net
3 www.bharatpetroleum.com/corporate/csr.asp
4 Mr. K Subramanya, CEO, Tata BP Solar, said while delivering the keynote address at the **CII Conclave on Integrating CSR with Business Strategy** in Bangalore on 18 March 2008.
5 Boli and Hartsukar, 2001, as quoted in ASSOCHAM and KMPG white paper 2008 on Corporate Social responsibility-Towards Sustainable Future- A White Paper KPMG IN INDIA https://download.clib.psu.ac.th/datawebclib/e_resource/trial_database/WileyInterScienceCD/pdf/CSR/CSR_2.pdf, presented at the 1st international summit on CSR on 29–30 January 2008 organized by the Indian Ministry of Corporate Affairs and Industry association Associated chamber of Commerce (ASSOCHAM). https://www.in.kpmg.com/pdf/csr_whitepaper.pdf
6 Bryane Michael at www.interscience.willey.com, 10.10.02.
7 "Kejriwal's Poll Promises to RWAs: Mini-councillor Status, Funds", Latest News Delhi, *Hindustan Times*.
8 The Times of India, 16 June 2009.
9 New York Times and agencies, as reported in the Times of India on 31 January 2009.
10 www.csrwire.com/News/8871.html
11 Ibid.
12 Ibid.
13 www.ic.gc.ca/eic/site/csr-rse.nsf/eng/Home
14 T. Macalister, "Investors Urged to Back Climate Change Awareness with Action", *The Guardian*, September 2006.
15 "Climate Change Performance Index 2023: India Ranked 8th in the List", adda247.com.
16 M. Kahn, " California Sues Car Makers over Global Warming", *Reuter*, 20 September 2006.
17 "Marking the Kyoto Protocol's 25th Anniversary", United Nations, https://www.un.org/en/climatechange/marking-kyoto-protocol%E2%80%99s-25th-anniversary.
18 A. Revkin, " Branson Pledges Billions to Fight Global Warming", *The New York Times*, 20 September 2006.
19 The of "Promise Thinkers", 3, no. 24, 19 June 2006.
20 www.mca.gov.in/Ministry/pdf/FAQ_CSR.pdf, accessed on 27 August 2017.
21 http://tiss.edu/view/11/projects/all-projects/national-corporate-social-responsibility-hub/, accessed on 27 August 2017.
22 www.forbesindia.com/article/real-issue/csr-report-card-where-companies-stand/34893/1, accessed on 28 August 2017.
23 Ibid.
24 Press Information Bureau, pib.gov.in.
25 https://assets.kpmg.com/content/dam/kpmg/in/pdf/2020/02/india-s-csr-reporting-survey-2019.pdf
26 www.chdgroup.org/wp-content/uploads/2020/10/csr_whitepaper-kpmg-chd.pdf
27 Ibid.

28 "The Gazette of India Companies (CSR Policy) Amendment Rules, 2021.pdf", Google Drive.
29 https://indiacsr.in/corporate-responsibility-in-action-the-top-10-companies-leading-the-way-in-csr-for-fy-2021-22/
30 "Warren Buffett Has Now Given Record $48 Billion to Charity", forbes.com.
31 Ibid.
32 "Bill Gates Made 2022's Biggest Charitable Donation", *Los Angeles Times*, latimes.com.
33 Ibid.
34 www.moneycontrol.com/news/business/markets/nse-gets-the-final-sebi-approval-to-launch-social-stock-exchange-10147071.html.

9

FINANCIAL COMMUNICATION

9.1 Introduction

Financial communication has grown to be an important part of corporate communication. The seamless markets *sans* international boundaries, the growing aspirational middle class, double-income-generating households, risk-taking attitude, desire for a secure future for self and children have all contributed in creating a large target audience who are interested in the capital market and investment options. India is said to be a nation that attracts maximum saving in the world. The emergence of various financial institutions is indicative of the trend. Therefore, from the perspective of organizations that are seeking finance, there is a need for informing and educating this class of consumers.

9.1.1 Evolution of financial communication in India

The economic liberalization in the 1990s in India brought with it many players from overseas. The market saw FDI (Foreign Direct Investment) pouring in many sectors, including the financial sector, necessitating both the national and international players to reach out to the existing customers and potential ones with their USPs and promises of value additions. The life Insurance Corporation of India (LIC), an unchallenged player for about five decades in the independent India, understood the onslaught of competition as never before. It quickly changed its mission statement from "zindagi ke saath bhi. Zindagi ke baad bhi" to "We Understand India Better." Liberalization also brought about an unprecedented spurt in media growth, especially in the electronic segment. In India today there are more than 400 news channels and about half a dozen exclusive business channels. In the print media, the most visible trend was the proliferation in trade media. The number of financial newspapers and magazines increased considerably. Mainstream newspapers also added special business pages to satisfy the need of an average reader in the capital market and the growing investment opportunities.

With a liberalized economy in the 1990s, several companies in various sectors like IT, infrastructure, and power felt the need to expand, for which they needed finances. The

DOI: 10.4324/9781032694702-9

government of India encouraged public sector companies to explore the primary market for financing their projects. With such changes, the organizations in general felt the need for interfacing with institutional investors and shareholders through the primary market.

9.1.2 Financial communication function

In general, the corporate communication department of an organization looks after communication relating to "public issues" and investor relations. The internal department often takes the help of ad agencies and PR firms, which have experience in handling financial advertising and investor relationship management respectively.

9.1.3 What should the corporate communication manager know of financial communication?

Analysts believe that financial communication is an "important factor in reducing the cost of capital, provided the company discloses full, timely, and relevant information about its financial situation. The corner stone of financial communication policy is the signal, the managers of a company send to investors."[1]

The corporate communication manager is expected to have a good hang of the capital market functioning, the role and scope and functions of various regulatory bodies and institutions, and, most importantly, an acquaintance with the entire process of going to primary market and the legal aspects of financial advertising. A good knowledge of various financial instruments/products is crucial for the success of a corporate communication manager in financial communication.

The corporate communication manager needs to have a working knowledge of the methods of corporate reporting in different corporate setups, viz., public sector, private sector, and NGO sector; how the financial information can be used innovatively to keep the organization in positive focus in the media; and the role of auditing and financial information in corporate governance.[2]

9.2 Key publics for financial communication

Dolphin lists the following key target audience for financial communication by an organization:

1. Analysts
2. The city
3. Financial journalists
4. Institutional investors (for investor relations)
5. Merchant bankers
6. Private investors (for investor relations)
7. Stockbrokers[3]

Post Enron and Satyam Computer frauds and the buzz created by the Hindenburg exposé, which upset the capital market, people's exposure to various scams and scandals in the corporate world has increased. They are now expecting better accountability from organizations where they have invested. The information sought encompasses various areas like measurement, disclosure, impact of financial results on shareholders' wealth, and the options they have when the market has toughened.

Corporate annual report is the basic document for the purpose. However, when investor confidence is shaken for some reason, it is important for the organization to touch base with its shareholder community, both the private and institutional investors, to clear doubts and restore its confidence. The early 1990s witnessed shaky investor confidence in various scrips, resulting in frantic selling of various financial instruments. Voltas came out with an ad campaign assuring its investors that everything was fine with the company. "Another Quiet Day for Voltas at the Stock Exchange" was the headline of its print ad. In the copy, the ad informed the readers that over 90% of shareholders with Voltas had never sold their instruments, thereby assuring the investors that its shareholders had confidence in the company. Stock exchanges, before the transactions became automated and electronic, were a hyperactive place with thousands of people trading, creating a cacophony of sorts. The ad appropriately had the picture of a crowd of people engaged in trading at a stock exchange, thus qualifying the headline "Another Quiet day. . ."[4]

Trillions of dollars were lost when the stock markets across the world tanked amid the horrendous Covid-19 between 2020–22. Media often is the first one to ring the alarm bells on the stock market as was seen during the economic depression on 2008. Trillions of dollars were lost between 2020 and 2022 amidst the Covid-19 pandemic, but media was busy reporting on the havoc caused by the disease which claimed millions of lives, and not covering the stock market, that in normal times, it would done.

Many scholars feel that financial markets represent not just the capital, numbers, and figures, which an average person can hardly decipher, but also a very complex social reality. What media carries may be in bits and pieces, which may or may not be the whole truth. Therefore, it is important for listed companies to share information fully with shareholders not only through the annual report that is available once in a year but continuously through the company's interactive website or direct mailers. The case of ICICI Bank is an apt example of how it lost no time in interfacing with its existing customers and the public at large, when grapevine adversely affected its image in the aftermath of the falling of financial behemoths in 2008. The bank undertook a generic customer education campaign, which lasted for months. The full case study may be referred in the chapter on crises communication.

In the following paragraphs, we shall discuss the following to have a basic understanding of the subject matter, before we take up the process of financial communication and investor relations:

- Working of various financial institutions in India
- Capital market
- Various financial instruments

9.3 Working of various financial institutions in India

9.3.1 Reserve Bank of India (RBI)

RBI is the apex monetary institution of India, also referred to as the central bank of the country. Established in 1935 in pre-independent India, by the RBI act of 1934, it acts as

TABLE 9.1 Major financial institutions in India[5]

Financial institution	*Date of starting*
Imperial Bank of India	1921
Reserve Bank of India	1 April 1935
Industrial Finance corporation of India	1948
State Bank of India	1 July 1955
Unit Trust of India	February1,1964
IDBI	July 1964
NABARD	12 July 1982
SIDBI	1990
EXIM Bank	1 January 1982
National Housing Bank	July 1988
Life Insurance Corporation (LIC)	September 1956
General Insurance Corporation (GIC)	November 1972
Regional Rural Banks	2 October 1975
Risk Capital and Technology Finance Corporation Ltd.	March 1975
Technology Development & Information Co. of India Ltd.	1989
Infrastructure Leasing & Financial Services Ltd.	1988
Housing Development Finance Corporation Ltd. (HDFC)	1977

Source: Author

the apex body in monetary matters. Its preamble reads: "to regulate the issue of bank notes and keeping of reserves with a view to securing and maintaining stability of India and generally to operate the currency and credit system of the country to its advantage." RBI is very active in issuing instructions on interest rates on various kinds of savings and borrowings to the public sector banks, which they must follow.

9.3.2 Securities and Exchange Board of India (SEBI)

SEBI was established in 1988, as a non-statutory body for regulating the securities market. It became an autonomous body in 1992, gaining more powers through an ordinance. SEBI has been regulating the market with the following objectives:

1. To develop the securities market
2. To promote investor interest
3. To make rules and regulations for securities market

9.3.2.1 Functions of SEBI

SEBI was basically established to protect the interests of investors in securities and to permit the development and effective regulation of the securities markets.

SEBI is responsible for registering and regulating the operations of various intermediaries in the securities markets including stockbrokers, foreign institutional investors, merchant bankers, underwriters, and portfolio managers. It also regulates venture capital funds and investment schemes including mutual funds. SEBI also has the primary responsibility for preventing, prohibiting, and punishing fraudulent and unfair trade practices relating to the securities markets and investor relations. SEBI exerts complete control over all mutual funds in India.

The brokers and sub-brokers are required to get themselves registered in any of the stock exchanges in India. For working as underwriters, a minimum asset limit of Rs. 20.00 lakhs has been fixed as reflected in the SEBI (Underwriters) Act.[6]

9.3.3 National Stock Exchange (NSE)

On the recommendation of the Pherwani Committee, the government of India authorized the IDBI to establish the NSE in 1992. The NSE deals in the trading of equity shares, bonds, and government securities. The NSE has the reputation of being one of the best-run stock exchanges globally.

There are 28 stock exchanges in India.[7] Every stock exchange is required to maintain an index, which refers to the movement of scrips according to their value of transactions.

The Interconnected Stock Exchange of India Limited (ISE) is promoted by several regional stock exchanges in Mumbai with nationwide trading facilities. The NSE, OTECI, ISE, and regional stock exchanges use electronic facilities for trading with access to investors all over the country. The new NSE Reference rates are drawn from MIBOR (Mumbai interbank offer rates) and MIBID (Mumbai interbank bid rates). Both MIBOR and MIBID work in tandem, the former indicating lending rates and the latter the rate of receipts.[8]

9.3.4 Bombay Stock Exchange (BSE)

Bombay (now Mumbai) is called the financial city of India. One of the oldest stock exchanges in Asia, the BSE was established in 1875 under the name "The Native Share and Stock Brokers Association." The BSE launched its first BSE 200 Index in 1994, under which 200 companies were selected based on market capitalization, value of turnover, and other fundamental factors, keeping 1989–90 as the base year. The BSE Index 500 was announced in 1999, which had the scrips of 500 companies, encompassing 90% of the total market capitalization of BSE Ltd. The BSE-PSU Index that began in 2001 includes major public sector companies listed in the exchange.

9.3.5 Foreign Investment Promotion Board (FIPD)

The FIPD is a specialized agency in India dealing with matters relating to Foreign Direct Investment. The aim behind setting up FIPD was to create a base in the country by which large volumes of investment can be drawn to India. FIPD was transferred to the Department of Economic Affairs (CDEA) in 2003. Some of the functions of FIPD include the following:

- Formulating proposals for promoting investments
- Creating processes for implementation of proposals
- Setting friendly guidelines for facilitating more investors
- Inviting more and more companies to make investments
- To recommend to the government of India to take necessary actions for attracting more investments

The high-powered FIPD has top-rung bureaucrats on its board, viz., the Secretary, Economic Affairs, Secretary, Department of Industrial Policy and Promotion (Ministry of Commerce and Industry), Secretary Commerce, Secretary, Economic relations, Ministry of External Affairs, and Secretary, Ministry of Overseas India affairs.[9]

9.4 Capital market

Capital market defines the source of funds for the industry. The finances are sourced through two means from the capital market:

1. Primary market
2. Secondary market

In primary market, new issues of shares, debentures, and bonds are available to investors who apply directly to the issuer of allotment and pay application fee to the issuer's account.

Under the primary market, companies go "public," a term used to denote that the company is borrowing money directly from the public through a public issue. All the securities issued in the primary market are listed on the stock exchanges to enable trading.

The pricing of an IPO is dependent on three factors—the state of the capital markets, sector fundamentals, and company performance. According to market analysts, one needs the tailwinds of all these three to achieve good IPO response and post-listing performance.

The secondary market denotes a place where shares and securities are issued and traded. The transactions happen in various stock exchanges. Securities comprise shares, debentures, or bonds issued by government, semi-government authorities, and various mutual funds issued by public and private sector players.

Both the primary and secondary markets complement each other. The two markets are not to be taken as separate entities, cautions E C Thomas, a financial journalist: "Primary markets only mean the first investment in new shares or debentures by the public directly to the issuing company, whereas the secondary market refers to the subsequent trading in those shares and debenture i.e., the stock exchange."[10]

9.4.1 Stock index

A stock index is a statistical tool to capture and measure the price behavior of the overall market. The most effective index reflects the total market. This is achieved by averaging the price of scrips in the index—not the simple but weighted one. Thus, each stock gets a weight proportional to its market capitalization (market capitalization is the share price multiplied by the number of shares making up its equity capital).

Companies are very sensitive to how are they are commented upon by media and, more importantly, by investment banking or varying stock exchanges.

9.4.2 Market index

Market index is a term used for measurement of the trend of share prices. The index provides with an idea of the value change in share prices rather than just price change. A gain in index is referred as "bullish" trend, and the downward index is referred as "bearish." Media, especially the trade media, reflects the points the Senex has gone up and down to indicate how the market is doing. As soon as the news of R Raju's resignation from Satyam Computers became public, the stock market tanked within minutes. The extent of fraud, when unearthed, made it only worse, but the initial shock made people frantically sell their shares. Similarly, one found Adani stock fluctuating after the Hindenburg report in 2023.

Other widely known global share price indices include the Dow Jones Industrial Average, Standard and Poor (S&P) 500; the National association of Securities Dealers automated Quotations system (NASDAQ); Nikkes-225, stock average of Tokyo's Exchange; Hang Seung of Hong Kong exchange; Financial Times Exchange Index (FTSE-100) of London and Euro next; European Exchange; Frankfurt DAX index; CAC=40 index of Paris; Singapore's STI Index; South Korea's KOSPI Index; Australia's benchmark S&P/ASX=200 Index; and Morgan Stanley Capital International (MSCI). All the stock market indices now include new economy stocks that comprise information, entertainment, and communication.[11]

Both the countries and the companies are constantly on the radar of various national and international rating agencies. Any adverse comment by them does affect the market sentiment. Here are two examples:

Standard & Poor (S&P) revised India outlook from "stable to "negative" for 2008–09, citing various policies that, in its view, would put pressure on country's finances, reported the media. To quote S&P, "The outlook revisions reflect our view that India's fiscal position has deteriorated to a level that it is unsustainable in the medium term. The government has implemented various policies that increased stress on its fiscal position." The agency retained India's long-term credit rating to "BBB," the lowest investment grade. India's total deficit, including off-budget items like oil and fertilizer bonds, it said, would increase to 11.4% in 2008–09 from 5.7% in 2007–08. Similarly, the center's deficit has risen to 6.1% from 2.5% projected for 2008–09. The statement, commented the *Times of India*, came just before the announcement of the third stimulus package by the finance minister, "which will cost the exchequer an additional Rs. 29,000 Crores in 2008–09, which will push the fiscal deficit to 6% against the projection of 5.5%."[12]

When investment banker Goldman Sachs's report criticized the corporate governance standards of the gas behemoth Oil and Natural Gas Organization (ONGC) because it was subsidizing fuel prices under government orders, the company did not lose a breadth in sending a "point-by-point rebuttal," as reported by media, on Goldman's claim that the government as promoter had taken $20 billion "in cash" from the company over the last six years without consulting the minority shareholders. ONGC questioned its benchmarks in certain parts like its interpretation that the discounts given on crude sold to government-run subsidiaries so that they could sell cheaper oil. The company clarified that subsidy discounts were given on crude produced from nominated fields only where there was no production sharing or profit oil sharing with the government. And this practice, it said, was not uncommon in many countries.[13]

Here there is a lesson for corporate communication practitioners, that is, to take a strategic decision on whether to respond to criticism, keeping all the facts and arguments in place or not. In this case, the company even went to the media, giving a clarification before the Goldman Report could do harm to its reputation. Interestingly, the media also unearthed rifts between the two in the past. The information possibly could have been shared by ONGC to question Goldman's ethics in its corporate governance. It brought from the closet a case in 2008 when the then minister Mani Shankar Aiyer had accused Goldman of "lack of propriety and transparency" in presiding over an auction of a Kazakhstan oil firm. In this case it was alleged that ONGC and its partner steel magnate Lakshmi Mittal's $3.96 billion offer was rejected, while the China National Petroleum Corporation was asked to revise its higher bid in the following days and sale was announced before office hours on 22 August 2008.[14]

9.4.3 Fraudulent practices—impact on investors' wealth

No study of Indian capital market can be complete without a reference to three cases that duped the system of thousands of crore rupees. These are what came to be known as the Harshad Mehta case in the early 1990s, which forever changed the way the Indian stock market was to function, the Home Trade scam in 2002, and the Satyam Computers fraud in 2008. In between, there were some more scams, glimpses of which have been provided after the discussion of the Harshad Mehta and Home Trade case studies. The Satyam case has been dealt with in detail in the chapter on crises communication.

Harshad Mehta is said to be responsible for various regulations and acts that have been formulated post the scam through which he is believed to have duped the financial institutions of hundreds of crores of rupees in the 1990s. Home Trade, a virtually non-existent company, used smart ad campaign and celebrity endorsement to mesmerize investors and systems into believing what was non-existent. Satyam Computers, one of the largest IT companies with great brand equity in India and elsewhere, was caught engaging in fraudulent practices in the late 2008. The CEO, in his confessional letter to the regulator, said that the cash and bank balances were inflated to the extent of Rs 5,040 crore, accrued interest of Rs 376 crore did not exist, a liability of Rs 1,230 crore was understated, and the debtors' position was overstated by Rs 490 crore. The September quarter (2008) results of the company reported a revenue of Rs 2,700 crore and an operating margin of Rs 649 crore (24% of revenue) as against the actual revenues of Rs 2,112 crore and an actual operating margin of Rs 61 crore (3% of revenues). "This has resulted in artificial cash and bank balances going up by Rs 588 crore in Q2 alone. The gap in the balance sheet has arisen purely on account of inflated profits over several years," the letter stated. In all, the fraud was worth at least Rs 7,000 crore and, as investigations continue, could be much more.[15]

Here are the case studies:

9.4.3.1 The Harshad Mehta case

Arrested by the Central Bureau of Investigations for misappropriating in 1992 more than 27 lakhs shares of about 90 companies including some reputed ones like ACC and Hindalco through forged share transfer forms, the total value of shares was placed at Rs. 250 crores at that time.

By 1991, Harshad Mehta, a young man in his late twenties, was the most awe-inspiring stockbroker, who was considered a financial genius and referred to as Mr. Big Bull, who single-handedly decided the course the market would play. He wrote columns in media and had his website, giving advice to potential investors on where to invest. It is a different matter that the scam also unearthed that he was in league with some unscrupulous small companies, whose shares he was recommending. His "bull run," as termed by the media, came to an end in April 1992, when the stock market scam broke out, bringing down many financial institutions, but not before causing agony and loss to millions of investors. Mehta is estimated to have caused a loss of Rs. 4000 crores to various entities.[16]

The person responsible for unearthing the scam on 23 April 1992 was journalist Sucheta Dalal who then worked for the *Times of India*.

Cunning as he was, he also tried to rope in the former prime minister late Narsimha Rao in a scandal that came to be known as the "Suitcase" controversy. He alleged that he paid the former prime minister Rs. one crore to help him get "off the hook." The media covered the story for weeks on the possibility. He also did not stop; when the media asked him how could he fit in so many currency notes in one suitcase, he held a press conference and showed a video clip in which Rs. one crore worth of currency notes were being fitted in. The people and media lost interest soon when they found a goof up in the date, and not many believed that the prime minister of a country would take such a paltry amount for the party funding from a tainted person!

9.4.3.2 What was Mehta's modus operandi?

In their book *The Great Indian Scam: Story of Missing Rs. 4000 Crore*, authors Samir K. Barua and Jayanth R. Varma explain the critical mechanism through which the scam was affected through the Ready Forward (RF) deal. The RF is, in essence, a secured short-term loan, typically a 15-day loan, from one bank to another. Crudely put, the bank lends the money against government securities, as a pawnbroker would give loan against jewelry. In the case of RF, the borrowing bank sells the securities to the lending bank and buys them back at the end of the loan period, typically at a slightly higher price. In a typical RF deal, a broker brings together two banks for which he earns commission. He does not handle cash or securities. In the case of Mehta, this was not followed.

In his case, the deliveries of securities and payment were made through the broker. So neither the buyer nor the seller probably knew whom they had traded with, a fact known only to the broker. Smartly, the broker traded on behalf of the bank to bring some credibility aspect. In this case, the other factor was known as the Bank Receipt (BR). In RF, the securities were not moved back or forth in reality. Instead, the borrower and the seller of securities gave the buyer of the securities a BR. Once Mehta figured this out, then he was looking for banks that could give him BR without the backing of the government securities. Two banks came in the trap, viz., Bank of Karad and Metropolitan Cooperative bank, which were willing to issue BRs as and, when asked, for a fee. Once these fake BRs were obtained, these were passed on to the other banks for loans. The banks did not question, presuming the BRs had the backing of government securities. The money thus obtained was used to drive up prices of certain stocks in the stock market. When time came to return the money, the stocks were sold for a profit. The banks got their money back. When the scam was unearthed, the banks and financial institutions were said to be responsible for swindling Rs. 4000 Crores.

It took the investigating agencies a lot of effort and time to understand the scam and the involvement of various individuals and institutions. Harshad Mehta had 28 cases against him, but even after years, he was being tried only for one, when a massive heart attack claimed his life at the age of 47 in 2002 while undergoing a jail term along with his two brothers.[17]

His life seemed to lose no interest years after his passing away, when a film by the name *The Big Bull* was conceived in Bollywood with mainstream actor Abhishek Bachchan essaying the role of the scamster. Due to Covid-19, the screening was delayed and at last could be seen on the OTT platform.[18] There was also a web series: *Scam 1992: the Harshad Mehta Story* in 2020, which evinced keen interest among the audience, the series bagging some awards.[19]

9.4.4 The story of a non-existent brand—Home Trade

The Home Trade story would go down in the history of capital market and advertising industry as one of the most dubious ones in which celebrities were used as cover-up for a meticulously planned financial scam. By claiming a foreign source of money supply, the company—which was only a financial dot-com—launched a mega endorsement campaign with the most expensive celebrities in the country, like superstar cricketer Sachin Tendulkar, Bollywood superstars Shahrukh Khan and Hritik Roshan, to brand a financial product that nobody could figure out what it was. The company is believed to have spent around Rs. 60 crores on advertising and publicity even though nobody knew what Home Trade did or what it sold, or even whether a financial portal could afford to throw around that sort of advertising money that it did. The advertisements kicked off with the signature line *Life Means More*, whatever it meant in tangible terms for those who put in their money. The people behind the brand were Sanjay Agarwal, Ketan Sheth (who was already a broker), Nandkishore Trivedi, and one Baluchan Rai (a Hong Kong–based non-resident Indian).[20]

9.4.4.1 The modus operandi

Euro Discover Technology Ventures, based in Mauritius, funded the venture. The group bought off Lloyds Brokerage Ltd from its owners—the Guptas—for a nominal Rs 1.50 per share. It later made an offer for sale at several times that sum to get it listed. Lloyds Brokerage changed to Euro Asia Securities, which was listed at the Pune and Bangalore stock exchanges, and it started a nonstop effort for a listing on the Mumbai stock exchange. Euro Asia Securities soon announced the Home Trade company with a lot of hype and hoopla. Its high profile, commented analysts, ensured that nobody, including high-profile organizations and individuals, bothered to check its background for over two years—in fact, right until the bubble burst.

As per its own website, some of the best names got associated with it. For instance, PricewaterhouseCoopers ran its back-office operations, an advanced centralized customer contact center was powered by Siebel, A T Kearney helped define customer-centric strategies, Andersen Consulting assisted the company in focusing on stock broking and risk management, Dow Jones and Reuters delivered up-to-the-minute news, while Multex, CMIE, Dun & Bradstreet, et al provided content. It received credit from HDFC Bank until 2002, when the cheques started bouncing.

Home Trade claimed on its website,

> You've seen the ads splashed across media. You've heard Shah Rukh, Hrithik and Sachin. Exciting and innovative things are set to happen in the investment bazaar, as these revolutionary new FMFG products herald the next generation of financial services available to consumers. Productised and packaged, available "off the shelf" at convenient locations across the country, these services are driven by a simple philosophy—"life means more." Add to this the firm belief that finance can be fun, and you've got the secret to what makes them special. Designed to address specific needs across a wide spectrum, these boxed products are backed by state-of-the-art infrastructure and the latest CRM technologies. And of course, the financial expertise and strong credentials of Home Trade.[21]

If one were to analyze celebrity endorsement and smart communication, these were the driving force behind the strategy which, in effect, meant nothing, Rediff Money commented thus: "Productised," "boxed products"—what on earth does it mean in the absence of a specific service?"[22]

The company pretended to buy G-secs (government securities) to earn credibility with banks for borrowing money. It used the money for some time and then repeated the deal with another cooperative bank to repay the first. However, after a while, it could no longer repay over Rs 125 crore to the Nagpur Co-operative Bank. Very soon it was clear that the Osmanabad Central Co-operative Bank, the Wardha Co-operative Bank, and a couple of other cooperative banks from Pune and Ahmedabad also faced the same problem. The cooperative banks were duped of about Rs. 500 crores. The scam could not have happened without the active collusion of some employees of these banks. Cooperative banks have generally been embroiled in many controversies, including lack of accountability, corruption, and active political interference. This only reinforced the situation in some such banks.

As per media reports, neither the celebrities nor the ad agencies were paid fully for the task.

Home Trade was a registered broker with SEBI. When the bubble burst, it issued instruction to Home Trade to stop transaction in the capital market till it held a post-decisional hearing for the accused company on 3 May 2002.

SEBI was cautioned by the Reserve Bank of India on the Nagpur District Co-op Bank Ltd. about Home Trade that had allegedly entered "certain transactions of government securities with Home Trade Ltd.," which the apex bank said seemed fraudulent.[23]

Some other scams since liberalization include the following:

9.4.5.1 Preferential allotment of stocks

In this case, some companies, including Colgate and Castrol, began allotting shares to themselves on preferential basis at a substantial discount to the market. This resulted in a benefit of about Rs. 5000 crores (in relation to the then-prevailing market price) to retail investors. SEBI intervened to block the practice

9.4.5.2 Fly-by-night companies

Many companies that were not listed on any SE surfaced, promising, in some cases, 1000% growth in seven years for various plantation projects. Their issue offers were often accompanied by huge media blitzkrieg. These companies swindled more than Rs 8000 crores of gullible investors.

9.4.5.3 Mutual fund disaster

The MF operators, including GOI-backed UTI, messed up with thousands of crores in investing in manipulated scrips. Middle-class people, retired people, many NGOs could not even get the basic amount invested when the failure surfaced. The government bailed out UTI by paying Rs. 4800 crores of taxpayers' money.

9.4.5.4 The K-10 gimmick

Stock broker Ketan Parikh, along with some others, hammered down prices with the active collusion of some companies and banks to divert funds to the market. A joint parliamentary committee later was set up to look into the scam.[24]

9.5 Various financial instruments in the capital market

9.5.1 Government securities

Referred to as G-secs, these are very popular among institutional purchasers like central government and state government public sector organizations, commercial banks, etc. Government issues these to collect money for various developmental projects. The government issues the risk of default for these.

9.5.2 Bonds/debentures

An instrument of loan floated by government or a company against a specified interest rate and a promised date of repayment. A bond/debenture holder is a creditor to the company who loans funds for a fixed period of three to ten years against a fixed interest.

Company bonds that are secured against company assets are referred to as debentures. Companies often raise money through what is known as IPO (initial public offering), whereby individuals directly deal with the company by paying it an application fee.

9.5.3 Rights issue

The rights issue refers to the additional equity shares that are issued to the existing shareholders on a pre-emptive basis. Normally the subscription price of a rights issue is significantly lower than the market price of the shares.

9.5.4 Preference shares

Preference shares carry a fixed dividend rate and a special right to dividend over the private equity holders. These have a fixed period of maturity.

9.5.5 Certificate of deposit

Certificates of deposit, commonly known as CDs, are like commercial papers and are mainly issued by banks.

9.5.6 Commercial papers

Commercial papers are issued by corporate businessmen to fund their working capital needs. Commercial papers are issued generally for short-term maturities. Commercial papers are not secure; they are subject to market risks.

9.5.7 Call money market

The loans made in the call money market mainly deal with the interbank markets. The banks that have a problem of cash deficit borrow cap from the call money market at interest rates that vary with the market rate.

9.5.8 Industrial securities

Big business houses generally issue industrial securities to fulfill their long-term requirements regarding working capital. Debentures and equity shares fall in this category.

9.6 Mutual funds (MFs)

Various kinds of organizations that include banks, insurance companies, corporate organizations, and financial institutions can offer different kinds of mutual funds. The basic premise behind a mutual fund is that the investor looks for higher non-flexible returns and is ready to take a risk if the investment by the organization in the market has not done well. The economic recession phase that has engulfed the world since late 2008 has impacted the mutual funds market adversely.

The most efficient method of starting a classification or categorization of all schemes that are offered in the Mutual Fund Investments Market would be to group these into two broad classifications: *portfolio classification* and *operational classification*. Let us look at them closely.

9.6.1 Portfolio funds

The portfolio classification of funds can be divided into five kinds.

9.6.1.1 Return-based classification

The investors of the mutual fund schemes are made to enjoy a good return in the form of regular dividends or capital appreciation or a combination of both.

1. **Income Funds:** Income funds are floated for the interest of investors who want to maximize their current income. These funds distribute periodically the income earned by them, in the form of either a constant income at relatively low risk or in the form of maximum income possibly with higher risk using leverage.
2. **Growth Funds:** These schemes have the objective to achieve an increase in the value of the underlying investments through capital appreciation, and they invest in growth-oriented securities.
3. **Conservative Funds:** These funds offer a blend of good average returns and reasonable capital appreciation. These funds are very popular and are ideal for the investors who want both growth and income from their investment.
4. **Investment-Based Classification:** Mutual funds may also be classified on the basis of the kind of securities that they invest in.
5. **Equity Funds:** These funds invest most of their investible shares in equity shares of companies and undertake the risk associated with the investment in equity shares.

In a developed market, equity funds can be of different categories. For example, "blue chip," FMCG (fast-moving consumer goods), PSUs (public sector undertakings), etc.

Schemes launched by Indian MFs like GIC MF, UTI LIC MF, SBI MF, Canbank MF, Bank of Baroda MF, Bank of India MF, Morgan Stanley, Templeton, and Alliance. Offshore funds can invest in securities of foreign companies, after requisite permission from RBI. The objective behind launching offshore funds is to attract foreign capital for investment in the country of the issuing company. These funds facilitate cross-border fund flow, which is a direct route for getting foreign currency. From the investment point of view, offshore funds open domestic capital markets to the international investors and global portfolio investments.

9.6.2 Operational classification

Operational classification highlights the two main types of schemes, that is, open-ended and close-ended, offered by the mutual funds.

9.6.2.1 Open-ended schemes

As the name implies, the size of the scheme (fund) is open and not specified or predetermined. Entry to the fund is always open to the investor who can subscribe at any time. Such fund stands ready to buy or sell its securities at any time. The units are normally not traded on the stock exchange, but are repurchased by the fund at announced rates. Open-ended schemes have comparatively better liquidity even though these are not listed. No minute-to-minute fluctuations in rates haunt the investors. Open-end funds keep some portion of their assets in short-term and money market securities to provide available funds for redemptions. A large portion of most open mutual funds is invested in highly liquid securities, which enables the fund to raise money by selling securities at prices very close to those used for valuations.

9.6.2.2 Close-ended schemes

Such schemes have a definite period after which their shares/units are redeemed. Unlike open-ended funds, these funds have fixed capitalization, that is, their corpus normally does not change throughout its life period. Their price is determined based on demand and supply in the market. A premium may exist only on account of speculative activities.

Once underwritten, close-ended funds trade on stock exchanges like stocks or bonds. The market price of close-ended funds is determined by supply and demand and not by net asset value (NAV), as is the case in open-ended funds. Usually, closed mutual funds trade at discounts to their underlying asset value. For instance, the State Bank of India has many mutual funds of this nature that it announces from time to time. Trade papers often reflect the current value of shares continuously. The bank gets in touch with the investors just before the closure of the lock-in period to checks whether the investor would like his/her money back at the existing share value, or invest in some other schemes.

9.6.3 Various genres of mutual funds

9.6.3.1 Large-cap funds

Large-cap funds are those mutual funds that seek capital appreciation by investing primarily in stocks of large blue-chip companies with above-average prospects for earnings growth. Different mutual funds have different criteria for classifying companies as large cap. Generally, companies with a market capitalization in excess of Rs 1000 crore are known as large-cap companies. Investing in large caps is a lower risk–lower return proposition (vis-à-vis mid-cap stocks), because such companies are well established, and people have a good idea about their market standing.

9.6.3.2 Mid-cap funds

Mid-cap funds are those mutual funds which invest in small/medium-sized companies. Generally, companies with a market capitalization of up to Rs 500 crore are classified as small. Those companies that have a market capitalization between Rs 500 crore and Rs 1,000 crore are classified as medium sized.

As per the analysis of the capital market, it has been noticed that big investors like mutual funds and foreign institutional investors are increasingly investing in mid caps nowadays, because the price of large caps has increased substantially.

9.6.3.3 Equity mutual funds

Equity mutual funds are also known as stock mutual funds. Equity mutual funds invest pooled amounts of money in the stocks of public companies.

As per analysts, equity fund managers employ various styles of stock picking when they make investment decisions for their portfolios. Some fund managers use a value approach to stocks, searching for stocks that are undervalued when compared to other similar companies. Another approach to picking is to look primarily at growth, trying to find stocks that are growing faster than their competitors or the market. Some managers buy both kinds of stocks, building a portfolio of both growth and value stocks.

9.6.3.4 Balanced funds

Equity fund managers in this kind of mutual fund employ various styles of stock picking when they make investment decisions for their portfolios. Some fund managers use a value approach to stocks, searching for stocks that are undervalued when compared to other, similar companies. Another approach to picking is to look primarily at growth, trying to find stocks that are growing faster than their competitors or the market. Some managers buy both kinds of stocks, building a portfolio of both growth and value stocks.

9.6.3.5 Growth funds

Growth funds are those mutual funds that aim to achieve capital appreciation by investing in growth stocks. They focus on those companies, which are experiencing significant earnings or revenue growth, rather than companies that pay out dividends.

In general, growth funds are said to be more volatile than other types of funds, rising more than other funds in bull markets and falling more in bear markets. Only aggressive investors, or those with enough time to make up for short-term market losses, buy these funds.

9.6.3.6 No-load mutual funds

Growth funds are those mutual funds that aim to achieve capital appreciation by investing in growth stocks. They focus on those companies, which are experiencing significant earnings or revenue growth, rather than companies that pay out dividends. Growth funds tend to look for the fastest-growing companies in the market. Growth managers are willing to take more risk and pay a premium for their stocks in an effort to build a portfolio of companies with above-average earnings momentum or price appreciation.

9.6.3.7 Exchange-traded funds

Exchange-traded funds (ETFs) represent a basket of securities that are traded on an exchange. An exchange-traded fund is like an index fund in that it will primarily invest in the securities of companies that are included in a selected market index. An ETF will invest in either all the securities or a representative sample of the securities included in the index. The investment objective of an ETF is to achieve the same return as a particular market index.

Exchange-traded funds rely on an arbitrage mechanism to keep the prices at which they trade roughly in line with the net asset values of their underlying portfolios.

9.6.3.8 Value funds

Value funds are those mutual funds that tend to focus on safety rather than growth, and often choose investments providing dividends as well as capital appreciation. They invest in companies that the market has overlooked, and stocks that have fallen out of favor with mainstream investors, either due to changing investor preferences, a poor quarterly earnings report, or hard times in a particular industry. Value stocks are often mature companies that have stopped growing and that use their earnings to pay dividends. Thus, value funds produce current income (from the dividends) as well as long-term growth (from capital appreciation once the stocks become popular again). They tend to have more conservative and less volatile returns than growth funds.

9.6.3.9 Money market mutual funds

A money market fund is a mutual fund that invests solely in money market instruments. Money market instruments are forms of debt that mature in less than one year and are very liquid. Treasury bills make up the bulk of the money market instruments. Securities in the money market are relatively risk-free.

9.6.3.10 International mutual funds

International mutual funds are those funds that invest in non-domestic securities markets throughout the world. Investing in international markets provides greater portfolio diversification and lets you capitalize on some of the world's best opportunities. If investments are chosen carefully, international mutual fund may be profitable when some markets are rising and others are declining.

9.6.3.11 Regional mutual funds

Regional mutual fund is a mutual fund that confines itself to investments in securities from a specified geographical area, usually the fund's local region. A regional mutual fund generally looks to own a diversified portfolio of companies based in and operating out of its specified geographical area. The objective is to take advantage of regional growth potential before the national investment community does.

9.6.3.12 Sector mutual funds

Sector mutual funds are those mutual funds that restrict their investments to a particular segment or sector of the economy. These funds concentrate on one industry such as infrastructure, heathcare, utilities, pharmaceuticals, etc. The idea is to allow investors to place bets on specific industries or sectors, which have strong growth potential. Tata's have an infrastructures mutual fund. They later also floated a global infrastructure fund.

9.6.3.13 Index funds

An index fund is a type of mutual fund that builds its portfolio by buying stock in all the companies of a particular index and thereby reproducing the performance of an entire section of the market. The most popular index of stock index funds is the Standard & Poor's 500. An S&P 500 stock index fund owns 500 stocks of all the companies that are included in the index.

Investing in an index fund is a form of passive investing. Passive investing has two big advantages over active investing. First, a passive stock market mutual fund is much cheaper to run than an active fund. Second, most mutual funds fail to beat broad indexes such as the S&P 500.

9.6.3.14 Fund of funds

An index fund is a type of mutual fund that builds its portfolio by buying stock in all the companies of a particular index and thereby reproducing the performance of an entire section of the market. The most popular index of stock index funds is the Standard & Poor's 500. An S&P 500 stock index fund owns 500 stocks-all companies that are included in the index.

Investing in an index fund is a form of passive investing. Passive investing has two big advantages over active investing. First, a passive stock market mutual fund is much cheaper to run than an active fund. Second, many mutual funds fail to beat broad indexes, such as the S&P 500.

9.6.4 Various phases of mutual funds in India

Analysts put the Indian mutual fund in three distinct periods.

9.6.4.1 Phase I: 1964 to 1987

During this phase, the only player was government's the Unit Trust of India (UTI), which had a total asset of Rs. 6,700/- crores at the end of 1988.

9.6.4.2 Phase II: 1987 to 1993

During this period, eight more funds were established (six by banks and one each by LIC and GIC).

9.6.4.3 Phase III: 1993 till date

The third phase began with the entry of private and foreign sectors in the Mutual Fund industry in 1993. Kothari Pioneer Mutual fund 18 was the first fund to be established by the private sector in association with a foreign fund, and a host of companies followed suit.

With an influx of various mutual funds both from the public and private players, the regulator has issued renewed instructions to MF operators to educate the investors clearly that the money they invest in its MF is subject to market fluctuations, hence risky.

The Securities and Exchange Board of India has put a stop on the haste with which mutual fund advertisements deliver their standard warnings: "Mutual fund investments are subject to market risks, read the offer document carefully before investing." Now the fund operators have to display and read out the warning for at least five seconds in television and radio ads, said SEBI in a circular issued in February 2008.[25] The time allowed before was just two seconds. The detailed code of conduct for MF operators can be referred in Annexure II at the end of the chapter.

9.7 Trade media in India

Trade media is indispensable for financial communication. The circulation and reach of trade media may not be able to match to the level of the mainstream media in most of the cases, but there is no denying that it commands a niche readership and viewership of people who are interested in the stock market, besides the opinion makers and political class. The last one and a half decades has witnessed a tremendous spurt in trade media growth and access in the country. In the following tables, some glimpses have been provided to understand the reach and access of trade media, both print and electronic. The 24-7 specialized trade channels have changed the way trade media is being perceived now. In fact, some trade channels boast of more viewership than many mainstream news channels.

The 24-7 trade channels, both in English and Hindi, have a variety of programs that include, expert opinion, continuous stock market update, interviews with company heads, financial aspect of events/happenings, marketing-based programs, phone-in programs with investors, financial/investment experts' advice, et al.

The proliferation of news and trade channels have provided corporate communication managers with a great opportunity to showcase the achievements of their organizations and get interview-based programs for their top management. However, in today's commercial and cutthroat environment, it is not impossible to organize positive publicity at a cost, which may go against the interests of gullible investors, who depend a great deal on media about their stock options.

The corporate communication professionals need to keep a close watch on the trade media, its editorial content, and its reporters for strategic use both in proactive and reactive times. In retrospect, it was trade journalist Sucheta Dalal who unearthed the Harshad Mehta scam in the early 1990s.

The information requirements of trade media are slightly different from the mainstream media; hence, it is important for the corporate communication professionals to feed such media accordingly.

A good hang of the capital market operations, company's profit and loss analysis, its financial instruments, how they are doing, and market terminology come in handy while preparing press releases and press notes for trade media. A glossary of market terms is provided at the end of the chapter to facilitate easy comprehension.

9.8 Financial advertising for various financial instruments

Financial advertising is a term used for communication that is aimed at raising money from the capital market. The ad campaign for an IPO has to undergo various phases of advertising described later, besides following stringent stipulation from the regulator, SEBI.

9.8.1 The pre-issue phase

During this phase, the companies advertise about the public issue in the offing, giving various details of the portfolio manager, the merchant bankers, the size of the issue, the value of the share/price, and the risk factors. Most of the organizations, however, precede this with an image building campaign, which does not give any indication about the ensuing financial campaign. The companies, through an institutional campaign, aim at warming up the investors about the positive aspects of the company.

9.8.2 Issue phase

This phase of ads has all the details about the issue, including the closing date. Companies whose issues get oversubscribed must go to the regulatory authorities, in case they wish to retain the oversubscribed amount. This may or may not be approved by the concerned authorities, the reason being that if there were more issues in the pipeline, they would not like to saturate the market in advance.

9.8.3 Post-issue phase

In this phase, a formal announcement about the closure of the issue is made. Some companies also issue "thank you" ads for the investors.

9.9 Financial advertising

Financial advertising is defined as a paid form of communication relating to various financial instruments using mass media. Hundreds of crores of rupees are spent by various companies and financial institutions with a view to attract investment. Critics believe that financial ads have become drab and lackluster thanks to the restrictions imposed by regulatory authorities from time to time. The three major scams, viz., the Harshad Mehta, Home Trade, and, more recently, the Satyam computers fraud, have duped the system of thousands of crore rupees.

The Indian capital market has gone from strength to strength, but critics point out that the regulators may have become stringent before the launch of issue, but there is not much to suggest that post any issue, any measures are in place to safeguard the interests of the investors till a major scam breaks out and people and media raise a hue and cry.

It has been observed that companies create immense hype through paid-for-publicity and also through third-party endorsement route when the issue is open. The media publicity through editorial endorsement is really a cause for concern as the gullible investor is taken for a ride, believing that what appeared in the media must be legitimate.

The financial campaigns, by and large, were quite innovative during the 1980s, but some became too innovative, alerting SEBI to issue stringent norms. One such ad campaign that earned the ire of SEBI was by West Coast Breweries that had bikini-clad cine star Pooja Bhat in its issue ad. Besides attracting the attention of the readers, it also exposed the thoughtlessness of the company in using glamour that in no way educated the potential investor about the issue *per se*.

SEBI reacted in 1996 with comprehensive guidelines, which, among other things, prescribed that issue ads could use only information contained in the prospectus. Celebrity endorsements were ruled out. Issuers onwards then had to deal with stringent entry norms, public scrutiny of offer documents, and substantive due diligence by stock exchanges. The issue of real concern, according to Haldea, was not as much the paid advertising as the editorial content.[26]

> Issuers and merchant bankers often talk to the media about matters outside the prospectus. While they can be deterred, the bigger problem is with non-company people writing or talking about IPOs. Television, for instance, is flooded with analysts voicing views and recommendations. Channels invite managements of issuer companies. Worse, while issuers cannot talk about their day-to-day over-subscription details, channels broadcast them hour on hour. There are other issues like paid editorials and the practice of exchanging shares for advertising space. The ideal way would be

> for Sebi to formulate a code of conduct for media, even probe media that colludes to mislead investors.
>
> *(Haldea in his column)*[27]

Interestingly, Sachin Tendulkar, Rahul Dravid, and Kapil Dev continued for long to endorse products of insurers such as Aviva, Max New York, etc. SEBI bars mutual funds from getting celebrities to advertise their schemes. The rub-off effect on the mutual funds of these organizations could have been possible through this strategy on the issues, overlooked by the regulators so far. Even in 2023, one has seen a generic campaign on investing in mutual funds, called "Future ki Tayyari" (Planning for Future) in the new AMFI ad being endorsed by cricketers MS Dhoni and Sachin Tendulkar. The campaign is financed by the Association of Mutual Funds in India.[28]

It has been seen that a large number companies are putting a premium on their shares. To create the necessary hype, the issue announcement is preceded with a multimedia blitzkrieg through institutional campaigns. For instance, India's largest company in the public sector, the Oil and Natural Gas Corporation (ONGC), launched its mega issue in 2004 on a very high premium. It spent a huge amount as a build-up to the issue. Many critics wondered as to why a blue-chip company that was the largest and commanded great respect in the market had to spend so much money on an institutional campaign. As expected, the issue was oversubscribed many times, much before the closure date. When expectations are raised, the companies are also put on the public opinion radar, and ONGC's case was no different. Media soon carried front-page stories about some problem in the allocation of shares. It pointed out that while some people got more shares than asked for, others were denied. The then disinvestments minister, Arun Shourie, quickly convened a press conference, promising to look in to the matter, at the same time underplaying any goof-up by ascribing the problem to some computer virus. The company had to issue advertisements asking the investors to check the status of their allotments.[29] At the end of the chapter, some financial ads had been analyzed to see the content and whether they inform and educated the public to take informed decisions about their investments.

NSE has issued a fresh code for advertising in 2023. Some of the salient features include the following:

Information which is accurate, true, and complete in unambiguous and concise language.

1. Standard warning in legible fonts (minimum 10 font size) which states "Investment in securities market are subject to market risks. Read all the related documents carefully before investing." No addition or deletion of words shall be made to/from the standard warning.
2. In audio-visual-media-based advertisements, the standard warning in visual-media-based advertisement and accompanying voice-over reiteration shall be audible in a clear and understandable manner. For example, in standard warning, both the visual and the voice-over reiteration containing 20 words running for at least ten seconds may be considered as clear and understandable.

3. Whenever the advertisement is being issued in a language other than English, it will be ensured that the standard warning is accurately translated in the language of the advertisement.

   In case the mode of advertisement is SMS/message/pop-up, social media, etc., and the details such as full name, logo/brand name, full registered office address, SEBI registration number, membership number of a SEBI-recognized supervisory body and standard disclaimer are not mentioned, then an official website hyperlink should be provided in such SMS/message/pop-up, etc., and the website must contain all such details.
4. In case any specific security/securities are displayed in the advertisement as examples, a disclaimer that "the securities quoted are for illustration only and are not recommendatory" should be mentioned.
5. Advertisements and communications/correspondences with clients shall include the disclaimer that "registration granted by SEBI, membership of BASL (in case of IAs) and certification from NISM in no way guarantee performance of the intermediary or provide any assurance of returns to investors."

Prohibitions in the advertisement:

The advertisement shall not contain:

i. Anything which is prohibited for publication under the law.
ii. Statements which are false, misleading, biased or deceptive, based on assumptions or projections.
iii. Any misleading or deceptive testimonials.
iv. Statements which, directly or by implication or by omission, may mislead the investor.
v. Any statement likely to be misunderstood or likely to disguise the significance of the same or any other statement contained in the advertisement.

For details, log on to: SEBI | Advertisement code for Investment Advisers (IA) and Research Analysts (RA)

9.10 Investor relations (IR)

Effective investor relations are said to be the backbone of successful financial communication. Perceptions about companies are not just formed via the happenings at the stock markets or what gets reflected in the media, but also within communities both at individual and group levels.

Paul A. Argenti et al suggest that corporate communication need to have the following at the back of their mind when planning financial communication:

> How is your company valued at the stock market? If it is undervalued, what could be the possible reasons? Could it be that investors don't know enough about the company? How does the company currently communicate with its shareholders, financial analysts and the media? And more importantly, where does the investor relations function on the company's organizational chart?[30]

9.10.1 Defining investor relations

The investor relations vertical in a company is expected to maintain communication with current and potential investors through dissemination of information about the company and its financial performance.

Doorley and Garcia define investor relations as the

> subset of Public Relations and corporate communication that deals with a company's relationship with the investment community. Both current investors (who own a corporation's stocks and bonds) and potential investors (who might be persuaded to own these stocks and bonds) make up the primary audience for investor relations.[31]

According to CIRI (Canadian Investor Relations Institute), "Investor Relations is the strategic management responsibility that integrates the disciplines of finance, communication and marketing to achieve an effective two-way flow of information between a company and the investment community in order to enable fair and efficient capital market."[32]

CIRI argues that maintaining corporate and personal credibility is essential to an effective IR program. Credibility can be established only when information is based on honesty, reliability, and integrity. The information needs to be shared continuously with timely disclosure rules and presented in a clear and truthful manner.[33]

Analysts believe that the foremost goal of a successful IR is that it ensures a company's securities to be fairly and fully valued in the stock market.[34]

9.10.2 Who handles investor relations?

Investor relation, according to experts, is a "strategic function of corporate management, combining the disciplines of marketing, finance and communication."[35] As per the practice in most companies, IR function is handled by a company's staff and not outsourced, except for technical support. But there are others who do outsource IR to specialized agencies.

In the new media age, it is rather easier for companies to create an online interface with the investing communities. Many research studies indicate that people who invest, especially the educated ones, do wish to know about their investments and redress their grievances through the company sites.

Research also reveals that the capital market can function efficiently when information is widely available to the investment community. The quality and quantum of information is crucial to the investment process. Information and data can be sourced from various places, like putting together a jigsaw puzzle, recommends Stephen D. Barlow in his article.[36]

There is no gainsaying that a successful IR program depends a great deal on the extent of commitment of the senior management and the board of directors. Effective IR, in fact, is based on how a company discloses information required, both to the regulatory authorities and the investing communities. Many believe that public limited companies need also to invest in building internal brand advocates and champions from within the employees.

9.10.3 Communication channels for effective IR

The good and the bad news about IR is that the investors are loaded with information—that is a good part of the news. The bad part is that information flows from all directions all the time—the authorized company information, opinionated information from the trade media, the Internet, the bloggers, and the live chat room on the social networking sites. All this can be quite a plateful, but not necessarily appetizing, either for the investor or the company. Some of the communication channels for an effective investor relations management include the following:

9.10.3.1 Annual report

Annual report is the traditional tool of IR. It is also statutory in nature. All shareholders have a right to receive a run on the company accounts at least once in a year through the annual report.

9.10.3.2 Press release

Corporate communication managers use press releases often to disseminate information to the market on various developments in the company that may have to do with achievements/progress, policy change to get positive mileage in the media, at the same time to feed the investment and financial analysts.

9.10.3.3 Interactive media

The new age media, especially the interactive, interface with investors is the latest tool in IR that is being befittingly used by many companies.

9.10.3.4 Interpersonal media

Corporate communication mangers assist the top management in addressing investment conferences, often organized by investment bankers and broker firms for the investment community.

9.10.3.5 Trade channels

The 24-7 trade news channels have become an important media of informing and educating the investing community. It is not uncommon to find company CEOs being interviewed during the pre-issue, issue, and post-issue phases. In case of turmoil in the capital market, trade channels often invite experts who are seen responding to callers' anxieties and queries through phone-in programs.

9.10.3.6 Paid for communication

Advertising is an important tool for financial communication, especially when an IPO is floated. Various phases of financial advertising have been discussed elsewhere in the chapter.

Financial communication to shareholders, recommend experts, need to be honest, accurate, pertinent, and timely so that investors can make informed decisions on the buying, selling, or holding of securities. Thanks to the new age media, most of the companies now use their websites to provide updated information and redress the grievances online. The investor relations page of the Colgate website, for instance, opens with a three-minute video of its CEO, who tells the investors about how the company is doing, its core philosophy, corporate governance, and what it believes in.

Dell is another innovative company that has even started a dialogue with the financial analysts through the blogs.

With social media platforms, one has seen an emerging community of social influencers on the Net, who wield a lot of power due to their following. Many among them comment on stocks which may influence positively or negatively the community of investors. Corporate communication practitioners, therefore, must increase the bandwidth of their media relations management to also loop in these influencers in the interest of their organizations.

9.10.4 Case study

Dell innovating IR by creating virtual communities

In May 2007, Dell launched its PartnerDirect program to engage the value-added resellers and system integrators in the channel. Though there was some skepticism in the beginning about its functioning, in about a year's time, it had more than 37,000 registered partners worldwide. The channel, according to the company, generated nearly $12 billion in run-rate revenue. From 31 December 2008, PartnerDirect was run as one global organization, connecting 148 countries in 19 languages.

The company created a Partner Advisory Council where it hosted face-to-face meetings with its partners twice a year and teleconferences every month. The Partner Advisory Council, held in every region, included special councils tied to Dell's certification paths. This provided the company a forum to listen and implement changes from the feedback the channel partners gave it.

The company kick-started its World Money Show in early 2009, which planned to feature 300 workshops and 150 speakers with an "opportunity to hear leading experts talk about the global economy, investment and personal finance."

Individual investors owned about 20% of Dell, so the World Money Show provided them with an opportunity to meet current and potential investors.[37]

Dellshares.com, a website for interfacing with the investing community, was perceived to be a place for serious discussion about the strategy and direction of the company. Its two postings, viz., how should Dell use its cash and "21 Century IR," are said to have drawn tremendous response from the IR team and investors. Dell's approach received good coverage in the media and from bloggers. Dell's experiment was seen as an example of how organizations can build a virtual community.

Dell's slip, however, showed when it sent a legal notice to a blogger (an ex-Dell manager) in 2007 for what it alleged was sharing of propriety information. The issue gathered momentum against the company's policy on discount that was shared by the blogger. Losing no time, the company apologized. The case study has been dealt with in detail in the chapter on corporate reputation management.

Let us now argue from the flip side of all this. There are thousands of people. All of them may not be necessarily happy with a company's brands, experience, or governance. There is a chance that some competing companies may also enter the adverse dialogue in a surrogate manner. The bloggers may also bring in issues that may not necessarily relate to the subject under discussion, thus digressing the argument. So is it worth to be proactive when the companies are under the bloggers and media scrutiny anyway?

We live in the media age, where all this comes as a part of the package. Engaging the communities proactively in a transparent manner as stakeholders surely would not work against the long-term interest of any company. The redeeming thing about the blogosphere is that what one writes will be reinforced, expanded, or questioned by others, making it, hopefully, a balanced argument. This would provide constant feedback to the company and also keep it alerted about issues that people are sensitive or worried about.

In his Blogspot, Dominic Jones talks about the influence of bloggers on investor relations and how much influence the bloggers, especially the financial bloggers, have in stock purchasing decisions.[38]

9.11 How well is the Indian investing community cared for?

The Indian capital market is considered still nascent by analysts, especially when it comes to educating the investors or encouraging investor advocacy. Many believe that unless the investors join under a strong association that has a voice, they will continue to be treated badly by the system and the market. The system, argues Sucheta Dalal, is badly loaded against the investor. The maximum penalty is only Rs. 5 lakhs, and that too is not payable to the investors who keep losing millions of rupees by fraudulent practices of some companies and individuals. If any one wishes to take a legal recourse, there is also no respite for the investor, as the legal suits take years and can be cost-intensive for the people. In India, in fact there are no monetary costs attached to corporate crimes.[39]

A survey by a global marketing communications firm found out that despite India having stock exchanges that are among the world's oldest and the biggest, when it comes to trading, a third of the country's investing community felt duped by brokers. The survey brought out a startling fact that the more the broker's experience was in the stock market, the higher were the chances of people being cheated. The research was conducted by Starcom Worldwide, a part of the Starcom MediaVest Group that has 110 offices in 76 countries, including India.

Three out of five respondents knew someone who had been deceived by a broker. And several of those who may not have been cheated did know of others who have had bitter experiences with brokers.

Even agencies like the Society for Consumers' and Investors' Protection—among several institutions for investor protection that are registered with the market's watchdog, Securities and Exchange Board of India (SEBI)—feel rather helpless, pointed out the survey.

The survey reflected that more than half of the respondents had a salaried position in the private sector, 16% had their own businesses, 9% each were public sector employees or self-employed, and 4% were students.

Most replies were to the said survey from Mumbai (22%), followed by National Capital Region—New Delhi and satellite towns—(14%), Bangalore (9%), Kolkata (6%), Pune (4%), and Chennai and Hyderabad (4% each).[40]

In an age and time when there are dozens of trade papers, magazines, and 24-7 trade channels, it is not uncommon to find constant advice given by sundry financial and investment advisors on various financial instruments. There are programs in which these experts are invited by channels to advise investors in phone-in programs.

In retrospect, one of the all-time dubious scamsters Harshad Mehta, who resurfaced in 1998 through his website and various columns he was writing in some mainstream newspapers, was seen advising in favor of some scrips rigging BPL, Videocon, and Sterlite shares, which, according to financial journalist Sucheta Dalal, "ended with the inevitable collapse and a cover up operation involving an illegal opening of the trading system in the middle of the night by the Bombay Stock Exchange officials. It cost the BSE President and Executive Director their jobs."[41]

As a part of a series of initiatives to protect investors' interest, SEBI has granted, in principle, the approval for the introduction of "optional grading" of public issues of those companies which are not listed with the stock exchanges (viz., initial public offerings [IPOs]). IPO grading service is provided by some credit rating agencies (CRAs), including ICRA, CRISIL, Fitch Ratings India, and CARE, registered with SEBI.

According to SEBI, the IPO grading would not be mandatory and would be solely at the option of the issuer company. SEBI will not certify the assessment made by the grading agency. The main objective of such IPO grading is to enable investors to have an independent opinion from credible entities about the equity issue of an unlisted company.[42]

To make the investors' grievance redressed quickly, the SEBI has directed all the stock exchanges/registered brokers/sub-brokers/depositories/listed companies/registered depository participants to make a provision for a special e-mail/ID of the grievance redressal division/compliance officer, so that the investors can register the complaints easily. Besides this, all the aforesaid organizations have been advised to display this e-mail ID prominently on their websites and other promotional materials.[43]

Watchoutinvestors.com is a national web-based registry, partly funded by the ministry of corporate affairs, that has names of entities including companies, intermediaries, and individuals who have been indicted for some economic defaults and/or have been non-compliant of laws/guidelines and/or are no longer in the specified activity.

The investor community is waking up, and it is hoped that a self-motivated movement will soon gather momentum and work as a pressure group to exert influence on the capital market to safeguard their own interest.

As per the information on the website, its mission is "to prevent unscrupulous entities/persons from harming investors and thereby help build public confidence in the financial system enabling greater flow of public investment to the right avenues."

The watchoutinvestors.com is basically a database of economic offenders that includes the names of companies and individuals under two categories: willful defaulters and politically exposed persons.

9.12 Awards—the efficacy and relevance

It is commonplace for professional bodies, investment institutions, and trade media to bestow awards to companies on their performance in financial communication. Awards work like trophies for companies to showcase their recognition. The corporate communication departments and PR firms use these as opportunities to gain media mileage. It is not uncommon to hear critics questioning the locus standi of certain organizations that institute such awards. There, however, are also some genuine bodies who recognize the work of organizations in various categories.

One of the admired companies in the IT sector in India, viz., Infosys, has reflected on its website various awards received by it in financial communication. Some such awards include the 2008 platinum award for its annual report from LACP; global ranking 2008 in APAC categories; 2007 in best investor relations website; and the company with the best corporate governance practice in IR. About 20 other awards are mentioned that it has received since 1999.[44]

Competitor Satyam Computers, before its fraudulent practices surfaced, was also a recipient of several awards in corporate governance, investor relations, and other categories. Just before the scam was unearthed in 2008, it received the prestigious Global Investor Relations Award. The company was ranked "number one in India and among the top 5 in Asia/Pacific regions" in the financial disclosure category. In the corporate governance category, Satyam Computers was ranked "number one in the Asia/Pacific region." The global rankings were based on a "comprehensive methodology developed by MZ Consult, an investor relations and financial communication firm." The ranking entailed "extensive research by several respected companies and investors" and included "input from audit, corporate governance, and legal experts, such as KPMG, independent auditors, Linklaters, and JP Morgan."

> Satyam is participating in the IR global review for the fourth consecutive year and we clearly identify the Company's commitment with the continuous improvement of its investor relations program, in line with the principles of transparency, access to information, and equal treatment.
>
> *(Rodolfo Zabisky, IR Global Rankings coordinator, MZ Consult)*

The evaluation process considered the following:

1. Management accountability to promote the alignment of interests of shareholders and managers.
2. The performance of the two fundamental duties of the board of directors, which are the supervision of setting the company's executive management and long-term goals.
3. Minority shareholder protection, capital structure and other policies, transparency, and equality.[45]

Commenting on the award, the chief financial officer of Satyam, Srinivas Valdamani, said, "We are pleased to be recognized for the excellence of our financial earnings, releases and financial disclosure practices. Our practices are designed to provide complete, accurate, timely information in clear formats."

"Our top-ranking highlights Satyam's emphasis on governance," said Srinivas.

> It demonstrates our commitment to being a responsible corporate citizen who leverage best practices wherever possible. It also shows that we continuously strive to find creative, productive ways to delight associates, investors, customers, and society.

> Delighting stakeholders is one of Satyam's key principles, and an element of everything we do at Satyam.[46]

The Satyam case puts a question mark on such awards and the seriousness the awarding institutions give to researching about organizations and the rating indicators they follow in short-listing companies for awards. It is not known whether the awarding institutions are planning to divest such companies of the awards to gain some credibility for themselves.

Summary

In this chapter, we started with an understanding of financial communication and its role and scope. The various financial institutions were discussed with their functions. Capital market is a place for money generation and transaction through primary and secondary market dynamics. How the capital market functions, who are the major players from within and outside the country, what kind of financial instruments are available were discussed in detail. Case studies of some infamous stock market scams that happened either because there were loopholes in the system or because institutions and individuals got together to dupe the system and gullible investors were discussed, foremost among them being the Harshad Mehta scam and Home Trade scam. Whether investors are protected by regulations was discussed in detail, encompassing various regulations to protect the interests and the problems in the system.

Trade media and its role with reach and access were covered in the chapter, followed by the process of going to primary market and the role of financial advertising. A few ads of mutual funds have been analyzed to see if these really educated the people on investment.

The capital market evolution in the last two decades or so was seen through media coverage, selected randomly to provide a perspective.

Later, investor relations, its pros and cons, were taken up for discussion. Investor relations in the digital age was discussed, giving a case study of Dell computers to see how a virtual community has been created by the company involving investors through social media.

In the end, the efficacy and relevance of awards by financial institutions and industry associations were discussed in the wake of Satyam computers that duped millions of their hard-earned money but was the recipient of several awards in the category of corporate governance and investor relations.

Key terms and financial glossary

Allotment of shares: after a company has issued a prospectus and application forms for shares, it receives applications from the investing public. In case the total number of shares applied for equals or is less than applied for, full allotment is made. However, if more shares are applied for than the number offered, then a basis of allotment is finalized in consultation with the stock exchange where the company is listed.

Annual general meeting: a meeting that is required to be held statutorily by companies once in a year, where the directors report to the shareholders on the year's performance. In this meeting, the Director also receives auditor's report and appoints auditors.

Annual report: this is a report that the directors of a company present to its shareholders at the end of every accounting year. It must contain the following: director's report, auditor's report, balance sheet, profit and loss account, and schedules explaining various items on the balance sheet and profit and loss account.

Anti-trust law: laws designed to control monopoly power and practices.

Application money: the amount an investor is asked to pay with the application form for new issues, usually less than the full value of the shares. The balance is collected at the time of actual allotment.

Appreciation: increase in the price of share and the value of assets, which is called capital appreciation.

Appropriation: an amount kept aside from the after-tax profit for a specific purpose. A term used in the balance sheet of a company showing how net profits are deployed, viz., distribution of dividends, transfer to general reserves, and balance carried forward. It reflects the utilization of disposable profits.

At a premium: a price higher than that printed on the share certificate, called above par.

At par: a price equal to the face value of a share.

Authorized share capital: the maximum number of shares that a company may issue, as stated in the memorandum and articles of association of the company.

Net asset value: a term used by mutual funds and other investment trusts to indicate the net tangible asset value of each share, calculated by taking the total value of an investment portfolio at market rates on a certain date and dividing it by the number of outstanding shares.

Balance of payment: the difference between a country's total payments to foreign countries and its total receipts from foreign countries. It, in fact, is the record of the transactions of the residents of a country with the rest of the world during a year. The main accounts of BOP are the current account and the capital account.

Balance of payment-surplus/deficit: a positive or negative balance of payments.

Balance sheet: the statement of a company's financial position at a particular time, showing its assets, liabilities, and net worth.

Bank rate: the minimum rate at which the Central Bank is prepared to discount or rediscount the bills of exchange brought to it by members of the money market.

Base year: the reference year, given the value of 100, when constructing a price index or other time series.

Bear market: a prolonged period of falling share prices, dominated by selling pressure in the marketplace brought about by bears or economic or political factors.

Bear: a term used for a stock market operator who expects the price to fall and keeps selling, to pick up shares later at a lower price, causing selling pressure and lowering the prices further. The term is said to be derived from the way a bear attacks, that is, pushing downwards.

Below par: a price lower than the face value of a share.

Bill of exchange: it is an order in writing signed by a person giving it, requiring the term to whom it is addressed to pay on demand a sum of money to a person or to the order of that person or to a bearer.

Bill rate: the discount rate on bills of exchange.

Black market: a market in which sales take place at a price above the legal maximum.

Blue chips: shares of well-known companies, which have shown consistent growth over the years. In stock market terminology, a first-class equity share is called a blue chip because it is hoped that purchase of this share entails little risk.

Bond: an instrument of loan rose by government or a company against a specified interest rate and a promised date of repayment. Company bonds that are secured against company assets are referred to as debentures, as distinct from fixed deposits, accepted by companies, which are unsecured.

Bonus share: extra shares given to shareholders in proportion to their holding without any payment by the shareholder. When company reserves are high, it may choose to capitalize part of it by issuing bonus shares to existing shareholders in proportion to their holdings, to convert the reserves in to equity.

Breakeven point: the output levels where costs equal revenues and therefore profit is zero.

Bull cycle: an extended period during which share prices are on the rise and stock market indices show an upward trend.

Bull market: a prolonged rise in the price of shares, sustained by buying pressure of actual investors, news of favorable economic growth, and a stable political scene.

Authorized capital: the amount of share capital fixed by a company's memorandum of association.

Call provision: the price at which a bond can be repaid before maturity under a call provision.

Capital expenditure: expenditure on acquiring land, machinery, and other fixed rather than liquid assets.

Capital issue: the issue of shares by a company.

Capital market: a market in which long-term capital is raised for the setting up and growth of companies. The stock exchange is a part of the capital market where various financial instruments like shares and bonds are bought and sold.

Cartels: formal agreements among firms to set price and or market shares.

Central bank: a banker's bank whose responsibility is to control money supply. It also performs other functions such as cheques clearing and inspection of commercial banks. It is an institution that is charged with controlling a country's money and banking system. The Reserve Bank of India is the central bank in the country.

Convertible debenture: loan certificates which carry a provision of conversion into a certain number of shares. When a part of the loan can be converted, the certificate is called a partly convertible debenture. When the entire debenture amount is converted, it is called a fully convertible debenture.

Cost of living index: a price index measuring the general level of prices of goods and services. The index is used by the government to make a wage adjustment to nullify the effects of inflation on wages, pension, etc.

Deficit financing: deliberately budgeting for a deficit. It is a tool of fiscal policy to influence the level of demand and employment in the economy.

Debentures: an instrument of debt, also called bond in the USA. A debenture holder is a creditor to the company who loans funds for a fixed period of three to ten years against a fixed interest.

Depression: a period of receding economic activity characterized by falling prices, rising unemployment, and excess supply over demand.

Devaluation: reduction in the value of currency against the exchange rate of another country's currency; devaluation requires deliberate action of monetary authorities, whereas depreciation happens as a result of market forces in the foreign exchange market.

Double-digit inflation: a rate of inflation between 10% to 99%.

Earnings per share (EPS): it shows what a company has earned for each of its shares; it is a ratio calculated by dividing the net profit after tax by the number of equity shares of a company.

Equity: shares of companies as distinguished from other kinds of investments such as gold, real estate, debentures, fixed d deposits, units in mutual funds, and government bonds.

ESOPS: employees stock option plan is an employee benefit plan which makes the employees of that company owners of stock of that company.

Fair market value: the price that an item is valued at in an open market.

FERA: the Foreign Exchange Regulation Act, 1973, that lapsed in May 2000.

FEMA: the Foreign Exchange Management Act, 1999, that came in to effect in June 2000, replacing FERA. The current act is in conformity with the liberalized market for foreign exchange.

Foreign exchange reserves: foreign currencies held by the government or the central bank.

Free trade: trade that is unimpeded by tariffs, import and export quotas, and other devices, which obstruct the free movement of goods and services between countries.

Gross domestic product (GDP): the monetary value of all the goods and services produced by a country over a specific period of time, normally a year. It is obtained by valuing and aggregating the output of all goods and services at market prices.

Gross national product (GNP): the GDP with addition of net dividends received from abroad by domestic residents. The growth of GNP indicates the health of an economy.

Hawala: a trade system that bypasses the official foreign exchange channel. Operators in India take payment in rupees and supply dollars and other currencies abroad. The hawala trade works through a network of agents who are under an operator's control. Payment made in dollars or pounds made abroad can be paid in rupees in India. This is a method of money laundering. Hawala rates differ from place to place in the country.

Inflation: a rise in the average level of prices, resulting in the real value of money, which can buy only less.

Insider trading: an illegal activity in which persons in a company having confidential information, such as expansion plans, financial results, takeover bids, etc. take advantage of such information to make a profit on the stock exchange by buying or selling shares.

Liquidity: the degree to which an asset can be quickly and cheaply turned into money. A current bank account is a liquid asset because money can be withdrawn immediately at little cost. An office building or machinery is not a liquid asset.

Liquidity ratio: the proportion of the total asset of a bank, which is held in the form of cash and liquid assets.

Limited company: a company in which liability of members is limited, which is confined to the face value of shares they hold.

Liquidation: winding up of business of a company either through bankruptcy or through resolution passed by the shareholders when the purpose of the company has been fulfilled.

Listed shares: shares that are registered by a stock exchange for trading on floor.

Merchant bank: a bank that underwrites corporate securities, manages public offerings, and advises clients on corporate mergers, etc.

Million: one million is equivalent to Rs. 10,000,000.

Mega issue: an issue of shares of debentures running in to several crores.

National income: this is regarded either as money value of total volume of production of goods and services or the total income derived from economic activity during a specific period usually a year after allowance made for capital consumption.

Net worth: the value of total assets minus liabilities.

Price index: it is the weighted average of prices of all the goods and services produced in an economy measured over time.

Preferential shares: the shares having preference over equity shares in distribution of post-tax profit and a prior claim of the assets of a company in the event of liquidation.

Rights issue: the issue of additional equity shares to the existing shareholders on a pre-emptive basis. Normally the subscription price of a rights issue is significantly lower than the market price of the shares.

Share certificate: a share is one unit of ownership of a company.

Sunrise industries: new industries that are coming up in the growth areas and play an important role in a country's economy.

Underwriter: a broker or a financial institution which agrees to buy up an unsubscribed portion of a new issue of shares. The payment to the underwriter is called underwriting commission.

Venture capital: investment in a new business carrying considerable financial risk, but with an above-average prospect for reward. They include business investment companies and merchant banks.

Venture capital fund: a limited company formed to provide venture capital to new industries.

Vote on account: it is a grant made by the Lok Sabha in advance of the estimated expenditure of the government of India for a part of the financial year pending the voting of demands for grants for the financial year.

Yield to maturity: the return earned on debt instrument if it is helped till maturity. It is computed using the discounted cash flow method.

Yo-Yo-stock: highly volatile shares, the price of which go up and down like a yo-yo.

Concept review questions

Q.1. Define financial communication and its role in corporate communication.

Q.2. What do you understand by capital market, how does it function, and who are the major players?

Q.3. Discuss in short the role and functions of various financial institutions.

Q.4. What do you understand by mutual funds? How are these different from other instruments like bonds and debentures?

Q.5. Define trade media. Which are the trade publications and news channels you know of?

Q.6. What are the various phases in issue advertising? Discuss various restrictions imposed by SEBI on such advertising.

Q.7. Why should companies care for investors? Discuss with arguments.

Critical thinking exercise

Study closely the various case studies relating to stock market scams reflected in the chapter, and analyze the modus operandi employed in each case. Go through the guidelines provided by the SEBI, and make an argument on investor education and what it should contain.

Field work (this can be a groupwork among three to four class fellows):

Choose six to eight mutual fund print ads and commercials, and conduct a survey among at least 20–25 investors to know whether the ads educate them on various financial products. Also, camouflage the company logo/name from print ads, and remove the voice-over/logo from the television commercial to check on the brand recall, keeping in view the ad content.

*

Case study

Analysis of some financial ads

A study conducted in the early 1990s by the *Economic Times* reflected that financial ad campaign surpassed brand advertising.[47] The scenario has only strengthened since then. The television channels are flooded with commercials on mutual funds, pension schemes, life insurance schemes, and pure banking from various financial institutions.

Because of a general clutter of mutual fund ads, some companies are using the emotional route to catch the attention of potential investors, while others are run-of the-mill ads. Remove the name, and you cannot make out whom the mutual funds belong to.

Some storylines:

1. Bajaj allianz

The ad starts as an obese man eating noodles makes lewd gestures at a Chinese woman. She calls out for help, and a few Chinese men come to her rescue. They surround the fat man in order to attack him.

The man pulls at a lever and is suspended in the air, with people pulling at the ropes. Next, we see that there is a film shoot taking place. The obese man performs all sorts of kung-fu antics and is rescued from getting hurt by the crew members.

VO: ***Safety hai to sab hero, Bajaj Allianz ke Safe Plans***

2. Tata capital

There are two little girls playing in a room when they find an old coin. They grab the coin; an idea strikes them, and they run out of the house towards the market. They go to buy ice candy and hand over the coin to the vendor.

He looks at the old coin and refuses to give them the ice candy. They take back the coin, looking morose, when a boy approaches them and asks them to give him the coin that he takes to an antique shop and gets it exchanged for some money. He comes back and buys two ice candies for the girls.

VO: Is not it nice when genuine care and financial expertise come together?
The ad ends with the super and logo: Tata Capital. *Karein wahi jo aapke hit mein.*

3. *UTI mutual fund*

Just as a girl stands gazing at a guy, her friend comes and warns, "Short-term investment *hai.*" A woman in a hospital tells a lady that she is expecting twin babies. In reply, the lady asks, "*Do-do* asset manage *karne padenge?*"

"Bottom line *ka kuch karo,*" says an instructor of a gym, pointing at the protruding tummy of a bulky fellow. Short of cash to buy an expensive shirt, a man tells his wife, "Liquidity *kam hai.*"

Trying to sell off an uninviting house to a customer, a property dealer tells him, "Face value *pe mat jaaiye. Andar se mast hai.*

Getting a samosa for four people, a waiter wonders, "*Ek samosa, chaar log,* mutual fund *hai kya?*"

VO: **"*Suna? Saara* India *bol raha hai* investment *ki bhaasha. Kisne sikhaayi?* UTI Mutual Fund."**

4. *Reliance money*

The story is of one Sameer Gupta who wins a mega prize in a lottery. A crowd of journalists gathers outside his house and asks him what he would do with the big money. Avoiding everyone, he runs out of the home. There too a man advises him to buy a car.

Soon the whole city is after Sameer, suggesting him to invest in what they thought was the best. Chasing the fellow, among the crowd was a nurse who advises him on medical insurance: "Mediclaim *ka socha?*"

Two guys even put up a hoarding, hinting him to put his money in fixed deposits. The man becomes the subject of discussion between two executives, who thought foreign investments would be the best choice for him. Running for his life, he got inside a building. There too a man demanded, "Sir, bonds?"

Escaping everyone, Sameer reached the top of the building and finally announced, "*Main* ek call *karoonga* 3988 6000!"

VO: **"*Jab maan mein ho paison ka* confusion, just phone a friend. Reliance Capital launches. . . (whenever there is a confusion about money, call a friend. . . Reliance Capital)**

Reliance Money, *Jahan aap kisi bhi* financial product *jaise* equity, mutual funds, IPOs, insurance *aur bahut kuch mein* invest *kar sakte hain. Jab bhi sawaal ho aapke paison ka, jawaab*, Reliance

5. AIG vyas

A little boy approaches an old woman and offers to pick up her vegetable bag. Sharing the burden, he drops her home. The woman gives the little master a one-rupee coin for his sweet help.

With the money "earned," he goes to his father's office and finds him busy in a meeting.

The father, surprised to see his son there, comes out of the meeting and asks, "*Beta, kya hua?*"

The kid innocently informs, "Papa, *meri pehli* salary," and gives him his first earned money. Moved by the gesture, the father lets him keep it.

VO: **"We understand how much every single rupee means to you. AIG. We appreciate the value of your money."**

6. UTI mutual fund

With eyes wide open, a guy looks at a gleaming blue imported car. Seeing his liking for the vehicle, the owner hands over the keys to him, saying, "*Rakh lo.*" Not believing what he just heard, the guy starts jumping with joy. Jingle: "*Lekin aapke saath aisa na hoga*, no-no."

In his office, his boss calls him to his cabin, giving him an airline ticket, saying, "*Teen mahine ki chhuti* Switzerland *mein*. Enjoy.

Alien to such treatment, the guy starts dancing like a madman. Jingle: "*Parantu, aapke saath aisa na hoga*, no-no." Cut to the shot of the guy with his date at a restaurant. He starts sweating upon seeing the bill brought by the waiter.

To his surprise, a fat rich man comes to his rescue, assuring, "I'll pay it." The guy expresses his gratitude to the savior.

Jingle: "*Kintu, aapke saath aisa na hoga*, no-no." Lending voice to the ad, a man says, "*Isiliye aapko ameer. . . banna hoga, apne dum pe*. Invest keejiye UTI Mutual Fund *mein*.

UTI Mutual Fund. "Let's plan to get rich."

7. SBI mutual fund

The film opens on a couple sitting in pin-drop silence in their home. They get alerted as Miss North arrives with dishes for them. Miss East, Miss South, and Miss West follow her with the best dishes for the couple.

VO: **"Imagine the best from the four regions of India working for you. Introducing SBI One India Fund, which invests in most promising companies from the four regions of India."**

8. ICICI mutual fund

Two men are on their way to the office when it suddenly starts raining. To take shelter in this downpour, they run to the nearest tea stall, but with a leak in its roof, they get uncomfortable.

VO: "Your life savings are meant to shelter you from a rainy day. . . but inflation—it's a leak in that shelter." Without waiting any longer, one of them gets out and starts running towards the office. While running, the man slips and falls midway.

VO: "Nothing to rush though. . . " His smarter friend follows him but takes small steps on some steppingstones.

VO: "Just small steps one at a time. Presenting the Systematic Investment Plan. From Prudential ICICI mutual fund. Invest in regular monthly installments." Taking small steps, the smart man finally reaches the office safely.

VO: "For a more secure future, get smart, get systematic.

Analysis

If we were to analyze the earlier ads, none of them educates the investor on the scheme *per se*. If the voice-over about the company names was removed, any ad would fit any brand! The core brand values of the company are also not reflected in any of the ads. In a clutter, it surely is difficult for people to take a call on a particular financial product based on the ad stimuli. Some studies suggest that when making a decision on various stocks, people mostly depend on the advice from agents and known people.

UTI's ad was pompous when it said, "Saara India bol raha hai investment ki bhaasha. Kisne sikhaayi?" It easily seemed to have forgotten that public memory is short, but not to that extent, especially of those who were duped of their money in UTI in 2001.

It is not clear if UTI has conducted any study to find out whether any of those institutions and individuals who lost money have invested in UTI after that. It will be worthwhile doing it.

Commenting on mutual funds, a *Business Today* study said thus:

> Just like a Starbucks coffee store, where you can go nuts trying to decide whether to order a Guatemala Antigua Decaf, a Caffe Verona, or just a plain and simple Starbucks Breakfast Blend, for first-time investors tip-toeing into the Indian mutual funds market, choosing a fund to invest in can be hair-tearingly frustrating. At the last count, there were 341 mutual fund schemes, which come, just like Starbucks' coffee, in a confusing array of flavors: open- and close-ended funds, tax-saving funds, ice-skewed funds, cyclical stock funds, debt funds, diversified funds, sector funds. . . Enough to frazzle the most cool-headed investor.[48]

Way back in 1986, British Airways did an excellent campaign by educating the potential investors "that it is a much smaller sale (than British Gas) and not a guaranteed safe bet." The campaign aimed at educating the investing community that BA was a capital-intensive industry that relied heavily on international trade. An early corporate communication effort was to guide 120 financial/investment analysts and fund managers through BA's training village at Heathrow and to demonstrate BA operations.[49]

Question on case study

Go through the earlier scripts carefully, and analyze which ads, in your view, aim at educating the potential subscriber in making decision based on SEBI's Code of Advertisements.

Notes

1 www.verimmen.com.
2 www.cardiffac.uk.
3 Richard R. Dolphin, *The Fundamentals of Corporate Communication*, 2001 (London: Butterworth-Heinemann), p. 95.
4 Jaishri N. Jethwaney, Adrash Kumar Varma and N. N. Sarkar, *Public Relations Concepts, Strategies and Tools*, 1994 (New Delhi: Sterling Publishers), pp. 169–170.
5 www.economywatch.com/financial-regulatory-body/
6 "Underwriters and Underwriting Commission and Judicial Remedies Present in Cases of Illegal Acts Committed by the Underwriter", legalserviceindia.com.
7 SEBI | Details of Stock Exchanges.
8 www.nse.co.in.
9 www.economywatch.com.
10 E. C. Thomas, *Economic and Business Journalism*, 2001 (New Delhi: Sterling Publishers), pp. 87–88.
11 Ibid., p. 92.
12 The Times of India, 16 March 2009.
13 The Times of India, 9 March 2009.
14 Ibid.
15 Outlook Money, 11 February 2009.
16 www.thehindubuisnessline.com.
17 www.sify.com.
18 The Big Bull (2021)—IMDb.
19 Scam 1992: The Harshad Mehta Story (TV Series 2020)—IMDb.
20 www.rediff.com/money/2002/may/03dalal.htm
21 Ibid.
22 Ibid.
23 www.rediff.com/money/2002/apr/30sebi.htm.
24 www.suchetadala.com.
25 www.thehindubusinessline.com/, 28 February 2008.
26 The Indian Express-Express Money, 31 July 2006.
27 Ibid.
28 "Mutual Funds Sahi Hai Campaign: Sachin and Dhoni Suggest Mutual Funds for 'Future Ki Tayyari' in New AMFI Ad", *ET BrandEquity*, indiatimes.com.
29 Ibid., p. n443.
30 Paul A. Argenti and Janis Forman, *The Power of Corporate Communication*, 2002 (New York: McGraw Hill), p. 159.
31 John Drooley and Helio Fred Garcia, *Reputation Management*, 2007 (New York: Routledge), p. 210.
32 Canadian Investor Relations Institute, www.ciri.co.in.
33 Ibid.

34 John Drooley and Helio Fred Garcia, *Reputation Management*, 2007 (New York: Routledge), p. 210.
35 Ibid.
36 Stephen D. Barlow, *Canadian Business Review*, 22 September 1989.
37 http://en.community.dell.com.
38 Investorrealations.blogspot.com.
39 www.suchetadalal.com.
40 www.whereincity.com/news/2/7660.
41 www.sucetadalal.com
42 Sidharath Shankar Saha, www.icai.org/resource_file/10180116-
43 http://blogs.ibibo.com/editor/investor-s-grievance-mechanism-a-sebi-initia.
44 www.infosys.com/about/awards/about-awards-
45 www.indiaprwire.com/pressrelease/information-technology/200704042445.htm.
46 www.satyam.com/media/pr1april07.asp.
47 The Economic Times, Brand Equity, 1993, quoted by Jaishri Jethwaney and Shruti Jain in *Advertising Management*, 2006 (New Delhi: OUP), pp. 442–443.
48 www.india-today.com/btoday/20000807/feature3.html
49 PR Week, 16 December 1986 as quoted by Frank Jefkins in *Public for Your Business*, 1995 (New Delhi: Excel), pp. 94–95.

10

CRISES COMMUNICATION

Chapter objectives

After reading this chapter, you will learn:

Various classifications of crises
Role and scope of crises communication
Corporate governance—need for and importance of securing positive image
Case studies in crises communication—insights and lessons learned (Bhopal gas, Satyam, Jet Airways, ICICI Bank, Tata Nano-Singur, 26/11 Mumbai terrorist attack, Covid-19)
Media coverage of Delhi bomb blasts
Media survey on disaster coverage

10.1 Defining crisis

A crisis can be defined as an adverse event, a great and sudden calamity that needs immediate addressing. Crises can be man-made or may occur due to natural reasons. Famines, droughts, cyclones, earthquakes, tidal waves, insurgency, terrorism, wars, epidemics, corporate warfare, employee agitations, project closures, product recalls, and scams, et al all qualify to be called as crises. Each crisis is unique and needs special handling, keeping in view the enormity of the crisis, stakeholders involved, and who would oversee crisis management. One thing, however, common among all kinds of crises is the important role of communication in various stages of managing a crisis. Let us look at various phases of a crisis.

DOI: 10.4324/9781032694702-10

10.1.1 Phases of crisis management

10.1.1.1 Pre-crisis phases

Preparedness
Mitigation
Prevention

10.1.1.2 Crisis phase

Response
Recovery
Development

10.1.1.3 Post-crisis phase

Relief
Recovery
Rehabilitation

10.1.2 Role of communication in various phases of disaster management

- Identifying stakeholders
- Identifying channels of communication for reaching out to various stakeholders
- Articulating flow of information

The success of each phase of crises management impinges on effective communication.

Hill and Knowlton, a leading PR consultancy in the USA, has classified crises in the following four segments:

1. Actual disasters such as fires, explosions, accidents, earthquakes, floods, famines, etc. These can be termed as *exploding crises*.
2. Controversial or scandalous incidents, involving companies, individuals, governments, et al. These are referred to as *immediate crises*.
3. Anticipated crisis due to premeditated decisions like closure of a plant, discontinuance of a service, retrenchment, etc. Crises falling in this category are classified as *building crises*.
4. *Continuing crisis*—when an organization, a product, or a service is under long-term attack from some stakeholders like special interest groups, media, judiciary, consumer groups, et al.

The National Disaster Management Authority in India defines disasters/crises as under the following:

- Natural sudden disasters (earthquakes, cyclones, tidal waves, tropical storms, volcanic eruptions, landslides, floods)
- Slow-impact disasters (droughts, famine, environmental degradation, deforestation, pest infestation)

- Man-made, complex emergencies (industrial, displacement, terrorism, food scarcity, food insecurity, et al)

A disaster plan is always patterned to fit the organization's own potential exposure to calamity. To illustrate, the disaster plan of a nuclear plant would be very different from that of an FMCG plant because the potential risk areas are quite different in the two cases. In times of a terrorist strike in a particular city, the police are generally put on "red alert" in other cities, which amounts to gearing up to the immediate possibility of similar strikes in other cities.

Grunig posits four principles of crisis communication:

1. ***The relationship principle***: an organization can withstand crises if it has a well-established relationship with key stakeholders.
2. ***The accountability principle***: an organization should accept responsibility for a crisis even if it was not its fault (he cites the example of a product recall that has been threatened or tainted by an extortionist).
3. ***The disclosure principle***: in a crisis, an organization should disclose all it knows about a crisis or problem. If it does not have immediate answers, it must promise full disclosure once it has additional information.
4. ***The symmetrical communication principle***: in a crisis, the public interest should be considered as equal in importance as the organization's intent.[1]

How would one know that there is a crisis? All crises are not sudden like an earthquake, an accident, or a tsunami; there are crises that simmer for some time before they explode, like employee attitude, absenteeism, drug use at workplace, lifestyle behavior, or a long-drawn case with an inquiry committee that is being waited upon. A management, corporate or political, that does not have the "sixth sense" about dormant critical issues is doomed to face larger crises anytime soon. Early corrective action often helps in solving the problem when at a nascent stage. It saves time, effort, resources, both manpower and financial, besides reputation. The memory of 1984 riots against innocent Sikhs keeps surfacing every time the Congress party tries to reinstate the alleged accused in the public sphere. The Central Bureau of Investigation exonerated Mr. Jagdeesh Tytler and Mr. Sajjan Kumar of any role in the episode when the Congress party announced their candidature for the Parliamentary elections in April–May 2009. A large section of the Sikh community does feel betrayed as even after close to four decades, the guilty have not been brought to book. When the then home minister, P Chidambaram, was addressing a press conference in April 2009 (not on this issue), Jarnail Singh, a journalist, was not satisfied when his question on the subject was skirted, leading him to hurl his shoe at the home minister. The news channels kept repeating the visuals soon after. The minister, of course, reflected his graciousness and did not make a case against him. The man also regretted having done it. The episode sent strong signals, when the Congress party quickly decided to withdraw the candidature of both the persons, who may have been given a "clean chit" by the CBI but were perceived guilty by some sections of the concerned community.

Commenting on the episode, Sir Meghanand Desai, in an opinioned article, "Mera Joota Jadugar" in the *Indian Express*, said that the shoe-throwing had cheered things up. When Bush received the first shoe, he thought it was the sort of a futile gesture resorted by weak and powerless people. "But Jarnail Singh," wrote Desai, "has now proved me wrong. If you have a vibrant democracy and a 24-7 media, then you can leverage a shoe into a political whirlwind." Desai commented that the shoe throwers were now "articulate and middleclass," who brought to the surface "the seething outrage that those in power, even as they pretend to be humble and prattle on about serving the public, have insulated themselves from law."[2]

10.2 The importance of communication

Whenever an organization is faced with a crisis, it must communicate with several stakeholders who are important from its perspective and respond to the information needs of these stakeholders. Media, which represents the public voice, is the most critical stakeholder to handle in times of a crisis. The strength of character of a person, as goes the age-old adage, is judged in adversity; such can also be said for an organization. Every crisis poses a test about how the organization in the eye of the storm responds to an emergency, how it takes care of the people who are affected, and how it is going to rebound after a crisis. When an organization is undergoing a crisis, its leadership is constantly in public gaze and on media radar, so the resilience of the top management and its action plan to avoid a similar kind of disaster is important, both from the perspective of the organization and its stakeholders. To quote an instance, Ratan Tata, chairman of the Tata Group, displayed enormous grit and resilience, at the same time firmness, in analyzing the situation and taking charge after the hotel Taj, a Tata property, became the target of a terrorist siege in November 2008. He did not mince words when he said that the emergency response from authorities was less than adequate and announced that, for the safety of the guests and employees, the Tata Group would put its own security in place "to serve as an impediment" to such happenings and "not to create heroes" after the event had occurred. Ratan Tata's whole demeanor reflected that here was a person who was in command. On the other hand, as will be reflected in the case study given later in the chapter, it cost both the chief minister and the state home minister their jobs for appearing indifferent and insensitive.

Each category of crises, whether it is man-made or natural, requires careful handling, especially when life is involved. When a crisis has occurred, one cannot turn back the clock. The damage to reputation may be a reality, but honest intentions, coupled with effective communication, would help an organization to tide an image problem sooner or later. Communication takes center stage from the perspective of various stakeholders. Everyone wishes to be told the truth—the employees, the shareholders, the suppliers, the policy makers, the financial institutions, and, above all, the media. While it may take some time to know the reasons behind that crisis, communication cannot wait. In almost every crisis, confidence of the alleged victims and those who empathize with them need to be restored. Following are critical in a crisis:

- Enormity of the disaster/loss of human life
- Perceived abettors and victims
- Perceptions about the crisis
- Media coverage/media stand
- Action plan to deal with the crisis at hand

Two aspects from a disaster manager's perspective become crucial. In fact, the success of a crisis management impinges on the following:

- How the organization responds to the victims
- If it is communicating what it is doing and how it shall rebound

Exactly after a month, both the hotels the Taj and the Trident, victims of terrorists' strike in Mumbai in November 2008, were back serving their clients, notwithstanding the fact that a lot of repairing work was still going on in many areas. The whole idea behind that was to convey that despite what they underwent, their spirit could not be killed. Media wholeheartedly covered the incident, talking about stories of human courage, determination, and resilience.

10.2.1 The importance of sharing information

It is generally said of news persons that they feast on crises. The bigger the crises, the better they feel, because it gives them the opportunity to showcase their alertness in bringing issues to the public domain, pull up authorities and get closer to their viewers/readers, and, of course, the TRPs rise as more and more people sit glued to their television sets, read newspapers, and get updates from the Internet and social media platforms. In the aftermath of a crisis, or even while a crisis has not subsided, getting hold of information, and as fast as possible, is very important for media. Due to fierce competition among various channels and in print media, every channel/newspaper wishes to give the "breaking news." Therefore, it is important for a corporate communication practitioner to understand that media will get information somehow, so it is in the interest of the organization to share an official version and be heard constantly. Ducking or not sharing information can be suicidal. The 24-hour channels can be seen as a problem or an opportunity. The Internet, especially the social networking sites and live chat rooms, has brought about a paradigm shift in how the organization must change their communication strategies and media options. The official version of the organization needs to be placed on the Net immediately after a crisis has occurred, along with the action plan of the organization to mitigate the crisis. The information needs to be updated as soon as new facts about the emergency emerge. It is not uncommon that no sooner than a major crisis strikes, many blog sites emerge, and not all would say complementary things. Tracking the social networking sites, following the social media influencers, addressing the concerns of the people, and thanking those who stand by the organization is important from the perspective of managing the reputation of the organization.

In a crisis scenario, the stereotypes for media and organizations only get reinforced, viz., "They smell only bad" vs. "They are going to conceal," said for media and organizations respectively.

Allegations, fault-finding, charges of insensitivity are commonplace in a crisis, which the crisis team should take in their stride and in no way get bogged down by criticism that may even be unwarranted from their point of view. People ultimately would appreciate the display of maturity, sensitivity, and empathy, coupled with honest intentions, to manage the crisis, keeping the human concern uppermost.

Corporate communication practitioners are often criticized for "engineering consent" and "manipulating" the minds of the stakeholders in critical times to salvage damage done to their organizations, even when they may know that their organizations were guilty of unethical practices or poor corporate governance. This may not always be true, but exceptions are always there.

10.2.2 The advisory role of corporate communication

Corporate communication is a "staff function" that advises the top management on information management both in routine and critical times. Many case studies, be it the Watergate scandal, the taking of embedded journalist for coverage to Iraq, the Enron or Satyam frauds, all amply tell that communication of any kind cannot help individuals or organizations to come out clean if they indulge in unethical practices. Critics often call the corporate communication department the "whitewash cell." Can any amount of whitewashing save a crumbling wall? Bill Clinton's initial lies about his affair with an intern did not help him in the long run. Led by the events, Satyam CEO R Raju had to send a confessional letter that helped unearth the scam. If corporate communication strategies are used to get fair comments in the media through unfair means (of which media would be equally guilty), it may only end up doing many times more damage to the organization once the truth surfaces. On the other hand, if media gets to know of the crisis through its sources, criticizing it may not help. Shooting the messenger is a bad strategy and does not help.

10.2.3 Use of words and imagery—what should one communicate in crises?

In the pre-crisis phase relating to natural disasters, alerting the people on preparedness is important. Local governments, as soon as they get data from the metrological department, announce to people about impending cyclones, rainfall, possible tidal waves and make arrangements to evacuate them. After the disaster has occurred, informing people about succor, rehabilitation, medical facilities, compensation, etc. is equally important. Involving people in rescue operations and holding a constant two-way dialogue will result in ownership of operations by the communities.

One has watched in the past some very impactful disaster preparedness campaigns, especially on earthquakes, mounted by the Disaster Management Authority in various media. As a precautionary measure, people were being asked to get their houses checked for earthquake resistance and how to go about correcting them if there was a problem.

On the other hand, in cases of man-made crises, the strategy cannot always be preempted, especially in cases of frauds and scams. When the Satyam fraud was unearthed after a confessional letter from the CEO of the company, the company obviously remained silent for a while till a new board was in place. However, thousands of blogs surfaced in no time. Communication was coming from various sources that included the regulatory bodies, industry, media, and, of course, the political class. Prior to that, when the Harshad Mehta stock market scam was unearthed in the 1990s, it led to various regulations and policies to strengthen the stock market.

10.2.4 Message action plan

From the perspective of corporate communication, the message action plan in a crisis, according to Lawrence Warner, should include the following: "public's message elements, communication techniques, responsibilities, time and schedule commitments, and accountability factors."[3]

The stakeholders need to be listed in order of importance. The critical ones must be reached on priority. The concepts need to be communicated to the target audience, keeping in view the core message. The techniques of communication will include the decision about various channels, both paid and unpaid. Provision must also be made for budgeting and evaluation and feedback. In a crisis, free media coverage may not suffice. The crisis team may think it prudent to buy space and put across its viewpoint without the fear of its curtailment, if sent as a press release. Ratan Tata, after pulling out the Nano car production from West Bengal, issued a large advertisement expressing his angst against those he thought were responsible for the mess. The case study of the Nano car and the full text of the letter have been included later in the chapter.

The readers/viewers deduce visual and textual information according to their understanding, experience, and cultural and social milieu. The picture of a little girl afire changed the course of the Vietnam War against the USA in the 1960s. *Life* magazine commented that it was not only the first "Living Room War" (TV) but also "Coffee Table War." The cover story on India's involvement in Sri Lanka's war with its dissidents in *India Today* in the late 1980, which had the picture of a dead soldier being devoured by a dog, or when the *Frontline* cover story included pictures of a dead Rajiv Gandhi, killed by a human bomb in 1992, allegedly by LITTE sympathizers, raised debate about media's insensitivity in showing blood and gore. A field visit to tsunami-affected areas in 2004 reflected that media reports on the tsunami frightened the survivors immensely.

In a free society and an independent media, one expects plurality of view. However, due ideological divide, it is not uncommon to see media polarized in its coverage, as many stories bear that out.

10.2.5 Caselets

10.2.5.1 Wild rumors caused reputation damage

There can be times when an organization may get involved in a crisis not because of its doing, but due to factors not under its control, as in the case of Procter & Gamble which became the victim of a wild rumor from certain religious groups that it was in "league with Satan" and was funding the "Church of Satan." The rumor probably arose from its logo, which had evolved over a century, which showed a man in the moon and stars. To deal with negative propaganda that refused to die, P&G challenged it in the court and used media to manage misperceptions. However, P&G, despite getting respite from the court, decided to change the logo in 1985 to avoid any more trouble on that front.[4]

10.2.5.2 Sexist approach cost Archie's dear

There are times when lack of sensitivity may cost an organization dear, as Archie's learned the hard way. A chain of departmental stores, Archie's, among other things, also sells cards for all occasions. During the early nineties, it thought it could have some fun at others' expense, but thanks to the increasing awareness of consumer rights, its strategy boomeranged. Archie's had displayed for sale a variety of thematic greeting cards, including on Holi celebrations, christening them "(Un)holy" cards to commemorate

Holi, a festival of color and gaiety in India. The cards were sexually suggestive and not in good taste, which could have embarrassed women if they were at the receiving end. A couple of Delhi University girls took it upon themselves to organize public opinion against the departmental store near the university campus. Soon many women activists' groups organized "*dharnas*" and demonstrations all over the country in various cities, outside Archie's departmental stores. The company was sued in the court. Thanks to the exposure in the media and the quick response of the police, the offender (owner of Archie's) was taken into police custody. Stocks of the offending cards were confiscated. Archie's was taken totally unaware, as their image took a nosedive. Their cards and other mementos are very popular with people. In fact, their promotional campaign had been quite visible in the media around that time. Noting the loss of face and the public outcry, the company soon came out with an institutional campaign, apologizing. The message "Salute to Indian Womanhood" appeared on large billboards at important sites in major cities. The company was quick to realize the negative swing in public opinion and took a corrective action.[5]

10.2.5.3 Bhopal gas—a catastrophe that remains unresolved

A multinational corporation, viz., the Union Carbide, was involved in a holocaust that remains unseen and unheard of until it happened on 3 December 1984 in Bhopal, the capital city of Madhya Pradesh, the central part of India. The tragedy left over 10,000 people dead and many more rendered homeless, when the killer, methyl isocyanate, spread through the city at the dead of night. Despite almost four decades of the happening, the issue is still not resolved to the satisfaction of the victims.

It is not uncommon to see a ritual rally by some spirited people led by some NGOs taking place on every anniversary, which does not really matter to powers that be to settle affected people's claims.

The company seemed in no mood to pay beyond a pittance. It argued that since it had only 50.9% share, the state and central governments were also responsible. It also said that the company had no control over its affiliate in India, which was a blatant lie as all strategic decisions were taken by it.

In 1989, the Supreme Court of India passed a judgment that the Union Carbide should pay US $470 million as compensation in full and final settlement. The company agreed on the condition that it would not entertain any further claims. The government of India agreed without consulting the victims. Analysts believe that with this amount the average would not work out to more than Rs. 10,000 a victim.

Late Warren Anderson, the CEO of the company, who died in the US in 2014, avoided all along receiving warrants for appearing before the Indian court until his passing.

India must take the blame squarely on itself for mishandling the crisis. In the meantime, both the plants in India and the US have changed hands to BM Khaitan Group and Dow Chemicals respectively.

10.2.5.4 Wrong representation of facts—a perceived cause for war (1990)

In times of a crisis, the temptation more often is to overdo things or camouflage reality for strategic gains. That is where the credibility of corporate communication comes under public focus. PR consultancy Hill+Knowlton got embroiled for what was seen by critics as an attempt at the "manipulation of minds" of opinion makers, before the Gulf War. In October 1990, a 15-year-old Kuwaiti girl—Nayriah-al-Sabah—testified before the US Congress about the atrocities that the Iraqis were committing against Kuwaiti citizens. She specifically mentioned that Iraqis were taking Kuwaiti babies from incubators in area hospitals. What she said was believed, looking at her disposition, an innocent face with tearful eyes. The episode came to be referred as the "Incubator Atrocities." Many senators voted for war and cited the story. It came to notice later that Hill+Knowlton was paid $10.5 million by a group called the "Citizens for a Free Kuwait," which was represented primarily by wealthy members of the Kuwaiti ruling class to manage perceptions of various stakeholders. The aim behind the strategy was to "offset unfavorable publicity about Kuwait's form of government as well as its human rights record." It was also revealed that the girl who testified was the daughter of Kuwait's ambassador to the USA. There was even a doubt if the girl was in Kuwait at the time of the alleged atrocities that she testified about. Amnesty International had a difficult time corroborating her allegations. The Kroll Report that came out in 1992 concluded that there had been no mass scale atrocities on babies. It was, however, a fact that seven babies died because medical equipment was moved from a hospital.

The PR agency later admitted having coached the girl about the incubator imagery. The agency, nonetheless, defended its action in the interest of drawing public attention. Thomas J. Mickey, in one of his articles, questioned the use of signs, which may or may not necessarily represent reality.[6]

Image issues often surface when an organization is guilty or is perceived to be guilty of a certain malpractice, human rights violation, or a fraudulent or unethical practice. Often poor practice of corporate governance has led many an organization in deep trouble. Once the scams and issues of poor ethics surface, the task of image building is passed on to the corporate communication or PR department. Before some case studies are taken up for discussion, let us understand corporate governance as a concept and practice.

10.3 Corporate governance

The *Financial Times* once described corporate governance "as the relationship of a company to its shareholders or more broadly as its relationship to society." J Wolfensohn, president of World Bank in 1999, defined corporate governance thus: "Corporate governance is about promoting corporate fairness, transparency, and accountability.[7]

The paper *Corporate Governance: Value for who and how*, prepared by the Confederation of Indian Industries (CII) and Ernst & Young, lays emphasis on the need for an effective model of corporate governance to ensure that the interests of relevant stakeholders are guarded without hampering the development of enterprises. This would be imperative for restoring market confidence, the efficiency of capital allocation, the growth and development of a country's industrial bases, and, ultimately, the nation's total wealth and welfare. The paper also addresses the challenges faced by various stakeholders such as family in family-owned business, institutional investors, and private equity investors in the execution of corporate governance.[8]

10.3.1 Why corporate governance has become a globally discussed issue

The term corporate governance was not commonplace until the Enron fallout surfaced around the turn of the century, when everyone started talking of the need for ethical practices in the corporate sector. Some of the reasons ascribed by analysts include the following:

- Unethical business practices
- Lack of transparency
- Inefficient management boards
- Lack of concern for small investors

India woke up to the challenge of corporate governance practices in the 1990, the era of liberalization. The entry of multinationals, the Foreign Direct Investment in a few sectors, new structures of ownership, increasing exposure to international practices are cited as some of the reasons. This was followed by the Harshad Mehta scam, the allotment of equities at discounted rates to controlling groups, the siphoning of more than thousands of crores worth of public money by fly-by-night companies through public issues between 1993–95, which made India Inc and the government serious about bringing reforms in the sector.

The CII circulated a draft code called the *Desirable Corporate Governance: A Code* for comments in 1997. When this was released in 1998, around 25 companies followed the code voluntarily.

The Securities Exchange Board of India (SEBI) set up a committee under Kumar Mangalam Birla to design mandatory-cum-recommendatory code for listed companies in 1999. By and by, many companies with various paid-up capital started following the code.

The Department of Corporate Affairs (DCA) modified the Companies Act in 1956 to include specific corporate governance provisions regarding independent directors and audit companies. The DCA also appointed a task force on corporate excellence in 2000. A high-level committee under Mr. Naresh Chandra was appointed in 2002 to examine corporate auditing and role of independent directors following the collapse of Enron in 2001 and enactment of Sarbanes-Oxley Act in 2002.

The SEBI formed a new committee under N R Narayana Murthy to study the adequacy of existing corporate governance practices and to bring further improvement.[9]

The Ministry of Corporate Affairs in India has the following vision:

> To be a leader and partner in initiatives for corporate reforms, good governance, and enlightened regulation with a view to promote and facilitate effective corporate functioning and investor protection.[10]

The Ministry's website clearly indicates what the companies are required to do and the consequences of not complying with the regulation. To quote:

> All companies are required to file balance sheet and profit and loss account within 30 days and annual return within 60 days of holding their annual general meeting (AGM) to avoid:

1. Prosecution under the company's Act 1956
2. Payment of additional fee
3. Publication of name of your company in the list of defaulters
4. Information to your banker/financial institution.[11]

10.3.2 Policy dialogue on corporate governance in India 2006

In February 2006, the Ministry of Company Affairs co-hosted a conference along with the Organization for Economic Cooperation and Development (OECD) on "Policy Dialogue on Corporate Governance in India." The conference addressed the following issues:

- The role of the board in dealing with related party transactions
- The role of institutional investors in dealing with non-controlling shareholders
- Developments on compliance with international accounting and auditing standards
- Corporate governance of state-owned enterprises, including the OECD Guidelines on Corporate Governance of State-Owned Enterprises
- Corporate governance and capital markets
- Insolvency and corporate governance

The conference was widely attended by many Indian participants and international experts.[12]

The Ministry of Corporate Affairs, like other ministries, ran institutional campaigns just before the parliamentary election held in April–May 2009 was announced, to educate and inform the public of its initiatives and achievements.

In the backdrop of corporate governance concepts, let us analyze the Satyam fraud, considered the worst of its kind in the corporate history of India.

10.4 Case studies

10.4.1 Satyam computers—a case of poor corporate governance

Called "India's Enron" and "Mother of all scams" in corporate India, Satyam computers hit the headlines just a week after the new year ushered in, sending shock waves across the markets as the share price of the company tanked, post revelation by the company CEO, B Ramalingam Raju, that he had been fudging figures for many years. Although he was led by events, in his confession letter, he said he wished to "ease the burden on his conscience."

Shareholders, said the trade media, lost Rs. 9,374 crores in one day, when the news broke.

Satyam founder and former chairman Ramalingam Raju, his brother, Rama Raju, who was managing director, and former chief financial officer Vadlamani Srinivas were arrested in January 2009, soon after the chairman's resignation and confession letter.

Raju confessed to the investigating team that he orchestrated doctoring of company's books to inflate sales, profits, and cash balances for years. The investigating agencies at the beginning of the probe felt that much of the money existed and could have been diverted in buying assets within and outside the country.[13]

As soon as the fraud was unearthed, the government of India appointed a new board of directors, which immediately retained KPMG Deloitte to restate accounts that were overstated for six years.

10.4.1.1 About Satyam computers

Founded in 1987 by the US-educated Ramalingam Raju, Satyam computers soon became one of the top five software services exporters from India. The company has also been listed on the NYSE. Some of its competitors from India included Tata Consultancy Services and Infosys Technologies as well as global majors such as IBM and Accenture.

Satyam specialized in business software and offered back-office outsourcing and consulting. The company, at the time of the scam, had more than 600 clients, some of the prominent among being General Electric, Cisco Systems, and Qantas Airways.

Satyam claimed to have 53,000 employees (a fact later refuted by investigating agencies who felt that thousands of names were fictitious but their salaries were drawn that filled the personal coffers of the family).

The falsification of accounts by the company for years put a question mark on the integrity of the global auditing firm PricewaterhouseCooper (PWC), which works in India as Pricewaterhouse. After about three weeks of the exposure of the fraud, sleuths arrested two of its top officers, viz., S Gopalakrishna, relationship manager, and T Srinivas, engagement leader. They reportedly told the investigating officers that the CEO, R Raju, did not allow them to ask "unnecessary questions" but expected them to follow his instructions. The complicity of the firm was also investigated closely.[14] The *Economic Times* commented that their arrest on charges of alleged falsification of accounts, first time in the history of corporate India, had sent "shockwaves among the 1,50,000 odd chartered accountants' fraternity here."[15]

The investigative agencies found out that despite that the scope of work remained almost same, Pricewaterhouse, which was retained at less than Rs 1 crore fee per annum, started getting over Rs. 4.00 crores during the last few years of the scam. When compared with rates of other competitive IT firms, the fee was much higher than any company paid to its auditors.[16]

DSP Merrill Lynch, which handled the company's oversees equity offerings in all probability, as speculated by a section of media, told SEBI of serious accounting flaws, just before R Raju sent his confession letter.

Sunil Singhania, executive VP of Reliance MF, commented, "This is the worst thing to have happened. It reflects poorly on the corporate governance of the company. From the foreign investors' perspective, the image of corporate India would be dented in a big way."[17]

IT stalwarts, like N R Naryana Murthy of Infosys, were unsparing in their comments. Murthy said of the scam, "What's happened is shocking. It will have a deep impact on the entire Indian industry. I believe it is a bad taste, but an isolated case. The need of the hour is for IT sector to walk that extra mile."[18]

The chairman of regulatory authority SEBI, G B Bhave, spoke tough, saying,

> It is an event of horrifying magnitude. We are in touch with the Ministry of Company Affairs for coordinated action. We need to learn a few lessons from this. The

> development will have serious from this. This development will have serious implications for the market.[19]

Later, during the *Economic Times* Excellence Awards function in Mumbai on 18 January 2009, Prime Minister Manmohan Singh said that the Satyam computers scandal was a blot on India's corporate image. The government, he said, was determined to unravel the nature of the fraud. To quote him, "Satyam episode is a blot on our corporate image. It indicates how far malfeasance in one company can inflict suffering on many. . . The government is determined to unravel the full nature of the fraud."[20]

Expressing shock over Satyam's revelation of accounting fraud, US-based technology giant Cognizant said the entire episode reinforced the importance of strong corporate governance. "We are shocked and dismayed by today's announcement of fraudulent accounting by Satyam. Such a situation reinforces the value and importance of strong corporate governance and many other additional controls imposed on US companies that are subject to the Sarbanes-Oxley Act," Gordon Coburn, chief financial and operating officer of Cognizant, said. "At Cognizant, we follow rigorous corporate governance practices. In addition to independent testing of our annual compliance with the Sarbanes-Oxley Act, Cognizant retains both outside legal counsel and independent accountants to ensure that good governance practices and regulations are followed," he added.[21]

Commenting on the fraud, Sumeet Chatterjee of Reuters writes,

> At the height of the boom, top software firms Tata Consultancy Services, Infosys Technologies, Wipro, and Satyam consistently reported annual 50-percent increases in profits every quarter. Pressure to maintain this pace of growth, please investors and shareholders and justify inflated P/E multiples during a six-year bull run on the stock market have all been cited as reasons why Satyam cooked the books.[22]

10.4.1.2 Anatomy of the fraud

Analysts believe that on the face of it, Satyam did everything by the rule book. It had an international firm auditing its books, its declaration of accounts was in accordance with Indian and US standards. It had the requisite number of independent directors with good credentials, including a Harvard business school professor and a former federal cabinet secretary. Despite all that, the accounting books were cooked for years with inflated figures of profit and revenue, exaggerated cash, and bank balance, besides an understatement of what was owed and overstatement of what was due to the company.

The statutory auditing firm PWC either overlooked fudging of figures or were hand in glove with the management; either way, both conducts are not expected of an auditing firm.

Responding to stories in media about the role of independent directors in various companies, one could feel a visible anxiety among the clan. Many independent directors either quit their jobs or were planning to quit, especially in the realty sector.

"Even the best independent director of a company cannot detect a fraud if the auditor cannot detect it. And most independent directors are not involved in the workings of a company for more than 15 days," said Omkar Goswami, founder and chairman of Corporate and Economic Research Group (CERG) Advisory Private Limited, and an independent director of companies such as Infosys, Crompton Greaves, and Godrej Consumer Products.[23]

Another independent director in a few companies, Gurcharan Das, a former CEO of Procter & Gamble, said, "It is an impossible job for an independent director to penetrate the company from outside. Unless the independent director does not get deeply involved with the activities of the company, such kind of malpractice cannot be detected."[24]

Ramalingam Raju, in his letter outlining the deception, said no other board member—past or present—was aware of the financial irregularities. Here is the full text of the letter.

EXHIBIT 10.1 TEXT OF B RAMALINGAM RAJU'S LETTER

It is with deep regret and tremendous burden that I am carrying on my conscience, that I would like to bring the following facts to your notice:

1. The Balance Sheet carries as of September 30, 2008,
   a) Inflated (non-existent) cash and bank balances of Rs 5,040 crore (as against Rs 5,361 crore reflected in the books);
   b) An accrued interest of Rs 376 crore, which is non-existent;
   c) An understated liability of Rs 1,230 crore on account of funds arranged by me;
   d) An overstated debtors' position of Rs 490 crore (as against Rs 2,651 reflected in the books);
2. For the September quarter(Q2) we reported a revenue of Rs 2,700 crore and an operating margin of Rs 649 crore (24 per cent of revenue) as against the actual revenues of Rs 2,112 crore and an actual operating margin of Rs 61 crore (3 per cent of revenues). This has resulted in artificial cash and bank balances going up by Rs 588 crore in Q2 alone.

The gap in the balance sheet has arisen purely on account of inflated profits over several years (limited only to Satyam standalone, books of subsidiaries reflecting true performance).

What started as a marginal gap between actual operating profit and the one reflected in the books of accounts continued to grow over the years.

It has attained unmanageable proportions as the size of the company operations grew significantly (annualised revenue run rate of Rs 11,276 crore in the September quarter, 2008, and official reserves of Rs 8,392 crore).

The differential in the real profits and the one reflected in the books was further accentuated by the fact that the company had to carry additional resources and assets to justify a higher level of operations thereby significantly increasing the costs.

Every attempt made to eliminate the gap failed. As the promoters held a small percentage of equity, the concern was that poor performance would result in the takeover, thereby exposing the gap. It was like riding a tiger, not knowing how to get off without being eaten.

The aborted Maytas acquisition deal was the last attempt to fill the fictitious assets with real ones. Maytas' investors were convinced that this is a good divestment opportunity and a strategic fit.

One Satyam's problem was solved, it was hoped that Maytas' payments can be delayed. But that was not to be. What followed in the last several days is common knowledge.

I would like the board to know:

1. That neither myself, nor the Managing Director (including our spouses) sold any shares in the last eight years—excepting for a small proportion declared and sold for philanthropic purposes.
2. That in the last two years a net amount of Rs 1,230 crore was arranged to Satyam (not reflected in the books of Satyam) to keep the operations going by resorting to pledging all the promoter shares and raising funds from known sources by giving all kinds of assurances (statement enclosed only to the members of the board).

   Significant dividend payments, acquisitions, capital expenditure to provide for growth did not help matters. Every attempt was made to keep the wheel moving and to ensure prompt payment of salaries to the associates. The last straw was the selling of most of the pledged shares by the lenders on account of margin triggers.
3. That neither me nor the managing director took even one rupee/dollar from the company and have not benefited in financial terms on account of the inflated results.
4. None of the board members, past or present, had any knowledge of the situation in which the company is placed.

Even business leaders and senior executives in the company, such as, Ram Mynampati, Subu D, T R Anand, Keshab Panda, Virender Agarwal, A S Murthy, Hari T, S V Krishnan, Vijay Prasad, Manish Mehta, Murli V, Shriram Papani, Kiran Kavale, Joe Lagioia, Ravindra Penumetsa, Jayaraman and Prabhakar Gupta are unaware of the real situation as against the books of accounts. None of my or managing directors' immediate or extended family members has any idea about these issues.

Having put these facts before you, I leave it to the wisdom of the board to take the matters forward. However, I am also taking the liberty to recommend the following steps:

1. A task force has been formed in the last few days to address the situation arising out of the failed Maytas acquisition attempt.

   This consists of some of the most accomplished leaders of Satyam: Subu D, T.R. Anand, Keshab Panda and Virendra Agarwal, representing business functions, and A S Murthy, Hari T and Murali V representing support functions.

   I suggest that Ram Mynampati be made the chairman of this Task Force to immediately address some of the operational matters on hand. Ram can also act as an interim CEO reporting to the board.
2. Merrill Lynch can be entrusted with the task of quickly exploring some merger opportunities.
3. You may have a 'restatement of accounts' prepared by the auditors in light of the facts that I have placed before you.

I have promoted and have been associated with Satyam for well over 20 years now. I have seen it grow from few people to 53,000 people, with 185 Fortune 500 companies as customers and operations in 66 countries. Satyam has established an excellent leadership and competency base at all levels.

I sincerely apologise to all Satyamites and stakeholders, who have made Satyam a special organisation, for the current situation. I am confident they will stand by the company in this hour of crisis.

In light of the above, I fervently appeal to the board to hold together to take some important steps. TR Prasad is well placed to mobilise a support from the government at this crucial time.

With the hope that members of the Task Force and the financial advisor, Merrill Lynch (now Bank of America), will stand by the company at this crucial hour, I am marking copies of the statement to them as well.

Under the circumstances, I am tendering the resignation as the chairman of Satyam and shall continue in this position only till such time the current board is expanded. My continuance is just to ensure enhancement of the board over the next several days or as early as possible.

I am now prepared to subject myself to the laws of the land and face the consequences thereof.

(B Ramalinga Raju)

Copies marked to:

1. Chairman SEBI
2. Stock Exchanges.[25]

Analysts believe that $1 billion, or 94% of the cash, on the company's books was fictitious. The manipulation of the cash flow may be a reason why the fraud remained undetected. "Companies have manipulated P&L (profit and loss) accounts before, but cash flow is the Holy Grail—you don't tamper with it," said Saurabh Mukherjea, an analyst at UK-based research firm Noble Group.[26]

The Central Bureau of Investigation (CBI) issued a statement on 7 April 2009, that is, after three months of the exposure of the scam, filing charges against nine people including Satyam Computer Services' founder and former chairman, Ramalinga Raju, for alleged involvement in accounting fraud at the outsourcing firm. The charges included criminal conspiracy, cheating, forgery, and falsification of accounts. Media, quoting CBI sources, said that the agency had a feeling that R Raju may not have shared all the frauds in his letter. The agency may seek permission from the government to question Raju further and may put him on a lie detector.[27]

The *Indian Express*, in its Sunday supplement, carried a long story titled "The Charge Sheet Factory," mentioning that it was a mammoth report prepared by the CBI, running to 65,000 pages. The synopsis ran to 300 pages, and statements of 433 witnesses, mainly Satyam employees, bank officers, and realty sector representatives ran to thousands of pages. Besides that, 1,532 documents seized from the office and residences of Raju and family were attached with the report. The CBI had to make nine copies of the report that were loaded in 22 boxes and transported in a mini truck to reach the destinations.[28]

Imagery plays an important role in communication. By giving graphic details of the quantum of work to the media, the investigating agency probably wished to reflect the enormity of work that it had to do in a tight schedule and the depth of investigations.

10.4.1.3 Satyam corporate governance

The Satyam computers story has opened a Pandora's box on various issues relating to ethical corporate governance. Questions are being raised about various companies and sectors that have benefited largely from various schemes to boost business. The complicity of the political class in many cases is also not ruled out. Media has been full of stories on what all possibly went into making the Satyam computers the fourth largest company in the IT sector in India. Satyam founder Ramalinga Raju "allegedly used his political connections, first with the previous government headed by the then TDP chief minister Chandrababu Naidu, and later the current congress (I) Chief Minister to further his ambition," wrote the *Indian Express*.[29]

The newspapers commented that for Naidu and Raju, it was mutual—Naidu needed Satyam to promote Hyderabad as its next IT destination, while Raju needed a "Chief minister's zeal to fuel his own ambition of emulating the success of IT majors like the Infosys." He received large chunks of land for the IT parks and huge facilities.[30]

In 1997, Satyam established a school at the Indian Institute of Information Technology in Hyderabad, joining the league of a select brand of global IT giants like IBM, Microsoft, and Oracle that also had similar schools.

During Clinton's 2000 visit to India, Naidu lobbied to put Hyderabad on his itinerary, in which he succeeded. Raju was on the list of VVIPs who were introduced to the US president. That meeting, believed analysts, opened many doors for Satyam to do business with companies in the Fortune 500 list and their clients. Raju was invited to make a speech organized by the Confederation of Indian Industries (CII) on "India and US: Leaders in Science and Technology." Stalwarts like Azim Premji of Wipro and Ratan Tata of the Tata Group were ignored, while Raju shared the dais with the US president.

The economic offences wing of the CBI wondered as to how various banks and financial institutions never questioned his thousands of accounts or providing statements about his company's finances.

Critics believe that Raju invariably had inside information on government policies and development plans even before the blueprints were prepared. The modus operandi of the family, believe critics, was that it would buy huge chunks of land before a development project was announced. The international airport and IT areas in Madhapur and Ranga Reddy were definite pointers in that direction.

Raju's transfer of loyalty from TDP to the Congress was smooth. The chief minster may have taken some time, but it was not difficult as the favors given to the company later reflected, especially for the family-run infrastructure development firm Maytas, which ironically proved to be the nemesis for the family. The company was able to garner works worth more than Rs. 30,000 crores from the Congress government.

The Congress government chose the Byrraju Foundation set up by B Satyamaryan Raju, father of Ramalinga Raju, to start 108 emergency services under the Emergency Management and Research Institute (EMRI) started by Satyam.

In its article, "Is corporate governance a mere lip service?" the *Economic Times* invited experts to debate on the issue. N Balasubramanian, professor of corporate governance at IIM (B), said that the most important part in practice of ethical corporate governance was the independence and objectivity of the chosen directors, who were expected to "stand up to any potential breaches in the equitable accounting and transmission of created wealth in their companies to the rightful claimants, the shareholders." He further said that for this mechanism to work effectively, at least two critical criteria must be concurrently fulfilled: "First, the independence and objectivity of the chosen directors have to be established beyond doubt, and second there should be enabling processes in place that would help successful operation of the scheme."[31]

In the same article, Rohit Kochhar said that it was unfair to conclude that corporate governance failed at Satyam and "turn all guns at the regulators, or even the promoters involved." The institutional shareholders in Satyam, he argued, were able to force a reversal of questionable decision on the Maytas. Echoing the sentiment of N Balasubramanian, Kochhar felt that one of the biggest malaises in the corporate governance was the lack of authority of independent directors, who in his view were "mere puppets, dancing to the tunes of the promoters or a block of shareholders in control."[32]

"The culture of corporate governance," according to N K Jain, the then CEO of the Institute of Company Secretaries,

> need to be spread amongst the entire corporate world, more specifically, in respect of small and medium sized enterprises. This will not only ensure sustainability, but will also ensure development of the country at large. Some sporadic incidence of mis-governance should not wish away the sincere and exemplary efforts of corporate India towards good corporate governance.[33]

NR Narayana Murthy, founder chairman of Infosys Technologies, in an interview to the ET, said, "Feudalism was responsible for what happened at Satyam." He was harsh on certain individual promoters about whom he said, "Honesty is not something they want to pursue as hard as profits. They want to make money any which way. by avoid paying taxes, cooking books and payoffs."[34]

What all these experts say make a lot of sense, especially when India has the largest listed companies than anywhere else in the world.

10.4.1.4 What are the corporate communication insights?

- A crisis is a challenge but at the same time a great learning opportunity. Satyam's case hopefully cautioned corporate Inc. on the risks of poor corporate governance.
- Resilience in time of a crisis is very important. When in trouble, the company may have to sail alone, so it is important that the management and corporate communication team need to work on a communication strategy that not only responds to the communication needs of the stakeholders but also aims at restoring the confidence in the organization.
- It is important to know of "friends" and "adversaries" so that one can make strategic use of intervention from the allies.

- Tracking media, including social media, to keep a finger on the pulse of public opinion and addressing the genuine concerns of the stakeholders is extremely important amid a crisis and thereafter.
- In trying times, informed employees can be used as goodwill ambassadors.
- It is no guarantee that a company that won many awards for excellence in corporate governance, including the Golden Peacock Global Award twice, including one just before the scam surfaced in 2008, would be so unethical in its dealings. This also puts a question mark on the sanctity of such awards and organizations instituting such awards. When companies are short-listed for awards, what goes into the process of selection is an area that needs serious addressing.
- Business in general does not elicit much respect. People invariably do not trust a businessman. It is often believed that a businessman only sees the profit angle in whatever he does, including relationships. The coverage of media on tainted business and businessmen has not been very different in the last one century.

Investigative and opinionated journalists, who were referred as muckrakers in the beginning of the last century, wrote about businessmen more scathingly. Let us sample one of the dispatches of "muckraker" Lincoln Steffens in 1904, to appreciate that not much has changed in media's perceptions:

> The typical businessman is a bad citizen; he is busy, he does not neglect, he is busy with politics, oh, very busy and very businesslike. I found him buying boodlers (thieves and swindlers) in St. Louis, defending grafters in Minneapolis, originating corruption in Pittsburgh, sharing with bosses in Philadelphia, deploring reform in Chicago, and beating good government with corruption funds in New York. He is a self-righteous fraud, this big business man. He is the chief source of corruption and it were a boon if he would neglect politics.[35]

- Thousands of blogs surfaced on the Satyam fraud within weeks, most of them critical, some going into the what and how of the fraud, while a miniscule were remembering how their "friends" appreciated Satyam as a great employer!
- Social networking sites have become sources of "consumer insights." It will do well if the corporate communication department of Satyam computers trails these sites, gather insights, sift, and share with the management for a better understanding of the stakeholder concerns.
- Media took potshots at the beleaguered CEO of Satyam, on his life in jail, giving graphic details about the size of the room that he was sharing with other criminals, the toilet that he would be sharing with 40 other inmates, and, of course, the food, not forgetting to write that he came in his Mercedes Benz to the police station for his arrest! It was probably the sadist pleasure they wished to provide to all those who were hurt by his misdemeanor and misdeeds.
- When the news of Satyam buying Maytas broke, creating a problem of confidence within the group, the company used media vigorously to assure that it was withdrawing from the deal, reiterating at the same time that despite that they were rightful in doing it, but at the same time, the interests of the shareholders and employees would be supreme for the board. No one except probably those involved in the fraud could

have imagined that the malady was deep rooted, till the CEO shared in his confessional letter the fraud he had been committing. He surely lost face among his internal stakeholders, as just a day before that, he was talking about their "interests" being supreme!

- While most of the employees avoided talking to media about their state of mind, one newspaper published a picture of the exterior of the jail where R Raju was lodged, which had a few ply cards pledging support to their boss. One of them read: "With you, always." In adversity, one is not left with many friends and well-wishers. The heartfelt gestures by some of his employees hopefully would have given the former CEO some food for thought on valuing trust and sincerity.
- After about three weeks, when the new board was in the saddle, media reports indicated that the employees had formed a union and were demanding their representation on the board to ensure the interests of the employees were addressed adequately.[36]
- Seized of the anxiety on the part of the employees, the new dispensation released a video referred to as "Inspirational video" by media, in which most of the board members assured the employees about the steps taken by the company that would address their concerns. The internal auditing officer also spoke about auditing that was underway to look at the financial health of the company. One of the board members also hoped that the company would be able to borrow money from the banks and other institutions soon to make payments and get over difficult times.[37]
- Headhunters interviewed by various news and business channels said that in just few hours of the unearthing of the scandal, various job portals were inundated with thousands of applications that reflected the anxiety of employees. In a box item with the caption "Infy not to hire Satyam employees," the story in a newspaper quoted Infosys Technologies HR, Education & Administration Director T V Mohandas Pai about the decision on the company on this issue, thus: "We have asked our Recruitment staff not to poach anybody from Satyam. The company is in the middle of a crisis and people will jump ship." The impression sought to be given was that in tough times, one must help a fellow company. This, however, was in contravention to the stand of its chief mentor, who, a day before, had said, "We will not touch such a tainted company." As reported by the media, Infosys management had also instructed its staff not to entertain telephone calls or CVs of Satyam employees.
- Thanks to the powers that be, the company soon had a new owner, Tech Mahindra, that bid the highest for a 51% share at Rs. 2889 crores. The industry feels the company would be able to cover the lost ground. The *Economic Times*, in the banner headline "Satyam@techmahindra," said on a hopeful note, "Four months on, the scammed company, now on the mend, has gone to a new owner. Four months from a deep hole, the markets have hit 11k. Are these glimmers of hope?"[38] However, within a short period, news surfaced that at least 10,000 employees expected pink slips.
- Last but not the least, the government of India, especially the Ministry of Corporate Affairs, did a tremendous job of taking control of the situation, thus restoring the confidence of various stakeholders, de-bureaucratizing the whole process of finding a new buyer, putting in place the new buyer within three months, and, most importantly, separating the process from the "consequence of fraud." Industry watchers wondered if the impeccable handling of the Satyam issue would set a precedent and enhance expectations from the government.[39]

10.4.2 *The Jet Airways imbroglio*

The dust had not even settled on the issue of Kingfisher and Jet Airlines entering a strategic alliance to share resources to tide over mounting losses and trying times of global recession, and Captain Gopinath wishing to "buy back" his Air Deccan from the "King of Good Times," Malaya, when the media gave the lead story on 16 October 2008 that Jet had fired 850 cabin crew members and about 1,100 staffers were facing the axe soon. It created quite a turmoil in the aviation industry. Not to be left behind, Raj Thakre of Maharashtra Navnirman Sena (MNS) threatened Jet Airways to reinstate the employees forthwith or face the consequences. And what were the consequences he was talking about? Grounding of Jet Airways flights from Mumbai!

The print media was full of pictures of young airline staff in yellow (official dress code) with agonized expressions. The central government made it clear that it will not bail out the aviation sector. The then aviation minister Praful Patel expressed his "deep disappointment" with some central ministers for not easing up the credit flow to the industry. Murli Deora, the then oil minister, reacted sharply to the aviation minster's outburst by saying that he was doing his best to help the airlines, even though oil companies were also going through a rough patch. The next day, the media reported that both Jet Airways and Kingfisher owed more than Rs. 2000 crores to public sector oil companies on account of purchase of fuel.

On the issue of sacking, there was a complete volte-face by Jet patriarch Naresh Goyal within 24 hours. "It's conscience, not pressure," he said in a press conference that he called in Mumbai at 11.30 p.m. on 16 October 2008 to announce that the sacking orders were being withdrawn and all employees who were given pink slips could return to work on Friday, the 17th of October. Making it clear that he was not a part of the decision (of sacking), he subtly said, "The management might not like my decision but sometimes there are disagreements within the family and as the head of the family, I am taking this decision." The media reported that distancing himself from the decision taken by the management based on the prevailing economic condition, Goyal said he was not even aware as to how many employees were being sacked.

Both Raj Thakre and cousin Udhav Thakre took credit for forcing Jet Airways to make a decision in favor of the sacked employees.

Interestingly, as the announcement from Mr. Goyal came late at night, most of the inside pages of various newspapers had stories of sacking with pictures of the employees. As the front page is published last of all, it did carry the breaking news of reinstating the employees, announced almost at the midnight hour by Jet Airways chairman.[40]

Corporate dossier, *Economic Times*, in its article "The dreaded f-word," commented on the Jet story, thus: "The whole nation saw Naresh Goyal pussyfoot around the lay-off issue. He was not the first to, either. What makes India Ink's honchos falter when it comes to mass firing even when it could save their business?" Swearing on his dead mother, he said, "I swear on my dead mother that I have not spoken to any politician," while announcing reinstatement of fired employees. His bluff was called when the union aviation minister claimed that he had indeed spoken with Goyal on the issue. The Jet scrip fell by 17% (from Rs. 259.50 on 16 October to Rs. 182 on 18 October 2008) in two days. It clearly was a case of financial stakeholders losing to internal stakeholders.

"At some point you have to think about those 2000 people who were let go but the other 13000 Jet employees, if the company collapses because of it," commented management expert Gurcharan Das.[41]

10.4.2.1 What are the lessons for corporate communicators?

- It is important to have pre-thinking on the issue before "letting the cat out of the bag." The pros and cons and probable players need to be worked on.
- It is important to keep the employees informed of impending management decisions so that issues do not take a political turn and vested interests do not have a field day.
- The government needs to have a unified opinion. Various ministers should not use verbal salvo against each other, which hurts the reputation of the government. In this case, this strategy may not have been possible as the UPA was a coalition of parties which had ministers from various partner political parties. So trading charges against one another and not speaking in unison was only expected.
- Timing is also an important consideration. The oil minister, as reported by the media, accused Naresh Goyal of "breaking the promise of not defaulting on fuel bills and acting in an amateur manner in sacking people just before Diwali. I don't know what country he lives in," he was quoted saying. The Indian Oil Corporation, in sync, issued information to media that both Jet and Kingfisher put together owed Rs. 2,024.33 crore to public sector companies.
- Under the prevailing circumstances, Naresh Goyal's strategy was a face-saving device, which did work for the company, albeit as a short-term solution.

10.4.3 ICICI case study

Economic recession—image impact on ICICI

As soon as the news of the crashing of Lehman Brothers, a financial behemoth in the USA, poured in, whispers about the ICICI Bank also surfaced, sending panic waves among depositors and investors in October 2008. A Google search on ICICI brought in 99,200 responses in 0.28 seconds on 22 October 2008.

10.4.3.1 Third-party endorsements

Bank CEO Kamath appeared in many news channels, assuring stakeholders that the bank was extremely healthy and had ample capital. In its effort for damage control, Joint MD Chandra Kochar also joined in interfacing with the media.[42]

Weekly journal *Business World* reported: "ICICI Bank, India's biggest bank said on Tuesday that rumors being repeatedly circulated about its financial strength were baseless and malicious, saying the bank had a strong capital position."[43]

10.4.3.2 Paid advertising to manage perception

The bank also roped in Shahrukh Khan for their TV commercials, who talked of "trust" and "faith." "ICICI bank. It's a smart choice. Take my word for it," said Shahrukh. He further said he had his money in ICICI and would continue to have it there. Their earlier "Mein hoon naa" campaign could not have worked in troubled times when the bank's stock plummeted to a 52-week low in the second week of October 2008. To arrest gossip mongering and an overactive grapevine, the bank, in an unprecedented move, sent SMS messages to its customers, requesting them not to believe any rumors surrounding the bank, with the message "Your deposits with the ICICI Bank are safe. Your bank is well capitalized with good liquidity. Please don't listen to baseless rumors. Happy festive season." The bank simultaneously issued print ads to highlight its strong liquidity. One of the ads had the copy "At the end of the day, truth and trust have no equal." In the body copy, it spoke of malicious rumors about the bank. The ad spoke about the following areas, viz., sound banking system, healthy capital, large net worth, and strong credit rating, in various subheads, to support its claims through robust data and testimonials.

It later mounted a long-drawn generic campaign, educating the people on various aspects of banking. Here is one of the ads from the series.

In an in-depth study of the banking sector, in the article "Agony Time Marketing," in Brand Equity, Ashley Coutnho argued that in the face of the global turmoil which was affecting the Indian banks as well, it was important that banks brought back the good old plank of faith and trust, as the ICICI Bank did.[44]

10.4.3.3 Corporate communication insights

- Timeliness is the essence of crisis communication. The ICICI bank did not lose any time in launching its campaign to avoid giving chance to gossipmongers.
- The top management was in unison in its communication strategy. In fact, they complemented each other.
- Community interface was a smart move, which helped put to rest wild rumors.
- Shahrukh Khan's entry through advertisements was quite timely. It was a smart strategy not to overdo it.

10.4.4 The Tata "Nano" story—a crisis aggravated by political forces

Nano, the smallest and most economical car from one of the globally respected conglomerate, the Tata Group, faced major hassles before the little car was seen test-driving in media programs as a build-up before the bookings for the car began in April 2009. The company got embroiled in the state politics as soon as Ratan Tata, the group chairman, announced a small car project that he wished to set up in the Left-run West Bengal. The project incidentally was announced on the day Buddhadeb Bhattacharya was sworn in as the chief minister of West Bengal in May 2006.

10.4.4.1 What was the issue?

The Tata Group was allotted 404 hectares of land to build its factory in a place called Singur, which later became the bone of contention. Some farmers led by Trinamool Congress chief Mamta Banerjee questioned the decision of the state government in taking away "forcibly" a multi-crop fertile land by revoking the archaic Land Acquisition Act of 1894.

The construction work developing the infrastructure was in full swing, and the Tatas had put its first batch of engineers in place from January 2007.

All the while, the Tata Group kept itself out of direct dialogue with the agitators, who held demonstration many a times. Once, they were joined by social activist Medha Patekar of *Save Narmada* fame, who was booked on charges of rioting and disturbing the peace of the place, the movement against the Tatas gained prominence in the mainstream and local media.

Things took a turn, and the agitation gained momentum when the Trinamool Congress was able to garner majority seats in the local self-governing bodies in May 2007. This gave a momentum to agitation. Ratan Tata, however, categorically said there was no pulling out from Singur.

The chief protagonist went for a 25-day-long hunger strike in December 2007.

The governor of West Bengal played the informal arbitrator, but nothing came out of it. The various agitations that also included torching of the fence of the factory had the Tata employees worried about their life and security, when a disheartened Ratan Tata took a call and decided to pull out of West Bengal, amidst promises from the state government that things would be sorted out. The entire industry rallied around Ratan Tata. FICCI publicly said that such events might lead other industrialists to pull out from West Bengal.

Many chief ministers offered Ratan Tata to shift to their states when he settled for Gujarat in October 2008. This meant a loss of Rs. 500 crores to the company and settling of claims of vendors who put up cumulative claims of over Rs 250 crores on the company for their investment and borrowings from the banks, as reported by the media.

The central government, by and large, kept out of the controversy.

All the while, Ratan Tata resisted from making any comment on the agitators, led by Mamta Bannerjee. All he would say was that since the lives of the employees were at stake, Tata Motors had no alternative but to withdraw from the state. However, three weeks later, in an "Open Letter to the Citizens of West Bengal" that appeared in a few newspapers in West Bengal, Ratan Tata minced no words when he openly criticized the Trinamool Congress led by Mamata Banerjee who he alleged was supported by "vested interests and certain political parties" that caused serious disruption to the progress of the Nano plant.

EXHIBIT 10.2 RATAN TATA'S OPEN LETTER

THE TELEGRAPH
Date: 17.10.08
TATA Motors

Open letter to the citizens of the West Bengal

Over the past three weeks there have been statements by vested interests criticizing the decision taken by Tata motors to move the Nano car project out of Singur claiming that the decision was hasty and politically motivated. I therefore feel compelled to address this letter to the people of West Bengal, to explain how our dreams of contributing to the industrial revival of west Bengal has been shattered by an environment of politically-motivated agitation and the hostility that finally left us with no option but to withdraw the Nano project from West Bengal.

Two years ago, when Tata Motors decided to locate the Nano car project in West Bengal, it reflected the tremendous faith and confidence we had, and still have, in the investor-friendly policies of Mr. Buddhadeb Bhattacharjee's government. All through the two years that we have been constructing the plant at Singur, this feeling of faith and confidence in the vision of objective of the state government has been reinforced. All our interaction with the chief minister and the industry minister in particular, as also with several other officers, have been exemplary. We had therefore hoped that this project would reinstate confidence for further investments in West Bengal and would create a large number of jobs for the younger citizens, directly in the company and its suppliers, as also foster a large number of small enterprises in the Singur area which would provide livelihood to the citizens of that area. We had also taken medical and other community services in the Singur region. Our fervent desire has always been to be a good, contributing corporate citizen enhancing the quality of life of the people around the plant.

Unfortunately, the confrontative actions by the Trinamool Congress led by Ms. Mamta Banerjee and supported by vested interests and certain political parties, opposing the acquisition of land by the state government, have caused serious disruption to the progress of the Nano plant. The land acquired by the state government at Singur and leased to Tata Motors has been, we believe, through a transparent process and fair compensation. The Trinamool Congress's position has been that this land acquisition by the state government is illegal. In response to Public interest litigation, the Hon'ble Calcutta High Court has ruled that the land acquisition is totally legal but the same plaintiffs have filed against this judgment in the Supreme Court, which is pending a hearing

Throughout the construction of the plant, the Company has had to endure constant acts of open aggression on the site, occasional acts of violence, breakage of the compound perimeter walls, theft of construction material from within the project area, as well as intimidation and even physical assault of employees, contract labor and residents of the area to be absorbed in the project. Country bombs have been lobbed into the premise, obstructing the movement of material and personnel into and out of the plant.

Various attempts at finding solutions were thwarted by the Trinamool Congress's consistent demand that land acquired for the Nano plant and/or its integrated vendor park be returned to the segment of the land owners which the Trinamool Congress party claims to represent. Tata Motors has always maintained that this project has been conceived of as an integrated campus of manufacturing facilities and suppliers, so as to maximize integration and minimize logistics and material flow costs. Disruption of this integrated campus would make it extremely difficult for the Company to meet its product price and productivity goals.

On August 22nd, I addressed a Press Conference in Kolkata, generally referring to the hostility and difficult environment we were facing and appealing for a more congenial environment, failing which we would have no option but to consider taking the project out of West Bengal. Unfortunately, the response to this appeal was an escalation of the hostilities through a dharna on the highway in front of the plant, some more incidents of physical assault and considerable amount of intimidation of personnel working at the site, which finally resulted in the suspension of the completion work on the plant for almost a month. All of you will therefore appreciate that the final and painful decision to move the project out of West Bengal has not been a decision taken in haste, but a decision taken with great regret after a great deal of deliberation and a final assessment that it was unlikely that a sustainable, peaceful environment would develop in which our project could operate.

We are conscious of the disappointment and despondency that may be felt by some of the residents of Singur who may have hoped for an improvement in their quality of life after the plant was operational. We believe the responsibility for this would lie with the Trinamool Congress, which has created the hostile environment that has obliged the Company to move the project from Singur.

In the future, in the state of West Bengal many Tata Motors-type projects may come and go, many political ideologies may come and go, but the future of the state of West Bengal will depend on the path its leaders and citizens take in developing and retaining an environment which will result in the prosperity of the state in the years to come. Many may have forgotten that West Bengal was the major centre for heavy industry and steel fabrication, Agitation and violence drove away many industries around 30 years ago, and it has only been in recent times that the present government has been able to rebuild the confidence of investors to invest in the state.

It is therefore ironic that, at this crucial time and moment of hope for the state, history appears to be repeating itself. Agitation, violence and terror are overtaking the state in the name of the agricultural community, to serve political goals—stalling progress and destroying the newfound confidence in the state, while doing nothing for the rural poor, other than making promises. West Bengal's agriculture was a success story in the 1970s and 1980s but the farm sector's growth has slowed in the recent past. It is self-evident that industrial growth and agricultural growth must happen together in peace and harmony, and not through agitation and activism.

The people of West Bengal—particularly the younger citizens—will need to express their views and aspirations as to what they would like to see West Bengal become in the years ahead. Would they like to support the present Government of Mr. Buddhadeb Bhattacharjee to build a prosperous state with the rule of law, modern infrastructure and industrial growth, supporting a harmonious investment in the agricultural sector to give the people in the state a better life? Or would they like to see the state consumed by a destructive political environment of confrontation, agitation, violence and lawlessness? Do they want education and jobs in the industrial and high-tech sectors or does the future generation see their future prosperity achieved on "stay as we are" basis?

The future destiny of West Bengal lies with its citizens. They will need to decide whether they wish to stand still and let growth take place elsewhere, or move forward with the present Government's progressive policy, so that West Bengal can take its rightful place with other states—sharing in the future prosperity of India.

Ratan Tata

10.4.4.2 What are corporate communication insights?

- In a crisis, many stakeholders get embroiled, who may or may not be the concerned "parties" in the crisis per se but can wield influence. The political environment is an important constant factor which needs to be taken into account by the industry. In other words, the importance of "pre-thinking" should not be underestimated.

- The goodwill of the Tata Group was amply visible when the entire industry rallied around Tata Group in its struggle in Singur.
- Taking land through the state government meant the company did not invest much effort, if at all, in interfacing with the community, who, rightly or not, could be indoctrinated by vested interests. The compensation received by the farmers for their land was presumably much lower, despite that the land was supposedly fertile when compared with other states where the farmers are said to have received many more times the amount even for non-fertile land.
- Companies often conduct baseline surveys and social audits before deciding on a place. To quote an example, Reliance Industries Limited (RIL), which had acquired thousands of acres of land in the state of Haryana SEZ around the same time. It had put in place an extensive corporate social responsibility (CSR) initiative to win the trust of the local communities before land deals could materialize. However, even this did not help; the company decided to withdraw from there.
- To Ratan Tata's letter, analysts reacted variously. The tone and tenor of the letter was angry and political in nature when he exhorted the young people of West Bengal to decide whether they would like to support

  the then Government of Mr. Buddhadeb Bhattacharjee to build a prosperous state with the rule of law, modern infrastructure, and industrial growth, supporting a harmonious investment in the agricultural sector to give the people in the state a better life? Or would they like to see the state consumed by a destructive political environment of confrontation, agitation, violence, and lawlessness?

  Interestingly a few months later, the Left government was routed in elections. On a media question, Mamta Banerjee, after her unprecedented victory, said that her party was not against industrialization, but if factories must be set up, these would to be on barren land and not at the cost of fertile land. Some felt that it did not really suit the stature of an industrialist like Ratan Tata to openly criticize a political party and its leader, reflecting his political prejudice, while others felt that after losing so much on time, effort, and money, he had nothing more to lose. Calling a spade a spade, therefore, was a good strategy.

- Tatas, by and large, had a very supportive press, especially the national media.
- When the car was demonstrated at the India International Fair in 2007, it created a near frenzy among Delhi citizens. The media played on the sentiment. It covered front-page stories on how Ratan Tata had once seen a family of four riding a scooter, when he pledged that he would soon produce a car that will be affordable to the common man. The design and the designers of the car were kept in a closet until the day the car was demonstrated to people at last. With a highly cluttered car market, especially in the low category, the company was not able to generate as many bookings as it probably expected. As per media reports, the company could attract 2.5 lakhs of bookings, the highest at 50% in the top category, costing Rs. 1.84 Lakhs. Nano, Ratan Tata's dream venture, unfortunately failed in people's expectation and in the marketplace.

The Tata Group, hopefully, later analyzed the Singur Saga ardently and drew some useful insights on crises management.

10.4.5 *Mumbai siege—an exploding crisis that had the the whole world watching it live*

The Indian Institute of Mass Communication had conducted an exploratory field survey post 9/11 among Delhiites to see its impact on the psyche of the people as they were exposed to the happenings through several news channels beaming images 24-7 for weeks. One of the questions was whether the 9/11 kind of event was relevant to India, when a whopping majority had replied in the affirmative. India and indeed the world at large were witness to the terror theater, live for days, when ten armed terrorists from the neighboring country sneaked into the financial capital of India, Mumbai on 26 November 2008 and created mayhem for 64 hours, shooting at people indiscriminately at a railway station, making hundreds of people hostages in two five-star hotels and a Jewish family from Israel in their own home. About 200 hundred people died, and double the number injured in one of the worst terrorist carnages witnessed by the country in its history.

For some time, even the police thought the shoot-out in one of the hotels was the result of a gang rivalry, before the truth dawned on them.

10.4.5.1 Sensitivity to situation under watch

In a crisis, the intent and integrity of those in charge of solving the situation is under a constant scanner. The crisis managers also must be careful in their use of verbal and non-verbal communication. It cost both the Maharashtra chief minister at the time of the terrorist attack, late Vilas Rao Deshmukh, and the state home minister, R R Patil, their jobs. The chief minister was vehemently criticized by media for an act that seemed so insipid and unexpected of a person in charge of the state. A day after the hotel Taj was being sanitized, he, along with his entourage, visited the venue, an exercise in PR, so would anyone infer. However, in his party were two persons that raised eyebrows instantly, namely filmmaker Ram Gopal Verma, who has made a few films on the underworld's nexus in city crimes, and film star Ritesh Deshmukh, who happened to be the chief minister's son. Images appeared in the media immediately criticizing the CM for bringing the filmmaker and his son for a reconnaissance that would probably be a plot for Ram Gopal Verma's next film in which his son would act! Calling it "Terror Tourism," one of the news channels in an interview program titled "Lacking: Sense and Sensibility," the anchor grilled the CM on the issue.

"Insensitive, inconsiderate, mindless and cruel" were some of the adjectives the young people have used to describe Indian politicians on their Facebook pages, blogs, chat rooms, and public space.[45]

10.4.5.2 Failure to handle a crisis ends up finding easy scapegoats

In a crisis, it is not uncommon to find scapegoats. The incident also caused the Union home minister Shivraj Patil his job, despite that there was not much criticism in the media about his actions or decisions, unlike at the time of the Delhi bombing on 13 September 2008, when he survived the axe amidst media speculation. The Union home minister, in fact, had accompanied the NSG commandoes in the plane to reach Mumbai. The case study of the Delhi bombing has also been included in the chapter.

The electronic media coverage received a lot of criticism from the viewers on various blogs. The live coverage had all the ingredients of a horror movie, commented a blogger. One journalist was seen speaking in whispers somewhere from the venue where the Jewish family was made hostage; another journalist was seen hugging a victim and crying while reporting from the site. One channel claimed they were talking to one of the terrorists.[46]

10.4.5.3 No one seemed in command

In case of hostage incidents, one expects that some authorized negotiator would speak to the tormentors to get to know their identity, their nationality, and their demands, if any. The strategy is also to buy time, distract their attention, and weaken their defense. Despite that the siege went on for two nights and three days, no such attempt was made by authorities to get to the terrorists, if not in person, at least through loudspeakers, public address system, or cable network. The tormentors were either watching the television themselves to know the tactical moves of the security agencies or were briefed by their masters over phone who were watching the live coverage, as brought out by government reports later. The electric power to the hotels was disconnected much later, when it could have taken a minute to disconnect the supplies to handicap the terrorists. In fact, nobody seemed to be in charge to give instructions to passersby or media who were also exposed to danger.

10.4.5.4 Media under public glare

The news media is no longer alone in the business of disseminating information. The social networking sites, a parallel channel, got activated as soon as the siege took place. One of the blogs commenting on media's role had this to say:

> They (meaning the news channels) have to be told how to behave in times like these. Their actions have to be considered criminal conduct if they in any way compromise security operations. And really, if a channel puts a terrorist on air and airs his views in the middle of operations, it should be legally considered a criminal act.[47]

The viewers, in general, were aghast to find self-promotion by channels during the live coverage, claiming being the first ones to break news, a highly insensitive thing to do.[48]

India Today, *Outlook*, and *The Week* hiked the price of their issues that carried the 26/11 coverage, which invited people to criticize them for their unjustifiable act of making money on death and destruction. E-mails were circulated for boycotting the magazines. One recalls, after 9/11, *Time b*rought out a special issue, but without any advertisements to avoid being seen as insensitive. Many advertisers withdrew their ads from channels during that period for the same reasons.

10.4.5.5 Soothing frayed nerves—an important strategy

when the atmosphere is charged with anxiety and restlessness, it is a good strategy on the part of communicators to reflect the human spirit and grit to give readers/viewers the necessary break from tense moments. It was a good strategy on the part of the media to cover human-interest stories in between, to relax the nerves of people, watching blood and gore with batted breaths for days together. As soon as the Taj was cleared of the terrorists, hundreds of media men, covering live, said that, from the body language of the security forces, one could make out that the flushing was complete, even before a formal announcement was made. It was a great site to find a few security personnel from police, the commandoes from the National Security Guards and other agencies taking out cell phones from their pockets and engaging in small talk, beaming all through. There was no mistaking that the calls were from or to their harnessed family members and well-wishers, who must have heaved a sigh of relief seeing their loved ones alive.[49]

People holding red roses appeared in hundreds from nowhere. Roses were presented to security personnel as they boarded the buses to take them away after their task was over. A soldier feeding the pigeons also made an interesting shot.

The public is very sharp when it comes to visual imagery. A channel had a person from the public who criticized the local government for sending the mundane BEST buses to take the security personnel back after they successfully accomplished the task. He minced no words when he said if it were the cricket team returning from somewhere, it would have been a luxurious coach for them, but not for the real heroes who did not bother about their lives so that others could live!

Some Mumbai politicians who, in the past, had raised slogans against "outsiders" occupying Mumbai came in for a lot of flak from media and bloggers who spared no efforts in challenging them on their narrow vision and parochialism. "Who have come to save Mumbai (referring to security forces), would you call them outsiders or Indians?" wrote a blogger.

10.4.5.6 Lessons for crises managers

- In a crisis of this kind and magnitude, who really was the crisis manger—the central government, the state government, or the spokesperson of the security forces grappling with crisis on field? It is important to know beforehand who would do the media briefing. It can be more than one, after clear-cut roles are ordained for them. In the case of the Mumbai siege, hundreds of media persons had assembled, who were seen moving about in all directions. There were no instructions about their security. One could even see on live television people moving around while a bloody battle was going on inside the hotels.
- As the coverage was live for the whole world see, the responses from various countries through their news channels was also constant. One of the international channels commented on the rudimentary way the security agencies handled the whole episode until the NSG commandoes entered the scene.
- In various functions organized by civil society organizations to express their solidarity against the perpetrators of violence and bring about unity among various groups, the media reported some goof-ups. Some corporate organizations did not resist from reflecting their names on the banners.
- India used its diplomatic channels befittingly to garner support from various countries. Both the prime minister and the external affairs minister used various fora to put forth India's point of view, without getting hyper or emotional, unlike their counterparts in Pakistan who were not consistent in their views.
- Armed with investigation and insights on how the direct telecast helped the terrorists in changing their tactics, keeping in view the movement of the rescue team, the government put together a code of conduct in January 2009 for media for future coverage. Media, in general, cried hoarse against the impending restriction on their freedom,

calling in "gag order." However, most of them agreed to work together on a code of ethics that was acceptable to the media. Prime Minister Manmohan Singh assured the media that nothing would be done unless a wider dialogue and discussion was conducted in the matter. Media associations need to voluntarily put forth self-regulations.

- It is easier to do a postmortem after a crisis is over. Critics often find holes in the crisis handling and have many handy suggestions on what could have been a better solution. The person/group that makes a decision probably is the best judge of taking stock of the situation and deciding on the line of strategy in resolving a particular crisis. It is quite possible that later it may be felt that strategy could have been different. In retrospect, the BJP government came in for a lot of flak from all quarters, including the Congress party for bargaining the security of the country when terrorists were exchanged for hostages in 2000 in the hijack drama at Kandahar in Afghanistan. The then foreign minister Jaswant Singh had personally gone to strike the deal with the terrorists. The Congress party bigwigs were openly charging the BJP during their election rallies for letting out the terror mastermind, who they alleged had been steering terror attacks in India after that.
- When the then NDTV reporter Barkha Dutt asked the home minister P Chidambaram during an award ceremony in January 2009 if he would subscribe to the theory of no negotiations with terrorists, whatever the price, he said he probably would not know the answer. When families of 155 hostages had pleaded with him to ensure the safety of their loved ones (referring to the Kandahar highjack), he said there was no one easy answer.[50] The lesson one gets here is that political rhetoric besides, when it comes to a sensitive issue like this one, restraint is very important. The home minister's response was significant, even if it contradicted with the viewpoint of some congressmen.

Summary

In this chapter, the concepts, role, and scope of crisis communication was discussed. The role of corporate communication in crises and the misperceptions surrounding it were deliberated upon. Poor corporate governance and non-perusal of ethical principles often put organizations on public opinion radar. Communication not based on honest intentions often boomerang. Several case studies from various genres of crises, like the Satyam computers fraud, Tata pullout from West Bengal, the Jet Airways fiasco after sacking employees, wild rumors about ICICI Bank, the terrorist siege of Mumbai, and the Delhi bomb attack were included in the chapter. As the chapter on corporate reputation management carries many crisis case studies relating to brands and product recalls, stories from genre were not covered here. Highlights of an exploratory survey conducted among media persons on disaster coverage has been included in the chapter.

Key terms

Corporate social responsibility: operating a business in a manner that meets or exceeds the ethical, legal, commercial, and public expectations that society has of business.

Corporate governance: a term used for the legal and ethical norms followed by a corporate organization.

Crises communication: refers to the term for how an organization responds to various stakeholders while managing a crisis.

Social audit: refers to conducting surveys among the communities to make needs assessment.
Employee communication: aims at managing relationships with employees through various forms of communication and media.
Employee blogs: term used when a management encourages its employees to create their blogs and interface with various communities.
Internal communication: refers to communication within an organization.
Internal publics: refers to employees, their families, and other shareholders.
New media: refers to the Internet, social networking sites, and the blogosphere.
Media reach: refers to the percentage of people in various SEC categories accessing media.
Media characteristics: refers to the relative strengths and weaknesses of each medium, keeping in view its inherent characteristics.

Critical thinking exercise

The media is full of stories on crises of one kind or another. Follow a crisis as long as it has held media's interest to analyze the crisis from various perspectives and stakeholders. Besides the print and electronic media, visit the organization's website to look at its efforts at sharing information, and also some social networking sites and blogosphere to map public opinion. Draw your conclusions on corporate communication efforts and what, in your view, are the lessons learned.

Concept review questions

Q.1. How would you define a crisis? What are the various classifications of crises?
Q.2. Why is corporate communication often criticized especially in crises times? Discuss with relevant cases in point.
Q.3. Define corporate governance and its role in the functioning of an organization.
Q.4. What communication strategy would you suggest for government in dealing with a crisis of an exploding kind, like earthquake, floods, droughts? Make a message action plan.

Critical thinking exercise

Follow a crisis in various media platforms to gain an understanding on how the crisis has been dealt with from stakeholders' perspectives. Now go to the organization's website and see how responsive it is to people's concerns and the actions taken by it to mitigate the crisis.

Case study

Media coverage of subversive activities

Being in the business of news, events created by the perpetrators of violence attract media attention like nothing else. Many studies suggest that news media is often "stage-managed" by subversive forces without media even realizing it. Many a times, media men have tried to solve situations, which really is not the right thing to do. News media has to be an independent interpreter of events and not a part of it.

Indian media, especially the electronic media, literally goes overboard as far as images are concerned. Not a drop of blood was shown on American television in the aftermath of 9/11, but some of the Indian channels had added the images of falling towers in their montages. The Mumbai pictures of blood and gore could be seen even after months on almost all the channels whenever the issue came for discussion.

EXHIBIT 10.3 MEDIA'S ETHICAL PRINCIPLES AND CONTENT OF GUIDELINES

To avoid, where possible, unchallenged terrorist propaganda
To ensure that human suffering is not overshadowed by terrorist acts
Do not serve as a spokesperson for terrorists
Use caution in order not to endanger lives (hostages)
Avoid cooperation by participating in events that are specially and exclusively organized for the media
Portray the cowardice, blindness, and frequent barbarian acts of terrorists
Try not to get involved—being there can trigger action
Never solve a situation

Delhi media coverage on Delhi bomb blasts (2008)

The capital city of India, Delhi, faced serial bomb attacks from terrorists on 13 September 2008. A dipstick study was conducted by the Indian Institution of Mass Communication to look at the media coverage quantitatively and qualitatively through content analyses. Here are the highlights:

Media tracking study

Serial bomb blasts in Delhi (13 September 2008)

A print media tracking study of disaster communication over five days from 14 to 18 September 2008 included analyses of seven newspapers, four English, two Hindi, and one trade paper, to gauge the quantum of coverage and a content analysis of what was being written about. The following newspapers were included in the study: the *Hindustan Times* (*HT*), the *Times of India* (*TOI*), the *Indian Express* (*IE*), the *Hindu*, the *Economic Times* (*ET*), *Jansatta* (Hindi), and *Navbharat Times* (*NBT*, Hindi). A random viewing of some TV news channels like CNN-IBN, NDTV24X7, NDTV-India, AajTaak, India TV, and Sahara NCR was also done during the period of study.[51]

As the incident happened on the evening of 13 September, it was television that broke the news first. Most of the channels had their OB vans at various places of disaster, beaming live coverage. With many dozens of news channels with 24-7 newscasts, the newspapers obviously could not be "first with the news" or the "breaking news."

With the proliferation of electronic media, one has witnessed a changing paradigm in newspaper coverage of disasters. The news stories have become a featurized version of reporting. There are more and more human-interest stories, in-depth analysis, op-eds, and discussion on broader issues. The case of Delhi carnage was not different. Some newspapers also provided a sense of history by including similar past disasters in Delhi and elsewhere. Most newspapers criticized the government's indifferent attitude to the kin of those who died, including police personnel who laid down their lives fighting terrorists, once the heat was over. Memories of Parliament attack and previous Delhi blasts came alive through some articles.

The quantitative analysis was done on the following broad parameters:

Coverage in terms of column cum centimeters, total number of stories, pictures, op-eds, editorials, broader view on terrorism, politicians covered, bites, and people's perceptions. A table of quantitative coverage may be referred to at the end of the chapter as Annexure I.

Survey highlights

The *TOI* topped the list in overall coverage in terms of space. It used 4,828 column centimeters in five days in 115 stories, followed by *Indian Express*, using 4615 CC space in 68 stories. *NBT* carried 100 stories spread on 3236 column centimeter space. *HT* came in fourth position with 77 stories in a total space of 2940 CC space. The *Hindu* used 2409 CC space in 46 stories. *Jansatta* carried 40 stories on 1611 column cum centimeters space in five days. *ET*, as expected, used the least space when compared with other mainstream papers, that is, 1317 column centimeters on 27 stories spread over five days.

The maximum numbers of editorials were written by *NBT*, five in all, followed by *TOI*, which wrote four edits. *HT*, *IE*, and *ET* wrote two each, and the *Hindu* and *Jansatta*, one each.

TOI published as many as 90 pictures, followed by *HT*, which had 71 pictures in five days. *NBT* covered 57 pictures; *IE*, close at 53 pix; *Hindu*, 15; *Jansatta*, seven; and least, at six, *ET*.

A crisis usually opens a Pandora's box. *Times of India* wrote 13 stories on the broader views on terrorism, followed by *IE* with 11 stories; and *NBT*, ten stories; and *HT*, nine stories. *ET* wrote seven stories, followed by *Hindu* and *Jansatta*, writing five stories each on a broader perspective on terrorism. Most of the stories were full of pictures. In some cases, full pages were devoted on the issue with a collage of pictures appearing across the page.

More space was given to human-interest stories with pictures of the injured, survivors, and wailing kith and kin of those who lost their lives. Politicians also jostled for space. Interestingly, it was not a mainstream by an economic paper like *ET* that topped the list of papers in covering 15 politicians, followed by *Hindu* that gave space to 14 politicians, *TOI* and *IE* covered 12 politicians each, and HT covered nine. Interestingly, both Hindi newspapers, viz., the *NBT* and *Jansatta*, covered eight and five politicians respectively.

Among the politicians who were covered were PM Manmohan Singh, Home Minister Shivraj Patil Gujarat, CM Narender Modi, Sonia Gandhi, Lalu Prasad Yadav, L K Advani, Rajnath Singh, and communist leader Vrinda Karat.

The balloon seller, a witness who saw two persons placing a packet in a dustbin that exploded in a few minutes, was first mistaken to be a human bomb, but the media soon corrected itself, saying he was a witness. As live television has no scope for editing, the harassed child who was running and being followed by many policemen was shown on every TV channel. The *TOI* the next day, referring to the child witness, said that they had the picture but had withheld it from publishing. His name was also changed to protect his identity. It was a matter of fact that the child's face was already exposed the previous day on television, but *TOI* still resisted from giving the picture because the child was a minor and could also be exposed to danger—a good case of self-regulation.

The home minister was at the receiving end both in print and electronic media for wrong reasons. He was criticized vehemently and made fun of for changing three dresses while Delhi was burning; the reference obviously was to the proverb "When Rome was burning, Niro was fiddling." One media report talked about his well-coiffured hair; another channel reasoned that Patil wore white so that he could stand out in the flash-light of cameras amid darkness! *Times of India* had on the front page the picture of a composed Patil with the headline "Words of Wisdom," giving his quotes on the last few disasters with an aim to reflect the acute indifference on the part of the top person in charge of security. It is quite possible that the quotes were selectively chosen from his long bite, making them look insipid when published in that manner.

The HM, under speculation of being sacked, invited press people in his office to give his side of the story. He was visibly agitated and asked a reporter as to what was media's problem if he wore decent clothes (*Dhang ke kapade*). Did media see him on a dance floor, or playing cards? If yes, then it made sense to write or say what they did, he retorted. Mercifully, that put a stop on such stories in the following days. He, however, was sacked about two months later after the Mumbai blasts in November 2008.

Here, there is a lesson both for the media and people who occupy space in the public domain. In solemn times, it is important to be careful about one's appearance. Media's intention is always to symbolize an issue or use metaphors to drive home a point. Similarly, the people on the receiving end of media's wrath have to strategize their communication, deciding on whether to remain quiet and let it go or take it head-on with the media. The home minister's strategy paid off, at least during that period.

As usual, the media reflected blood, gore, and mayhem for days on end. Electronic media was obviously the first one to show the happenings from site. People witnessed the diffusing of a bomb live on television. Various television channels included scrolls that had police asking people to remain calm, inviting people to donate blood, and reflected the telephone numbers of Red Cross for contact.

Then Police Commissioner Dadwal was at the site immediately, but he did not give a bite to assure people that the security agencies were in control of the situation. Next day, when he held the press conference in his office, he was peeved when a journalist asked him about developments; he shot back, "This is not a cricket match. We cannot share every development in the case."

On the third day, the big story from the media perspective was the graphics of the suspects released by the Delhi police PRO, Rajan Bhagat. When someone asked him if there was a possibility of suspects being caught on this basis, he matter-of-factly said no suspect had ever been caught based on the pictures released anytime in the past, but at the same time he exhorted people to help the police in finding the suspects. It sure brought down the enthusiasm level of viewers and the media alike.

Television reporting reached its *nadir* when Indian TV went on with a live program of about half an hour talking to six-year-old Khushi, flanked by her parents, one of whom was injured at one of the blast sites. Pictures of Khushi sitting beside her injured father in one of the hospitals the previous day were shown from the file shots. The anchor asked her whether she saw a lot of blood around and what were her feelings when she saw her father injured. "*Aapne papa ko kya kaha* (What did you tell your father?)" to which she said, "*Mama ke pass jana hai* (I want to go to my mother)." Not satisfied with the answer, the anchor went on prodding her again and again, till she asked her what was her message for "*Atankvadi* uncle," to which she rattled a mugged up line (it seemed so).

"*Aap ne mera papa ko kyu chot pahuchaya*" (Why did you injure my father?), then the anchor asked her what should be done to the *atankvadi*, "jail" or "phansi" (gallows), to which she had the tutored one-liner "*Unko fansi milni chahiye*."

A child of Khushi's age would obviously not know what and who is an *atankvadi* and what is *phansi*, but words were put in her mouth. Kushi's ordeal was, at last, over, after some phone-ins were included in the program, wherein people from all over the country wanted to talk to the "brave" Khushi and applaud her.

Playing with the psyche of children as young as Khushi was uncalled for and certainly not in good taste.

When you look at the Delhi serial bombing, some of the channels and print media went overboard writing about the softer side of at least one terrorist who died. His profile on a social networking site, or that he had a girlfriend and who she was, appeared. About an hour-long dramatized version on his supposed love affair was telecast by one of the news channels, interspersing clips from some Bollywood films on terrorism and an artist's impression of his girlfriend, which the anchor kept on repeating was from the "North East" and stayed in "South Delhi." What purpose did it serve except glamorizing the life of a terrorist, who had already died in the encounter or ridiculing the girl? Only the channel could answer. It is important that the media does not portray terrorism as glamorous or adventurous!

A newspaper wrote about the sadist pleasures the terrorists drew when they asked each other how many were down by their individual acts, or when one of them stopped to enjoy an ice cream after planting the bomb.

Blogosphere

Social networking sites, accessed by millions across the globe, reflect people's views, anxieties, annoyance, but at the same time, often, emotional and subjective opinions. The Delhi blasts received tremendous response from the bloggers. Here is a reproduction of one such posting:

> Just when the story of the bomb blasts in Delhi was unfolding, Aajtak committed a colossal blunder. It ran a flash that "a kid with bomb tied around him" was caught. Just when the people were trying to cope with the gravity of New Delhi being attacked on the evening of September 13 2008, the news further surcharged the atmosphere. It kept on showing that the "boy was arrested and taken away by police." In fact, it was totally baseless and represented the height of irresponsible reporting. The child,

Rahul, had seen a suspicious person, who probably planted the bomb or left it in polythene. The police took the boy away for quizzing him about the man. Aajtak aired this unconfirmed story without bothering about its consequences. This is not just irresponsible but dangerous reporting. Such "flashes" do create panic. Any news organization, whether a paper or a channel, that claims to be doing journalism, should first confirm and then telecast a news let alone causing scare. Within an hour, there was more panic as people thought that if a "fidayeen" kid was used what could be the magnitude of terror attacks in future. The channel sheepishly showed a flash later that it was wrong information but did not bother to apologies. It did not feel responsible enough to say that and pretended as if the earlier report of "boy used as suicide bomber" was not telecast on Aajtak. So much in the name of journalism![52]

Some pointers

- Live reporting: both from the perspective of the media and those covered by the media needs addressing. Sensitivity on the part of anchors when taking bites from the injured, those affected, administration, and the general public is expected.
- Visuals: Scenes of disaster, people bleeding, dying, crying shown on all channels. Should they not be more sensitive, selective, and responsible?
- Provocative reporting: The administration/government is generally at the receiving end. They need to articulate their responses so that they are not seen as indifferent.
- Media, especially TV channels, arouse the sentiments of people against the government.
- Media coverage, at times, becomes like a theater of the absurd. When the issue is grim, should they focus on inane issues? Point in case: Home Minister Shivraj Patil and his clothes. Should that be a focus area for hours together across channels and newspapers, or playing with the psyche of a child who was caught in the blast?
- Live discussions on TV: Can they bring about a healthy debate and suggest some remedies instead of bringing people to accuse each other?
- Interviews with witnesses: Can they be used to suggest some dos and don'ts for the public?
- Media in general do not reflect a sense of history in their coverage. For them every disaster seems worse than the previous one. This may not always be true. How disaster preparedness, the incident command system, helped in mitigating, rescuing, and providing relief to the affected rarely, if at all, gets reflected in media stories.
- Print coverage: Thanks to losing their right to "breaking news," the newspaper reporting seemed more balanced, analytical, and more in-depth when compared with the news channels.
- Straight reporting vs. opinionated articles: Shouldn't news media focus more on straight reporting, rather than provide a direct/indirect slant to every story?
- Talk about the positives also: What were the positive steps taken? Who helped the victims? How did they escape? Have any voluntary organizations come forward for relief work?
- Instead of only criticizing the government, the media should also talk about what could be government's strategy to tackle the situation in the future. Are they going to do anything to improve the disaster preparedness for the future?

- POTA or TADA: While media kept discussing whether the Prevention of Terrorist Activities Act (POTA) and Terrorists and Disruptive (Prevention) Activities Act (TADA) should be implemented or not, there was no in-depth coverage on how far these laws have been useful in the past. Did they help the government in bringing to book notorious terrorists/organizations? If not, what could have been the areas that needed to be addressed?
- Media's sensitivity to gender, caste, and religion in disaster coverage is important. A terrorist's bullet does not recognize gender, caste, color, or religion, but in the aftermath of a strike, it is not uncommon to find fingers pointed at communities, thus igniting passions.

Survey of media personnel

A purposive sample of 20 media personnel from mainstream and regional newspapers and electronic media was selected, some of whom were reached through personal contacts and others through e-mail for their inputs on disaster reporting, gaps in prevailing practices, and their experience of getting information from government sources in times of disasters. The questionnaire/research guide and list of journalists covered in the survey may be referred to as Annexure II and III (at the end of the chapter).

Media plays a vital role at the time of disasters by providing timely information, alerting the concerned authorities, facilitating disaster preparation, and rehabilitation through effective communication. But an analysis of disaster reporting by Indian media reflects a somewhat mixed picture. Media organizations, particularly some television news channels, are driven more by their objective of attracting eyeballs, which results in avoidable sensationalism and blowing up of issues. Journalists need to approach these incidents with more sensitivity and better understanding of the situation. Organizational objectives should not overpower a journalist's basic responsibility of reflecting the happenings as objectively as possible. A survey conducted by IIMC across various media organizations highlighted the need for a specific training program for journalists covering disasters.

Key findings and insights

Out of the 20 media organizations the survey covered, only four organizations had some specific guidelines for covering disasters. Although some of them did mention any implicit guidelines that were followed, considering the sensitivity of the situation, there seemed no consistency or clarity on many issues. A senior journalist from the *Hindustan Times* explained that in such situations, reporters usually have to follow the instructions given by the editor or bureau chief anchoring the coverage. Another journalist from the *Hindu* pointed out that in many situations, a reporter covering the disaster may have to exercise his/her own individual discretion or sense of judgment. The Prasar Bharati has laid down an extensive set of guidelines on their role in covering disasters (some highlight of AIR in the box). Among the private channels, NDTV follows a three-phase strategy: immediate reports, reports on rescue and rehabilitation, and follow-up. *Down to Earth*, published by the Center for Science and Environment, being a niche magazine in this area, also follows some guidelines on the aspects they would examine while writing their reports or features.

Approach to government data

AIR guidelines for national calamities

1. Give due priority for all news about calamities such as cyclones, floods, fires, etc.
2. Only authentic news should be disseminated.
3. Figures about death, losses, etc. should be based on official or equally reliable sources.
4. Where forewarning can prevent widespread damage and reduce human misery and avert loss of life, break into the program and issue the warning. All the bulletins particularly beamed toward the affected region must carry and give high position to warnings, announcements regarding relief measures, and such statements of leaders as these would build up the morale of the affected people. In serious situations, transmissions should be kept open whole day long and not restricted merely to their regular transmission hours.
5. In case of drought or cyclone, avoid giving monetary quantification of loss to crops until a figure is available from an official source.

Source: Style Book, News Services Division, All India Radio,
Detailed guidelines may be referred in Annexures

Highlights

In the research, it was found that the media usually tried to tap its own sources to get immediate access to data and accurate information. Government data, if required, was used, at best, to verify and confirm facts. Most journalists blamed government sources for hiding or underplaying facts in the interest of the higher authorities. They not only expressed doubts on the accuracy of government data but also pointed towards a lack of ability to measure the extent of damage in an accurate manner. Some journalists commented that information from the government usually came in too late, and the information officers were not able to provide answers to all their queries. A TV Today news producer explained that as television news channels are usually running against time to give live reports, it is not possible for them to wait for data from government sources.

When asked about their opinion about the state information machinery, most media personnel felt it functioned in a reactive rather than proactive manner. Though at times some bureaucrats and senior officials who were media savvy did try to speak to the media or provided information, when asked for.

Disaster coverage by Indian media

Most journalists admitted to a lack of sensitivity and understanding among their fraternity on disaster issues. In general, media decides to take a stand based on their organization's interests. For example, if they decide to focus on government apathy, the slant of all their stories would be in that direction. Some candidly admitted that reporting was rarely fair and unbiased as expected by the public.

A rise in the number of television news channels has had both negative and positive repercussions. There is no doubt that television has a greater impact and reaches a larger audience. TV channels can show what is happening live on the spot. This can be leveraged in a positive manner to speed up the government's rehabilitation and mitigation efforts.

But the downside is that the electronic media, as echoed by television journalists, was that it was usually running against time so did not use much discretion while showing visuals. The effort of some channels was directed more on catching eyeballs rather than covering the important aspects, said the journalist from TV Today. As a result, electronic media ends up unnecessarily glamorizing and sensationalizing such incidents.

Assessment of skills required

Among the journalists interviewed, many had covered disasters such as the Kargil War, the Latur earthquake, and floods in Bihar and Orissa. When asked how they approached such disasters, they said it was important to have empathy towards human suffering and a vision to anticipate the impact. When asked whether journalists needed to cultivate any specific skills, most of them were not sure if disaster reporting required any specific skills, almost all of them unanimously agreed the need to groom journalists on the dos and don'ts.

Based on the insights of the study, it was felt that reporters needed to be sensitized on the human aspect of such situations. Despite being independent in its own way, the media has a certain responsibility towards the public. Therefore, journalists need to develop a fair sense of judgment and clarity on issues. They not only need to maintain integrity and honesty; they also need to look at such situations without bias.

To understand the issue well and go into the depth of the problem, reporters need to cultivate their local sources also. They also require the ability to make quick decisions and analyze facts and figures in a balanced manner. Television journalists need to be trained on how to conduct interviews and avoid being unnecessarily aggressive or pushy. Both print and electronic media need to relook at the way they have handled such situations in the past and develop a set of guidelines and best practices.

Seamless media—the challenges

In a crisis, voices, opinions, and noises are commonplace. With the world becoming flat, thanks to the seamless media, how the overseas media covers an event, at times without understanding the sensitivities and cultural and social reality of the place, such coverage can cause a flutter. When the Bihar floods in 2008 claimed more than 1,000 lives and displaced about 30 lakhs people, the Associated Press posted the following on its website on 2 September 2008: "Even in flood, India's 'untouchables' last rescued." The story alleged that India's "untouchables" were the last to be rescued, if at all, from a deluge that had killed hundreds and many times more homeless. Quoting some "Dalits," the story said that when it came to rescue operations, it appeared that the upper caste and rich came first, leaving the Dalits to suffer without food and water. The story quoted a disaster management officer, who was reported to have said, "We are aware of these complaints." The story then went on talking about the plights of Dalits in India per se. It sure did some damage to the reputation of the disaster managers of Bihar.

Interestingly, in an opinion poll preceding the parliamentary elections in April–May 2009 in India, NDTV figures revealed that chief minister Nitish Kumar received an approval from 63% of the electorate, that is, every three out of five respondents were satisfied with him on whether it was handling the Kosi floods or developmental work;

the chief minister received a thumbs-up on various issues.[53] The election results only reinforced when he swept the results, reducing rival Lalu Yadav's RJD to a mere four seats.

These case studies, each reflecting a different kind of crisis and their analysis, would hopefully help the readers understand the role, scope, and strategy required in communication. Crisis communication case studies relating to some famous brands and product recall have been included in the chapter on corporate reputation management.

Case study question

Critically analyze the role of media in the backdrop of the Mumbai and Delhi terrorist attacks. What, in your view, should be a few areas of self-regulation for media while reporting subversive activities?

Notes

1 J. Grunig, as quoted in Tom Watson and Paul Noble, *Evaluating Public Relations*, second edition, 2008 (New Delhi: Kogan Page), p. 193.
2 Meghananad Desai, "Mera Joota Jadugar", *The Indian Express*, 12 April 2009.
3 Lawrence Warner, *PR Journal*, 1990.
4 Jaishri N. Jethwaney, A. K. Varma and N. N. Sarkar, *Public Relations Concepts, Strategies and Tools*, 1994 (New Delhi: Sterling Publishers), p. 181.
5 Jaishri Jethwaney and N. N. Sarkar, *Public Relations*, 2002 (New Delhi: Sterling Publishers), pp. 171–172.
6 Thomas J. Mickey, *PR Review*, Fall 1997.
7 www.encygov.com.
8 www.cii.in.
9 Prof Himachalam Dasaraju, www.essex.ac.uk.
10 www.mca.gov.in.
11 Ibid.
12 http://economictimes.indiatimes.com.
13 The Economic Times, 19 January 2009.
14 The Indian Express, 25 January 2009.
15 The Economic Times, 25 January 2009.
16 The Times of India, 26 January 2009.
17 The Economic Times, 8 January 2009.
18 The Times of India, 8 January 2009. The quote along with his picture appeared on the ear-panel of the newspaper.
19 The Times of India, 8 January 2008.
20 The Economic Times, The Asian age and The Indian Express, 19 January 2009.
21 http://economictimes.indiatimes.com.
22 http://in.reuters.com/article/businessNews/.
23 Ibid.
24 www.business-standard.com.
25 www.expressindia.com/latest-news/Satyam-fraud-Full-text-of-Rajus-letter-to-board/407799/.
26 Quoted by Sumeet Chatterjee in http://in.reuters.com/article/businessNews/idINIndia-37326120090107.
27 The Indian Express and The Times of India, 8 April 2009.
28 The Indian Express, 12 April 2009.
29 The Indian Express, 18 January 2009.
30 Ibid.
31 N. Balasubramanian in the Economic Times, 23 December 2008.
32 Ibid.
33 N. K. Jain, CEO, ICSI, in The Economic Times, 23 December 2008.
34 The Economic Times, 20 April 2009.

35 As quoted in Paul A. Argenti and Janis Forman, *The Power of Corporate Communication*, 2002 (New York: McGraw-Hill), pp. 18–19.
36 Times Now and Headlines Today, 25 January 2009.
37 Times Now, evening bulletin, 27 January 2009.
38 The Economic Times, 14 April 2009.
39 The Economic Times, 8 May 2009.
40 Sources: The Times of India, The Economic Times, The Hindustan Times, 15/16/17 October 2008.
41 The Economic Times, 31 October 2008.
42 When Mr. Kamath retired a couple of weeks later, he took over as the chairman, and Ms. Chanda Kochar became the MD of ICICI bank.
43 Business World, 30th September 2008 issue.
44 The Economic Times, Brand Equity, 30 October 2008.
45 The Hindustan Times- HT City, 2 December 2008.
46 Barkha Dutt of ND TV was lampooned by a newspaper columnists on her getting overtly hyper and reflecting her emotions too loudly.
47 www.smallchange.com.
48 Aaj Tak went on bragging a number of time during the live coverage that the channel was always the first with the news, something that seemed very outplace given the grim situation.
49 CNN-IBN and Times TV, 28 November 2008.
50 The NDTV Evening News Bulletin, 23 January 2009.
51 α The Institute was working on the development of course curriculum on disaster communication, aimed at various stakeholders, viz., policy makers, program officers from government, information officers and media based on the training needs assessment, when Delhi was rocked by serial bombing on 13 September. The IIMC team took the opportunity to do a dipstick study of media content analysis to gather fresh insights on the issue.
52 *Source*: Editindia.blogspot.com.
53 ndtv.com, 2 April 2009 and The Indian Express, 2 April 2009.

11

CORPORATE COMMUNICATION RESEARCH

Chapter objectives

After reading this chapter you will learn:

The role, scope, and need for research in corporate communication
Theoretical underpinnings of corporate communication research
Various kinds of research and methodologies

11.1 Introduction

Any profession, to become robust, must have a body of knowledge supporting it, and corporate communication is no exception. Research in the profession and about the profession is very important to make it relevant. As the profession of corporation communication has emerged out of public relations, the chapter would invariably be using references from the PR research.

James Gruning is one of the ardent research minds in public relations who received the Distinguished Service Award from the Arthur W. Page Society in 2008 for his many contributions to the profession. He, in his acceptance speech, spoke of three kinds of research that concern the profession:

1. Research *in* the profession is research that communication professionals use in the practice of public relations. It includes formative research to learn how publics are affected by organizations, to find out how publics view organizational actions, and to plan communication programs to build relationships with publics. It also includes evaluative research to measure the effectiveness of communication programs and to determine what contribution the corporate communication (CC) or PR function contributes to organizational success.

DOI: 10.4324/9781032694702-11

2. Research *on* the profession is conducted by scholars who explain, evaluate, and criticize the behavior of CC/PR practitioners.
3. Research *for* the profession also is mostly done by scholars, although many professional consultants and counselors also conduct it. The purpose of research *for* the profession is to build from research *on* the profession to develop and test new ideas and techniques that practitioners can use to improve their effectiveness.[1]

Frank Jefkins writes that PR research can be used in two ways: first, to reveal the current situation so that a PR method can be applied to solve communication problems; second, it can be used to test the extent to which the PR program is succeeding or failing to solve those problems.[2]

James Grunig in 1983 argued that the key contributor to the image problem of public relations was the lack of objective research methodology for evaluating PR programs. To quote him: "Although considerable lip service is paid to the importance of program evaluation in public relations, the rhetorical line is much more enthusiastic than actual Utilization."[3]

A study conducted by Dr Lloyd Kirban around the same time in 1983 among Public Relations Society of America (PRSA) members in the Chicago Chapter found that more than half the practitioners expressed a "fear of being measured."[4]

In *Managing Public Relations* (1984), James Grunig and Todd Hunt comment: "The majority of practitioners. . . still prefer to 'fly by the seat of their pants' and use intuition rather than intellectual procedures to solve public relations problems."[5]

Research, many analysts feel, is not a favored tool with practitioners. It is often viewed narrowly. Many may not have the confidence to undertake it, while others may not have the educational background and exposure to social science research to undertake research and evaluation studies. Many practitioners rely on output measurement through media coverage to reflect the program contribution.

Some of the other reasons for not undertaking research could be that management does not support expenditure on a discipline, which may be perceived as intangible by it; research is time-consuming and cumbersome, hence not initiated by the corporate communication manager. Good research, it is believed, reflects problem areas, which the practitioner would rather wish to remain dormant in order not to get "exposed" on failure. Many undertake a semblance of research to impress the management or client, which does not achieve anything.

11.1.1 Pseudo research

Stewart A. Smith explains the various reasons of pseudo research as follows:

11.1.1.1 Organizational politics

In this case, research is used to gain power, justify decisions, or serve as a scapegoat.

111.1.2 Service promotion

To impress clients or prospects that the sponsor is sophisticated, modern, or sincere.

11.1.1.3 Personal satisfaction

Here, in this case, the research is an exercise in ego bolstering activity to keep up with fads or to demonstrate acquired skills.[6]

A CC/PR practitioner does not need to be a research expert but should believe in research, and it will help if he/she has working knowledge of the research process so as to get work done from outside research agencies. Someone has rightly said that in order to drive a car, one does not need to be a motor mechanic, but it helps to know a few things about car mechanics when you visit a garage.

In this chapter we shall look at the following broadly: areas of research in corporate communication, various kinds of research that would be suitable for corporate communication, research methodology, and random case studies, to understand various kinds of research and evaluation.

11.1.2 Research is instinctive

Researchers believe that research is instinctive to most people. As human beings who aspire to have the best, we are frequently doing research. For instance, when we go to a supermarket, we look at various brands of a commodity before we settle for the one that suits our need/desire, purse, and satisfaction level. When working on a college admission, students often go for desk and primary research while applying in various universities. They collect information on the ranking of universities and reach out to the faculty and maybe some alumni before settling for one when they have more than two universities to choose from. Similarly, corporate communication managers have relied on research in one form or the other to demonstrate to the client that what they implemented had a) impacted some public/audience, b) they have examined media vehicles to see whether they have carried the news through the press release.[7] Research in any activity or program, according to Stacks, is the "beginning of a process that seeks to bring about a specific objective."[8] As corporate communication is a management function, decision cannot be taken without a research base.

11.1.3 Research is strategic

Research, according to Dolphin, not only serves a purpose; it also aims at finding out if the means of communication are appropriate, and it also helps establish what kinds of messages and themes may be required to bring about a better perception about the organization or establish a new image.[9] To facilitate decision-making, corporate communication uses two kinds of research techniques, viz., informal and formal. We shall look at various techniques in both the genres of research after discussing a few models used in corporate communication and PR research.

11.2 Theoretical underpinnings in corporate communication research

Corporate communication scholars believe that practitioners soon would have to turn to corporate communication as an interdisciplinary body of knowledge. "Communication expertise," argues Sandra Oliver, "is proactive, protagonist, catalytic, soothsaying and supportive, whose traditional methods of strategic programming with detailed plans now incorporate post-technological management thinking."[10]

Mintzberg feels that the detailed plans address the role of communication and serve in three directions, viz., to external environment, into the organization, and back to the input end of the strategy formation process in a feedback loop. For instance, Mintzberg argues that the challenge for the role of stakeholder relation in policy and practice of research of corporate strategy would be to ensure that the research focus is based on what he describes "re-conceived strategic programming and not pre-conceived strategic programming."[11]

The Institute of PR suggests a measurement called PRE (the planning, research evaluation process). As a part of a program, stage 1, relating to audit, *"Where are we?"*, is concerned with conducting research and gathering data to form a foundation on which the program campaign is based. Stage 2, *"Where we need to be?"*, would determine the objectives that would need to be aligned with organizational goals and objectives. In stage 3, *"How do we go there?"*, research and evaluation must be in the forefront, with decisions made about selecting the type of measurement to be used and what pre-testing techniques would be employed. Stage 4, *"Are we going there?"*, concerns ongoing research to ensure that the program is on track and decisions are made about any adjustment required. It may also suggest that the program needs to be suspended with. Stage 5, *"How did we do?"*, concerning results and evaluation, examines as to what degree the objectives for the campaign or program were achieved. The dynamic circular feedback, circular process, can be mapped on to a four-layered pyramid.[12]

Research methods

Research from the client's context is often driven by a desire to understand the root of the problem, the possible communication solution to that. The client may or may not be interested in whether the agency is getting to the crux of the problem by using secondary data or suggesting primary research, so long as the problem is defined.

In the following paragraphs, we shall look at various informal and formal techniques of research and evaluation.

11.3 Informal research techniques

Many believe that informal research techniques still dominate the field of corporate communication, despite that highly sophisticated research tools are now available. Some of the informal research techniques include the following:

11.3.1 Personal contacts

Networking with people who can be important contacts is a trait that all managers develop, and corporate communication managers are no exception. Since corporate communication is all about information, images, perceptions, and reputation, having personal contacts within the organization and among various stakeholders outside the organization really helps in gauging the pulse of various TA groups. Many believe that no survey can provide the insights that come through personal contacts.

11.3.2 Gatekeepers

Gatekeepers are defined as opinion leaders whose opinion matters to those groups of people who depend on them for various supports, viz., social, economic, political, or emotional. Gatekeepers are found in all kinds of professions and social groups. A doctor, engineer, a teacher, a politician, a celebrity, a village head can be an opinion leader. In the Indian context, it is often said that postmen in rural areas and village barbers are influential opinion leaders because it is not uncommon for a postman to read the letters to the recipients and help them in sending replies. It is not uncommon to seek his point of view also, taking him as a wise person. Similarly, in Indian villages, it is a common day-to-day scenario to find people chatting in groups at various barbershops which are often set under trees. Many political leaders in India swear by the prognosis offered by these opinion leaders as more accurate than those offered by psephologists!

It is believed that if the gatekeepers are influenced, so can be people who see them as knowledgeable and, in some cases, their role models.

11.3.3 Through mail analysis

Companies in the product line receive tremendous amount of mail from their consumers, most of which may not be complimentary. A periodic analysis of mail can help reflect areas of disfavor and concern. Many companies now use their website for dealing with customer complaints. Customers in the digital age have also become vocal about their rights and do not spare a moment in rating the products and companies on the social media platforms.

11.3.4 Through field reports

Marketing-oriented companies generally have agents, field officers, and marketing officers stationed at various places. They send their periodic field reports. The Hindustan Unilever Ltd., a FMCG company that has a huge market in the rural hinterland of the country, sends all its new recruits, whichever discipline they may join, for village posting to understand the dynamics of the rural market.

The Department of Field Publicity of the Ministry of Information and Broadcasting has a bevy of field publicity officers who visit the nook and cranny of the country to disseminate information on various social issues and the achievements of the government in the welfare sector and bring back feedback for the government to take corrective actions.

11.3.5 Media reflections

Scanning media on a day-to-day basis is one of the important activities of a corporate communication manager to get a hang of the environment and to know how media is reacting to that. Scanning media regularly also indicates issues of public concern and agenda setting by the media. Tracking the media scientifically through quantitative methods and content analyses through formal research techniques is discussed later in the chapter.

11.3.6 Social media influencers

The new age media has brought about a paradigm shift in people's engagement with the media. The obtrusive media, which touches almost everything under the sun and comes from all sides and directions, cutting across the geographical divide, has left the organizations only more worried about maintaining their image. Any disgruntled employee, a client, or an adversary can play havoc with the reputation of an individual or an organization. Tracking the blogosphere and social media influencers, sifting through the opinions, can provide a vast array of views and opinions. Various kinds of software are now available to track the issues and opinions quickly to have a holistic view about the concerns. When the Satyam computers fraud was unearthed, thousands of bloggers wrote on various aspects of the fraud, some giving the reasons how it went undetected for years, others providing solutions. Many were concerned about their investments, while a few were nostalgic of the company when they worked there.

11.4 Formal research methods

Formal research methods include, attitude/opinion studies, image surveys, communications audits, media studies, and secondary data analysis, et al. Besides, a lot of syndicated research is available about communities, media, and media habits of the people, at a certain price, which the corporate communication practitioners can have access to.

11.4.1 Research is a program planning tool

Corporate communication and PR departments, from time to time, launch campaigns and programs on various issues, like institutional advertising, using various mass media, or motivational programs for employees to enhance productivity, or information dissemination programs during a crisis, to name a few. The research, therefore, must be undertaken as a planning tool and not as an afterthought. Organizational objectives need to outline the scope of the research. Research that is not specific, but vague, achieves little. The practitioner must determine the most relevant information for decision to direct the study. Many scholars feel that research is a tool which should complement experience and judgment and not necessarily replace it.

Gaunt and Wright conducted an interesting online survey gaining responses of various practitioners from 25 countries in 2004. The research provides some useful insights that include the following:

- Demand of measurement is driven by the CEOs, who considered measurement as an integral part of the program.
- In external communication, more practitioners measured outputs than outcomes with media evaluation.
- Opinion survey was seen as most effective. Dashboards and advertising value equivalents (AVEs) were seen as least effective.

- In internal communication, feedback tools were used by many organizations. Twenty three percent of practitioners, however, depended on instinct.
- The main impediments to measurement were cited as cost (77%), time (59%), and lack of expertise and questionable value of results (58% each).
- Sixty five percent of respondents felt that return on investment (ROI) could be applied to their programs.[13]

11.4.2 What to research?

Research, as the word indicates, is searching what is already there (that is, "re-search") but is not manifest. In other words, we are seeking to investigate something which is either latent or hazy. The first step, hence, is setting the objective, that is, what is it that we are trying to find out? Is it the access of the target audience to a message, its recall, assimilation/comprehension and action, or is it what the reaction of a certain stakeholder group is after a certain decision was taken. It can also include evaluating the extent of coverage received after a press conference. A further area of research could be to do media content analysis to find out quality of coverage, that is, percentage of negative, positive, and neutral coverage. In this case, one must decide beforehand what would be positive, negative, and neutral coverage from an organization's perspective.

Research is not a stand-alone discipline, but must be in-built in a program from the word go. In fact, the objectives of the program need to be articulated in a manner that they indicate the research task. The research objective would also facilitate the choice of research methodology.

For instance, if the objective of a program is to create awareness about a CSR initiative by the organization, then the measurement criteria could be how many people in the defined target audience category accessed information through which media (used for information dissemination). The other could possibly be what they think about the initiative.

Let us take a hypothetical case of the plant management of a company that wishes to devise a program to motivate the employees to achieve enhanced productivity, with the active assistance of its corporate communication department. In this case, the program would use various media like shop-floor discussions, brainstorming sessions, bulletin board, pamphlets, house journal, Intranet, et al. As the TA in this kind of research is defined, that is, the internal stakeholders, the program team should ideally get an access to their demographic profile to decide on the most appropriate media. The data can be easily accessed through the HR department.

In the evaluation, the study would aim at finding out whether the messages reached the intended TA, the employees, and whether the messages were comprehended and assimilated by the employees. It would also aim at finding out whether the program was able to achieve its goal of enhanced productivity over a designated time frame. If there are different shifts and assembly lines, one can also find out the relative change of behavior among employees working in different shifts/assembly lines. The evaluation may also aim at finding out which media was considered more credible.

The other area of evaluation can be to find out the appropriateness of a certain messages that appeared in the house magazine aimed at employees. Yet another area of research could be to find out exposure, readability, legibility, believability, and the desired action.

If the evaluation is through an opinion survey aimed at the general public, then the number of messages placed and number of media vehicles used would determine whether the intended target audience had the opportunity to see/read the message. In other words, the research would aim at finding out if the message achieved the desired OTS (opportunity to see). Exposure of messages in the media is, however, no guarantee that the intended audiences attended to the message. Not everything that comes in the media is seen/read and comprehended. In other words, reach is not necessarily equivalent to access; access may not necessarily mean comprehending the message; the messages may be comprehended but may not be found credible. There could be a situation when all these may be positive for the organization, but the intended TA still does not act for various reasons like social conditioning, self-interest, or no motivation to act.

For research of this kind, one can't rely on cut and dry data, but aim at gathering insights about why people take or do not take action, despite access and comprehension through qualitative research by in-depth and focus group interviews.

It is important for the corporate communication researcher to keep the management or client continuously informed of the findings of the research and what corrective actions are being recommended. One-time research is never sufficient; it may reflect findings relevant only for that time. Research must be a continuous activity. All research adds to a body of knowledge, which must be kept for future reference.

When program implementers use mass media, then for evaluation, an analysis of mass media reach and access is studied to make an assessment about how many people were exposed to the messages. We shall take up this for discussion later.

11.4.3 Formative research

Formative research is conducted by program implementers generally with the help of experts to define the problem that the proposed program is aiming to tackle through communication intervention. The PRE model discussed earlier includes research process for formative research in the first three steps, viz., "Where are we?", "Where do we need to be?", and "How do we go there?"

The case study included at the end of the chapter would enable the readers to understand the program goals and the extent of formative research conducted.

11.4.4 Opinion surveys

Surveys: The surveys are a mode of primary research that can be both quantitative and qualitative in form. The former refers to gathering data in terms of number/quantum and objectivity, which can be scientifically projected; using close-ended questions to get tight answers. The qualitative research denotes somewhat subjective but in-depth probing of the respondents through open-ended or freewheeling method of response. The basic aim behind a survey is to gauge how a target audience feels about a company, product, service, or issue. The intended target audience may be very vast, so researchers work on a scientific method to select a cross section of people from that group to be able to arrive at the average opinion of the entire group. A margin of error is also taken into account. Opinion polls are not restricted just for political prediction; these can be used for a variety of areas. For example, a research agency may provide weekly charts on music by analyzing the sale of cassettes/CDs/downloads or retrieving data on sale from, say, 500 shops.[14] An opinion poll, similarly, can be held among a niche group to rate various companies on their CSR or corporate governance score.

11.4.5 Research imperatives

11.4.5.1 Research rationale

The researcher must have a fair idea of what the research is supposed to find out.

11.4.5.2 Methodology

The objective often would help decide the methodology. A decision needs to be made on whether it is going to be based on secondary research or primary research. If it is the latter, then decide whether it would be quantitative research through a questionnaire or qualitative research through in-depth interviews or focus group discussions through a research guide.

11.4.5.3 Universe

It is important to know your target audience, whose views the research is seeking. This will help in defining the research universe.

Let us look at some of these in details.

11.4.5.4 Research instrument

Researchers use a questionnaire and administer it in person, mail, or telephone to ask respondents about their opinions on various issues addressed by the research. Personal interview surveys, also referred to as "mall intercepts," happen in shopping arcades, homes, or public places. Questionnaires can be straight with one, two, or more options to tick mark, or a combination of close-ended and open-ended questions. In the latter case, it is expected to get more candid answers. In the case of the open-ended question, the respondents write their answer descriptively, which can give good insights about his/her attitudes, which is not possible through a "yes" or "no" answer.

Instrument aimed at capturing this evaluative data is called *attitude scale* that includes *Likert scale, Semantic Differential scale, and Rank-order scale.* The Likert scale is the most used form of attitude scale, as it is easy to prepare and analyze. It is also simple for respondents to answer. The options for respondents could be as follows: "Agree/Don't Agree/Neither agree nor disagree." The Semantic Differential scale is also easy to administer. The scale has bipolar adjectives to choose from such as "Expensive/Cheap, Beautiful/Ugly," etc. In the Rank-order scale, respondents are asked to rank items in order of preference in terms of some criterion, like quality or value for money. This enables researchers to gather data also for competitive products.

For example, in a global survey using the Rank-order scale methodology, Edelman, a US-based PR firm, asked respondents to rate various institutions on a scale of 1 ("I don't trust at all") to 9 ("I trust them a great deal"). No specific companies or organizations were mentioned in the survey. Some interesting findings emerged. Some highlights:

Among the countries where business was trusted more than the government were Mexico, India, Japan, Brazil, South Korea, Spain, Ireland, Britain, and Russia.

Countries where government was trusted more than business included Germany, Italy, Canada, France, China, the Netherlands, and Australia, in that survey.

Despite that the economic turndown happened in the USA, respondents around the world (52%) said they trusted companies based in the US. Companies based in Britain, Sweden, Germany, and Canada were the most trusted, ranging between 68% for Britain to 75% for Sweden. At the bottom of the scale, at 24%, were companies in China and Russia.[15] There could be bias in the rating, depending on the country of the respondents.

11.4.6 Defining sampling

Sampling is an important part of a research design and must address the following—whom to survey, how many to survey, and how to select them. In other words, the sample unit, sample size, and sampling procedure is to be selected. The size of the sample depends on the availability of funds, time, and the extent of accuracy being looked for by the researcher. Sampling is both probability and non-probability.

11.4.6.1 Probability sampling

Simple random sampling: In this kind of sampling, every member of the population has the equal chance of being selected. To illustrate, if there are 100 students in a class, the random sampling can be every fifth or tenth or any decided number which must be followed scientifically, leading to every person getting an equal chance of being included.

Stratified random sampling: The population is divided into mutually exclusive groups, and random samples are drawn from those groups. For example, if the class of 100 has students both from urban and rural areas, then for the purpose of sampling, the class will be first divided based on urban/rural divide and then it could be random selection within those groups. In this case, both the groups would get equal representation vis-à-vis their population in the class.

Cluster (area) group: The population is divided into mutually exclusive groups and then the researcher draws a sample of the groups to interview. It is a multistage research in which natural groups are sampled initially, then with members of each group subsampled later for interviews. To illustrate, a researcher may draw a sample of universities teaching mass communication and draw a sample of some students from each university. Later, out of those selected, a subsample is selected for in-depth interviews.

11.4.6.2 Non-probability sampling

Convenience sampling: The researcher selects the most accessible population members from whom to obtain information. To illustrate, the researcher conducts interviews in his neighborhood to know about certain trends.

Judgment sampling: The researcher uses his judgment to select people to gather information. For example, experts in the relevant area of study, say cardiologists, to know about cardiac issues, or environmental scientists to understand the state of environment etc.

Quota sampling: The researcher selects a prescribed number of respondents from one or many categories, based on age, sex, income group, etc.

11.4.7 In-depth interviews

One of the forms of survey is conducting interviews by telephone or face-to-face. Interviews can be through a well-structured questionnaire or a research guide that is prepared by the researcher to facilitate a sequence of questions. Face-to-face interviews can be expensive and time-consuming. However, the refusal rate would invariably be lower when compared with telephonic interviews. It may not be the right time when the researcher calls. The respondent, if not interested, could give an excuse of being occupied or may simply refuse until the researcher, on the other hand, is apt in his/her work and is able to motivate the person on the other side of the phone to be interviewed.

The researcher needs also to choose this sample scientifically, viz., randomly, purposively, or representatively.

11.4.8 Focus group interviews

The focus group interview technique is said to be drawn from the marketing research technique, which has been adapted by social science researchers very usefully.

A combination of surveys, secondary data analyses, and focus group can be useful for executing corporate communication and public relations campaigns.[16]

This technique of research carries the potential of acquiring a deep understanding of the attitudes and opinions of the target group. However, only trained researchers can articulate them. The key features of focus group research, according to Daymon and Holloway: "They provide evidence from many voices on the same topic; they are interactive; they provide a supportive forum for expressing suppressed views; and they allow you to collect a large amount of data fairly quickly."[17]

11.4.9 Research analysis

In qualitative research, the moderator or test researcher usually analyses the responses; in quantitative research, the researcher supervises the analysis. In a close-ended questionnaire, the responses are statistically analyzed in terms of numbers. Open-ended responses are coded and quantified into a numerical score, and then responses are tabulated and analyzed. Most such surveys are computer-analyzed.

Report: Both in qualitative and quantitative survey, the research report includes a brief executive summary of the findings, besides detailed findings through tables, graphs, and charts. At times, it may also include recommendations, if asked for.

11.5 Campaign/program evaluation

As discussed elsewhere, formative research is the first step in the campaign to define the problem that is being addressed.

Evaluation research according to Cutlip et al is used "to learn what happened and why, not to prove or do something."

Noble talks of seven principles of evaluation:

1. *Evaluation is research*: evaluation is a research-based discipline with the purpose to inform and clarify, and it operates on a high standard of rigor and logic.
2. *Evaluation looks both ways*: evaluation is a proactive, forward-looking, and formative activity that provides feedback to enhance program management.
3. *Evaluation is user and situation dependent*: evaluation is ideally undertaken according to the objective and criteria that are relevant to the organization and concerned campaigns. It is the responsibility of the corporate communication department to know the expectations of the organization from corporate communication activities.
4. *Evaluation is short-term*: evaluation is generally campaign or project based. The campaigns are frequently concerned with raising awareness using media coverage techniques. One may not be able to fine-tune the project on hand, but the evaluation enhances the effectiveness of future campaigns.
5. *Evaluation is long-term*: this kind of an evaluation study is undertaken for issue management, corporate reputation, or brand positioning. In a continuous evaluation, there is scope to revisit the project, reposition it, adapt it vis-à-vis the insights the evaluation throws while the project is still on.
6. *Evaluation is comparative*: evaluation often does not give absolute judgments, but instead draws comparative conclusions. It may also compare the messages transmitted by the media against those directed at journalists.
7. *Evaluation is multifaceted*: PR/CC are multifaceted disciplines; hence, a range of different evaluation methodologies are required at each step.[18]

Once the campaign input based on the problem definition is ready, the materials and messages should ideally be pre-tested among a small group of the targeted audience to ensure that the campaign is understood and assimilated for a desired action. Changes are brought about, if required at this stage, before launching the campaign. For long-term campaigns/programs, midterm appraisals are undertaken to ensure the campaign has the desired impact on the targeted audience. The program team can bring about changes in the message, media selection, or strategy at this point in time, if required. Finally, an evaluation of the impact on the targeted group at the end of the campaign is required to gauge the usefulness of the campaign.

A few years ago, the UNICEF and Human Rights Commission of India spearheaded a campaign on the theme of child sexual abuse. The objective of the campaign was to inform that a) having sex with a girl below the age of 16 was a criminal offence, even if it was with her consent; and b) the punishment for the offence was up to life imprisonment. An ad agency had prepared the campaign for the sponsoring organizations. The present author, along with another researcher and a group of her students, got the opportunity to pre-test the campaign. The universe was carefully drawn that encompassed a cross section of TA, including probable and real "clients," victims at brothels, those who ran the brothels, the "madams" and the "pimps" and parents of children from slum clusters, who often left their young children back home when on work. The sample was reached at interstate bus terminals, railway stations, slum clusters, and a couple of brothels in the red-light area of Delhi. The help of local police was sought to gain entry to brothels.

A visit to the brothels made the research team expand its universe to include educated college youth from affluent families, because quite a few youngsters from elite colleges were found there.

Interestingly, most of the campaign input, including imagery and messages, were recast after gathering insights from the pre-test. The campaign was launched in Delhi only for a short time using only the outdoor media. The same team was asked to evaluate the impact of the campaign after a few months. The evaluation was done on campaign and message recall, comprehension, and credibility. The campaign was able to achieve a multiplier impact as some news channels included it in their discussions programs.

11.6 Image surveys/studies

An image study, as the name suggests, is undertaken to gauge the image of an organization in comparison with its competitors on various parameters, viz., brand equity, brand salience, price, quality, corporate governance, CSR initiative, technology, and a host of other areas.

Such research studies are taken up by rating agencies also. For instance, Ipsos MORI has been conducting image surveys for over a quarter century for its various clients across the world, to discover how well or poorly the companies are perceived by the consumers. By its reckoning, the consumer image surveys work as ideal vehicles for "evaluating the public's perception of companies; discovering how well companies are regarded in comparison to their competitors among both customers and non-customers; and monitoring how perceptions of a company changes over time."

For an average consumer image survey in Great Britain, Ipsos MORI interviews about 2,000 adults using its Ipsos MORI Omnibus survey. Companies are expected to have a subscription of the surveys to access findings.[19]

Individual organizations, industry associations, NGOs may go in for image surveys from time to time to gauge their reputation. For instance, Rotary International conducted a survey in 2007 across various continents, selecting one country each, to find out how well it was known among people of various countries.

11.6.1 Case study of image survey by Rotary International

Here are some interesting insights on the questions and the findings.

The universe of the survey was spread over six countries, viz., Argentina (Latin America), Australia (Pacific), Germany (Europe), Japan (Asia), South Africa (Africa), and USA (North America). The purpose of the survey was to gauge awareness about Rotary and its image.

The survey reached at least 675 individuals in each country. The sample group represented a cross section of the general population (gender, age, income, education, etc.). The method of survey were face-to-face interviews and telephonic survey.

The questions were an interesting mix of dichotomous, with an option of yes/no and open-ended questions, wherein the respondent had to give his/her opinion.

Some interesting insights emerged across various countries, and if we carefully look at the replies to an open-ended question and when a question is posed with the option of a yes/no or agree/disagree, the replies were not always consistent. Researchers intentionally put questions in a manner that would gauge the efficacy of answers.

One of the questions was "Have you heard of an organization or a group called Rotary?" The maximum number of people, at 87%, in Australia said yes, followed by Argentina at 72%. Close on the heels was the US at 71%. Fifty one percent of respondents in South Africa knew about Rotary, followed by 33% in Japan, and the least at 31% in Germany.

From the simple question, now the second question was open-ended, asking the respondents: "How would you describe Rotary?" The responses were quite interesting from various countries:

Argentina (Humanitarian/charitable organization; Non-profit organization; Club for entertainment and exchange)
Australia (Public/community service organization; Charitable organization; Organization that helps children/education)
Germany (Know name only; No further information; Humanitarian organization; Organization for rich people)
South Africa (Charitable/funding organization; Charitable organization for needy, poor, hungry, and elderly; Organization that organizes events)
USA (Public conscience organization; Networking organization for business/professional leaders; Social organization)

The third question was "Do you agree or disagree that Rotary is a group of charitable people trying to help and serve community?" with three options "Agree," "Disagree," "Don't know/Can't say." Here you see that in the earlier open-ended question, many respondents did say that Rotary was a charitable institution, so this question should ideally reiterate the above, which it did. In South Africa, 97% agreed, followed by 95% in Australia, 76% in the USA, 71% in Argentina, 68% in Japan, and the least at 53% in Germany.

The fourth question was reversed with a negative presumption, which asked: "Do you agree or disagree that Rotary is group of self-seeking people trying to help themselves?"

Even if it was not a majority, quite a few agreed, as the responses reflect. In Japan, 48% agreed, followed by 45% from Argentina. Twenty-three percent from Germany, 16% each from the US and Australia, and 11% from South Africa agreed that rotary was a group of self-seeking people trying to help themselves. If we compare both the responses, we do find some discrepancies in the responses.

For another question: "Do you happen to know anyone who belongs to Rotary?" the response was between 50% to 26% from various countries, interestingly the highest from Japan, which recorded the highest at 48% in the previous question, believing that Rotary was a group of self-seeking people trying to help themselves.

As said earlier, the researchers intentionally ask double-barreled questions to find out goof-ups in replies. The next question in the image survey was: "How likely would you respond to contribute your time, or money to support a nearby Rotary club to do community service work?" Here the response was Australia at 40%, South Africa and US at 29% each, Germany at 20%, and Japan the least at 17%. Japan, in fact, has been consistent in its responses.

The overall conclusions of the image survey were as follows:

Individuals reporting higher income and education levels were more likely to be aware of Rotary.
Gender was not a major factor when it came to awareness or perception of Rotary.
Fifty percent or fewer of respondents in all countries who had heard of Rotary personally knew a Rotarian.
Respondents who personally knew a Rotarian were more likely to perceive the organization positively to support a local club.
More than half of all respondents who had heard of Rotary agreed that it was a charitable organization trying to help the communities.[20]

11.7 Community surveys

Unlike the image surveys where the objective is to find out how an organization is perceived by the people, a community survey could have a very different objective. Community survey could be sought on safety, healthcare, social security, and a host of issues.

Harvard University, along with various community foundations and funding organizations covering a sample of 30,000, conducted a survey to understand the civic engagements of Americans.[21]

11.8 Communication audit

As the nomenclature signifies, it is the auditing of communication undertaken by an organization over a period. As in an accounts audit at the end of a period, the auditors try and find out the investment/expenditure and the return of investment to make a balance sheet of profit and loss, so a communication audit also makes a "balance sheet" of communication efforts vis-à-vis the outcome. Every corporate communication program or campaign addresses the need for communication and defines the stakeholder group that is required to be reached through a choice of media vehicles that have the maximum reach and are cost-effective. At other times, routine communication activities are undertaken, like employee communication, media relations, investor relations, etc., in order to find out that the activities are fetching the "desired response" an audit is required to. The basic aim behind a communication audit is to find gray areas and make changes, if required.

Experts believe that a communication audit is a broad-scale, loosely structured examination of communication assets—systems, strengths and weaknesses, and communication styles. It is employed to know if they are compatible with the basic management philosophy of the company.

When used to gauge the outside stakeholders, the communication audit helps assessing the difference between how an organization's stakeholders perceive the organization and how it wishes to be seen; if it matches, then there is no need to change the communication activities, but in case there is a mismatch, then differences could be bridged by changing the contents or methods of communication.

Corporate communication, by the very nature of its job, uses various kinds of media and processes to reach out to its disparate set of internal and external target audience.

The choice of media should ideally depend on where the stakeholders are located and what are their communication habits and media choices. Ideally, the decision to choose media for a stakeholder group should be based on formative research about the demographic profile of the audience and their media access habits. For instance, the choice of Intranet for a telecom or software company would be ideal as most of the workforce is expected to be new-age media savvy. This may, however, be a waste of money for an organization where the employees may not be literate, say, in Coal India, which has a workforce of about five lakhs of employees, most of whom cannot read and write. Even a written house journal may not be the right choice of media for Coal India.

Experts believe that, like content analysis, the communication audit is rather a specific procedure, but in general use it has come to mean almost like any set of questions that assesses the adequacy or effectiveness of communication. A communication audit is used with various aims such as to analyze advertising, a corporate communication program, relationship with customers, sales/service response, and internal communication among employees.

11.8.1 When is communication audit more useful?

Communication audit can be used periodically but would be useful in the following situations:

- Before an organization is bringing about some strategic changes
- When it is apparent that employees are de-motivated for any reason, say, cut in pay, holding back of bonus, lack of business et al.
- Recall of products, when customer complaints are a concern
- When the organization is working on long-term plans and strategies
- When large-scale expenditure or new technology is considered
- When there is an obvious communication problem

11.8.2 What is a comprehensive audit schedule?

Communication audit can be handled by an internal group or an outside group. However, when it has a representation of concerned executives from within and outside experts, it makes the team better placed to conduct the audit.

An audit, to be successful, needs to be aided by a steering group, drawn from among senior decision-makers, executed by a working group from various functional areas, and a project coordinator, and may also include internal/external consultants/researchers.

Let us take an example; if the communication audit were on employee communication, then what process would need to be required?

A formal audit should ideally take a time span of three months, starting with a workshop with senior managers to discuss their approaches to employee communication, to build consensus, and elicit senior management's support from the beginning. The corporate communication manager must be in the center of the audit process.

Most organizations have some data available. Hence, the second step is to do the data analysis of the existing studies, annual attitude surveys, personal records, employee complaints, issues addressed by unions, and whether there are any pending issues that need to be resolved.

Once a fair idea about the stakeholders' profile and concerns is in place, the team should access samples of various forms of communication emanating from all the departments and corporate communication department.

The audit would look at two areas:

- Content analysis of communication materials.
- Choice of survey methodology, viz., through in-depth interviews/focus group interviews or by using a pre-tested questionnaire. It can even be a combination of all three, keeping in view the various echelons in the management hierarchy, with the objective of finding out how well the organization communicates with its own employees.

The objectives of the said study would be to gauge the following:

- Do the employees understand the organizational goals, philosophy, and ethos?
- Do they understand their role in achieving the objectives?
- How well do they feel the organization communicates its objectives to them?
- What are their sources of information about the organization they work for?
- What are their preferred sources of information?
- What are their information needs and desires?
- Do they find the current flow of information useful?
- Do they find the information trustworthy/credible?

The auditors, based on the findings, should provide management with an understanding of how employees identify with the company, division, department, or their peer group.

The nature of the relationship between individuals and subgroups can be gauged through network analysis and communication diaries.

An important facet of communication audit is "media audit," which means regular contact with the editor and beat reporter to check about satisfaction and usage of material sent from the organization. It would also reflect whether the media prefers transmission of material through e-mail, SMS, hard copy, Web link, or QR code through which they can access it.

11.8.3 Value of audit

The audit generates enough data, which can provide a better understanding of the flow of information in an organization. For employees, an audit means they are being listened to. The communication audit process should be repeated as soon as steps have been taken to remedy identified shortcomings. This will demonstrate the willingness of the management to "listen." This will improve staff morale and bring about greater efficiency and higher productivity. For conducting audit scientifically among employees, they may be given diaries to maintain their communication engagement, such as time consumed in reading, on phone, in meetings, et al.

If the audit wishes to know the reach of certain important messages and the use of channels among employees, it can address questions including whether the message was received by them, when, through which channel, that is, formal channel of notice board/memo/circular/intranet or peers/superior officer/grapevine.

11.9 Dashboard and scorecards

Dashboards and scorecards are the new research tools used by corporate communication practitioners to apprise the top management in a short and succinct style of reporting.

The term has its genesis from the car dashboard, which reflects various gauges of performance, including speed, rpm, fuel, engine, temperature, and battery charge. Taking the analogy further, Watson and Noble write that how the engine (campaign) is performing and whether there are any threats (low fuel, high engine temperature, or battery discharge). The tool argues the authors has arisen from corporate information systems that brought together various performance data into a single, easily read document for senior management.[22]

According to Paine, the success of this depends on how the corporate communication manager has articulated the "definitions of excellence." She posits six steps to design and implement a dashboard:

1. To ensure that all those operating the program work as team when developing it. It should not be imposed from outside.
2. To identify the measurement priorities by ranking the audience in order of importance.
3. To choose individual measures of effectiveness for each of its target audience.
4. To set benchmarks for comparing the current year's performance with corresponding years in the past and against similar organizations.
5. To seek the integration of various tools of measurement.
6. To make the dashboard report simple and short, no more than a page or two.[23]

11.10 Media research

A lot of corporate communication is achieved through mass media. Similarly, media reflections of organizations do impact their reputation and their engagement with various stakeholders. What is media writing? Why is it writing? Are there biases in media's stand? Do media writing impact perceptions and attitudes? are some of the perennial questions that haunt an average corporate communication practitioner. The issue of relationship has been dealt with in detail in Chapter 6. Here we shall discuss what to track as far as media is concerned, how to do it, and discuss a couple of case studies to understand media coverage and their stand in normal and critical times.

11.10.1 Media content analysis

Content analysis is defined as the application of a systematic procedure for objectively determining what is being said in the media. The press clippings and broadcast monitors only tell what was covered, and not necessarily what is being read and viewed. Besides stories, researchers also track editorials, op-eds, and letters to the editor to understand media's stand and bias on issues that concern the organizations, and readers' letters and phone-in calls to know the pulse of public opinion.

Grunig and Hunt refer to effects of research, which must point out the following:

- Was the message received?
- Was it understood?

- Was the message recalled/remembered?
- Was action taken up based on the message?

In case of media, it should address how the media covered the story, was it based on the press release, was some more input added, and what was the overall impact of the story, that is, positive, neutral, or negative.

Organizations generally have a system of keeping track of some media, at least through press clippings, and may use a scientific or crude method to reach a conclusion on media coverage, being positive, negative, or neutral. Outside PR/CC firms are engaged by many organizations to track media, including print, electronic, and Internet, including social media platforms, to keep themselves informed about its coverage in the media and the stand of the media on issues that concerns it. Professional media tracking agencies use appropriate technology and software to track media scientifically.

11.10.2 What to find out in media research

There are many areas that can be tracked in media coverage. Here is a checklist:

1. Which publications and electronic media covered the news?
2. How often?
3. How many articles have bylines?
4. How many articles are sourced from wire agencies?
5. Coverage of competitors
6. Have pictures and graphics been used?
7. What are the key messages carried?
8. What is the space covered by articles?
9. Are their company spokesperson's quotes in the articles?
10. Mention of competitors in the same story
11. Big picture about the issue/sector
12. Slant in the stories, viz., positive, negative, and neutral

It is a hotly debated issue in professional circles, but many corporate communication and PR practitioners quantify the coverage in terms of ad space and present it to the management or clients to express the worth of effort in ad space terms. The issue has been dealt with in detail in Chapter 12.

11.11 Web search

The ephemeral nature of web content on the web made it challenging in the beginning for researchers to monitor it. Now there are various tools and software to accurately find what one is looking for.

All that is available on the Net can be tracked through various search engines, but there can be material that is protected with password access. Information generated in chat rooms and discussion forums cannot be accessed without the requisite proprietary software.

The "conversation tracker" software is said to produce a summary picture from the participants' comments, news graphs, mailing lists, and message boards. There are various kinds of software available to track content. For instance, ComAduit, media monitor CARMA Asia Pacific, window-based COMA Audit are some of the software used by researchers for most world markets. Many practitioners use spreadsheet software, notably Microsoft Excel. The proliferation of websites has seen more and more software being promoted. A new software called Vocus aims at tracking social networking sites and promises a "fully integrated PR software solution that empowers you to engage, monitor and analyze traditional media, bloggers and the world of social media."

Many in the West use an appraise system developed by the Hallmark PR consultancy in England. Through the process, six messages are chosen by the organization on which the tracking is done (the number is restricted to six at a time to avoid confusion with too many issues). The messages are linked to corporate objectives, products, promotions, key contact information, etc. The media targets one set and monitor by regular scanning of publications, broadcast, and Internet media. The data entry, feel critics, may be a clerical grind, but it is the analyses that add value.[24] The appraisal system allows for the collection of alternative messages such as a negative comment and a competitor's response. It collects information on media versus the activity that generated the media coverage, journalists who are writing about the organization, corporate spokesperson quoted by the media, and placement of article by position in print and electronic media.[25]

When evaluating websites, the Treadwells recommend the following:

Ownership: Whose website it is? Does an identifiable person or organization sponsor it?

Authorship: Who has written the content? What are the credentials of the author/institution?

Bias: Is the bias apparent or latent in favor or against an issue, organization, or individual? To get the other side of the story, we need to search other sites.

Authority: Is the content reviewed? Are there identifiable criteria, reviewers, or editors by which the material is screened or chosen for the website?

Links: Are there credible links? Do you know of any credible websites that find a link here?

Currency: Is the information up to date? Websites not updated speak of lack of professionalism and reflect negatively on the author and website.[26]

Media content analysis can be both quantitative and qualitative. In case of the former, the research aims at finding out how much, that is, in terms of quantum, is being covered, and, in the latter case, what is being said and if there is a slant in the story.

11.12 Desk research

Desk research is also referred to as secondary research. A lot of useful information can be accessed through internal records/archives, published reports, information available in the public domain, the media, websites, books, reports, court judgments, etc. These are also referred as secondary data, as the information already exists, while the data gathered through surveys is called primary or raw data, which need to be sifted and made sense of. Going through secondary data sources can provide a mine of information to a corporate communication practitioner.

11.12.1 Secondary data sources

Media information is available from sources within the media itself as well as from some external sources. Some of the media source books in the Indian context and other database publications often used by media planners include the following:

11.12.1.1 Population census

Conducted every ten years, the census probably is the most broad-based database offering a profile of the Indian people. The census data provide information about the population size, population strata, age, sex ratio, literacy level, family size and forms, etc. The data also provides information about "human resources, demography, culture and economic structure at local, regional and national level."[27]

The last population census was conducted in India in 2011; the census which was supposed to be conducted in 2021 was deferred due to the Covid-19 pandemic. According to the government of India website, the forthcoming data collection will be taken digitally via a mobile app.

> The Mobile app for Census purpose has been devised to be very simple, convenient and user friendly to ensure its maximum acceptability by all the Enumerators and Supervisors. With the help of mobile app, all the data will be instantaneously ready for processing, without any need of extra Logistics for schedules and ICR processing. Also, self-enumeration facility will be provided for the first time in the forthcoming Census.
>
> *(Census Division)*[28]

11.12.1.2 Annual economic survey

This provides an industrial survey based on SEC (sex, education, and caste), income, and occupation, etc.

11.12.1.3 India year book

Brought out by the Publications Division of the Ministry of Information and Broadcasting, the India Year Book provides a holistic view of data on various aspects of governance, demographics, progress, etc. Since the data are compiled from various governmental sources, they have a high degree of accuracy and authenticity.

11.12.1.4 INFA

The Indian News & Feature Alliance Year Book, known as the INFA Year Book, is published every year from Delhi, and it details information on various newspapers and magazines. The data include basic information about India, who is who in the press, in marketing and advertising, a list of publications with details about number of editions, mechanical data about the size of the publication, what kind of ad material will be acceptable to them, circulation and names of the concerned persons in the ad department, etc. Besides INFA, the publishers also bring out two annuals, *India Who's Who* and *Press and Advertisers' Year Book*.[29]

11.12.1.5 Audit bureau of circulation

In the early days of advertising, each medium reflected its circulation figures. Inconsistencies in reporting and a tendency on the part of certain media to inflate figures put a question mark on the credibility of the figures. To provide an impartial assessment, an organization known as the Audit Bureau of Circulation, better known as ABC, came into being with the support of newspaper publishers, magazine publishers, advertisers, and advertising agencies. ABC provides advertisers with impartial and authentic check of circulation statements of member publications by looking at their circulation figures every six months.

In order to bring about more accuracy, the ABC has brought about certain changes in the system.

In a circular issued in 2023, some interesting information and insights can be gauged on how it works. A relevant portion of the circular is in the subsequent box.[30]

CRITERIA FOR CERTIFICATION OF CIRCULATION FIGURES W.E.F. JANUARY 2023 CHANGED TO MAXIMUM TRADE COMMISSION PAID TO THE TRADE: Bureau's Council of Management decided that w.e.f. January 2023 the criteria for certification of circulation figures of member publications would be changed to maximum trade Commission paid to the trade in lieu of the waste rate of newspapers (NRR) which would be prevalent only up to 31st December 2022. The maximum trade commission would be calculated as under: ABC certification for the period January–December 2023 would be considered for all those member publications whose maximum trade commission is below 45% of the cover price (maximum trade commission would include all allowances, trade discounts, gifts etc. or payment in any form/kind to the distribution trade). However, Council also decided that from the next audit period i.e. w.e.f. 1st January 2024 (since w.e.f. 1st January 2023 annual circulation audit would take place) the maximum trade commission limit would be reduced to 40% trade commission to the distribution trade from 45% earlier.

Source: auditbureau.org.

11.12.1.6 Syndicated research

Syndicated research is often based on a given sample or panel survey, of which the entire or part is supplied to various users. Several marketing research agencies like the Indian Marketing and Research Bureau (IMRB), Marketing and Research Group (MARG), MODE, and academic and economic outfits like the National Council of Applied Economic Research (NCAER) and others are constantly engaged in gauging the pulse of markets and behavior of consumers. Syndicated research can be initiated by client organizations also. Many blue-chip companies, especially in the consumer sector, go in for research of this kind, all with the basic purpose of understanding the market, the consumer psychology, and the shifting paradigms. In the last couple of decades, there has been an increasing urge to know about the "media consumer," his/her media habits, accessibility, and changing perceptions. This has been the result of the proliferation of media, especially in the context of the satellite channels and the ultimate power of "remote" to surf channels or prefer one media vehicle over the other. The National Readership Survey, IRS (NRS, now defunct) has fulfilled the need to a great extent.[31] The IRS 2013 especially encountered criticism from some media houses for its badly "flawed" data, demanding withdrawal of the survey and a change in methodology.[32] The last IRS came in 2019. It was suspended in 2020 by the MRUC India due to Covid-19-related restrictions. While there has been resumption of most activities in the post-Covid scenario, there is no sight of IRS even by the middle of 2023.

Summary

In this chapter, we discussed the role, scope, and need for research in corporate communication. As the discipline of corporate communication has, by and large, progressed from public relations, the nomenclature PR research should not be taken as something different from CC research.

Research has not been always a favorite choice among practitioners. The chapter discussed various reasons for the same.

We discussed various models of research and their use by practitioners.

What to research was discussed to facilitate practitioners in building research as an important ingredient in the overall corporate communication programming.

Various kinds of research, both primary and secondary, were taken up for detailed discussion, along with case studies to facilitate students and practitioners in undertaking research and evaluation studies.

Key terms

Communication audit: refers to the auditing of communication undertaken by an organization over a period

Community surveys: such surveys are conducted on a variety of issues such as on safety, healthcare, social security, social engagements, rituals, etc.

Dashboards: a new research tool used by corporate communication practitioners to apprise the top management in a short and succinct style of reporting.

Desk research: refers to secondary data analyses

Focus groups: this technique of research carries the potential of acquiring a deep understanding of the attitudes and opinions of the target group

Formative research: formative research is conducted by program implementers generally with the help of experts to define the problem that the proposed program is aiming to tackle through communication intervention

Gatekeepers: defined as opinion leaders whose opinion matters to those groups of people who depend on them for various supports, viz., social, economic, political, and emotional

Image surveys: an image study is undertaken to gauge the image of an organization in comparison with its competitors on various parameters

Media research: a term used for measuring quantitatively how much coverage has been received in media in terms of column centimeters and minutes and what has been written when media is content-analyzed

Opinion surveys: the surveys are a mode of primary research that can be both quantitative and qualitative in form

Research rationale: the researcher has to have a fair idea of what the research is supposed to find out

Research methodology: refers to the technique, that is, whether the research is going to be based on secondary research or primary research

Research universe: refers to the target audience whose views the research is seeking

Research instrument: researchers use a questionnaire, also known as instrument, that is administered in person, by mail, or telephone to ask respondents about their opinions on various issues addressed by the research

Research analysis: in a close-ended questionnaire, the responses are statistically analyzed in terms of numbers. Open-ended responses are coded and quantified into a numerical score, and then responses are tabulated and analyzed and the report prepared.

Sampling: defines how to select a cross section of people, that is, whom to survey, how many to survey, and how to select them

Web search: refers to tracking what is written on the Web on official sites as well as on social networking sites

Concept review questions

Q.1. What do you understand by the term research? Why do we need research? Discuss with arguments.

Q.2. What is formative research, and why do we need it?

Q.3. What is the difference between primary and secondary research?

Q.4. Define opinion survey and the various steps of conducting a survey.

Q.5. What is a communication audit, and what is it expected to achieve?

Q.6. Define various desk research options

Critical thinking exercise

What kind of research would an infrastructure development company in housing be interested in and why? Discuss with logical arguments.

Fieldwork

Research study (group work)

Prepare a three-stage research study design (formative research/baseline, midterm appraisal, and evaluation at the end of the campaign) for a proposed campaign that aims at changing the behavior of the youth by convincing them on why smoking is bad for them. Your design must be based on PRE (the planning, research, and evaluation process) discussed in the chapter.

Case study

Formative research for developing communication strategies for peer-led intervention for drug and other substance users

This was an NGO sponsored project taken by the present author along with a co-researcher in 2006 with the objective: To improve quality coverage of substance using populations, especially injecting drug users, to prevent the spread of HIV among this population in India.

The aims of the proposed communication program were to:

1. Raise awareness of the adverse consequences of drug use including HIV/AIDS.
2. Reduce risky behavior among drug using populations to break the chain of HIV transmission.
3. To suggest a behavior, change communication (BCC) plan.

   The basic premise of the proposed program was that the peer group would lead it, that is, former drug users who had quit drugs would be used as influencers to reach out to current drug users by sharing their story and how they quit and how they are maintaining the changed behavior of being drug-free.

   The broad aim of the project was to conduct formative research to define the problem and suggest appropriate communication strategies, including the choice of media to reach out to a disparate groups of drug users spread across the length and breadth of the country, cutting across demographic and psychographics divide.

Formative BCC assessment

The research was multi-pronged, which included the following:

1. Desk research: this included going through various research studies taken up in the past, experiences from various countries, studying various models and paradigms on behavior change, and communication interventions and their success rates.
2. Review of initiatives taken in India and impediments.
3. Government of India's policy and program on reaching out to drug users and the extent of political will. This was done through accessing information in the public domain and meeting government officers in charge of policy and program implementers from the National AIDS Control Organization (NACO) and media review.
4. Through a participatory workshop, in which a cross section of NGO representatives were invited to share their strategies and experiences.
5. Discussions with a peer group who was proposed to spearhead the program.
6. Survey of drug users in two states, viz., Manipur and Delhi.
7. Pre-test of BCC material among the target population and program implementers, that is, NGOs.

The workshop sought to gain from the experience of the participants in focusing on the following:

a. Identification of the problem areas
b. Identification of effective strategies

c. Identification of cultural factors

   i. Contributing to the effective implementation of project objectives
   ii. Preventing the effective implementation of project objectives

d. Identification of peer group or/and opinion leaders
e. Target groups/audience segments left out and reasons for their exclusion
f. Level of support and participation from the following:

   i. Local government
   ii. NGO groups other than those working for AIDS prevention
   iii. Media awareness programs/interface/sensitization
   iv. Media/local media
   v. Community
   vi. Cooption of cultural networks

g. Evaluation of existing tools:

   i. Appropriateness of the following:

      - Information inputs
      - Cultural perspectives
      - Comprehension choice of medium
      - Placement and structure

   ii. Reach, quantity
   iii. Meeting requirements of all key segments

h. Evaluating existing infrastructure facilities:

   i. Media effective implementation of strategy
   ii. Effective infrastructure to support implementation or effecting behavior change among the proposed target group.

Two days' extensive discussions in a seminar conducted in Manipur enabled participants to share experiences, evaluate and look at existing material, and give suggestions for the development of additional inputs. On the last day, participants were involved in developing what they thought were important communication inputs, which facilitated PIL on the ground to fulfill project objectives and get the project message across.

Focus group discussions and in-depth interviews were conducted at the project site with peer educators and IDUs, and all this material was compiled for analysis for the development of an appropriate communication strategy.

A field visit in Delhi at the Yamuna Bazaar area was conducted in May 2006, covering a migrant population who were users of drugs. In-depth interviews and focus group discussions were held with the peer educators from Sahara Sharan, an NGO, and about 25 clients. The age group ranged from early 20s to 40s. Some of the DUs and IDUs were on drugs for more than 30 years.

Based on the insights gathered from field visits and qualitative research, a campaign was prepared, which proposed to use a variety of linked communication channels based on field assessment. All proposed communication material was pre-tested in the field before formally integrating it within the BCC strategy.[33]

Question on formative research case study

Based on the insights from the earlier case study, make a formative research design before a campaign can be launched on initiating the youth in using their adult franchise.

Notes

1 www.culpwrit.com/?p=169.
2 Frank Jefkins, *PR for Your Business*, 1995 (New Delhi: Excel Books), p. 160.
3 James Grunig, "Basic Research Provides Knowledge That Makes Evaluation Possible in PR", *Public Relations, Quarterly*, no. 28, 1983, pp. 28–32.
4 John V. Pavlik, *Public Relations, What Research Tells Us*, 1987 (Sage Publication), p. 65 in Jim R. Macnamara, *Research in PR- A Review of the Use of Evaluation and Formative Research* (CARMA).
5 James Grunig and Todd Hunt, *Managing PR in Jim R Macnamara, Research in PR—A Review of the Use of Evaluation and Formative Research* (CARMA).
6 Stewart A. Smith, "Research and Pseudo Research in Marketing", *Harvard Business Review*, 52, no. 2, March–April 1974, pp. 73–76, in Scot M. Cutlip, Allen H. Center and Glen M. Broom, *Effective Public Relations*, 2000 (Harlow, UK: Pearson Education).
7 Don W. Stacks, *Primer on Public Relations Research*, p. 3, on preview @ books.google.co.in.
8 Ibid.
9 Richard R. Dolphin, *The Fundamentals of Corporate Communication*, 1999 (London: Butterworth-Heinemann), p. 103.
10 Sandra Oliver, *Corporate Communication*, 1997 (London: Kogan Page Limited), p. 179.
11 H. Mintezberg, "The Rise and Fall of Strategic Planning", in Sandra Oliver (Ed.), *Corporate Communication*, 1997 (London: Kogan Page Limited), p. 182.
12 Institute of Public Relations and Communications Directors' Forum, *Best Practices in the Measurement and Reporting of Public Relations and ROI*, 2004 (London: IPR) in Tom Watson and Paul Noble, *Evaluating Public Relations*, second edition, 2008 (New Delhi: Kogan Page), p. 90.
13 R. Gaunt and D. Wright, "PR Measurement", 2004, www.benchpoint.com/download/download.asp.
14 Frank Jefkins, *PR for Your Business*, 1995 (New Delhi: Excel Books), p. 164.
15 2009 Delman Trust Barometer.
16 Tom Watson and Paul Noble, quoting Grunig and Hunt in *Evaluating Public Relations*, 2008 (New Delhi: Kogan Page), pp. 68–69.
17 C. Daymon and I. Holloway, *Qualitative Research Methods in Public Relations and Marketing Communication*, 2002 (London: Routledge), p. 186.
18 P. Noble, "A Proper Role for Media Evaluation" at The International PR Research Symposium, Bled, Slovenia, 1994 in Scot M. Cutlip, Allen H. Center and Glen M. Broom, *Effective Public Relations*, 2000 (Harlow, UK: Pearson Education).
19 www.ipsos-mori.com/researchspecialisms/loyalty/sector/financial-services/general-public-corporate-image-survey.ashx.
20 Rotary International Public Image Survey, June 2007.
21 www.hsk.harvard.ed.
22 Tom Watson and Paul Noble, *Evaluating Public Relations*, second edition, 2008 (New Delhi: Kogan Page), pp. 101–102.
23 K. Paine, *How to Measure Your Results: Lessons Learned*, 2006, www.instituteforpr.org.
24 Tom Watson and Paul Noble, *Evaluating Public Relations*, second edition, 2008 (New Delhi: Kogan Page), pp. 116–117.
25 Ibid. The sample of evaluation sheet may be seen in Watson and Noble book at pp. 117–122.
26 Donald Treadwell and Jill B. Treadwell, *Public Relations Writing*, second edition, 2005 (New Delhi: Response Books), p. 104.
27 Census Division | Government of India (censusindia.gov.in).
28 Ibid.
29 India News and Features Alliance (INFA)—Publications.

30 194 (auditbureau.org).
31 Jaishri Jethwaney and Shruti Jain, *Advertising Management*, 2006 (New Delhi: OUP).
32 "18 Top Media Houses Rubbish Readership Survey Findings", *The Times of India*, Timesofindia.indiatimes.com, 31 January 2014.
33 The present author, Dr. J Jethwaney was the lead consultant with dr. Abhilasha Kumari as her Associate. The formative research was conducted in 2006 and the campaign input recommended was pre-tested among about 100 NGO representatives during a workshop conducted by the sponsoring NGO, namely Society for promotion of youth and Men 9SPYM) who have been doing pioneering work in HIV/AIDS and drug use communication.

12

LAWS AND ETHICS IN CORPORATE COMMUNICATION

Chapter objectives

After reading this chapter, you will learn:

Various laws, like the law of defamation, invasion of privacy, and Copyright Act, as relevant to the practice of corporate communication
Professional bodies and codes of professional ethics in corporate communication and journalism
Case studies
Abstracts/highlights of various codes of professional ethics/standards

12.1 Introduction

Every profession functions and operates within the precincts of a legal framework, the law of the land. There are certain expectations from each profession, an acid test, which it needs to pass to be respected. Professional bodies/associations pertaining to different professions, therefore, create certain self-regulations for its members, so that those who practice the profession do not succumb to wrong practices and be aboveboard. A professional code of ethics is like a ready reckoner to be referred to when in doubt.

A corporate communication practitioner, because of the nature of the profession, not only has to be acquainted with laws and code of ethics pertaining to his/her profession but also the laws and ethics pertaining to the corporate sector *per se* and the news media. During one's professional work, one interfaces with various stakeholders through a variety of channels including personal interfaces. At times, an organization, through its acts of omission and commission, gets embroiled in controversies, thus coming into public and media gaze. At other times, because of certain decisions, the organization may be

DOI: 10.4324/9781032694702-12

embroiled in legal hassles jeopardizing its reputation. Corporate communication is often called upon in such times to lend help in salvaging the damage and manage its reputation.

An overactive media and an overzealous NGO sector on the prowl have also necessitated organizations to be in readiness to respond, should a necessity arise.

As corporate communication is a staff function, rendering aid and advice to the management, it is important that the corporate communication practitioner has a good hang of various laws and enactments that are relevant to the organization. Similarly, professional codes of ethics and self-regulation propounded by the regulatory authorities and professional bodies within the corporate sector, media, and corporate communication/PR need to be gone through carefully.

It may not be necessary to have an expert view or understanding of various corporate laws, but a working knowledge would help, especially when dealing with issues relating to reputation management.

The Right to Information Act, 2005 in India has brought about a complete shift from the days of the Official Secrets Act, which empowered the government and public sector projects to keep every information under wraps. Now it is difficult to hold back any secrets about the functioning of the government departments and public-funded organizations. Government also intervenes in the governance of listed companies in the private sector, should there be a problem, as we read in the chapter on crisis communication in the case of Satyam computers. Therefore, a good working knowledge of laws and regulations pertaining to the financial sector will also help the corporate communicator immensely.

In the following paragraphs, we shall discuss various mass media laws, regulations, Right to Information, codes of conduct of various professional bodies, and a general overview of laws pertaining to the corporate sector.

12.2 Mass media laws

Corporate communication does not have any specific laws governing the profession, but all the mass media laws impact its practice. In the following paragraphs, we shall discuss the law of defamation, invasion of privacy, and the Copyright Act.

12.2.1 Defining defamation

Defamation is defined as a wrong done by one person to another's reputation by words, signs, or visible representation. It is different from wrongful acts which injure reputation, including assault involving disgrace, unlawful arrest or attachment, malicious prosecution, or breach of contract like promise of marriage, or a bank dishonoring a customer's cheque despite having money in his account.

The law of defamation widely made use of against the mass media occupies an important place in the Indian legal system. Under the Indian Constitution, the fundamental right to free speech (Article 19) is subject to "reasonable restrictions." What is reasonable is subjective, and the interpretation may vary from time to time, depending upon the prevailing circumstances. There are two independent components to this law, each of which operates independently of the other: the criminal law of defamation is contained in the Indian Penal Code, 1860, and the civil law of defamation in the Common Law. The civil law of defamation is less clearly defined. It is to be found not in any statutes but in that age-old repository of legal wisdom, the Common Law of England—which continues to be followed in India, with minor modifications to suit local situations.

The word defamation is generic, and libel and slander are its two forms. Let us define these two individually:

12.2.2 Libel

Any false statement published about a person that brings upon the person hatred, contempt, or inflicts mental torture or has an adverse impact on his occupation or business constitutes libel.

There have been many instances in the past when "aggrieved" persons and parties have sued media for libel. Corporate communication professionals, by the very nature of their profession, write for various publics, and this mundane job may cost someone her/his job if the practitioner is ignorant about the legal implications.

The author, when she edited a house journal, while working for a large infrastructure public sector company, once wrote a farewell note for a retiring officer in the house journal. A copy was sent to him, after which she received a complimentary letter from the gentleman appreciating what she wrote about him. However, out of the blue, after about four to five months, she received a typed letter from the same gentleman threatening to sue her in the court of law for what he thought was a libelous description of him in the said article which said "Mr. . . drew contrasts. He was the most loved and hated person simultaneously." He thought that by writing that he was "hated," she had diminished his chances of reemployment, which he was seriously contemplating. The letter came as a total shock to her. It was clear that he was quoting the line out of context. At the same time, if he sued her, she would have to undergo the torture of going to another city to fight the case. The letter he had written earlier after receiving a copy of the house journal came to her rescue. She immediately discussed the issue with the legal wing of the company. They made a suitable reply in the legal jargon and sent it to him, and that was last she heard of the gentleman. The moral of the example is to never take anything lightly. If in doubt, consult the rule book, the competent authority, or the experts. It is not worth hurting someone unwittingly or getting oneself in trouble.

Libel has four defenses, viz., truth, fair comment, criticism, and privilege.

If the writer can prove that what he has written is true with documentary proof, he can fight the libel suit to his advantage. For example, if the writer called someone a criminal and he faced a legal case, then he must prove through documentary evidence that indeed the man was convicted in a criminal case in a court of law. Similarly, while criticizing or commenting on someone's work, it must be restricted to the work of the person and without malice.

Some legal experts in the US opine that, typically, the following may constitute defamation per se:

- Attacks on a person's professional character or standing
- Allegations that an unmarried person is unchaste
- Allegations that a person is infected with a sexually transmitted disease
- Allegations that the person has committed a crime of moral turpitude

Experts believe that commencing a defamation action is not always a good idea, as they tend to be difficult to win. While people who are targeted may be genuinely hurt and quite angry to file a lawsuit, there are some very good reasons why actions for defamation may not be a good idea. The publicity that results from a defamation lawsuit, especially for public figures, can create a greater audience for the false statements than they previously enjoyed. For example, if a newspaper or news show picks up the story of the lawsuit, accusations that were previously known to only a small number of people may suddenly become known to the entire community, nation, or even to the world. The lawsuit may ultimately go in favor of the plaintiff, but it is no guarantee that media would be as enthusiastic to cover it.[1]

Celebrated author Late Khushwant Singh's preview of his biography in a publication earned the ire of Ms Maneka Gandhi, the daughter-in law of late Mrs. Indira Gandhi, who entered politics later, currently being a member of the Parliament (2019–24). She felt that some remarks about her in the book were libelous. She moved the court, urging it to order the author to expunge those references from the book which was being previewed in news media before it was put on general circulation/purchase. The honorable court gave the judgment in her favor, and the author was asked to edit the book accordingly, which he did.

On the other hand, there are some documents of official nature, which are immune to libel action. If quoted from such documents, libel action can be avoided under privilege.

The case of Sir Elton John is interesting from the perspective that he was not accused of anything but was the target of a spoof that hurt him to the extent that he filed a defamation suit against the *Guardian*. Here is the story in detail.

Sir Elton John, the famous singer, lost a defamation case in December 2008 against the *Guardian* for publishing a spoof column on his AIDS Charity Dinner, what he felt was defamatory. Sir Elton described the "A Peek At The Diary Of. . ." column, published on 5 July 2008, as having a "gratuitously offensive, nasty and snide tone." The newspaper defended its position, arguing that it was a satirical piece of comment rather than a factual account.

Sir Elton is known worldwide among music lovers, as well as his sexual orientation that he has not kept a secret.

EXHIBIT 12.1 THE COLUMN IN VERBATIM

"A peek at the diary of. . . Elton John

What a few days it's been. First I sang Happy Birthday to my dear, dear friend Nelson Mandela—I like to think I'm one of the few people privileged enough to call him Madiba—at a party specially organised to provide white celebrities with a chance to be photographed cuddling him, wearing that patronisingly awestruck smile they all have. It says: "I love you, you adorable, apartheid-fighting teddy bear."

The next night I welcomed the exact same crowd to my place for my annual White Tie & Tiaras ball. Lulu, Kelly Osbourne, Agyness Deyn, Richard Desmond, Liz Hurley, Bill Clinton—I met most of them 10 minutes ago, but we have something very special and magical in common: we're all members of the entertainment industry. You can't manufacture a connection like that Naturally, everyone could afford just to hand over the money if they gave that much of a toss about Aids research—as could the sponsors. But we like to give guests a preposterously lavish evening, because they're the kind of people who wouldn't turn up for anything less. They fork out small fortunes for new dresses and so on, the sponsors blow hundreds of thousands on creating what convention demands we call a "magical world", and everyone wears immensely smug "My diamonds are by Chopard" grins in the newspapers and OK!. Once we've subtracted all these costs, the leftovers go to my foundation. I call this care-o-nomics".

As seen by Marina Hyde

The interim judgment hearing decreed "the words complained of. . . could not be understood by a reasonable reader of the *Guardian* weekend section as containing the serious allegation pleaded."

Commenting on the judgment, the *Guardian* reported: "In a groundbreaking libel decision, the judge said that 'irony' and 'teasing' do not amount to defamation. The ruling offers protection to writers of satirical articles clearly not meant to be taken seriously and was welcomed last night by media lawyers and journalists."

Commenting on the judgment, the newspaper, in the article titled "A victory for irony as Elton John loses Guardian libel suit," said,

> Sir John Elton is well known for his quick temper and outrageous behavior. A documentary of his life said it all—it was called, knowingly, Tantrums and Tiara. But a High Court judge ruled that the singer's sense of humor failure over satirical piece by the Guardian was a tantrum too far.[2]

The judgment meant Sir Elton, who had sought damages and an apology, was ordered to pay the costs. He, however, had the option to go to court against the judgment.

In retrospect, Sir Elton's £3,000-a-head White Tie and Tiara Ball in June was able to raise £10 million from a celebrity auction that had the virtual who is who attending it, including former US President Bill Clinton, Elizabeth Hurley, Jemima Khan, and Uma Thurman.

The article quoted legal expert Robin Shaw, who said, "It is encouraging to have a judicial decision that recognises that a spoof should not be taken literally."

"It's significant," said another media law expert Mark Stephens of the ruling. "What Tugendhat has done is move us closer to the US system where you can't get damages for satire and humour, except in the most exceptional cases."[3]

12.2.2.1 The "virtual" libel

There are millions of bloggers, cutting across race, caste, color, religion, and language, who write on billions of subject matters ranging from politics to products, from crime to religion, from media to industry, from celebrities to the common man, and what have you. There are views, reviews, comments, apologies, threats, intimidations in their posts, using impeccable text to purple prose, using expletives and swear words.

Bloggers had a field day for long, till the Supreme Court of India refused to give reprieve to the petitioner despite a disclaimer on his blog. Reporting on the issue, the *Times of India* commented that it would no longer be "safe to start a blog and invite others to register their raunchy, caustic and even abusive comments on an issue while seeking protection behind the disclaimer-views expressed on the blog are that of the writers." The warning came from the bench comprising Chief Justice KG Balakrishnan and Justice P Sathasivam, who refused to protect a 19-year-old D. Ajith, who had started a community on a networking site against political party Shiv Sena, against summons received from a Maharashtra court on a criminal case filed against him.[4]

The redeeming thing, however, is that while the Internet users may face libel for what they write themselves, the "intermediaries" who host such content are liable only if they are consciously complicit to the offence or fail to remove the offending material immediately after it was brought to their notice by authorities.

The amendment to the Information Technology Act, which came into effect in February 2009, now postulates that where the intermediary, in effect, acts as no more than a distributor, he "shall not be liable for any third-party information, data or communication link made available or hosted by him." Section 79 provides that the intermediary is exempt from liability in all cases where

> the function of the intermediary is limited to providing access to a communication system over which information made available by third parties is transmitted or temporarily stored or hosted.

The intermediary does not, a) initiate the transmission, b) select the receiver of the transmission, and c) select or modify the information contained in the transmission; the intermediary observes the diligence while discharging his duties under this act and observes such other guidelines as the central government may prescribe in this behalf.

An "intermediary" has been defined in the amended law as

> any person who on behalf of another person receives, stores, or transmits the record or provides any service with respect to that record and includes telecom service providers, network service providers, web-hosting service providers, search engines, on-line payment sites, online auction sites, online market places and cyber cafes.

Analysts believe that the amendment saw careful drafting of provisions in the wake of industry-wide anxiety after the CEO of an auction site was arrested when the DPS-MMS scandal broke in 2004, in which a salacious clip was offered on sale by the user on baazee.com. The police defended its action of arresting the CEO on the grounds that he did not remove the clip for long. The amended Section 79 posits that the intermediary would attract criminal charges where "upon receiving actual knowledge, or on being notified by the appropriate government authority or its agency that any information. . . the intermediary fails to expeditiously remove. . . that material."[5]

What bloggers need to be cautious about

1. Bloggers are not intermediaries but authors (this entails that a blogger is liable for what he/she says online).
2. Look at the legal process as much as the provision (if caught on the wrong side of the law, it's a long tedious process that may take years).
3. Be careful of the service agreement with the intermediary who provides technical backup for the blog (to avail of the intermediary immunity, the intermediary has to, under the Intermediaries Guidelines, 2011, take down the content within 36 hours).
4. With wider audience cutting across geographical boundaries, the blogger can be dragged to a court anywhere to fight the case.
5. It is not just the government, but even the corporate sector, if hurt by a blog, who can take recourse to legal measures.[6]

12.2.3 Slander

Slander is very much like libel, except that it is verbal or spoken. It can occur in a broadcast, in a speech, or in an informal conversation. It becomes slander when a third party hears it. However, if someone wants to "fix" a person, it is not difficult for him to produce false witnesses.

Parliamentarians in India enjoy the privilege of immunity on what they speak within the House. Reporting on such comments also enjoys immunity from legal action, provided these are accurate. But the same privilege is not available while reporting the proceedings of the state legislatures. Interestingly, however, in an age when parliament and state assemblies are covered live on television, people have witnessed the hurling of chairs and shoes, not to speak of abuses, when the privilege does not seem to matter!

Caselets

12.2.3.1 Racial slur on a community

Indian Idol, a reality show on Sony Channel, led to riots in September 2007, because of a radio jockey's insensitive racial remarks.

The Information and Broadcasting Ministry served a show-cause notice on Radio Red FM, asking it to explain why action should not be initiated against it for airing racist slur against the Gorkhas after a Darjeeling boy, named Prashant Tamang, was crowned "Indian Idol."

The RJ, Jonathan Brady, who is popularly known as Nitin after a program called *Ulta Pulta Nitin* that he hosted on some other FM channel, apparently commented in a live broadcast that "shopkeepers will now have to make their own security arrangements as Gorkhas have taken to singing." The remark was made on his new program, *Khurafati Nitin*, on Red FM radio.

The issue kicked up a row and sparked off a mass movement in the Darjeeling Hills, leading to violence in Siliguri and strikes in several places like Kalimpong and Sukna. A Gorkha delegation moved a petition to the then union minister of information and broadcasting, late Priya Ranjan Dasmunshi, and former West Bengal Chief Minister Bengal Buddhadeb Bhattacharjee, demanding stern action against the radio channel.

The I&B Ministry also woke up to the controversy and served a show-cause notice on the radio channel, which read,

> It has been brought to the notice of the government by the West Bengal government and others that the permission holder of FM radio broadcasting station in the city of Delhi namely M/s Digital Radio (Delhi) Broadcasting Limited in their FM Radio channel named Red FM being aired on 93.5 MHz has carried a program on 24.9.2007 in which a Radio Jockey has made derogatory remarks about the Gorkha Community consequent upon the selection of Prashant Tamang as Indian Idol in a Sony television channel show.

The ministry cited para 11.2 of the Grant of Permission Agreement under which M/s Digital Radio (Delhi) Broadcasting Limited was supposed to follow the program code of All India Radio, which prohibits any program attacking communities, anything defamatory, incitement to violence, and anything against law and order.

"From the sequence of events, it is prima facie evident that the remarks are in violation of the program code of AIR and hence the permission holder has been given time till 1600 hours (IST) on October 1, 2007 to explain why action should not be taken against them," the notice said. Meanwhile, Red FM has apologized for the remark that led to violence and protests in Siliguri. In a statement, the channel said:

> Our shows and RJs use humour and satire in their presentation. There is nothing deliberate or intentional in anything that they do. We have not intentionally caused hurt to the sentiments of any person or any particular community, caste or creed. However, in the event any inadvertent slight or offence has been caused to the sentiments of any person or community, we tender our apology for the same.[7]

12.2.3.2 Defamatory comments in election campaigning

During the 15th Lok Sabha elections held in April–May 2009, Kapil Sibal, a candidate in Delhi, an attorney by profession, sued contender Vijender Gupta for making "abusive" remarks against him to mislead the public ahead of polls. Gupta, in an interview to a Hindi newspaper, had accused Sibal for fighting cases on behalf of some school management on fee hike, bringing hardship on parents. Sibal, in his notice, said that he had never been on any school management committee, and also since his election to parliament in 2004, as he could not practice under the code of conduct, he had not practiced law since then.[8] In a similar case, Bihar's ruling Janata Dal-United (JD-U) filed a defamation suit against Rashtriya Janata Dal (RJD) leader Rabri Devi for her alleged abusive remarks against Chief Minister Nitish Kumar and state JD-U Chief Rajiv Ranjan alias Lalan Singh, a party source said.

A JD-U leader, said Lalan Singh, filed the case in the Patna civil court over the former chief minister's remarks against JD-U leaders at a public meeting in Saran district. Her husband, then the railway minister and RJD chief, Lalu Prasad, was a candidate for the Saran Lok Sabha seat.[9]

In 2023, member of parliament and past president of the Indian National Congress Rahul Gandhi was sued for defamation in a Gujarat court for allegedly disrespecting and hurting a community that shares the surname of Prime Minister Modi, during an election rally in Karnataka in 2019.[10] He was convicted and awarded three years' jail term for "defaming" a community, the highest so far in the country against this law. He lost the case in Gujarat High Court. Now he has moved the Supreme Court in July 2023, but in the meantime, he lost his membership of the parliament and cannot contest election for six years. Rahul Gandhi's expulsion was based on the provisions of Article 102 (1) (e), read together with Section 8 of India's Representation of the People Act of 1951, under which any person who is "convicted of any offence and sentenced to imprisonment for not less than two years shall be disqualified for a further period of six years" after their release.[11] There have been allegations of bias against the speaker for being too hasty in acting, when a member from the ruling party who was convicted in the past for a criminal offence did not face the same action.

12.2.3.3 A bureaucrat takes on a politician

It is uncommon, especially in India, for a bureaucrat to slam a defamation threat to a politician, but it happened in 2008. A 1994 batch IPS officer, Paresh Saxena, sent a legal notice to Bihar Minster Bhola Singh warning him of defamation suit if he did not tender an apology for publicly humiliating him at a public function. According to the notice, Singh "badly insulted and demoralized" the officer by using "offending, libelous and defamatory" language at a function for not presenting a bouquet to the minister. The notice quoted the minister as saying "Shasan hum karte hain, adhikari nahi."[12]

It is not that the courts receive genuine cases always. It is not uncommon for some NGOs or some activists to file public interest litigation in the courts, even if the case does not warrant a second look. For instance, an office bearer of a slum dweller's body has filed a defamation case against music director AR Rahman and actor Anil Kapoor alleging that the award-winning film *Slumdog Millionaire* called Indians dogs and slum dwellers slum dogs.

In a complaint filed before a local court, Tapeshwar Vishwakarma, general secretary of Slum Dwellers Joint Action Committee, alleged that the film depicted slum dwellers in bad taste as it used the derogatory and objectionable title *Slumdog Millionaire*.[13] One wonders why he did not name the music director and actor and not the producer, director, and dialogue writer!

12.2.4 Defamation of a corporation

The reputation of a human being differs from that of a company or a body of persons. A company, for instance, cannot be accused of murder or immorality and cannot be sued for any such imputation. It can, however, complain of words in disparagement of its corporate property, business, and reputation. It would be libelous if someone said or published that the company was a bad paymaster or did not pay its contractors on time, if that were not true. Similarly, a political body, professional association, or social club may be able to sue when it suffers in public esteem from attacks on its corporate life or activities. For instance, if there was an allegation by someone or media that a political body promoted sedition, or a reputed social club was promoting immorality, it would amount to defamation if the allegation cannot be sustained.

12.2.4.1 Defamation while awarding contracts and writing

Corporate communication practitioners, in their day-to-day mundane functions, like writing letters, issuing press releases, editing company journal, giving work orders to agencies, printers/publishers can get in to trouble if not careful. This aspect, feels Philip Henslowe, can affect practitioners with damaging consequences.[14]

12.2.4.2 Defamation in cases of "passing off"

This aspect of defamation relates to misuse of a trade name of a company or product trade name. It encompasses imitation or the "getup" or packaging of the item, including type, size, shape of container, labeling, packaging of goods, etc. As corporate communication practitioners are generally in charge of corporate identity of a company, it is important for them to have a good hang of intellectual property rights.

For instance, when automobile company Volkswagen entered the Indian automobile market, it issued a public notice warning anyone from imitating its logo/trademark in any manner.

12.3 Invasion of privacy

There is no statutory enactment expressly guaranteeing a general right of privacy to Indian citizens, but elements of this right as traditionally contained in common law are recognized by courts in India. In addition, two pieces of legislation recognize this right viz., the Children's Act, 1960 and the Hindu Marriage Act, 1955, which impose similar restrictions on publication of reports concerning proceedings under the act. The Code of Criminal Procedure, 1973, also permits restrictions to be imposed on the publication of reports concerning certain proceedings, that is, rape trials.

Clarence Jones writes in her book *Winning with the News Media* that now more and more people don't sue for defamation but invasion of privacy against media, as privacy cases focus on personal and emotional beliefs in conflict with each other.[15]

The Supreme Court of India recognized the right to privacy as a fundamental right in *R Rajagopal vs. the state of Tamil Nadu* in 1994: "The right to privacy is implicit in the right to life and liberty to the citizens of this country by Article 21. It is a right to be left alone."[16]

The Press Council of India, in its norms of Journalistic Conduct (2005) says:

> The press shall not intrude or invade the privacy of an individual unless outweighed by genuine overriding public interest, not being a prurient or morbid curiosity. So, however, that once that matter becomes a matter of public record, the right of privacy no longer subsists and it becomes a legitimate subject for comment by the press and the media, among others.

12.3.1 Paparazzi mayhem

In the last few decades, no issue has been as much in public focus as the issue of invasion of privacy. The tragic death of Princess Diana was ascribed by her admirers as the outcome of invasion on her privacy. Her brother said publicly at her burial mass that the hands of the media were indeed bloodied by her death.

Photographer Galella was so much obsessed with the life of Jackie Kennedy that he followed her with his camera wherever she went. When tried through a lawsuit for invading her privacy, he pleaded innocence in the court of law, arguing that Mrs. Kennedy, wife of slain American President John F Kennedy, was a public figure, and he had every right to photograph her because that was his livelihood. In a landmark judgment, the court allowed him to continue with his professional job but from 50 yards and prohibited him from approaching within 100 yards of their New York apartment.[17]

In most recent times, photojournalist Jamie Fawcett, who was chasing Hollywood actress Nicole Kidman, lost a defamation case against an Australian newspaper that said he wanted to "wreak havoc" on actress Nicole Kidman's private life, with the court agreeing he was a "cowboy."

The New South Wales state supreme court ruled that the article saying photographer Jamie Fawcett was a "cowboy"—he once dubbed himself the "Prince of Paparazzi" and was determined "to wreak havoc on Kidman's private life"—was not defamatory.[18]

During the hearing, Kidman told the court that Fawcett chased her car across Sydney in 2005 at a speed which made her crouch on the back seat, tearful and frightened of crashing. The Hollywood star said Fawcett's car and another vehicle drove "dangerously, mounting concrete traffic barriers and driving through red traffic lights in the pursuit."

Judge Simpson justified this, keeping in view the nature of Fawcett's job, making a living from taking and selling candid photographs of famous people. The judge argued,

> Fawcett had made a goal of obtaining photographs of Ms. Kidman for which he had waited all day, un-rewarded, for a photograph of her. So, he was clearly motivated to obtain such a photograph, and he recognized that his remaining opportunities on that evening were very limited indeed."

Therefore, she said, "The evidence amply demonstrates that Mr. Fawcett's conduct was 'intrusive' and 'threatening.' "[19]

In a case relating to actress Monika Bedi, who had hit headlines being a close friend of the underworld don Abu Salem, the Supreme Court of India, on 24 August 2007, directed the Ministry of Information & Broadcasting to stop TV channels from telecasting photographs of Monica Bedi taken surreptitiously in a bathroom in Bhopal jail.[20]

Indian media, especially the news channels of late, have been drawing flak for coverage of crime, especially when they covered the Arushi murder case in 2008. The media sensationalism and their invasion of privacy received a comment from Chief Justice K G Balakrishnan when he said," Journalism must not encroach upon people's right to privacy." This, he said, while inaugurating a workshop on reporting at the Bombay high court. "Privacy of the person," he commented, "must be protected. Sometimes, damaging information is revealed during the investigation. It adversely affects people's right to a fair trial." The chief justice said that sometimes the media gave so much information on the victim, especially of sexual assault, that it was not difficult to know who the person was, even if the name was concealed. He, however, said, that newspapers cannot be as drab as government gazettes, so a "tinge of sensationalism is necessary." Commenting on the lack of editorial control on live coverage in the electronic media, he lamented, "In a paper, it is possible to edit material, but on television, when a reporter's version is directly broadcast, there is no editorial control."[21]

The basic premise behind the laws and lawsuits of this nature is to prevent anyone from knowing and spreading anything about a person which the person concerned does not wish to be known, to protect his/her reputation.

12.4 Copyright Act

India had its first Copyright Act in 1914, a replica of the English Copyright Act of 1911. The act was in use until we had the Copyright Act of 1957, which was later amended in 1999. The Indian Copyright law provides exclusive right for life of the creator and 50 years beyond for those who own the copyright, the exclusive right to publish, print, or reproduce an original literary, musical, or artistic work for a certain number of years. The Copyright Act was amended in 2012, which now has provisions of digital piracy. This has been discussed later in the chapter. The basic aim behind bringing the amended act in 2012 was to establish an equitable and just framework for the administration of copyright and sharing revenue to protect the rights of owners and authors incorporated in cinematography and audio recordings.[22]

In retrospect, the year 1992 marked the end of embargo on the works of Nobel Laureate Rabindra Nath Tagore. The copyright was vested with the VishwaBharti. The organization lobbied and was able to secure an extension of ten years of copyright from the government. This meant extension for others as well. Post 2002, Tagore's works are in the public domain for use and adaptation.

The copyright also extends to illustrations, plays, musical works, motion pictures, sound recordings, graphics, sculptures, pantomimes, and dances. The aim of a copyright is to secure for the creator of the material all the benefits accruing from the creation. The copyright act confers on the owner two rights, viz., the economic right and moral right.

12.4.1 Economic right

The copyright subsists in original literary, dramatic, musical, and artistic works, cinematographs, films, and sound recordings. The authors of copyright in the aforesaid works enjoy economic rights under Article 14 of the Act. The rights are mainly in respect of literary, dramatic, and musical, other than computer program, to reproduce the work in any material form including the storing of it in any medium by electronic means, to issue copies of the work to the public, to perform the work in public or communicating it to the public, to make any cinematograph film or sound recording in respect of the work, and to make any translation or adaptation of the work. These rights are similarly available to the author of sound recordings. In addition to the aforesaid rights, the author of a painting, sculpture, drawing, or of a manuscript of a literary, dramatic, or musical work, if he was the first owner of the copyright, shall be entitled to receive remuneration as per the provisions of law.

12.4.2 Moral right

Section 5 of the act defines the two basic "moral rights" of an author:

a) Right of paternity
b) Right of integrity

The right of paternity refers to the right of the author to claim ownership of work. Right of integrity empowers the author to prevent distortion, mutilation, or other alterations of his work, or any other work in relation to said work, which would be prejudiced to his honor or reputation.

12.4.3 Case studies in copyright infringement

With the amendment of the Copyright Act in 1994, which came into effect in 1995, the situation guarding copyright infringement seems to have improved. With copyright violation becoming a cognizable offence, it has now been possible to use the legal mechanism as a deterrent. Section 64 of the act provides:

> Any police officer, not below the rank of a sub-inspector, may, if he is satisfied that an offence under section 63 in respect of the infringement of copyright in any work has been, is likely to be committed, seize without warrant, all copies of the work, whenever found, and all copies and plates so seized shall, as soon as practicable, be produced before a magistrate.

In *Godrej soaps vs. Dora cosmetics*, the Delhi High Court held that where a carton was designed for valuable consideration by a person in the course of his employment for and behalf of the plaintiff and the defendant had led no evidence in his favor, the plaintiff is the assignee and the legal owner of the copyright in the carton, including the logo.

In *Eastern Book Co. vs. Navin J. Desai*, the issue was whether there was any copyright in reporting the judgment of a court. The High court observed:

> It is not denied that under section 2 (K) of the Copyright Act, a work which is made or published under the direction or control of any court or tribunal or other judicial authority in India is a government work under section 52 (Q), the reproduction or publication of any judgment or orders of a court, tribunal or other judicial authority shall not constitute infringement of copyright of the government in these works. It is thus clear that it is open to anybody to reproduce or publish the government work including the judgment/order of the court. However, in case, a person by extensive reading, careful study, and comparison and with exercise of taste and judgment has made certain comments about the judgment or written a commentary thereon, may be such a comment and commentary is entitled to protection under the Copyright Act.

The Delhi High Court, in a path-breaking judgment in April 2009, ruled that importing original DVDs and giving them on rent is also tantamount to copyright infringement. The court gave this verdict while hearing a writ petition by Warner Bros seeking to curb the practice of renting out its CDs and DVDs brought from the US. The defendant, a company by the name Paradisco, argued that its policy of giving on rent imported DVDs on hire was a part of the fundamental right to freedom of speech. It also said the films were critiqued at seminars organized by the company. Justice Bhat, however, concluded that screening rights of films can be territorial, and when rental rights are given in the US, it does not mean that these movies can be commercially exploited worldwide.[23]

Fair use for the purpose of criticism, comment, news reporting, teaching, scholarship, or research does not amount to infringement.

Imitating the voice or mannerisms of well-known personalities and artists for commercial purposes also tantamount to violating the right. Famous Hollywood actress Audrey Hepburn sued a fishing company for imitating her voice in a radio commercial. It is not uncommon in India to find imitated voices of celebrities in commercials, especially those of late Ajit and Amitabh Bachchan and Shahrukh Khan.

12.5 What is digital piracy?

The spurt in technology has made copying and duplicating films an easy job at a low cost. The biggest victim is the content owner, who is losing the control as the cost of content reproduction and dissemination has become dismally low. No sooner than a film is released, within hours one can have the CDs at a throwaway price. It is not difficult to get four films on a CD at a nominal price of Rs. 20 to 30 in the open market. There is a tremendous pressure on the government, especially the US, to improve its anti-piracy laws as it is believed that the US alone loses $496 million in India due to piracy.[24]

In India, Bollywood is an important copyright industry. It, however, became more relevant only when it attained the status of industry in 1998. This meant that financing of films has become more transparent and regulated. Bollywood has the distinction of producing the largest number of films in the world at about 1,000 a year, but the total contribution of the copyrighted industry in the Indian economy is not known. One finds a reference in the FICCI PricewaterhouseCoopers 2006 study which says that the Indian media and entertainment industry is worth 353 billion INR.

With the amendment in the Copyright Act in 2012, now various kinds of digital piracy have been put under its purview.[25] For instance, Section 65 states:

> Any person who circumvents an effective technological measure applied to protect any of the rights conferred by this Act, to infringe such rights, shall be punishable with imprisonment which may extend to two years and shall also be liable to fine.

Digital piracy has also been included in the Information Technology Act, 2000, which provides punishment of up to three years of imprisonment and fines up to R. 2.00 lakhs for illegally distributing copyrighted content.[26]

The Indian Performing Right Society Ltd. (IPRS) and Phonographic Performance Ltd. (PPL) issued an ad before the festive season in December 2008 that exhorted the people who organized parties to take the license before playing any music which was copyrighted. The ad read: "Good Food, Wine, Dance, but no Music!!!" The ad was addressed to "Event Organizers/Hotels/Restraints, X'Mas week and new year night party goers" who were warned that "playing music in public without obtaining the license from PPL and IPRS was an offence under the copyright Act 1957. Non-compliance with the requirement was tantamount to violation of the copyright Act, which was a cognizable and non-bailable offence, which would attract penalty up to Rs. 2.00 lakhs and 3 years of imprisonment." The ad then went on to warn: "More important your party may be stopped by the police." The ad ended with: "Issued in public Interest by The Indian Music Industry." The organization published the ad in many newspapers just before Christmas, on 25 December 2008.

Warning the event managers and the public at large is a sign of companies asserting about their rights. The copyright violation has been going unabated in India for decades, at times due to ignorance of the law. Over a period, however, it is almost institutionalized now that a certain fee will be paid before playing copyrighted music at any event. Functions held in hotels and banquet halls are allowed permission to play after paying the requisite amount to the concerned body. The bill is picked by the party hosting the function.

Under the arrangement, one or more of the three organizations IPRS, PPL, and Novex Communication Pvt. Ltd will have to be informed before deciding to play music at an event. An invoice of royalty, along with the certificate of holding the copyright, will be issued to the event organizer.[27]

12.6 Right to Information Act 2005

The issue of right to information was debated for years in the public domain, which at last saw the light of day in 2005 when the Right to Information (RTI) was passed, bringing much joy and relief to the civil society. The act which became functional in 2006 extends to the whole of India except the State of Jammu and Kashmir [S (12)].

This restriction was removed by the center in 2019. Now Jammu and Kashmir also come under the purview of the act, which entails that non-residents can also seek information from public offices of the J&K.[28]

The passing of the RTI means in brass tacks that all information in government files and public-funded organizations is open to public scrutiny. Anyone, by paying a certain nominal fee, can have access to the most confidential information, subject to some exceptions in the interest of the integrity and sovereignty of the country. Information is defined in the act as

> any material in any form including records, documents, memos, e-mails, opinions, advices, press releases, circulars, orders, logbooks, contracts, reports, papers, samples, models, data material held in any electronic form and information relating to any private body which can be accessed by a public authority under any other law for the time being in force but does not include "file noting" [S.2 (f)].

Right to information entails the following

i. "Inspect works, documents, and records.
ii. Take notes, extracts or certified copies of documents or records.
iii. Take certified samples of material."

Some highlights

12.6.1 Who is excluded?

Central Intelligence and security agencies specified in the Second Schedule, like IB, R&AW, Directorate of Revenue Intelligence, Central Economic Intelligence Bureau, Directorate of Enforcement, Narcotics Control Bureau, Aviation Research Center, Special Frontier Force, BSF, CRPF, ITBP, CISF, NSG, Assam Rifles, Special Service Bureau, Special Branch (CID), Andaman and Nicobar, the Crime Branch-CID-CB, Dadra and Nagar Haveli and Special Branch, Lakshadweep Police. Agencies specified by the state governments through a notification will also be excluded. The exclusion, however, is not absolute, and these organizations have an obligation to provide information pertaining to allegations of corruption and human rights violations. Further, information relating to allegations of human rights valuations could be given, but only with the approval of the Central or State Information Commission, as the case may be. [S.24)].

12.6.2 What is the application procedure for requesting information?

1. Apply in writing or through electronic means in English or Hindi or in the official language of the area to the PIO, specifying the particulars of the information sought for.
2. Reasons for seeking information are not required to be given.
3. Pay fees as may be prescribed (if not belonging to the below poverty line category).

12.6.3 What is the time limit to get the information?

1. Thirty days from the date of application
2. Forty-eight hours for information concerning the life and liberty of a person
3. Five days shall be added to the earlier response times, in case the application for information is given to the Assistant Public Information Officer.
4. If the interests of a third party are involved, then the time limit will be 40 days (maximum period plus time given to the party to make representation).
5. Failure to provide information within the specified period is a deemed refusal.

12.6.4 What is the fee?

1. Application fees to be prescribed, which must be reasonable.
2. If further fees are required, then the same must be intimated in writing with calculation details of how the figure was arrived at.
3. Applicant can seek review of the decision on fees charged by the PIO by applying to the appropriate Appellate Authority.
4. No fees will be charged from people living below the poverty line.
5. Applicant must be provided information free of cost if the PIO fails to comply with the prescribed time limit.

12.6.5 What could be the ground for rejection?

1. If it is covered by exemption from disclosure (S.8).
2. If it infringes copyright of any person other than the State (S.9).

The act can be downloaded from the GOI website. On its site are also FAQs that answer almost all the questions one may have.[29]

What does this mean for a corporate communication practitioner? It means that besides the contractors, vendors, NGOs, and general public, there would be requests even from the media to access information for filing their stories directly and also through the route of Right to Information Act.

12.6.6 Media and RTI

Late Justice Sawant, former head of the Press Council of India, remarked after the passage of RTI: "With the right to information on their side, media need no longer depend on questionable sources of information and can use RTI Act to access credible and authentic information."

Media has, in fact, been extensively making use of the RTI to write investigative pieces on issues that lay dormant for decades under the Official Secret Act. Besides that, as soon as the Right to Information Act was passed, several media houses took upon themselves to inform and educate their readers and viewers to make use of RTI. Here is a run on some such initiatives by the media:

NDTV, in partnership with leading civil society organizations, launched a nationwide campaign on RTI to build public awareness. It encouraged people not to pay bribes but ask for information through RTI to get their grievance redressed. In a two-week-long drive against bribes, the campaign had 1,500 trained volunteers at various centers in 48 cities. Eight media partners and more than 700 civil society groups were party to this initiative.[30]

The *Indian Express*, along with NGO Parivartan, guided the people in exercising their right to information through its regular column "Express Initiative" that carries reports of both successful and failed cases. It also includes sample questions for people to ask the authorities to get a response.[31]

Doordarshan launched a weekly half-hour program on the right to information, in which it presented the best examples of how the common man had used the RTI. Similarly, the *Hoot*, a web magazine on media issues, provided critical insights on the right to information.[32]

In some public-funded organizations, the person in charge of communication is also designated as public information officer, as in the case of the Delhi Development Authority. In the following paragraphs, a case study of the organization is given to facilitate understanding on how the right to information is used.

Media has been writing about problems and the intent of some organizations in dealing with RTI cases. Sample one of the dispatches in a mainstream newspaper with the headline: "Hospital stonewalls RTI queries of Shanno kin—MAMC forwards plea, LNJP takes refuge in rules." The story was about the death of an 11-year-old young girl, Shanno, allegedly due to corporal punishment at the hands of her teacher in school in April 2009. The story shared that RTI activists were aghast and condemned the replies provided to Shanno's well-wishers by two premier government hospitals—Loknayak Jaiprakash Hospital (LNJP) and Maulana Azad Medical College (MAMC) in response to the RTI queries on her death. The postmortem of the deceased was conducted at the MAMC. The hospital forwarded all the queries to LNJP, where the child had undergone treatment before her death. The letter said, "This information pertains to your hospital and is being transferred to you for appropriate disposal at your end." The LNJP quoted certain rules and provisions that cannot possibly be assimilated by an average reader: "This is to inform you that the life and liberty in this case is dead, hence the provision of section 7 (1) does not apply in this case. Moreover, information asked for cannot be provided as per provisions of section 8 (1) (j) of RTI Act."

The paper quoted the then leading RTI activist Arvind Kejriwal, who said, "Both replies are illegal under present conditions." Both the hospitals were slammed with criminal cases as society, he said, had the right to know what happened in the case.[33]

At the end of the chapter, a case study of the Delhi Development Authority has been included to understand the process of RTI.

The governments at the center and states have set up central information and state information commissions to deal with complaints of individuals who may like to approach it, when they are unable to get information through the direct application from organizations that come under the purview of the Right to Information Act as per the following provision in the Act:

> "**Section-18.** (1) Subject to the provisions of this Act, it shall be the duty of the Central Information Commission or State Information Commission to receive and inquire into a complaint from any person-
>
> (a) Who has been unable to submit a request to a Central Public Information Officer or State Public Information Officer, as the case may be, either by reason that no such officer has been appointed under this Act, or because the Central Assistant Public Information Officer or State Assistant Public Information Officer, as the case may be, has refused to accept his or her application for information or appeal under this Act for forwarding the same to the Central Public Information Officer or State Public Information Officer or senior officer specified in sub-section (1) of section 19 or the Central Information Commission or the State Information Commission, as the case may be;
> (b) Who has been refused access to any information requested under this Act;
> (c) Who has not been given a response to a request for information or access to information within the time limit specified under this Act;
> (d) Who has been required to pay an amount of fee which he or she considers unreasonable;
> (e) Who believes that he or she has been given incomplete, misleading, or false information under this Act; and
> (f) In respect of any other matter relating to requesting or obtaining access to records under this Act."[34]

As per media reports, the Central Information Commission halved the pendency of appeals and complaints with it in the last three years, according to data compiled by the transparency panel. The panel had 38,116 cases pending before it in 2020–21 which has reduced to 19,233 in 2022–23, officials said, referring to tentative figures compiled by the commission on 31 March 2023.[35]

12.7 The Press Council of India

The Press council of India (PCI) was set up in 1966 through an act of parliament to safeguard the freedom of the press and help maintain high standards in journalism. By convention, the PCI has always been headed by a retired judge of the supreme court. It functions through a fee levied on newspapers that have a circulation of 5000 and above. The shortfall is met through government grants.

It is not uncommon for individuals and corporate organizations to feel hurt sometimes on what the media writes or talks about them. The journalistic norms propounded by the PCI are contained in an elaborate document that has evolved based on its adjudications of cases from time to time. Though the code has emerged out of cases relating to print media, the fundamental principles evolved in the process are as much relevant to radio and television journalism. Similarly, journalists and media houses can also approach the PCI in case they feel their interests have been hurt by an action from an authority or an individual.

Here are some highlights that would help the corporate communication practitioners to use only in case of damage to the reputation of the individual or organization, which needs an extreme action as going to the Press Council. It is important to first understand the laid-out norms in the code.

12.7.1 Complaints procedure

The code provides that if a person with a complaint against a newspaper, for any publication, or non-publication of a material, which he finds objectionable and which affects him personally, he should first take it up with the editor or other authorized representative of the publication concerned. If the complaint is not resolved to satisfaction, he may refer it to the Press Council of India. The complaint must be specific and in writing and should be lodged within two months of the publication of the impugned news item in case of dailies and weeklies, and four months in all other cases, along with the original/Photostat copy of the impugned clipping (with English translation if the matter is in a language other than Hindi). It must state in what manner the publication/non-publication of the matter is objectionable within the meaning of the Press Council Act, 1978. The application to PCI needs to be accompanied with a copy of the letter sent to the editor, pointing out why the matter was objectionable. His reply thereto or published rejoinder, if any, may also be attached to it. A declaration stating that the subject matter of the complainant is not pending in any court of law is also required to be filed.

On receipt of a complaint made to it or otherwise, if the council is prima facie satisfied that the matter discloses sufficient ground for inquiry, it issues a show-cause notice to the respondents and then considers the matter through its Inquiry Committee based on written and oral evidence tendered before it. Appearance before the committee is not mandatory, and a complaint may be processed based on the written documents on record. If on inquiry the Council has reason to believe that the respondent newspaper has violated journalistic norms, the Council, keeping in view the gravity of the misconduct committed by the newspaper, warns, admonishes, or censures the newspaper or disapproves the conduct of the editor or the journalist. It may also direct the respondent newspaper to publish the contradiction of the complainant or a gist of the Council's decision in its forthcoming issue.

If a newspaper or journalist is aggrieved by any action or inaction of any authority that may impinge on the freedom of the press, he can also file a complaint with the Council. The aggrieved newspaper or journalist may inform the Council about the possible reason for the action/inaction of the authorities against him, that is, if it is a reprisal measure taken by the authorities due to critical writings or as a result of the policy that may affect the freedom of the press (supporting documents with English translation if they are in a language other than Hindi should be filed). Declaration regarding the non-pendency of the subject matter of the complaint in any court of law is also necessary.

On being prima facie satisfied of the admissibility of a complaint, the response of the authorities is called for and inquiry conducted through the inquiry committee of the Council. When the Council upholds the complaint of the aggrieved newspaper/journalist, the Council directs the concerned government to take appropriate steps, to redress the grievance of the complainant or records in observations regarding the conduct of that authority vis-à-vis the freedom of the press.[36]

12.8 Corporate laws

It is said in the context of India that with a legacy of the English legal system, India probably has the best corporate governance laws, but at the same time a poor implementation record.

Rajesh Chakraborty comments: "The enforcement of corporate laws remains the soft underbelly of the legal and corporate governance system."[37] World Bank's Reports on Observance of Standards and Codes (ROSC) found that while India observed most of the principles, it could do better in certain areas. The contribution of nominee directors from financial institutions to monitoring and supervising management is one such area.[38]

India inherited a truncated economy when it got freedom from the British yoke in 1947, but it had four functional stock markets with clearly defined rules governing, listing, trading and settlements, a well-to-do equity culture, even if it was for the urban rich, and a robust banking system with landing norms and recovery procedures.

The Industries Act, 1951 and the Companies Act of 1956, believe critics, paved the way for regimentation and license Raj, leading to corruption and nepotism. The economic liberalization of the 1990s brought about large-scale changes in laws and regulations. The establishment of SEBI in 1992 and its gradual empowerment has seen the implementation of regulations in place. It took only a few days for the government and the regulatory body to take control of Satyam computers, and within three months, the company had a new majority shareholding company through due process of law. Chapter 7 carries the case study of Satyam computers.

Corporate governance, as a concept, is not very old. Business is expected to be fair, but it is in the post Enron, WorldCom, and Satyam frauds that it has become a buzzword. The extent to which the 24-7 news channels have brought stories in the public domain was unknown until recently. People, in general, look at business distrustfully and businessmen not very kindly. Laws and ethics go hand in hand. It is when the law is lax or has certain loopholes that unscrupulous companies and businessman take advantage of it. Corporate organizations have been on the public radar for their acts of omission and commission. The following paragraphs are devoted in facilitating the students and practitioners of corporate communication about what they should know about corporate laws and governance.

It is important for a corporate communication practitioner to have a good understanding of the financial market, regulatory bodies, the statutory rules, and regulations relating to financial communication, etc. Since these have been included in Chapter 7, they will not be repeated here. Readers are advised to go through the relevant portions in Chapter 7 along with this chapter to gain a holistic understanding.

The Ministry of Corporate Affairs lays down rules and regulations relating to the corporate governance of companies. It is a must for corporate communication practitioners to be updated now and then to know the latest on the subject. The government of India's website has many useful postings and linkages, including the expectations from the companies for filing their annual accounts, penalty, and fines in case of non-compliance, role of auditing firms, list of fraudulent companies, how to register complaints, the "watch out investor" site supported by it for looking after the interests of shareholders and investors, and much more. In the following boxes are three reproductions on the code of corporate governance, Citizen's Charter, and investor watch site.

EXHIBIT 12.2 CORPORATE GOVERNANCE COUNTRY ASSESSMENT

Reports on the observance of standards and codes - Corporate governance country assessment India

"Corporate governance assessments are prepared within the framework of the joint World Bank/IMF Reports on the Observance of Standards and Codes (ROSC). This initiative is an important element of the response of the international community to the financial crises of the late 1990s, which has emphasized the role of international standards—such as the *OECD Principles of Corporate Governance*—in strengthening the international financial architecture. The ROSC corporate governance assessment covers corporate governance issues as they apply to listed firms. They assess the formal institutional framework underlying corporate governance of a country and the prevailing practices and enforcement against an internationally recognized benchmark, the OECD principles. While publication of the country ROSC is voluntary, ROSC assessments once approved are disseminated into the public arena through the ROSC website of the World Bank. The first *Report on the Observance of Standards and Codes (ROSC) Corporate Governance Assessment for India* was completed in July 2000. An update of the earlier ROSC on Corporate Governance for India was completed in June 2004 and has been published on the World Bank ROSC website."[39]

EXHIBIT 12.3 CITIZEN'S CHARTER

Citizen's charter

Our commitment

WE SHALL CARRY OUT OUR TASKS WITH
Integrity and Judiciousness
Courtesy and understanding,

Objectivity and Transparency
Promptness and Efficiency

Our expectations

We expect the corporate sector to be prompt and reasonable in fulfilling their duties and legal obligations and be true and honest in furnishing information to us.
OUR STANDARDS
WE SHALL

Acknowledge applications, returns and all communications within 7 days of their receipt.

Resolve expeditiously complaints regarding delay in issue of allotment letters & share/debenture certificates, refund of application money, delay in transfer of shares & non payment of dividends/interest on shares/debentures/fixed deposits etc. in close co-ordination with agencies.

Ensure that all applications submitted to the Ministry of Company Affairs, Regional Directors and Registrar of Companies, are processed within the time frame,

Be courteous, prompt, and effective & provide time bound services. All services shall be provided without charge or demanding any money other than remuneration prescribed by law.[40]

EXHIBIT 12.4 FOR INVESTORS

watchoutinvestors.com is a national web-based registry covering entities including companies, intermediaries and individuals who have been non-compliant of laws/guidelines and/or are no longer in the specified activity.

This information which was disorganized, difficult-to-use and was spread across a large number of sources i.e., websites, databases, publications, notifications and orders of the government and of other organizations, agencies, courts of law, tribunals and commissions, has now been aggregated, indexed, standardized, reformatted and re-presented on this website in a form and manner that can be accessed in a user-friendly manner.

Investors can use this information about entities/individuals before making any new investments with them for continuously reviewing their existing portfolio vis-à-vis such entities (Mywatchout) when dealing with them in any manner.[41]

12.9 Acts relating to advertising

As corporate communication practitioners, in most cases, also oversee advertising function in many organizations, it is important that they know about various laws pertaining to the field. Here in a nutshell:

12.9.1 Public morals and public policy

Section 292 and 293 of the Indian Penal Code, 1860 prohibits the dissemination of any obscene matter. The Indian Post Office Act, 1898 imposes a similar prohibition on the transmission of obscene matters through the post. The Customs Act, 1962 allows the detention and seizure of any obscene matter sought to be imported to the country.

12.9.2 The Young Person's [Harmful Publications] Act, 1956

It prohibits the dissemination of publication deemed to be harmful to persons under the age of twenty years.

12.9.3 The Indecent Representation of Women [Prohibition] Act, 1986

The act prohibits the depiction of women in an indecent or derogatory manner in the mass media.

12.9.4 The Children Act, 1960

Prohibits the disclosure of the name and address and other particulars of any child involved in certain proceedings.

12.9.5 The Emblems and Names [Prevention of Improper Use] Act, 1950

Forbids the use by any private party of certain names and emblems that are official insignia.

12.9.6 The Prevention of Insults to the National Honor Act, 1971

The act forbids the bringing into contempt of the national flag or the Constitution of India in any manner.

12.9.7 The Indian Penal Code, 1860

It prohibits the publication of any matter connected with unauthorized lotteries, while the Indian Post Office Act, 1998, imposes a similar prohibition on the transmission by post of such matter.

12.9.8 The Drugs and Magic Remedies [Objectionable Advertisements] Act, 1954

It prohibits advertisements for products and services claiming to cure certain medical conditions.

12.9.9 The Indian Penal Code, 1869

The act prohibits the publication of appeals using national symbols for furthering the prospects of any candidate at an election.

12.9.10 The Prize Competition Act, 1978

It prohibits the publication of matter with unauthorized prize competitions, while the Prize Chits and Money Circulation Schemes [Banning] Act, 1978 imposes a similar prohibition in respect of chits and money circulation schemes.

The provisions of law imposing limitations on message/content in the media apply *mutatis mutandis* to advertising as well, with such modifications as the context may require.

12.10 Professional ethics

As said earlier in the chapter, a legal framework and a professional code of ethics govern every profession. A professional code of ethics works as a reference point for principles and helps as a navigator when in doubt about a certain practice. Despite being there for over a century, PR/CC professionals still are not sure about the crux of the profession, that is, what is that one thing on which the profession rests, and that is the reason that there is often confusion among practitioners about what is ethical and what is not. For instance, one word that defines the profession of journalism in the context of ethics is "objectivity." Can this be said for PR/CC, when the practitioners are required to create a certain imagery and have the "desired response" in view before initiating a program? An honest answer would be a no. Many feel "advocacy" is better suited to the profession of PR/CC, as in the case of the legal profession.

12.10.1 Defining ethics

Breit (2004) defines ethics as "the personal values which underpin the behavior and moral choices made by an individual in response to a specific situation. Prioritizing moral values for an organization and ensuring its behaviors are aligned with those values."

Gruing and Hunt (1984) posit that "ethics is concerned with free intentional organizational conduct that affects or has consequences for a public or publics."

In terms of application of ethics in day-to-day work, experts talk of the following ethical systems and principles:

12.10.1.1 Deontological/duty ethics

This posits that ethics is duty-based and rests on moral obligations regardless of consequences. This treats actions as right or wrong and is principle-based. What would it mean in practice? One aspect could be not to disseminate false information, come what may.

12.10.1.2 Teleological ethics

This posits that ends justify means and stresses end results than action. In the chapter on crises communication, we have discussed the case of "incubator atrocities," which may fit in this category but would be termed unethical by many.

12.10.2 What are various ethical questions facing the profession?

There are numbers of issues that concern the profession of corporate communication and PR. Some of these are the following:

12.10.2.1 People without professional qualifications practicing CC/PR

It is not uncommon, especially in countries where accreditation is not required to practice CC, to find nonprofessionals practicing the profession. In the US, now the debate is not accreditation, but licensing to practice. In the US, certification is a must if one were to practice PR/CC there, that is, a professional education, accreditation from a professional body, and agreeing to a code of ethical conduct and to be subject to penalties for violating that code.

The Public Relations Society of America (PRSA), in fact, has an Ethics Committee that offers consultation to those who seek advice.

In India, the once-vibrant PR society with various state chapters has lost its relevance over the years. The practitioners also do not have a formal forum where they could seek advice or, when PR/CC is criticized, where the PR body can take up the issue on behalf of the profession. Most PR associations have a certain stand on issues of professional concern, but these are not manifest at the association's level through placing them in the public domain. The redeeming thing, however, is that many PR/CC specific blogs have been taking up this issue from time to time.

12.10.2.2 Paying for editorial coverage

It is not uncommon to find instances of garnering publicity by paying for editorial space. It is a different matter that many media houses have facilitated the process on their own behalf. The case of MediaNet has been discussed in detail in Chapter 2: Media dynamics and strategies.

12.10.2.3 Ambush marketing

Ambush marketing happens when an organization represents itself as being associated with an event when it has no official, legal, or moral right to do so. The instances would include putting signage at events for money when it has no relevance to the event, sponsorship of individual team, ad time around broadcasting, major promotion coinciding with event, and giveaway outside the event when it is not even a sponsor.

12.11 Professional bodies in CC/PR

It is not uncommon to have more than one professional body representing a profession having many kinds of codes of conduct. Within media also, there are some bodies of journalists who have issued codes of ethics. Individual media houses may also have their own codes of self-regulation. As the news media is in the public glare all the time for what they write or broadcast, it is not uncommon that those who are affected bash media. With the social media platforms making their presence felt all over, and the bloggers, often being individuals who may or may not know the legal or ethical implications of their writing, they find themselves at the wrong side of the law, as discussed in the chapter.

For long in India, there was one professional PR body, viz., the Public Relations Society of India, with various state chapters, which represented practitioners working in the public sector, private sector, and government. Later PR practitioners working in the public sector floated their association, Public Sector PR Forum (PSPRF). The economic liberalization in the 1990s in India witnessed a huge spurt in the growth of public relations consultancies. The PRCAI (Public Relations Consultants Association of India) was set up in 2001, and, as per the information posted on its website, it "represents over 70% of the organized public relations activity in India." It is "recognized and affiliated to the ICCO—International Communication Consultants Organization. The mission of the PRCAI is to establish and propagate the standards of excellence and ethical conduct through its professional charter amongst professional consultancies."[42]

12.11.1 About ICCO

The International Communications Consultancy Organization (ICCO) represents many public relations consultancies across the world. It is the umbrella organization for more than 850 consultancies through their trade associations in 24 countries. ICCO's charter, known as the Stockholm Charter, has been reproduced as Annexure II.

12.11.2 Professional bodies in media

There are a few professional bodies in the media also. Various states also have professional associations of local journalists and press clubs. The code of conduct of the All-India Editor's Conference has been reproduced as Annexure III. The *Business Standard*, a financial newspaper, has put its code of conduct for its staffers on its website, which is reproduced in Annexure IV.

12.11.3 Corporate communication and professional code of ethics

Even though in the last two to three decades one has seen corporate communication designations replacing PR designations and corporate communication emerging as an academic discipline at university level, the world over the public relations associations have not changed their names from PR to corporate communication. Therefore, we shall discuss the PR code of ethics that is being followed by the corporate communication practitioners all over the world.

When we talk about ethics in a profession, what is generally at the back of our minds is the fear of lack of ethics or the confusion about what is ethical and what is not.

Ethics in any profession is governed by two factors:

- A code of professional ethics developed by a professional body.
- Conscience and grooming of a PR practitioner as a human being.

The code of ethics in public relations, originally known as the "Code of Athens," issued in 1965, has been adopted by the Public Relations Societies in various countries. The PR code is inspired by the Universal Declaration of Human Rights of Man adopted by the United Nations Organization (UNO) on December 10, 1948.

Some of the *highlights of the code of Athens* include:

The PR persons *must not* do the following:

- Subordinate truth to any other considerations.
- Disseminate information not factually correct.

- Lend assistance to any enterprise, which might harm the moral, honesty, and dignity of the human race.
- Use words to make receivers act irrationally.

The Code of Athens has been reproduced as Annexure I, at the end of the chapter.

12.11.4 Bloggers' code of ethics

Is it possible for bloggers to get together and follow certain norms of ethical standards? There are millions of bloggers, who are spread across all the continents, cutting across geographical, racial, social, political, economic, age, and gender divide. Many corporate organizations also blog to network with communities. President Obama is said to reach out to youngsters on many social networking sites. The Information Technology Act, as referred elsewhere in the chapter, has clearly made bloggers responsible for their content, since they could be sued for defamation in case of infringement.

To reach out to a particular segment of stakeholders, corporate organizations are using social networking sites with their messages about their brands and services. Ogilvy PR has worked on a code of ethics, which probably is the first of its kind that may become the reference point for others to follow. Ogilvy's Code of Ethics for Blogger Outreach may be referred to in Annexure V.

12.11.5 Illustration

As most of corporate communication is achieved through various media, it is important that one understands their professional norms, and in case the corporate organizations feel affected by coverage, the norms could become a good reference point for resolving the issue. Let us illustrate with a hypothetical example. A media house has done a story clandestinely by, say, putting a spy camera and has recoded the interview without first informing the interviewee. If one were to refer to the journalistic norms of, say, the Press Council of India and the code of conduct of the professional bodies, we would know that this is in contravention to the professional code of ethics of these bodies. The matter can then be taken up with the concerned media house to resolve the issue, sue it for defamation, or go to the PCI, depending on the extent of perceived damage, the truth in the story, and the decision of the management, whether it would like to take on cudgels with the media. The following table quotes the relevant provisions from three separate codes of professional ethics to bring home the point.

EXHIBIT 12.5 COMPARATIVE ANALYSES OF PROFESSIONAL BODIES' STAND ON INVASION OF PRIVACY

"The Press shall not tape-record anyone's conversation without that person's knowledge or consent, except where the recording is necessary to protect the journalist in a legal action, or for other compelling good reason. The Press shall, prior to publication, delete offensive epithets used by a person whose statements are being reported. Intrusion through photography into moments of personal grief shall be avoided. However, photography of victims of accidents or natural calamity may be in larger public interest."

Source: NORMS OF JOURNALISTIC CONDUCT (Press Council of India)

*

"Any report found to be inaccurate and any comment on inaccurate reports shall be voluntarily rectified. It shall be obligatory to give fair publicity to a correlation of contradiction when a report published is shown to be false or inaccurate in material particulars."

Source: All-India Newspaper Editors' Conference: Code of Ethics.

*

"**Privacy:** Everyone is entitled to respect for his or her private and family life, home, health, and correspondence. Journalists of Business Standard will be expected to justify intrusions into any individual's private life without consent. Journalists of Business Standard should not use long lens photography to take pictures of people in private places without their consent."

Source: Business Standards' Code of Conduct for its staff (individual self-regulation)

There could also be instances when a particular media house feels that the professional body, of which it is a member, is being unfair to it, so it chooses to not abide by its decision. Here is one such case.

12.11.6 India TV alleges partisanship

India TV withdrew from its membership in the National Broadcasting Association (NBA) in April 2009. India TV, known for its typical style of reporting that at times is sensational and loud, was served with a notice and a fine of Rs. 1,00,000 from the National Broadcasting Association (NBA), a voluntary body of news broadcasters formed in October 2008. Former Supreme Court Chief Justice Late A N Verma headed the body at that time. The NBA was formed in October 2008, in the wake of concerns over media reporting of the Mumbai attacks, to create a self-regulatory mechanism and prevent any government intervention to control the electronic media in the form of a proposed Broadcasting Bill and Content Code.

In its first order, the NBA slapped a Rs.1-lakh fine on India TV for violating the "principles of self-regulation and specific guidelines" in handling the story based allegedly on an interview with Farhana Ali, a US-based writer, lecturer, and policy analyst. The NBA Standards Dispute Redressal Authority ordered that India TV pay the fine within a month and run an apology as a ticker on any one day between 8 p.m. and 9 p.m., five times, with a space of 12 minutes each, stating that Farhana's story was a "misrepresentation of facts."

The bone of contention was the allegation of Farhana Ali, who alleged that India TV had misused an interview she had given to Reuters news agency, by "deceptively dubbing" it in Hindi, a language she does not know or speak. She charged that this act was "factually incorrect, unethical and unjustified," a statement issued by the NBA said. The channel had run the said interview as part of its coverage of the 26/11 Mumbai attacks.

Alleging bias, India TV news channel withdrew from the News Broadcasters Association to protest the self-regulatory body's decision to slap a fine of Rs.100,000 on the channel for allegedly airing a fake interview with a US-based analyst of Pakistani origin in April 2009. India TV also protested the "partisan functioning of the NBA" and blamed its decision on the alleged machinations of the rival India Today Group. In its letter to the NBA president, India TV said, "We are compelled to notify our withdrawal from the membership of the NBA. This communication may also be kindly treated as a notice for withdrawal from the membership of the NBA with immediate effect."

In another letter to News Broadcasting Standards Disputes Redressal Authority, India TV contended that Farhana Ali has already "accepted and appreciated" an on-air apology run by the channel. "In fact, as a measure of her satisfaction with our sincerity, the complainant has gone on to voluntarily offer a live appearance on issues of her expertise," the letter said. Maintaining that the channel had followed "due diligence" in addressing Ali's grievances, India TV also argued that the NBA had not taken into consideration Farhana's letter before passing the order on 6 April 2009.

India TV argued that it telecast the wire copy in a short two-minute story after midnight, as what she said was important enough to be carried in the context of the Mumbai attacks. In the interview, Ali had said that there were more terrorists involved in the Mumbai mayhem. India TV, however, admitted that Ali's utterances were para-dubbed in Hindi.[43] Interestingly, after a few years, not only India TV was back as a member of NBA but Rajat Sharma held the position of president of NBA on more than one occasion.[44]

Summary

Discussing legal and ethical implications for a profession that is communication-based is challenging, if not impossible. Various laws concerning the profession of corporate communication, like the law of defamation, invasion of privacy, and the Copyright Acts were discussed with case studies and issues that need addressing.

It is important for a corporate communication practitioner to be aware of the corporate governance rules and regulations and the functioning of the financial market.

The question of ethics is always subjective. The chapter, on the issue, began with a debate on what is ethics, what are the issues facing the profession, and various codes of ethics, both by professional bodies in CC and media.

The right to information has empowered the common man and media to access information from government closets and public sector organizations and banks that hitherto were not possible. What are the implications of the act for those who represent the government and public-funded organizations was discussed, giving highlights of the act and a case study.

The chapter ended with a case study of popular Hindi news channel India TV, which withdrew its membership when the professional association of which it was member slammed it with a penalty.

Key terms

Copyright: refers to the exclusive right for life of the creator of an original work and 50 years beyond for those who own the copyright to publish, print, or reproduce an original literary, musical, or artistic work for a certain number of years.

Defamation: defamation is defined as a wrong done by one person to another's reputation by words, signs, or visible representation.

Digital piracy: refers to copying, duplicating, and distributing films on CDs/DVDs illegally.

Invasion of privacy: generally said in the context of media's intrusion in the private lives of people. The constitution of India treats it as a fundamental right that is implicit in the right to life and liberty to the citizens of this country by Article 21.

Libel: any false statement printed about a person which may lead to hatred and contempt or inflicts mental torture or has an adverse impact on his occupation or business.

Slander: a false statement about a person, which is verbal or spoken, unlike libel which is printed or broadcast. It can occur in a broadcast, in a speech, or in an informal conversation.

Concept review questions

Q.1. Define the law of defamation and its two kinds.

Q.2. What is the law concerning invasion of privacy? Discuss with some cases in point.

Q.3. What are the issues relating to violation of copyright? Discuss.

Q.4. "Right to Information has reduced the power of the government." Discuss the statement in the context of its role and scope.

Q.5. "Laws and ethics are the two sides of the same coin." Argue for or against it.

Critical thinking exercise

Follow any current defamation case through media coverage to understand the perspectives of the person who is alleged to have made a defamatory statement and the charges against him/her and the court's judgment on that. Critically analyze it, keeping in view the provisions of the act.

Case study

The Delhi Development Authority (DDA) and RTI

The department of corporate communication/public relations plays a dominant role in the implementation of RTI in the central government organization Delhi Development Authority since the implementation of the act in 2005.

About DDA

Set up over five decades ago, the Delhi Development Authority has come a long way. The company is responsible for more than 1 million dwelling units by way of constructing flats and allotting land to cooperative societies, developing more than 600 commercial centers, 22 industrial estates, and out of acquisition of land of approximately 67 thousand acres.

Being in an area that is supply-driven, there are thousands of people whose expectations are belied, every time there is draw of houses and they can't not make it. The huge gap between demand and supply of houses, inevitably, has brought in the role of the middlemen and touts who, in sync with some unscrupulous elements within and outside the DDA, hoodwink gullible people. The DDA has been on the public opinion and media radar constantly.

The organization has a large public interaction where people come for various transactions with various issues. The issues involved are diverse and vast because these involve property transactions, which encompass allotment or transfers of property, registrations, conversion from lease hold to free hold, delays, etc.

This vast public interface in DDA can be gauged from the fact that about 600 people visit the DDA office almost daily, and this number doubles on public hearing days when the public can meet DDA officers directly without appointments, that is, once in a week.

The RTI was implemented in DDA on 13 October 2005, exactly after 100 days of the enactment of the act in June 2005. A cell was created in the Public Relations Department under the sr. commissioner-cum-secretary with director (PR) as the assisting officer for ensuring the smooth implementation of the act.[45]

Responding under RTI meant putting the record of lakhs of properties in place that had accumulated over a period of half a century. It had its teething troubles with voluminous information with overlapping or contiguous responsibilities in DDA, intricate transaction procedures leading to difficulty in pinpointing the jurisdiction, and overlapping or multiplicity of authorities in the city of Delhi. Lack of computerization of records spread over more than 50 years made the retrieval of information difficult, if not impossible. A three-pronged model for receipt and disposal of RTI applications was used to facilitate fast disposal. Initially, the applicants were advised to apply on a format wherein, for easy identification of information, source of information, details like type of property, type of ownership was asked from the applicants. Requesting information from the applicant was objected to by CIC. The form was subsequently made optional, and it was decided to accept application on a plain paper or generated electronically as per the norms laid in the act. The issue of having one CPIO or separate PIO for various departments was also discussed, and, considering the huge organization and the number of transactions and records, it was decided that all the directors from various departments be appointed as PIO and heads of department as appellate authority. The Public Relations Department provided guidelines to all PIOs. The list of PIOs with all details has been made available to the public free of cost. It was decided that a single window system would be adopted for receipt of applications, and separate counters were opened at Vikas Sadan, Vikas Minar, Khel Gaon, Rohini, and Vasant Kunj, etc. for the convenience of the public. Under the single-window system, a person is aided with filling out the form or framing the application, and the fee is accepted at the counter after helping in identifying the right PIO, as per the information required by the applicant.

The performance of the RTI in DDA during the first year and subsequently, according to DDA sources, has been quite satisfactory. In fact, after the completion of a year, CIC invited DDA, the only public sector organization to make a presentation at Vigyan Bhawan to an invited audience to know about the implementation of RTI in a public-funded organization.

The DDA has received 33,109 numbers of applications until 31 December 2008, of which 32,604 have been disposed of, which is a record of sorts.

Questions on case study

The RTI is applicable only to the government departments and public-funded organizations. The case study of DDA reflects that thousands of cases have been disposed of in a matter of short time. Do you think the scope of RTI should be extended to encompass the entire corporate and NGO sector to make RTI more worthwhile? Discuss with arguments for or against it.

Practical work

Track the media for a few days, including the Web, to find out about people's experiences with DDA in the disposal of their grievances.

Annexure I

Professional code of ethics for PR/corporate communication practitioners

The Code of Athens

Adopted in 1965 and amended in 1968, the Code of Athens enjoins public relations practitioners worldwide to respect the Charter of the United Nations and the moral principles of the Universal Declaration of Human Rights. The code of Athens is based on the United Nations "Universal Declaration of Human Rights" and was and has, over the years, been translated into many languages.

CONSIDERING that all Member countries of the United Nations Organization have agreed to abide by its Charter which reaffirms "its faith in fundamental human rights, in the dignity and worth of the human person" and that having regard to the very nature of the profession, Public Relations practitioners in these countries should undertake to ascertain and observe the principles set out in this Charter:

CONSIDERING that, apart from "rights", human beings have not only physical or material needs but also intellectual, moral and social needs, and that their rights are of real benefit to them only insofar as these needs are essentially met;

CONSIDERING that, in the course of their professional duties and depending on how these duties are performed, Public Relations practitioners can substantially help to meet these intellectual, moral and social needs;

And lastly, CONSIDERING that the use of the techniques enabling them to come simultaneously into contact with millions of people gives Public Relations practitioners a power that has to be restrained by the observance of a strict moral code.

On all these grounds, all members of the International Public Relations Association agree to abide by this International Code of Ethics, and that if, in the light of evidence submitted to the Council, a member should be found to have infringed this Code in the course of his/her professional duties, he/she will be deemed to be guilty of serious misconduct calling for an appropriate penalty.

Accordingly, each member:

Shall endeavour

1. To contribute to the achievement of the moral and cultural conditions enabling human beings to reach their full stature and enjoy the indefeasible rights to which they are entitled under the "Universal declaration of Human Rights";
2. To establish communications patterns and channels which, by fostering the free flow of essential information, will make each member of the group feel that he/she is being kept informed, and also give him/her an awareness of his/her own personal involvement and responsibility, and of his/her solidarity with other members;
3. To conduct himself/herself always and in all circumstances in such a manner as to deserve and secure the confidence of those with whom he/she comes into contact;
4. To bear in mind that, because of the relationship between his/her profession and the public, his/her conduct—even in private—will have an impact on the way in which the profession as a whole is appraised;

Shall undertake

1. To observe in his/her professional duties, the moral principles and rules of the "Universal Declaration of Human Rights";
2. To pay due regard to, and uphold human dignity and to recognize the right of each individual to judge for himself/herself;
3. To establish the moral, psychological and intellectual conditions for dialogue in its true sense, and to recognize the rights of these parties involved to state their case and express their views;
4. To act, in all circumstances, in such a manner as to take account of the respective interests of the parties involved; both the interests of the organization which he/she serves and the interests of the publics concerned;
5. To carry out his/her undertakings and commitments which shall always be so worded as to avoid any misunderstanding, and to show loyalty and integrity in all circumstances so as to keep the confidence or his/her clients or employers, past or present, and all of the publics that are affected by his/her actions;

Shall refrain from

1. Subordinating the truth to other requirements;
2. Circulating information which is not based on established and ascertainable facts;
3. Taking part in any venture or undertaking which is unethical or dishonest or capable of impairing human dignity or integrity;

13. Using any "manipulative" methods or techniques designed to create subconscious motivations which the individual cannot control of his/her own free will and so cannot be held accountable for the action taken on them.

*

Annexure II

ICCOs code of conduct for members

Stockholm charter

All trade associations affiliated to ICCO and their member agencies have agreed to conform to the Stockholm Charter. This document was adopted in 2003 and replaced the Rome Charter, originally adopted by ICCO in 1986. The Stockholm Charter lays out a code of professional standards:

1. **Objective counsel and advocacy**
   PR consultancies may not have interests that might compromise their role as independent consultants. They should approach their clients with objectivity in order to help the client adopt the optimum communications strategy and behavior.
2. **Society**
   In an open society, freedom of speech and a free press create the context for the profession of PR. Consultants operates within the scope of this open society. They comply with its rules and they work with clients that share the same approach.
3. **Confidentiality**
   Trust is at the heart of the relationship between a client and a PR consultancy. Information that has been provided in confidence by a client and that is not publicly known should not be shared with other parties without the consent of the client.
4. **Integrity of information**
   PR consultancies should not knowingly mislead an audience about factual information or about the interests a client represents. Consultancies must make their best efforts to strive for accuracy.
5. **Delivering promises**
   Consultancies must work with clients to establish clear expectations in advance about the output of their efforts. They must define specific goals and then work to deliver on their promises. Consultancies must not offer guarantees which are not supportable or which compromise the integrity of the channels of communication.

6. **Conflicts**
   Consultancies may represent clients with conflicting interests. Work may not start for a conflicting interest without the current client first being offered the opportunity to exercise the rights under any contract between them and the consultancy.
7. **Representation**
   Consultancies may refuse or accept an assignment based on the personal opinions of the firm's management or the organization's focus.
8. **Governance and Business Practices**
   Public relations consultancies are committed to ethical behavior and implementation of best business practices in dealing with all audiences.[46]

Annexure III

All-India newspaper editors' conference: code of ethics

Code of Ethics of the All-India Newspaper Editors' Conference

1. As the press is a primary instrument in the creation of public opinion, journalists should regard their calling as a trust and be eager to serve and guard their public interests.
2. In the discharge of their duties, journalists should attach due value to fundamental, human and social rights and shall hold good faith and fair play in news reports and comments as essential professional obligations.
3. Journalists should observe special restraint in reports and comments dealing with tensions, likely to lead, or leading to civil disorder.

   a. Journalists shall particularly observe maximum restraint in publishing reports and comments relating to communal tension, incidents, riots, incipient situations likely to lead to communal disturbances. The identification of communities which may lead to chain reactions should be avoided.
   b. Journalists should endeavour at an rimes to promote the unity of the country and nation, pride in the country, its people, its achievements and its strength in diversity. Journalists should be most circumspect in dealing with movements and ideas which promote regionalism at the cost of national unity.
   c. Any reportage on ideas of fresh partition and secessionism must be treated with the greatest caution. Any comment likely to give comfort to the proponents of such ideas and further their interests should be avoided. The integrity of the country and of Indian peoples must be considered sacrosanct and beyond question.

4. Journalists should endeavour to ensure that information disseminated is factually accurate. No fact shall be distorted or the essential facts deliberately omitted. No information known to be false shall be published.
5. Responsibility shall be assumed for all information and comments published. If responsibility is disclaimed, this will be explicitly stated.

6. Confidences shall always be respected. Professional secrecy must be preserved.
7. Any report found to be inaccurate and any comment on inaccurate reports shall be voluntarily rectified. It shall be obligatory to give fair publicity to a correlation of contradiction when a report published is shown to be false or inaccurate in material particulars.
8. Journalists shall not exploit their status for non-journalistic purposes.
9. Journalists shall not allow personal interest to influence professional conduct.
10. There is nothing so unworthy as the acceptance or demand of a bribe or inducement for the exercise by a journalist of his power to give or deny publicity to news or comments.
11. Freedom in the honest collection and publication of news and facts and the rights of their comments and criticism and principles which every journalist should always defend.
12. Journalists shall be very conscious of their obligation to their fellows in the profession and shall not seek to deprive fellow-journalists of their livelihood by unfair means.
13. The carrying on of personal controversies in the press in which no public interest is involved shall be regarded as de-rogatory to the dignity of the profession.
14. It is unprofessional to give currency to rumours or loose talk affecting the private life of individuals. Even verifiable news affecting the private life of individuals shall not be published unless the public interest as distinguished from public curiosity demands its publication.
15. The Press shall refrain from publishing matters likely to encourage vice and crime.
    www.newswatch.in/print/344

Annexure IV

The business standards' code of conduct for its staff

All journalists of Business Standard have a duty to maintain the highest professional and ethical standards and the following code sets the benchmarks. It protects both the rights of the individual and upholds the public's right to know.

The Code sets standards designed to ensure the impartiality and independence of Business Standard. Employees are requested to keep it in safe custody and abide by it.

Correctness

Journalists of Business Standard should avoid any action, which, if it became publicly known, would jeopardize the newspapers reputation. If you would be embarrassed by public disclosure of something you are thinking of doing, don't do it. If you have done it tell your senior editor or the Editor. If you are uncertain whether something is ethical, discuss it with your senior editor or the Editor.

Gifts and favors

Journalists should not accept gifts, loans, holidays, discounts or other considerations, which could compromise them or the newspaper. Journalists may be given gifts (fruits, flowers, sweets, lunch), which have no real significance. Gifts of any significant value, if accepted should be given away in a manner which benefits a charity or the less advantaged. But in general they should be declined. If in doubt, decline the gift or consult your senior editor or the Editor.

Journalists should not seek or accept favors from competent authorities such as out-of-turn allotment of accommodation or land at subsidized rates, or similar privileges like company shares through a preferential allotment.

Travel

Business Standard does not normally accept invitations from companies and other organizations in which they pay for the invited journalists travel and accommodation within India. Travel and accommodation for professional purposes within India will be at Business Standard's expense, subject to normal expenses rules and approval of the relevant senior editor. Exceptions to this rule will be at the discretion of the Editor.

Business standard will sometimes allow companies or other organizations to pay for journalists to go abroad, at the Editors discretion. However, the invitation must go to Business Standard, not to the individual journalist. It will be the Editors decision to assign a journalist to take a sponsored trip abroad.

Accuracy

All journalists must take care not to publish inaccurate, misleading or distorted material including pictures.

Whenever it is recognized that a significant inaccuracy, misleading statement or distorted report has been published, it must be corrected promptly and with due prominence.

An apology must be published whenever appropriate. All Business Standard journalists must distinguish clearly between comment, conjecture and fact.

They must report fairly and accurately the outcome of an action for defamation to which the newspaper or they have been a party.

All Business Standard journalists must take extra care while reporting court proceedings and orders. Reportage of court proceedings and orders must be based on certified documents released by the court or the advocates concerned. Press releases issued by companies on a court order or proceedings should not be relied upon. Consult a senior editor at every stage of reporting court proceedings and orders.

Questions which are sensitive and which by implication level unsubstantiated charges against companies and individuals should not be sent by fax, unless the recipient has agreed to receive such questions by fax. Letters to companies and individuals, aimed at seeking comments and eliciting information, must be written with care and responsibility

While reporting, journalists of Business Standard must always correctly mention the source of their information and indicate if the source is a press release, seminar, press conference or a statement by a company or an individual. No report should be attributed to "sources". It is always better to identify the nature of the source (e.g. Company sources or government sources). Avoid attributing a report to informed or reliable sources. If you have contacted a company, individual or a government official and are using their comments in your report, you must make it clear that the comments were made in response to questions from Business Standard.

Allegations against actions of public servants (government officials) in the performance of their duties should be doubly checked before used in a report.

Suppression of facts under pressure is dereliction of duty. But statements and facts received on a non-attributable basis must not be attributed. While the right to protect the source should be exercised to the full limit of the law anonymity should not be allowed to become an instrument for the source to dish out falsehood. Journalists, therefore, should be cautious about sources, which mislead under the garb of anonymity.

Opportunity to reply

A fair opportunity to reply to inaccuracies must be given to individuals or organizations when reasonably called for.

Privacy

Everyone is entitled to respect for his or her private and family life, home, health and correspondence. Journalists of Business Standard will be expected to justify intrusions into any individual's private life without consent.

Journalists of Business Standard should not use long lens photography to take pictures of people in private places without their consent.

Harassment

Journalists of Business Standard must not obtain or seek to obtain information or pictures through intimidation, harassment or persistent pursuit.

Listening devices

Journalist of Business Standard must not obtain or publish material obtained by using clandestine devices or by intercepting private telephone conversations.

Institutions

While making enquiries at offices, hospitals or similar institutions, journalists of Business Standard must identify themselves to a responsible executive and obtain permission before entering non-public areas.

Reporting of crime

Journalist of Business Standard must avoid identifying relatives or persons convicted or accused of crime without their consent. Particular regard should be paid to the potentially vulnerable position of children who are witnesses to or victims of crime. This should not be interpreted by journalists as restricting the right to report judicial proceedings.

Misrepresentation

Journalists of Business Standard must not generally obtain or seek to obtain information or pictures through misrepresentation or subterfuge.

Documents or photographs should be removed only with the consent of the owner. Subterfuge can be justified only in the public interest and only when material cannot be obtained by any other means

Use of content and data

Journalists of Business Standard will always explicitly acknowledge in their reports the source of data, text, images, graphics or information, when they are borrowed from print publications, websites and television channels

Before using the Internet for sourcing ideas and information, all journalists are duty-bound to check whether the material being used by them is copyrighted and explicit permission must be sought. Wherever it is difficult to establish the ownership of the idea, data or image, you must explicitly indicate the source of information.

Published information and data, if used in reports, must be sourced, even when the source may be a rival publication

Investment disclosure

Journalists of Business Standard should disclose their investments to the Editor, and update the record when there are significant changes. The information will be kept in confidence by the Editor.

Even where the law does not prohibit it, journalists of Business Standard must not use for their own profit financial information they receive in advance of its general publication, nor should they pass such information to others. They should not discuss an article planned by Business Standard with people who could benefit or suffer from its publication.

They must not write about companies, shares, securities or other investments in whose performance they know that they or their close families have a significant financial interest, without disclosing the interest to the Editor. Whether or not disclosure of investments has been made, it is each journalist's responsibility to reveal any possible conflict of interest-financial or otherwise-as it arises.

They must not buy or sell, either directly or through nominees or agents, shares, securities or other investments about which they have written recently or about which they intend to write in the near future. They should not make recommendations in the newspaper about investments in which they personally have an interest.

Confidential sources

Journalists have a moral obligation to protect confidential sources of information. But this obligation is not superseded by their obligation to the organisation/the Editor/or anyone officiating as their supervisor to disclose the source in support of the authenticity of a story. The the/the Editor/or anyone officiating as their supervisor is in turn obliged to protect such confidential sources, divulged by the journalists under such circumstances.

Payment for articles

Journalists of Business Standard are prohibited from making any payment, directly or through agents, to anybody for obtaining any information.

Discrimination

Journalists of Business Standard must avoid prejudicial or pejorative reference to a person's race, color, religion, sex or sexual orientation or to any physical or mental illness or disability.

They must avoid publishing details of a person's race, color, religion, sexual orientation, physical or mental illness or disability unless these are directly relevant to the story/report.

What is public interest?

The public interest includes: Detecting or exposing crime or a serious misdemeanor; Protecting public health and safety; Preventing the public from being misled by some statement or action of an individual organization.

Journalists of Business Standard should be prepared to give a full explanation to the Editor whenever required to demonstrate how a certain action was needed to serve the public interest.

There is a public interest in freedom of expression itself.

www.business-standard.com/india/common/codeofconduct.php

Annexure V

Ogilvy's code of ethics for blogger outreach

- We reach out to bloggers because we respect your influence and feel that we might have something that is "remarkable" which could be of interest to you and/or your audience.
- We will only propose blogger outreach as a tactic if it complements our overall strategy. We will not recommend it as a panacea for every social media campaign.
- We will always be transparent and clearly disclose who we are and who we work for in our outreach email.
- Before we email you, we will check out your blog's about, Contact and Advertising page in an effort to see if you have blatantly said you would not like to be contacted by PR/Marketing companies. If so, we'll leave you alone.
- If you tell us there is a specific way you want to be reached, we'll adhere to those guidelines.
- We won't pretend to have read your blog if we haven't.
- In our email we will convey why we think you, in particular, might be interested in our client's product, issue, event or message.
- We won't leave you hanging. If your contact at Ogilvy PR is going out of town or will be unreachable, we will provide you with an alternate point of contact.
- We encourage you to disclose our relationship with you to your readers, and will never ask you to do otherwise.
- You are entitled to blog on information or products we give you in any way you see fit. (Yes, you can even say you hate it.)
- If you don't want to hear from us again, we will place you on our Do Not Contact list—which we will share with the rest of the Ogilvy PR agency.
- If you are initially interested in the campaign, but don't respond to one of our e-mails, we will follow up with you no more than once. If you don't respond to us at all, we'll leave you alone.
- Our initial outreach e-mail will always include a link to Ogilvy PR's Blog Outreach Code of Ethics.

- We won't pretend to have read your blog if we haven't.
- In our e-mail we will convey why we think you, in particular, might be interested in our client's product, issue, event or message.
- We won't leave you hanging. If your contact at Ogilvy PR is going out of town or will be unreachable, we will provide you with an alternate point of contact.
- We encourage you to disclose our relationship with you to your readers, and will never ask you to do otherwise.
- You are entitled to blog on information or products we give you in any way you see fit. (Yes, you can even say you hate it.)
- If you don't want to hear from us again, we will place you on our Do Not Contact list—which we will share with the rest of the Ogilvy PR agency.
- If you are initially interested in the campaign, but don't respond to one of our e-mails, we will follow up with you no more than once. If you don't respond to us at all, we'll leave you alone.
- Our initial outreach e-mail will always include a link to Ogilvy PR's Blog Outreach Code of Ethics.
- While you don't need to use your name in commenting, please identify yourself as a blogger and/or as an agency representative. Also, feel free to repost the current draft of the Code of Ethics on your own blog and solicit feedback from your readers (just give us a link back so we can follow the conversation too!).[47]

*

Notes

1 www.expertlaw.com/library/personal_injury/defamation.html.
2 www.guardian.co.uk/uk/2008/dec/13/law-press-and-publishing-elton-john-libel-guardian.
3 Ibid.
4 The Times of India, 23 February 2009.
5 The Times of India, 26 February 2009.
6 Apar Gupta, "Bloggers and the Law: Five Points to Keep in Mind", 25 March 2012, internet democracy.in.
7 www.mediawatchindia.in.
8 ANI, 15 April 2009.
9 ANI, 13 April 2009, www.thaindian.com.
10 "Rahul Convicted in Defamation Case, Congress Scrambles to Keep Him in House", Ahmedabad News, *The Indian Express*.
11 "What Are the Laws under Which Rahul Gandhi Has Been Disqualified?", Explained News, *The Indian Express*.
12 Friday, 31 October 2008, www.nerve.in/news:253500177192.
13 Press Trust of India, 21 January 2008.
14 Philip Henslone, *Public Relations—A Practical Guide to Basics*, 2003, second edition (New Delhi: Kogan Page), pp. 15–16.
15 Clarence Jones, "Winning with the News Media", www.winning.newsmedia.com
16 The Deccan Herald, 29 July 2008.
17 www.floridabar.com.
18 www.reuters.com.
19 Ibid.
20 The Deccan Herald, 29 July 2008.
21 The Times of India, 20 October 2008.
22 www.mondaq.com/india/copyright/750676/copyright-societies-and-the-copyright-amendment-act-2012#:~:text=The%20Copyright%20(Amendment)%20Act%2C%202012%20(2012%20Amendment),in%20cinematography%20and%20audio%20recordings.
23 The Times of India, 27 April 2009.
24 www.iipa.com.
25 https://copyright.gov.in/Documents/Notification/Copyright_Amendment_2012.pdf.
26 www.meity.gov.in/content/information-technology-act-2000-0.
27 https://m.economictimes.com/news/economy/policy/event-organisers-to-pay-royalty-to-use-copyrighted-songs/articleshow/56314037.cms.
28 https://thewire.in/law/central-rti-law-to-now-apply-to-jk-and-ladakh.
29 *Source*: www.righttoinformatio.gov.in.
30 www.ndtv.com/rti.
31 www.expressindia.com/initiatives/rti.
32 www.thehoot.org.
33 The Times of India, 2 May 2009.
34 https://cic.gov.in/who-are-we.
35 https://economictimes.indiatimes.com/news/india/central-information-commission-halves-pendency-of-cases-in-last-three-years-shows-data/articleshow/99962289.cms?from=mdr.
36 Detailed PCI' journalists norm may be accessed at https://presscouncil.nic.in.
37 unpn1.un.org/intradoc.
38 Ibid.
39 www.mca.gov.in.
40 www.mca.gov.in/MinistryWebsite/dca/citizencharter/citizencharter.html.
41 www.watchoutinvestors.com/default2a.asp.
42 Website: www.prcai.org.
43 http://blog.taragana.com.
44 "India TV Chairman Rajat Sharma Re-elected NBA President", *India News—India TV*, indiatv news.com.
45 Based on interview of the author with Ms Neemo Dhar, Director (PR) on 28 April 2009.
46 www.iccopr.com/content/view/126/84/.
47 http://blog.ogilvypr.com/2007/09/creating-a-blogger-outreach-code-of-ethics-take-1/.

INDEX

15th All India Public Relations Conference (1993) 9

Aaj Tak 119, 284
Accenture 101
active consumer 163
acts pertaining to equivalency 32, 39, 152
ad value 181; of corporate communication 31
advertising 2, 9–11, 19, 22, 27, 32–35, 39–40, 61–62, 65–67, 69–78, 80–81, 85–86, 90, 121, 123, 125, 152, 161–164, 170, 172, 176, 180, 182, 205, 213, 222–224, 227, 232, 236, 237, 264, 290, 300, 305–306, 334, 336, 356
Advertising Age Journal 162–163
agenda-setting theory 290
Aha moment 84
AIG Vyas 239
Air India Ltd 63, 72
Aiyer, Mani Shankar 211
Amar Ujala
Ambani, Anil 16
Ambani, Mukesh 16–17, 82
Ambani, Nita 16
ambush marketing 337
American Revolution 3
Amnesty International 127
announcement release 141, 159
Annual Economic Survey 305
annual general meeting 133, 232, 252
annual report 133, 206, 227, 231, 233
Arthur W. Page Society 285
Ashoka 3
Asian Paints 63
Associated Chambers of Commerce and Industry of India (ASSOCHAM) 112, 113–114, 196, 201–202
attitude change theory 89
audit, communication 299; definition of 299; objectives of 301; schedule of 300; uses of 300; value of 301
Audit Bureau of Circulation 23, 306

bad news release 227
Bahujan Samaj Party (BSP) 119
Bajaj Allianz 237
Balakrishnan, K.G. 48, 75, 318, 323
balanced funds 218
Barbour, Griffith and Rogers (BGR), lobbying firm 120
behaviour change communication (BCC) approach 309–310
behaviour change theory 89, 101
Bernays, Edward 3, 5–6, 20; Proctor & Gamble (P&G) campaign for Ivory Soap 191, 249; Torches for Freedom March assignment for American Tobacco Company 5
Bharatiya Janata Party (BJP) 117, 126, 143, 273
Bharat Petroleum Corporation Limited (BPCL) 185
Bharti/Bharti Airtel 111
Bharti, Sunil 111
Bhat, Pooja 223
Birla, Kumar Mangalam 99, 252
blogger(s) 16, 42–43, 45, 47–48, 56–57, 138, 153, 164–165, 172, 227–229, 271–272, 278, 290, 304, 317, 319, 337, 339, 356–358; code of ethics 339; Indian judiciary action on 48
blog tracking 30, 290
Board for Industrial and Financial Reconstruction (BIFR) 110

Bolshevik Revolution (1917) 3
Bombay Stock Exchange (BSE) 208, 230
bonds 118, 208–210, 215, 218, 226, 234, 236, 238
Brainstorming/brainstorming sessions 12, 75, 83, 87, 92, 94, 103, 291
brand building communication 11
branded identity 64, 72
brand image insensitivity 71
Brand India Campaign 113
brand PR 65
brand promotion(s) 25, 77, 161, 173, 174, 176, 178–179, 181; active consumer 163; area of discord 169; buying and selling of consumers, changing styles of 164; case studies 165, 175, 178, 179; events 161–162, 165–166, 170–171, 173–179, 182–183; innovative strategies to reach customers, case studies 165; management 173; third-party endorsements, in media 31, 169, 264
BSNL 44
bulletin boards 98, 101
bureaucratese 89
business and government, the relationship between 108; society functions under legal frameworks and regulations 107
business process outsourcing (BPO) sector 165

CAC 40 Index of Paris 210
call money market 216
Canadian Investor Relations Institute (CIRI) 226, 241
capital market 39, 112, 159, 200, 204–206, 209, 211, 213–215, 217–218, 222–223, 226–227, 229, 232, 234–235, 253; definition of 209; financial instruments in 215; fraudulent practices and its impact on investors 211; market index 209; media analysis of 218; primary 205, 209, 232; secondary 209, 232; stock index 209
CARE 230
cell revolution 25
Central Bureau of Investigation (CBI) 245, 258–259
central public sector enterprises (CPSEs) 194
CEO survey 52
certificate of deposit 216
Chandra, Naresh 252
Chatterjee, Sumeet 255
Children Act 322
cinema 4, 15, 18, 25, 28, 89, 141
Citi Bank 100
Citigroup 33–34
Civil Disobedience Movement 3
civilian casualties 89
civil servant 121
Clinton, Bill 120, 248, 259, 316–317
closed-circuit television 95
close-ended mutual fund scheme 217
clubs 298, 321–322
cluster (area) group sampling 294
coalition politics 122, 131
Cobrapost 119, 135
commercial papers 216
commissioning, concept to 174
Committee on Public Undertakings (COPU) on disinvestments and privatization of the Indian; audit; channels; communication(s) 129; effectiveness in the United Kingdom, case study; parlance; public sector 115; strategies
community surveys 299, 307
Company Act: 1956 252, 332; 2013 184, 191, 194, 196, 198
company blogs 30
Confederation of Indian Industries (CII) 62, 113, 259
conferences 12, 34, 69, 103, 138, 147–148, 173, 193, 227–228
Congress (I) 75, 111, 113, 117, 119, 120, 126, 133, 171, 190, 259
Congress Party 131, 245, 273
consumer: communication; segmentation
consumer behaviour: definition of; external influences on; investing communities in India; the psyche of an average consumer; traditional brand *vs.* financial brand; type of investor emerged from the financial brand
consumer PR campaign: case studies; meaning of
convenience sampling 294
copyright 326; definition of 324; economic right 324; moral right 325; need to protect 325
Copyright Act 313–314, 327–328, 341–342; 1911 324; 1957 65, 324, 327; 2012 324, 326
corporate: agenda building 36, 104, 130, 290; brands 162; communalization 85; image 2, 11, 19, 62, 67–68, 72–73; news, the credibility of 142; or institutional advertising 69, 73, 77; philanthropy 101, 198, 199, 202; signature 61, 73
corporate communication: definition of 2; evolution of 3; expectation from media 154; functions of 1; interface with other management functions 85; and media, interdependence between 153; need for 13; placement within organization

10; practitioner 12; professional bodies engaged in 12; Watergate scandal, in the United States 7
corporate governance: definition of 251; globally discuss issue 252; in India, policy dialogue in 2006 253; laws 332; reasons for 252
corporate identity: benefits of 62; branded identity 63; and corporate image, the difference between 67; endorsed identity 73; intangible characteristics of 73; legal aspects of 64; monolithic 73; need to protect intellectual property right 65; program 61; tangible characteristics of 73
corporate reputation: aims of 63; definition of 45; elements of 67; engagement with web 53; good, impact on stakeholders 46
corporate reputation diagnostic services 49
corporate reputation management (CRM): case studies 56; imperatives of 61
corporate sector, in India: growth of 108; regulation of 252
corporate social responsibility (CSR): Bennet Coleman & Co. Ltd. 23, 40; Coca-Cola Rainwater Harvesting 170; definition of 185; employees involvement in 188; expenditure by top companies 191; genesis of 186; global practice of 190; Hindustan Unilever Limited (HUL) 289; ITC 198; McDonald 47, 51, 58–59, 66, 171; Microsoft 65, 97, 199, 259; National Thermal Power Corporation (NTPC) 142; neoliberal school 186; Oil and Natural Gas Corporation (ONGC) 66.198, 224; Reliance Industries Limited (RIL) 269; sponsorship of theatre 175; state-centred school 186; Tata Consultancy Services (TCS) 194, 198, 255; third-way school 187
Corporate Sustainability Report 84, 106; created event 141; press release 138, 140–141, 144–145, 147, 152–155, 158–160; rating agencies
COVID-19 24, 100, 163, 206, 213, 304, 305, 307
Creel, George 6
CRISIL 30, 230
crisis: classification of 244; definition of 244
crisis communication 11, 19, 129, 273, 283, 314; advisory role of 248; corporate communication 314; importance of 247; message action plan 248; principles of 245; sharing information 247; words and imagery for 248
crisis management disaster management perspective 163, 247; phases of crisis 244; post-crisis 244; pre-crisis 244
current mindset 124
Customs Act, 1962 335

Dalal, Sucheta 212, 222, 229–230
Das, Gurcharan 256, 264
dashboards 290, 302, 307
DAX index of Frankfurt 210
DD News 329
debentures 215–216, 234–236, 334
defamation: case study 319; definition of 314; libel 315; in passing off cases 322; slander 319; while awarding contracts and writing 322
Delhi Metro Rail Corporation (DMRC) 151
Delhi serial bomb blasts (13 September 2008), media coverage of subversive activities 275
Deora, Murli 263
Department of Corporate Affairs (DCA) 252
Department of Economic Affairs (DEA) 208
Department of Industrial Policy and Promotion (DIPP) 209
Department of Public Enterprises (DPE) 115, 193–194
Desai, Meghanand 245
desired mindset 125
desk research 304, 307–308; definition of 304; secondary data sources 288
Dev, Kapil 224
Dil Chahta Hai film 90
disaster: definition of 244; plan 245
disaster management, communication role in 246
Doordarshan India 329
Dow Jones Industrial Average 210
Dravid, Rahul 224
Drugs and Magic Remedies (Objectionable Advertisements) Act, 1954 335
Dutt, Barkha 45

eBay 164, 167
e-Choupal 201
economic liberalization in 1990 204
Economic Times 79–78, 84, 106, 142, 237, 242, 254–255, 260, 262–263, 275, 283–284
election campaigns 117, 126
electronic media 39, 85, 138, 139, 154, 159, 270, 274–277, 280, 282, 303–304, 324, 340
e-mail interviews 158
Emblems and Names (Prevention of Improper Use) Act, 1950 335
employee blogs 96, 101

employee communication 101–102, 104–105, 178–179, 274, 299–300; bulletin boards 291; case studies 102; closed-circuit/in-house television 95; definition of; employee involvement in CSR initiatives 99; genesis of 84; house journal 101; idea boxes 101; induction literature/information kiosks 101; internal communication 87; media used in 102; new age media 101, 227–228, 290; organizational cultures 88, 93; Tata Group pioneer in 85; theories impact on 89; visits of top management 98
employee-oriented magazines 87
English Copyright Act of 1911 324
equity mutual funds 235, 239
Ethical companies attract better talent 53
Ethical Reputation Index 47
ethics/ethical corporate communication and professional code of 345; definition of 336; principles of 336
Euronext of the European Stock Exchange 210
evaluation research 296
event(s) 5, 11, 13, 28, 54–55, 160, 161–162, 164, 170–171, 173, 174–178, 179, 182–183, 222, 236, 243, 246, 248, 298, 326–327, 356–358; created; definition of 173, 179; for employees 83–87, 99, 101; facility management 127, 139–140; management case studies 41, 165–166, 253–254, 266, 270, 320, 337; media press briefings 137–139, 141, 143, 282; press conference 147–148, 152, 158, 173; press tour 159; spontaneous or reactive 146; technology use in the digital age 41, 174–175
evolutionary egalitarianism 14
Exchange Traded Funds (ETFs) 219
exhibitions 12
external stakeholders 12, 102

Facebook 25, 38, 47, 270
Facebook Messenger 26
face-to-face communication 11, 87, 98, 103, 156, 228, 297; interview 295
facility management 175
feature writing '; definition of 146; and news writing, the difference between 146
Federation of Indian Chambers of Commerce and Industry (FICCI) 112, 266, 326
field reports 289
financial advertising 223
financial communication 204–205; awards for good 261; awareness about 201, 291, 297; definition of 205; target audience for 205
financial institutions in India 206; capital market 39, 49, 112, 159, 200, 204–206, 209, 211, 213–214, 217–218, 226–227, 229, 232, 234, 236; financial instruments 215, 222; Foreign Investment Promotion Board (FIPD) 208; National Stock Exchange (NSE) 208; Reserve Bank of India (RBI) 206–207; Securities and Exchange Board of India (SEBI) 207–208, 214, 221, 224–225, 230, 236, 241, 252, 254, 258, 332; working of Bombay Stock Exchange (BSE) 208
Financial Times 251
Financial Times Exchange Index (FTSE-100) of London 210
first generation entrepreneurs 111
Fitch Ratings India 230
flashbulb marketing 162
fly-by-night companies 215
focus group(s): interviews 84, 292, 295, 301, 310
Foreign Direct Investment (FDI) 9
Foreign Exchange Regulation Act (FERA) 109, 235
Foreign Investment Promotion Board (FIPD) 208
formative research 286, 292, 295, 300, 307, 309, 311–312
Fortune 500 companies 2, 11, 186, 257, 259
Frontline 91

Games Management System (GMS) 175
Gandhi, Indira 8, 85, 109, 112, 131, 316
Gandhi, Rajiv 109, 249
gatekeepers 289, 307
General Electric (GE) 5, 33–34, 80, 254
Ghajini film 90, 106
glasnost 4
Goldman Sachs 190
Google Alerts 47
government relations 11, 107–108, 112, 116, 127, 130, 131, 135; handle visits of COPU projects 129; identification of concerned Nodal Ministry and Officers 128; issues identification 123–124; management of, critical factors 129; preparation of a list of crucial elected representatives; to safeguard interests within sector 129; work on the contact programme 128
Government Securities (G-Secs) 214–215
Great Economic Depression of the 1930s 3
Greenpeace 47, 51–52
growth funds 217, 219
Grunig, James 89, 106, 245, 286, 302, 311
Guha, Atulan 135
guilt-free purchase 163

Guinness World Records 166
Gupta, Nandini Sen 123

Hang Seung of Hong Kong exchange 210
Harshad Mehta case 211
HDFC Bank 213
Headlines Today 280, 284
Hindustan 284
Hindustan Unilever Limited (HUL) 289
Hitler, Adolf 7
Holbrook, Richard 120
home pages 30, 52, 360
Home Trade scam (2002) 211
house journal(s) 85, 91, 93–95, 101, 300, 315
HSBC 100, 106, 172
Hurley, Elizabeth 317
Hussein, Saddam 126

ICICI Bank 243; victim of Lehman Brothers bankruptcy in 2008 and crisis management 264
ICICI Mutual Fund 240
idea boxes 87, 97, 101
Idea Cellular 79
image repair theory 53, 55
image surveys/studies 61; definition of 297; by Rotary International, case study 297
implementation scenario post-Companies Act, 2013 196
Indecent Representation of Women (Prohibition) Act, 1986 335
in-depth interviews 130
index funds 220–221
Indian Express 44, 72, 81, 122, 241, 245, 258–259, 275–276, 283–284, 329, 358
Indian Institute of Mass Communication (IIMC), New Delhi 9, 270
Indian Marketing and Research Bureau (IMRB) 306
Indian News & Feature Alliance (INFA) yearbook 305, 311
Indian Penal Code: 1860 314, 335; 1869 335
Indian Readership Survey (IRS) 307
India's Most Admired Companies (IMAC) research (2014) 11, 231
India Today 23, 41, 205, 249, 271, 341
India TV, withdrawal of membership from NBA 341, 358
India Year Book 305
Indo-US civilian nuclear deal 120
induction literature 101
Industrial Policy Resolution of 1956 110
Industrial Policy Statement of 1991 110
industrial securities 216
Industries Act, 1951 332
information kiosk 93–94, 101
Infosys 14, 65–66, 82, 87, 92, 96–97, 106, 111, 189, 194, 198, 231, 242, 254–256, 259–260, 262
in-house television 95
initial public offering (IPO) 209, 215, 222, 227, 230; case studies; Coal India 92; issue phase 222; National Thermal Power Corporation (NTPC) 142; ONGC-2004 IPO 66; post-issue phase 223; pre-issue phase 222
Instagram 25
instant connectivity 25, 29, 47, 72
Institute for Public Relations (IPR), United States 65
institutional advertising 69–70, 73, 77–78, 80, 86, 290
integrated marketing communication (IMC) 162
Intel 34
intellectual property right (IPR) 64–65; brand management, relevance in 65; definition of 65; need to protect 65; role and relevance in corporate communication 65
interactive media 227
Interconnected Stock Exchange of India Limited (ISE) 208
internal communication 274
Internal Emergency in India during 1975 9, 23, 122, 131
internal publics, segmentation of 274
internal stakeholders 2, 12, 82, 86, 91; conditions for effective working relationship with 12; importance of 83; segmentation of internal publics 91
International Advertising Bureau 172
International Communications Consultancy Organization (ICCO) 338
international mutual funds 220
internet 4, 19, 25, 27, 29–30, 37, 39, 47–48, 64, 96, 102, 135, 149, 159, 164, 167, 172, 227, 247, 274, 303–304, 318, 354, 358
interpersonal communication 12; media 12
interview: in-depth 130; by e-mail 158; face-to-face 156, 293–295, 301, 310; focus group 84, 292–293, 295, 301, 307, 310; one-on-one 157; telephonic 157
intranet 95, 96, 300, 301
inverted pyramid style 144, 159
investing communities, in India 226
investor relations (IR) 62, 205–206, 208, 225–226; case study 228; communication channels for effective 227; definition of 226; handling of 226
issue/advocacy advertising 61, 69, 71, 74, 76

Jaago Re campaign 74
Jain, N.K. 260, 283

Janata Party 131
Jefkins, Frank 68
Jet Airways 263, 273
John Steve 117
judgement sampling 294

K-10 gimmick 215
key trade press 11
Khan, Amir 76, 90, 167, 182
Khan, Jemina 317
Kingfisher 176, 263–264
Kirban, Lloyd 286
Kor/Ferry's Global Corporate Affairs Practice 52
KOSPI Index of South Korea 210
KPMG CSR Survey 2016 196
Kroll Report 251
Kumar, Sajjan 245

large-cap funds 218
Lee, Ivy Ledbetter 4, 6
Lehman bankruptcy 125
liaison offices 133
libel 315–318, 342; virtual 317
Life magazine 249
lobbying: definition of 118; in India history of 119; murky affair; and petitioning, the difference between; role of media 122; steps in 121; in Western countries 119
lobbyists 121–123, 131, 135
Lok Sabha 131, 236, 320
Ludlow Massacre 4, 20

magazines 19, 23, 28, 29, 33, 41–42, 44, 69–70, 83, 87, 92, 93, 96, 159, 204, 230, 271, 305
Mahatma Gandhi 3, 112, 113
mail analysis 289
management communication 10
market index 209, 219
Marketing and Research Group (MARG) 306
Maruti 67, 76–77, 176–177
mass media 12, 18, 27, 39, 44, 69, 86, 121, 136, 146, 176, 223, 290, 292, 302; aims of 35; laws 314, 335; publicizing events through 177; reach 30
Matrix film 26
McDonald's Tops Index of Unethical Companies 47
Media Gag Order 122
media handling, strategy for 154
media/mass media: assessment of skills required 282; characteristics of 27; and corporate communication 27; corporate literature 139; crime and emergency calls 137; disaster coverage by Indian media 280; endorsement techniques 30–31; existence of guidelines 281; future trends 40; global and country reports 139; internet and social networking sites 159; interviews by e-mail 158; lessons for corporate communication professionals 69; letters to the editor 139; and lobbying/public affairs 116; measurement practices 33; newspaper advertisements 139; NGO sector 138; one-on-one interviews 157; one-on-one press interfaces 157; parallel media 138; personal contacts 137; personal, survey of approach to government data 281; persons used as lobbyists 121; politicians 121; pre-scheduled public events 139; press conferences 146; primary sources of academia and experts 137; procedure to write effective press release 140; professional bodies in 338; rejection of press release, reasons for, 144; seamless media, challenges for, 282; secondary sources of annual reports 138; social institution 136; style considerations 143; telephonic interviews 157; tip-offs 137; tracking study on the Delhi serial bomb blast in 2008 137, 244, 275, 278; when facing journalists 157; wire services 138; writing for press releases, types of, 139
media measurement 31, 39; definition of 31
medianet 37, 39–40, 42–43, 153, 337
media relations management: and corporate communication expectation of media 153; media and corporate communication, the interdependence of 153
Michaelson, David 32
Microsoft 97, 199, 304
mid-cap funds 218
mindset: Current 125; desired 125
Ministry of Corporate Affairs, India 128, 191, 198, 202, 230, 252, 262, 333
Ministry of Information and Broadcasting 289
mneumonic, communication through 63
mobile telephones/telephony 25
money market mutual funds 216
monolithic corporate identity 63–64
Monopolies and Restrictive Trade Practices (MRTP) Act 109
Morgan Stanley 33–34, 46, 79, 171, 217
Morgan Stanley Capital International (MSCI) 210
Mumbai Inter-bank Bid Rates (MIBOR) 208
Murthy, N.R. Narayana 82, 252, 254
mutual funds (MFs): equity mutual funds 218; Exchange Traded Funds (ETFs) 219;

growth funds 219; index funds 220; in India, phases of, 221; international mutual funds 220; large-cap funds 218; mid-cap funds 218; money market mutual funds 220; no load mutual funds 219; operational classification 217, 218; portfolio funds 216; Regional Mutual Funds (RMFs) 220; Sector Mutual Funds (SMFs) 220; types of balanced funds 219; value funds 219

Naidu, Chandrababu 259
National Aeronautics and Space Administration (NASA) 109
National AIDS Control Organization (NACO) 309
National Board of Review (NBR) Award 166
National Broadcasting Association (NBA) 340
National Corporate Social Responsibility (NCSR) Hub 193
National Council of Applied Economic Research (NCAER) 306
National Disaster Management Authority in India 244
National Hydroelectric Power Corporation (NHPC) 129–130, 134
National Readership Survey (NRS) 307
National Stock Exchange (NSE) 200, 208
National Union of Cooperative India (NUCI) 116
Native Share and Stock Broker Association 208
natural disaster, measures to bridge the gap between government sources and media conduct 48, 248; managing perceptions 3; PCI code of conduct 339; post-mortem 273, 329; revisiting of methods and strategies of media interface 154
Nayyar, Vineet 84
Nehru, Pandit Jawaharlal 8, 72, 109, 187
net asset value (NAV) 218–219, 233
new age media 290
new media 25, 29, 39, 102, 158–159, 226, 274
news item 92, 143, 146, 150, 159, 331
news release 140; body of 144; checklist on news writing 145; format of 145; ground rules for broadcasting media 145; inverted pyramid style 144–146, 159; news lead 143
Newsweek 165
news writing 146
New York Journal 4
New York Times 4, 36, 165, 202
New York World 4
Nikkes 225 Tokyo Exchange 210
no-load mutual funds 219
non-probability sampling 294
Nuclear Proliferation Treaty (NPT) 122

Obama, Barak 46, 79, 120, 171, 189, 339
Oil and Natural Gas Corporation (ONGC) 66, 198, 224
one-on-one interviews 157
online investing community, strategy to reach out to customers 229
online marketing 29, 163
online media relations management 149, 228
online sponsorship 172; definition of 172
open-ended mutual fund scheme 217
open house 99, 101–102
Operation Duryodhana 119
opinion surveys 292
opportunities to see (OTS) technique 29, 292
organizational communication 10, 19
organizational culture 88, 93
Organization for Economic Co-operation and Development (OECD) 253
outdoor (posters and billboards/hoardings) 29
over-the-top (OTT) messaging 213

paid communication 39, 69
Pai, T.V. Mohandas 262
Pandemic ix, 13, 24, 100, 163, 206, 305
Parikh, Ketan 215
Patil, Shivraj 270
perception(s) 3, 11–13, 18, 33–34, 45–46, 51, 54, 57–58, 66–67, 78, 97, 117, 123–127, 129, 131–134, 136, 143, 152–153, 155, 161, 170, 178, 184, 225, 246, 249, 251, 261, 264, 273, 287–288, 297, 299, 302, 307; influence on policy decision 126; in politics 126; unethical management 126
personal: contacts 128–129, 137, 280, 288–289; Culture 88
persuasion theories 89
petitioning 118
Pherwani Committee 208
placement of corporate communication, within the organization 10
policy agenda 121
policy decision, influence of perceptions on 126
population census 305
portfolio funds 216
power culture 88
Prasar Bharati 25, 280
preference shares 216
preferential allotments of stocks 214
Premji, Azim 259
press: brief 142, 147, 149, 159; conference 34, 69, 138, 141–142, 146–149, 154–157, 159–160, 164, 173, 212, 224, 245, 263, 267, 277, 291, 352; handouts 141–142; notes 140, 142, 159, 222; tour 149, 159

Press Council of India (PCI) 331, 339; complaint procedure 331; establishments of; functions of; principles of
press release 42, 43, 138, 144–145, 147, 153–155, 159–160, 196, 227; methods to write effectively 140; rejection of, reasons for 140; types of 141
Prevention of Insults to the National Honor Act, 1971 335
PricewaterhouseCoopers (PwC) 46, 255
primary capital market 209, 232
print media growth, in India 23
print media press 27
Privacy, invasion of, 313–314, 322–323, 339, 341, 342, 353
privy purses 8
Prize Competition Act, 1978 336
probability sampling 294
productivity enhancements 89, 290–291
program content 26
public affairs: agenda 121; and media 122; opinion 121; policy, making of 121
public relations: advertising 61; departments 85; effectiveness 92; function of 85; and marketing 86; origin of 8; practitioner as special pleader 338; professional bodies engaged in 338; research 20, 32; role of 162; situation 68
Public Relations Institute of Australia (PRIA) 32
public relations (PR) in India: and economic liberalization 9; foundation in public sector 8; teaching in schools 9
Public Relations Society of America (PRSA) 286, 337
public sector undertakings (PSUs), in India 85, 193; growth of 109
Purna Swarajay (complete self-rule as a bargain) 3

quota sampling 295

radio 4, 15, 18, 24–25, 27–28, 39, 42–43, 69, 79, 83, 96, 106, 149, 159, 221, 281, 319–320, 326, 331
Raju, B. Ramalinga 112, 258–259
Raju, Rama 253
Rajya Sabha News 131
Ranbaxy 123
Rao, Chalapati 111, 135
Rao, P.V. Narasimha 9, 212
Rashtriya Janata Dal (RJD) 320
rating research, CEO survey 52
reasoned action theory 90
Reddy, Jaipal 259
red tape 127
regional mutual funds (RMFs) 220
rejoinders 140, 143, 159
Reliance Money 238–239
reputation: definition of 45; management 45; recovery 53; Rx 49; survey 52; Xchange 49
research: instinctive 287; a programme planning tool 290; strategic 287
research, corporate 291; analysis of 293; blog tracking 30; campaign/programme evaluation 286; communication 287; Cutlip et al. PII Model 296; Dashboards 302; desk research 304; field reports 307; formal technique 290; formative research 292; gatekeepers 289; imperatives 293; informal techniques 288; instrument 293; mail analysis 289; McNamara pyramid model 31; media reflections 289; methodology 293; opinion survey 292; personal contacts 128; research a programme planning tool 290; research rationale 293; scorecards 302; study, fieldwork 308; universe 293; web search 304; what to research 291
research, media 302, 303, 308
return-based classification 216
Rights to Information (RTI) Act 2005 314; application procedure for requesting information 328; case study 330; exclusions under 328; fee to be charged to seek information 328; grounds for rejection 328; media and 329; time limit to receive information 328
rights issue 215
risk survey 53
risky business reputation online 49
role culture 89
Roosevelt, Franklin D. 120
Rotary International 297

S&P 500 of the National Association of Securities Dealers Automated Quotations (NASDAQ) 210
S&P/ASX= 200 Index of Australia 210
safeguarding reputation 49
Samajwadi Party 122
sampling: definition of 294; non-probability 294; probability 294
Sathasivam, P. 318
Satyam 83–84, 95, 111, 189, 231–232, 242–243, 248, 253–262
Satyam Computers 14, 52, 96, 141, 210, 211, 231, 232, 253, 258–259, 261, 314, 332
Satyam Computers fraud (2008) 14, 46, 108, 117, 189, 205, 211, 223, 248, 254–255, 261, 273, 283, 290, 332

Savvy and Society 23
SBI Mutual Fund 239
Scheduled Castes 193
Scheduled Tribes 193
scorecards 302
secondary capital market 209, 232
sector mutual funds (SMFs) 220
Securities and Exchange Board of India (SEBI) 207–208, 214, 221, 223–225, 230, 236, 241, 252, 254, 332; guidelines for advertisement by portfolio managers 207; regulations on ad campaigns 207
selective media 12
service sector in India: boom post liberalization 111
shareholder confidence 61
Shastri, Lal Bahadur 109
Shermer, Michael 21
shop-floor discussions 97
simple random samplings 294
Singh, Manmohan 129, 255, 273, 276
Singh, Sardar Jagjit 119
Sinha, Vivek 123
slander 342
Slumdog Millionaire 166, 167, 321
SMS messaging 26, 29, 48, 79, 175, 225, 265, 301
social: audit 199–201, 269, 274; gatherings 12; media x, 26, 45, 47–48, 53, 135, 163, 174, 228, 247, 289–290, 303, 337, 356; monitoring 33; responsibility 11–13, 17, 50, 185, 189, 191, 199, 202
social and political activists (SPAs) 53
societies 10, 90, 99, 338, 343, 358
Society for Consumers' and Investors' Protection 229
spokesperson preparation 156; for media interface 156
sponsorships 11, 162, 170–172; connecting with youth 170; definition of 170; improve public perceptions through 170
spot press release 141, 159
Stacks, Don W. 32
stakeholders or target audience (TA) 12–13, 31, 34, 62, 74, 90, 92, 116, 124–125, 131, 167, 173, 204–205, 249, 291–293, 299, 302, 308; definition of 12; types of 12
Standing Conference of Public Enterprises (SCOPE) 8, 112, 114–115, 130
State Bank of India 207, 218
Statesman 122
Steel Authority of India Limited (SAIL) 15
STI Index of Singapore 210
stock index 209, 220–221
stock market 4, 14, 206, 210–212, 220–222, 232–234, 237, 248, 255; Harshad Mehta Case 211
stratified random sampling 294
Sunday 23, 70
symbols, communication through 62–63, 335
syndicated research 290, 306
systems theory 89, 101

Taare Zameen Par film 90
task culture 88
Tata, J.R.D 85, 133
Tata, Ratan 143, 246, 249, 259, 265, 266, 268–269
Tata, Steel 85, 106, 194, 199
Tata Capital 237–238
Tata Consultancy Services (TCS) 194, 198, 255
Tata Iron and Steel Company Limited (TISCO) 123, 131–133, 186
Tata Motors 266–268
TATA Nano 141, 243, 265
Tech Mahindra 84
Telecom Regulatory Authority of India (TRAI) 141
Telegraph 79, 81, 266
telephonic interviews 157, 295
television
Tendulkar, Sachin 213, 224
third-party endorsements 31, 169, 264
Thomson, Stuart 117, 135
Thurman, Uma 317
The Times of India 23, 37, 41–44, 48, 72, 75–76, 79–81, 135, 140, 182, 202, 210, 212, 241, 275–277, 283–284, 312, 318, 358
Times magazine and newspaper 72, 168
Tracker 303
trade channels 222, 227
trademark(s) 64–67, 73, 322; as a brand communication tool 67; definition of 65; and patent, difference between 66; personal name as 67; redesigning 66
trade media, in India 39, 159, 221–222, 230, 232
trinity in corporate communication 11; communication channels 12; messages articulation 12; stakeholders identification 12
Twitter 25, 48, 97

UK Institute of Public Relations Research and Toolkit 32
unadulterated garbage 140
University Grants Commission (UGC) 9
UPA government 122; Nuclear Proliferation Treaty (NPT) with US in 2008 122
USA *Today* 165

US Postal Service 109
UTI Mutual Fund 238–239

value funds 219
value symbols 62
video 12, 38, 47, 91, 95–96, 134, 145, 154, 228, 262

Wall Street Journal 165
Washington Post 36, 120
Watergate scandal, in United States 7–8, 248
web: search 303, 308
WhatsApp x (Preface)
WIPRO 65–66, 92, 189, 255, 259
word-of-mouth marketing (WOMM) 167
World Bank Reports on Observance of Standards and Codes (ROSC) 333
World War: First 6; Second 7
World Wildlife Fund (WWF) 50

Young Person's (Harmful Publication) Act, 1956 335
YouTube 96

Zee TV 24

For Product Safety Concerns and Information please contact our EU
representative GPSR@taylorandfrancis.com
Taylor & Francis Verlag GmbH, Kaufingerstraße 24, 80331 München, Germany

www.ingramcontent.com/pod-product-compliance
Lightning Source LLC
LaVergne TN
LVHW081328011026
849161LV00013BB/2865

* 9 7 8 1 0 3 2 5 3 7 2 3 8 *